interchange

FOURTH EDITION

Jack C. Richards

With Jonathan Hull and Susan Proctor

CAMBRIDGE
UNIVERSITY PRESS

TEACHER'S EDITION

CAMBRIDGE UNIVERSITY PRESS
Cambridge, New York, Melbourne, Madrid, Cape Town,
Singapore, São Paulo, Delhi, Mexico City

Cambridge University Press
32 Avenue of the Americas, New York, NY 10013-2473, USA

www.cambridge.org
Information on this title: www.cambridge.org/9781107615069

First published 1992
Second edition 1998
Third edition 2005
2nd printing 2013

Printed in Hong Kong, China, by Golden Cup Printing Company Limited

A catalog record for this publication is available from the British Library.

ISBN 978-1-107-64870-8 Student's Book 3 with Self-study DVD-ROM
ISBN 978-1-107-69720-1 Student's Book 3A with Self-study DVD-ROM
ISBN 978-1-107-65269-9 Student's Book 3B with Self-study DVD-ROM
ISBN 978-1-107-64874-6 Workbook 3
ISBN 978-1-107-64685-8 Workbook 3A
ISBN 978-1-107-68752-3 Workbook 3B
ISBN 978-1-107-61506-9 Teacher's Edition 3 with Assessment Audio CD/CD-ROM
ISBN 978-1-107-66870-6 Class Audio CDs 3
ISBN 978-1-107-66684-9 Full Contact 3 with Self-study DVD-ROM
ISBN 978-1-107-62042-1 Full Contact 3A with Self-study DVD-ROM
ISBN 978-1-107-63667-5 Full Contact 3B with Self-study DVD-ROM

For a full list of components, visit www. cambridge.org/interchange

Art direction, book design, layout services, and photo research: Integra
Audio production: CityVox, NYC

Contents

Plan of Book 3

Titles/Topics	Speaking	Grammar
UNIT 1 — PAGES 2–7		
That's what friends are for! Personality types and qualities; relationships; turn ons and turn offs	Describing personalities; expressing likes and dislikes; agreeing and disagreeing; complaining	Relative pronouns as subjects and objects; *it* clauses + adverbial clauses with *when*
UNIT 2 — PAGES 8–13		
Career moves Jobs; careers of the future; job skills; summer jobs	Talking about possible careers; describing jobs; discussing the negative aspects of some jobs	Gerund phrases as subjects and objects; comparisons with adjectives, nouns, verbs, and past participles
PROGRESS CHECK — PAGES 14–15		
UNIT 3 — PAGES 16–21		
Could you do me a favor? Favors; formal and informal requests; messages	Making unusual requests; making direct and indirect requests; accepting and declining requests	Requests with modals, *if* clauses, and gerunds; indirect requests
UNIT 4 — PAGES 22–27		
What a story! The media; news stories; exceptional events	Narrating a story; describing events and experiences in the past	Past continuous vs. simple past; past perfect
PROGRESS CHECK — PAGES 28–29		
UNIT 5 — PAGES 30–35		
Crossing cultures Cultural comparisons and culture shock; moving abroad; emotions; customs; tourism and travel abroad	Talking about moving abroad; expressing emotions; describing cultural expectations; giving advice	Noun phrases containing relative clauses; expectations: *the custom to, (not) supposed to, expected to, (not) acceptable to*
UNIT 6 — PAGES 36–41		
What's wrong with it? Consumer complaints; everyday problems; electronics; repairs	Describing problems; making complaints; explaining something that needs to be done	Describing problems with past participles as adjectives and with nouns; describing problems with *need* + gerund, *need* + passive infinitive, and *keep* + gerund
PROGRESS CHECK — PAGES 42–43		
UNIT 7 — PAGES 44–49		
The world we live in The environment; world problems; current issues	Identifying and describing problems; coming up with solutions	Passive in the present continuous and present perfect; prepositions of cause; infinitive clauses and phrases
UNIT 8 — PAGES 50–55		
Lifelong learning Education; learner choices; strategies for learning; personal qualities	Asking about preferences; discussing pros and cons of different college majors; talking about learning methods; talking about personal qualities	*Would rather* and *would prefer; by* + gerund to describe how to do things
PROGRESS CHECK — PAGES 56–57		

Pronunciation/Listening	Writing/Reading	Interchange Activity
Linked sounds Listening for descriptions of people; listening for opinions	Writing a description of a best friend "To Friend or Unfriend?": Reading about choosing online friends	"Personality types": Interviewing a classmate to find out about personality characteristics **PAGE 114**
Stress with compound nouns Listening to descriptions of summer jobs; listening for likes and dislikes	Writing about career advantages and disadvantages "Help! How Can I Find a Job?": Reading a message board with advice on how to find a job	"The dinner party": Comparing people's careers and personalities to make a seating chart for a dinner party **PAGE 115**
Unreleased consonants Listening to people making, accepting, and declining requests	Writing emails with requests "Yes or No?": Reading about the way people in different cultures respond "yes" and "no"	"Borrowers and lenders": Asking classmates to borrow items; lending or refusing to lend items **PAGE 116**
Intonation in complex sentences Listening to news podcasts; listening to narratives about past events	Writing a news story "The Changing World of Blogging": Reading about the evolution of blogs	"A double ending": Completing a story with two different endings **PAGE 117**
Word stress in sentences Listening for information about living abroad; listening to opinions about customs	Writing a tourist pamphlet "Culture Shock": Reading blog entries about moving to another country	"Culture check": Comparing customs in different countries **PAGE 118**
Contrastive stress Listening to complaints; listening to people exchange things in a store; listening to repair people describe their jobs	Writing a critical online review "The Value of Upcycling": Reading about reusing materials to make things of greater value	"Fixer-upper": Comparing problems in two pictures of an apartment **PAGES 119, 120**
Reduction of auxiliary verbs Listening to environmental problems; listening for solutions	Writing a message on a community website "Saving a Coral Reef – An Eco Tipping Point": Reading about reviving marine life around Apo Island	"Make your voices heard!": Choosing an issue and deciding on an effective method of protest; devising a strategy **PAGE 121**
Intonation in questions of choice Listening to descriptions of courses; listening for additional information	Writing about a skill or a hobby "Learning Styles": Reading about different kinds of learning	"Learning curves": Choosing between different things you want to learn **PAGE 122**

Titles/Topics	Speaking	Grammar

Pronunciation/Listening	Writing/Reading	Interchange Activity
Sentence stress Listening to suggestions for self-improvement	Writing a letter of advice "Critical Thinking": Reading about the characteristics and benefits of critical thinking	"Put yourself in my shoes!": Discussing different points of view of parents and their children PAGE 123
Syllable stress Listening to predictions	Writing a biography "Tweet to Eat": Reading about a restaurant that uses social networking to reach customers	"History buff": Taking a history quiz PAGES 124, 126
Reduction of *have* and *been* Listening to descriptions of important events; listening to regrets and explanations	Writing a letter of apology "Milestones Around the World": Reading about important life events in Egypt, Mexico, and Vanuatu	"When I was younger,...": Playing a board game to talk about how you were and could have been PAGE 125
Reduced words Listening for features and slogans	Writing a radio or TV commercial "The Wrong Stuff": Reading about advertising failures	"Catchy slogans": Creating a slogan and logo for a product PAGE 127
Reduction in past modals Listening to explanations; listening for the best solution	Writing about a complicated situation "The Blue Lights of Silver Cliff": Reading a story about an unexplained phenomenon	"Photo plays": Drawing possible conclusions about situations PAGE 128
Review of stress in compound nouns Listening to a producer describe his work; listening for personality traits	Writing about a process "Hooray for Bollywood!": Reading about the kind of movies made in India	"Who makes it happen?": Putting together a crew for making a movie PAGE 129
Intonation in tag questions Listening for solutions to everyday annoyances; listening to issues and opinions	Writing a persuasive essay "How Serious Is Plagiarism?": Reading about plagiarism and people's opinions about its severity	"You be the judge!": Deciding on punishments for common offenses PAGE 130
Stress and rhythm Listening to challenges and rewards of people's work; listening for people's goals for the future	Writing a personal statement for an application "Young and Gifted": Reading about exceptionally gifted young people	"Viewpoints": Taking a survey about volunteering PAGE 131

Authors' acknowledgments

A great number of people contributed to the development of *Interchange Fourth Edition*. Particular thanks are owed to the reviewers using *Interchange, Third Edition* in the following schools and institutes – their insights and suggestions have helped define the content and format of the fourth edition:

Ian Geoffrey Hanley, **The Address Education Center**, Izmir, Turkey

James McBride, **AUA Language Center**, Bangkok, Thailand

Jane Merivale, **Centennial College**, Toronto, Ontario, Canada

Elva Elena Peña Andrade, **Centro de Auto Aprendizaje de Idiomas**, Nuevo León, Mexico

José Paredes, **Centro de Educación Continua de la Escuela Politécnica Nacional** (CEC-EPN), Quito, Ecuador

Chia-jung Tsai, **Changhua University of Education**, Changhua City, Taiwan

Kevin Liang, **Chinese Culture University**, Taipei, Taiwan

Roger Alberto Neira Perez, **Colegio Santo Tomás de Aquino**, Bogotá, Colombia

Teachers at **Escuela Miguel F. Martínez**, Monterrey, Mexico

Maria Virgínia Goulart Borges de Lebron, **Great Idiomas**, São Paulo, Brazil

Gina Kim, **Hoseo University**, Chungnam, South Korea

Heeyong Kim, Seoul, South Korea

Elisa Borges, **IBEU-Rio**, Rio de Janeiro, Brazil

Jason M. Ham, **Inha University**, Incheon, South Korea

Rita de Cássia S. Silva Miranda, **Instituto Batista de Idiomas**, Belo Horizonte, Brazil

Teachers at **Instituto Politécnico Nacional**, Mexico City, Mexico

Victoria M. Roberts and Regina Marie Williams, **Interactive College of Technology**, Chamblee, Georgia, USA

Teachers at **Internacional de Idiomas**, Mexico City, Mexico

Marcelo Serafim Godinho, **Life Idiomas**, São Paulo, Brazil

J. Kevin Varden, **Meiji Gakuin University**, Yokohama, Japan

Rosa Maria Valencia Rodríguez, Mexico City, Mexico

Chung-Ju Fan, **National Kinmen Institute of Technology**, Kinmen, Taiwan

Shawn Beasom, **Nihon Daigaku**, Tokyo, Japan

Gregory Hadley, **Niigata University of International and Information Studies**, Niigata, Japan

Chris Ruddenklau, **Osaka University of Economics and Law**, Osaka, Japan

Byron Roberts, **Our Lady of Providence Girls' High School**, Xindian City, Taiwan

Simon Banha, **Phil Young's English School**, Curitiba, Brazil

Flávia Gonçalves Carneiro Braathen, **Real English Center**, Viçosa, Brazil

Márcia Cristina Barboza de Miranda, **SENAC**, Recife, Brazil

Raymond Stone, **Seneca College of Applied Arts and Technology**, Toronto, Ontario, Canada

Gen Murai, **Takushoku University**, Tokyo, Japan

Teachers at **Tecnológico de Estudios Superiores de Ecatepec**, Mexico City, Mexico

Teachers at **Universidad Autónoma Metropolitana–Azcapotzalco**, Mexico City, Mexico

Teachers at **Universidad Autónoma de Nuevo León**, Monterrey, Mexico

Mary Grace Killian Reyes, **Universidad Autónoma de Tamaulipas**, Tampico Tamaulipas, Mexico

Teachers at **Universidad Estatal del Valle de Ecatepec**, Mexico City, Mexico

Teachers at **Universidad Nacional Autónoma de Mexico – Zaragoza**, Mexico City, Mexico

Teachers at **Universidad Nacional Autónoma de Mexico – Iztacala**, Mexico City, Mexico

Luz Edith Herrera Diaz, Veracruz, Mexico

Seri Park, **YBM PLS**, Seoul, South Korea

Self-assessment charts revised by Alex Tilbury

Grammar plus written by Karen Davy

A letter from the authors

Dear teachers and colleagues,

Together with Cambridge University Press, we have always been committed to ensuring that the *Interchange* series continues to provide you and your students with the best possible teaching and learning resources. This means we always seek ways to add new features to the course to make sure it reflects the best practices in language teaching. We are delighted to tell you that we have now prepared a new edition of the series to make sure it continues to be the market leader in English language teaching today.

Here are some of the things you can look forward to in the fourth edition:

- a fresh **new design, new illustrations** and **photos,** and **updated content**
- a new **Self-study DVD-ROM** in the back of each Student's Book that provides additional skills and video viewing practice
- a revised **Teacher's Edition** now with an **Assessment Audio CD/CD-ROM** that features ready-to-print PDFs and customizable Microsoft Word tests
- an array of **new technology** components to support teaching and enhance learning both inside and outside of the classroom
- the all-new *Interchange Video Program* and accompanying Video Resource materials

In addition, the features that have made *Interchange* the world's most popular and successful English course continue to be the hallmarks of the fourth edition:

- the same **trusted methodology** and proven approach
- **flexibility** for use in any teaching situation
- a wealth of resources for teacher training and professional development

We look forward to introducing you to the fourth edition of *Interchange*.

With best wishes and warmest regards,

Jack C. Richards
Jonathan Hull
Susan Proctor

The new edition

Interchange Fourth Edition is a fully revised edition of *Interchange Third Edition*, the world's most successful series for adult and young adult learners of English.

The course has been thoroughly updated, and it remains the innovative series teachers and students have grown to love, while incorporating suggestions from teachers and students all over the world. There is new content in every unit, additional grammar practice, as well as opportunities to develop speaking and listening skills.

What's new

Content – more than half of the readings are new and many others have been updated.

Grammar plus – the self-study section at the back of the Student's Book provides additional grammar practice that students can do in class or as homework. An answer key is also included at the back of the book, so students can check their work.

Progress checks – the Self-assessment charts have been revised to reflect student outcomes, and the statements are aligned with the Common European Framework of Reference (CEFR). This allows students to assess their ability to communicate effectively rather than focus on mastery of grammar.

Student's self-study DVD-ROM – contains brand new content at each level of the Student's Book. The interactive activities provide students with extra practice in vocabulary, grammar, listening, speaking, and reading. It also contains the complete video program with activities that allow students to check their comprehension themselves.

Assessment Audio CD / CD-ROM – contains eight oral and written quizzes plus a midterm and final exam. The quizzes are available in two formats – as ready-to-print PDFs and in Microsoft Word. The audio program, audio scripts, and answer keys are also included on this disc.

Core series components

Interchange Fourth Edition has a variety of components to help you and your students meet their language learning needs. Here is a list of the core components.

COMPONENT	DESCRIPTION
Student's Book with *NEW!* **Self-study DVD-ROM**	The Student's Book is intended for classroom use and contains 16 six-page units. The Self-study DVD-ROM provides additional vocabulary, grammar, listening, speaking, reading, and full class video–viewing practice.
Class Audio CDs	The Class Audio CDs are intended for classroom use. The CDs provide audio for all the audio sections in the Student's Book.
Teacher's Edition with *NEW!* **Assessment Audio CD / CD-ROM**	The interleaved Teacher's Edition with Assessment Audio CD / CD-ROM includes: • Page-by-page teaching notes with step-by-step lesson plans • Audio scripts and answer keys for the Student's Book, Workbook, and DVD • Language summaries of the new vocabulary and expressions in each unit • Supplementary Resource Overviews that make it easy to plan what to teach for each unit • A complete assessment program, including oral and written quizzes, as well as review unit tests in printable PDF and Microsoft Word formats
Workbook	The Workbook's six-page units can be used in class or for homework. Each unit provides students with additional grammar, vocabulary, and writing practice.
NEW! **Online Workbook**	The Online Workbook is an online version of the print workbook, optimized for online practice. The Online Workbook provides instant feedback for hundreds of activities as well as simple tools to monitor progress.
NEW! **Video Program**	Videos for each unit offer entertaining free-standing sequences that reinforce and extend the language presented in the Student's Book. Video Resource Books include step-by-step comprehension and conversation activities and detailed teaching suggestions.
NEW! **Classroom Presentation Software**	Classroom Presentation Software can be used on an interactive whiteboard, portable interactive software technology, or with a computer or projector. This software is intended for classroom use and presents the Student's Book, audio, and video.
NEW! **Animated Presentations**	Student's Book pages are reproduced digitally in MS PowerPoint format, allowing teachers to complete activities in front of the classroom using only a computer and a projector.
NEW! Interchange **Arcade**	*Interchange* Arcade is a free self-study website offering fun, interactive, self-scoring activities for each unit. The *Interchange* Arcade includes activities that help students practice listening, vocabulary, grammar, and reading skills. MP3s of the class audio program can also be found here.
Placement Test	The placement test provides three versions of the placement test and four achievement tests for each level of the Student's Book, as well as for *Passages* 1 and 2.

For a complete list of components, visit www.cambridge.org/interchange or contact your local Cambridge University Press representative.

Student's Book overview

Every unit in *Interchange Fourth Edition* contains two cycles, each of which has a specific topic, grammar point, and function. The units in Level 3 contain a variety of exercises, including a Snapshot, Conversation, Grammar focus, Pronunciation, Discussion (or Speaking / Role Play), Word power, Perspectives, Listening, Writing, Reading, and Interchange activity. The sequence of these exercises differs from unit to unit. Here is a sample unit from Level 3.

Cycle 1 (Exercises 1–6)

Topic: entertainment
Grammar: passive
Function: describe steps in a process

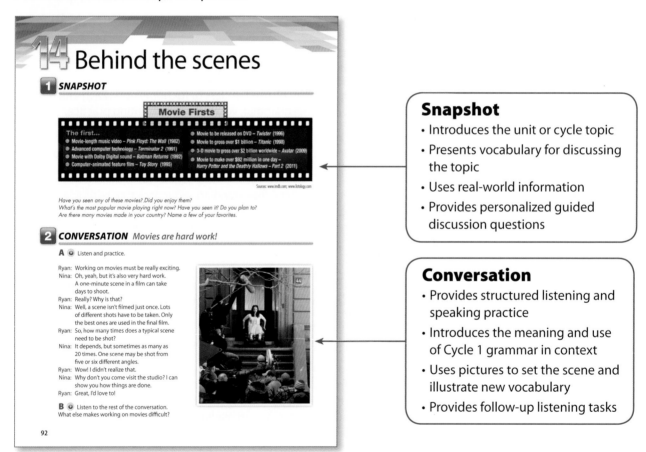

Snapshot
- Introduces the unit or cycle topic
- Presents vocabulary for discussing the topic
- Uses real-world information
- Provides personalized guided discussion questions

Conversation
- Provides structured listening and speaking practice
- Introduces the meaning and use of Cycle 1 grammar in context
- Uses pictures to set the scene and illustrate new vocabulary
- Provides follow-up listening tasks

Grammar focus

- Summarizes the Cycle 1 grammar
- Includes audio recordings of the grammar
- Provides controlled grammar practice in realistic contexts, such as short conversations
- Provides freer, more personalized speaking practice

Listening

- Provides pre-listening focus tasks or questions
- Develops a variety of listening skills, such as listening for main ideas and details
- Includes post-listening speaking tasks

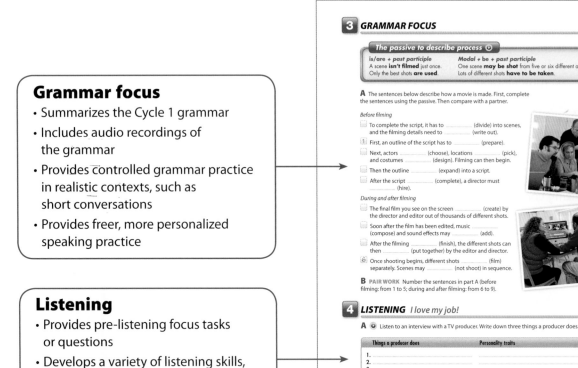

3 GRAMMAR FOCUS

The passive to describe process ⊙

is/are + past participle	Modal + be + past participle
A scene **isn't filmed** just once. Only the best shots **are used**.	One scene **may be shot** from five or six different angles. Lots of different shots **have to be taken**.

A The sentences below describe how a movie is made. First, complete the sentences using the passive. Then compare with a partner.

Before filming

☐ To complete the script, it has to .... (divide) into scenes, and the filming details need to .... (write out).

[1] First, an outline of the script has to .... (prepare).

☐ Next, actors .... (choose), locations .... (pick), and costumes .... (design). Filming can then begin.

☐ Then the outline .... (expand) into a script.

☐ After the script .... (complete), a director must .... (hire).

During and after filming

☐ The final film you see on the screen .... (create) by the director and editor out of thousands of different shots.

☐ Soon after the film has been edited, music .... (compose) and sound effects may .... (add).

☐ After the filming .... (finish), the different shots can then .... (put together) by the editor and director.

[6] Once shooting begins, different shots .... (film) separately. Scenes may .... (not shoot) in sequence.

B PAIR WORK Number the sentences in part A (before filming: from 1 to 5; during and after filming: from 6 to 9).

4 LISTENING *I love my job!*

A ⊙ Listen to an interview with a TV producer. Write down three things a producer does.

Things a producer does	Personality traits
1.	
2.	
3.	

B ⊙ Listen again. What are three personality traits a producer should have? Complete the chart.

Behind the scenes • 93

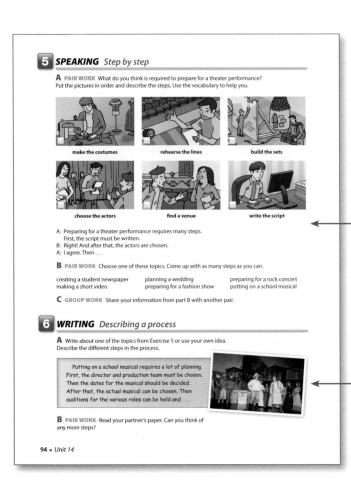

5 SPEAKING *Step by step*

A PAIR WORK What do you think is required to prepare for a theater performance? Put the pictures in order and describe the steps. Use the vocabulary to help you.

make the costumes
rehearse the lines
build the sets
choose the actors
find a venue
write the script

A: Preparing for a theater performance requires many steps. First, the script must be written.
B: Right! And after that, the actors are chosen.
A: I agree. Then . . .

B PAIR WORK Choose one of these topics. Come up with as many steps as you can.

creating a student newspaper
making a short video
planning a wedding
preparing for a fashion show
preparing for a rock concert
putting on a school musical

C GROUP WORK Share your information from part B with another pair.

6 WRITING *Describing a process*

A Write about one of the topics from Exercise 5 or use your own idea. Describe the different steps in the process.

Putting on a school musical requires a lot of planning. First, the director and production team must be chosen. Then the dates for the musical should be decided. After that, the actual musical can be chosen. Then auditions for the various roles can be held and . . .

B PAIR WORK Read your partner's paper. Can you think of any more steps?

94 ▪ Unit 14

Speaking

- Provides communicative tasks that help develop oral fluency
- Recycles grammar and vocabulary in the cycle
- Includes pair work, group work, and class activities

Writing

- Provides a model writing sample
- Develops skills in writing different texts, such as postcards and email messages
- Reinforces the vocabulary and grammar in the cycle or unit

Cycle 2 (Exercises 7–12)

Topic: jobs in entertainment and the media
Grammar: defining and non-defining
relative clauses
Function: describe careers in the media

Word power
- Presents vocabulary related to the unit topic
- Provides practice with collocations and categorizing vocabulary
- Promotes freer, more personalized practice

Perspectives
- Provides structured listening and speaking practice
- Introduces the meaning and use of the Cycle 2 grammar in context
- Presents people's opinions and experiences about a topic
- Introduces useful expressions and discourse features

Pronunciation
- Provides controlled practice in recognizing and producing sounds linked to the cycle grammar
- Promotes extended or personalized pronunciation practice

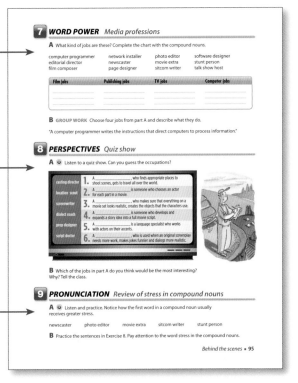

Grammar focus
- Summarizes the Cycle 2 grammar
- Includes audio recordings of the grammar
- Provides controlled grammar practice in realistic contexts, such as short conversations
- Provides freer, more personalized speaking practice

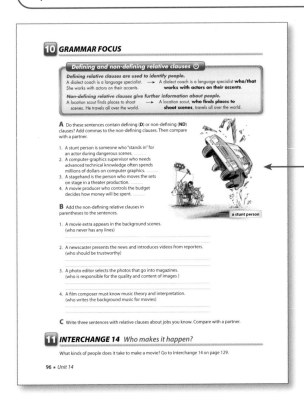

Reading

- Presents a variety of text types
- Introduces the text with a pre-reading task
- Develops a variety of reading skills, such as reading for main ideas, reading for details, and inferencing
- Promotes discussion that involves personalization and analysis

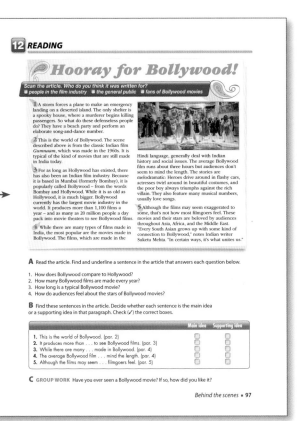

12 READING

Hooray for Bollywood!

Scan the article. Who do you think it was written for?
■ people in the film industry   ■ the general public   ■ fans of Bollywood movies

1 A storm forces a plane to make an emergency landing on a deserted island. The only shelter is a spooky house, where a murderer begins killing passengers. So what do these defenseless people do? They have a beach party and perform an elaborate song-and-dance number.

2 This is the world of Bollywood. The scene described above is from the classic Indian film *Gumnaam*, which was made in the 1960s. It is typical of the kind of movies that are still made in India today.

3 For as long as Hollywood has existed, there has also been an Indian film industry. Because it is based in Mumbai (formerly Bombay), it is popularly called Bollywood – from the words Bombay and Hollywood. While it is as old as Hollywood, it is much bigger. Bollywood currently has the largest movie industry in the world. It produces more than 1,100 films a year – and as many as 20 million people a day pack into movie theaters to see Bollywood films.

4 While there are many types of films made in India, the most popular are the movies made in Bollywood. The films, which are made in the Hindi language, generally deal with Indian history and social issues. The average Bollywood film runs about three hours but audiences don't seem to mind the length. The stories are melodramatic: Heroes drive around in flashy cars, actresses twirl around in beautiful costumes, and the poor boy always triumphs against the rich villain. They also feature many musical numbers, usually love songs.

5 Although the films may seem exaggerated to some, that's not how their stars feel. These movies and their stars are beloved by audiences throughout Asia, Africa, and the Middle East. "Every South Asian grows up with some kind of connection to Bollywood," notes Indian writer Suketu Mehta. "In certain ways, it's what unites us."

A Read the article. Find and underline a sentence in the article that answers each question below.

1. How does Bollywood compare to Hollywood?
2. How many Bollywood films are made every year?
3. How long is a typical Bollywood movie?
4. How do audiences feel about the stars of Bollywood movies?

B Find these sentences in the article. Decide whether each sentence is the main idea or a supporting idea in that paragraph. Check (✓) the correct boxes.

	Main idea	Supporting idea
1. This is the world of Bollywood. (par. 2)	☐	☐
2. It produces more than . . . to see Bollywood films. (par. 3)	☐	☐
3. While there are many . . . made in Bollywood. (par. 4)	☐	☐
4. The average Bollywood film . . . mind the length. (par. 4)	☐	☐
5. Although the films may seem . . . filmgoers feel. (par. 5)	☐	☐

C GROUP WORK Have you ever seen a Bollywood movie? If so, how did you like it?

Behind the scenes ■ 97

In the back of the book

Interchange activity

- Expands on the unit topic, vocabulary, and grammar
- Provides opportunities to consolidate new language in a creative or fun way
- Promotes fluency with communicative activities such as discussions, information gaps, and games

Grammar plus

- Explores the unit grammar in greater depth
- Practices the grammar with controlled exercises
- Can be done in class or assigned as homework

Interchange 14 *WHO MAKES IT HAPPEN?*

A GROUP WORK Here are some additional jobs in the movie industry. What do you think each person does?

art director   costume designer   makeup artist   sound-effects technician
cinematographer   lighting technician   set designer   special-effects designer

A: What does an art director do?
B: I know. An art director manages the people who build the sets.

B GROUP WORK Imagine you are going to make a movie. What kind of movie will it be? Decide what job each person in your group will do.

A: You should be the art director because you're a good leader.
B: Actually, I'd prefer to be the producer.
C: I think I'd like to be one of the actors.

C CLASS ACTIVITY Tell the class what kind of movie you are going to make. Explain how each person will contribute to the making of the film.

a cinematographer   *a makeup artist*

a lighting technician *a sound-effects technician*

Interchange 14 ■ 129

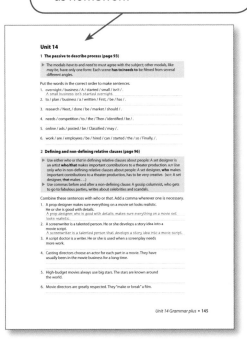

Unit 14

1 The passive to describe process (page 93)

▶ The modals *have to* and *need to* must agree with the subject; other modals, like *may be, have,* have only one form: Each scene **has to/needs to** be filmed from several different angles.

Put the words in the correct order to make sentences.

1. overnight / business // A / started / small / isn't / .
   A small business isn't started overnight.

2. to / plan / business / a / written / First, / be / has / .

3. research / Next, / done / be / market / should / .

4. needs / competition / to / the / Then / identified / be / .

5. online / ads / posted / be / Classified / may / .

6. work / are / employees / be / hired / can / started / the / so / Finally, / .

2 Defining and non-defining relative clauses (page 96)

▶ Use either *who* or *that* in defining relative clauses about people: A set designer is an artist **who/that** makes important contributions to a theater production. BUT Use only *who* in non-defining relative clauses about people: A set designer, **who** makes important contributions to a theater production, has to be very creative. (NOT: A set designer, *that* makes . . .)
▶ Use commas before and after a non-defining clause: A gossip columnist, **who** gets to go to fabulous parties, writes about celebrities and scandals.

Combine these sentences with *who* or *that*. Add a comma wherever one is necessary.

1. A prop designer makes sure everything on a movie set looks realistic. He or she is good with details.
   A prop designer, who is good with details, makes sure everything on a movie set looks realistic.

2. A screenwriter is a talented person. He or she develops a story idea into a movie script.
   A screenwriter is a talented person that develops a story idea into a movie script.

3. A script doctor is a writer. He or she is used when a screenplay needs more work.

4. Casting directors choose an actor for each part in a movie. They have usually been in the movie business for a long time.

5. High-budget movies always use big stars. The stars are known around the world.

6. Movie directors are greatly respected. They "make or break" a film.

Unit 14 Grammar plus ■ 145

Introduction ■ **xv**

Self-study DVD-ROM overview

Interchange Fourth Edition Self-study DVD-ROM in the back of the Student's Book provides students with hundreds of additional exercises to practice the language taught in the Student's Book on their own, in the classroom, or in the lab.

Interactive exercises

Hundreds of interactive exercises provide hours of additional:

- vocabulary practice
- grammar practice
- listening practice
- speaking practice
- reading practice

The complete *Interchange* video program

The entire *Interchange* video program for this level is included on the DVD-ROM with new exercises that allow the students to watch and check comprehension themselves.

Interchange Arcade overview

Interchange Arcade is a free self-study website for students that offers fun, interactive, self-scoring activities for each unit of each level of *Interchange Fourth Edition*. Using animated characters, sound effects, and illustrations, *Interchange* Arcade includes activities that help students practice listening, vocabulary, grammar, and reading skills.

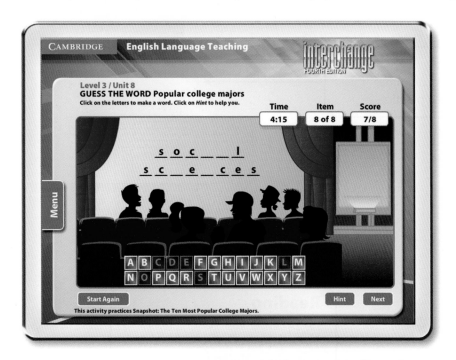

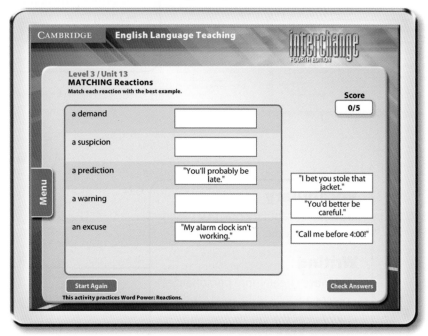

Workbook overview

Interchange Fourth Edition provides students with additional opportunities to practice the language taught in the Student's Book outside of the classroom by using the Workbook that accompanies each level.

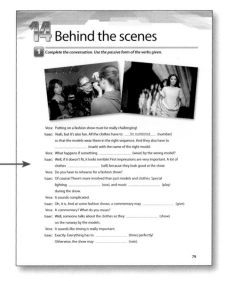

Grammar

Reinforces the unit grammar through controlled practice

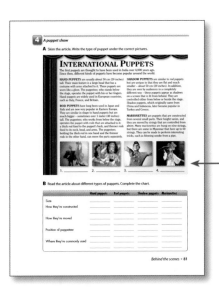

Reading

- Gives additional reading practice based on the theme of the unit
- Introduces the text with a pre-reading task
- Reinforces reading skills used in the Student's Book

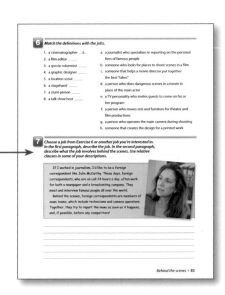

Vocabulary

Provides vocabulary practice based on the unit topic

Writing

- Promotes freer, more personalized practice
- Reinforces the vocabulary and grammar in the unit

Online Workbook overview

Each level of the *Interchange Fourth Edition Online Workbooks* provides additional activities to reinforce what is presented in the corresponding Student's Book. They provide all the familiarity of a traditional print workbook with the ease of online delivery. Each *Online Workbook* includes:

- A variety of interactive activities which correspond to each Student's Book lesson, allowing students to interact with workbook material in a fresh, lively way.
- Instant feedback for hundreds of activities, challenging students to focus on areas for improvement.
- Simple tools for teachers to monitor students' progress such as scores, attendance, and time spent online, providing instant information, saving valuable time for teachers.
- Intuitive navigation and clear, easy-to-follow instructions, fostering independent study practice.

The *Interchange Fourth Edition Online Workbooks* can be purchased in a variety of ways:

- directly online; using a credit card,
- as an institutional subscription,
- as a stand-alone access card, or
- as part of a Student's Book with Online Workbook Pack.

Please contact your local Cambridge representative for more details.

Teacher's Edition overview

The Teacher's Editions provide complete support for teachers who are using *Interchange Fourth Edition*. They contain Supplementary Resources Overview charts to help teachers plan their lessons (for more information see page xxiv), Language summaries, Workbook answer keys, Audio scripts, Fresh ideas, and Games. They also include detailed teaching notes for the units and Progress checks in the Student's Books.

Unit preview

Previews the topics, grammar, and functions in each unit

Teaching notes

- Includes Audio scripts
- Provides Tips that promote teacher training and development

Teaching notes

- Includes the Learning objectives for each exercise
- Provides step-by-step lesson plans
- Provides stimulating and fun Games to review or practice skills such as grammar and vocabulary.
- Includes Answers and Vocabulary definitions

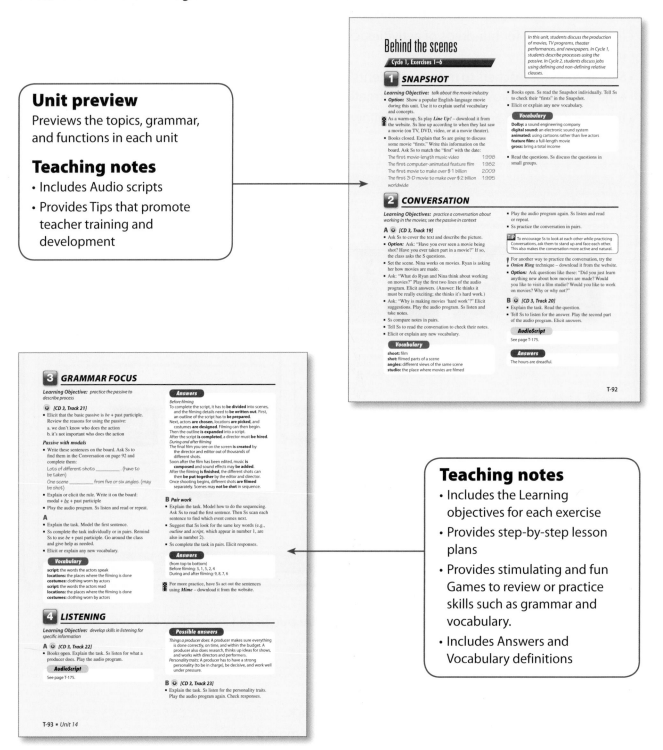

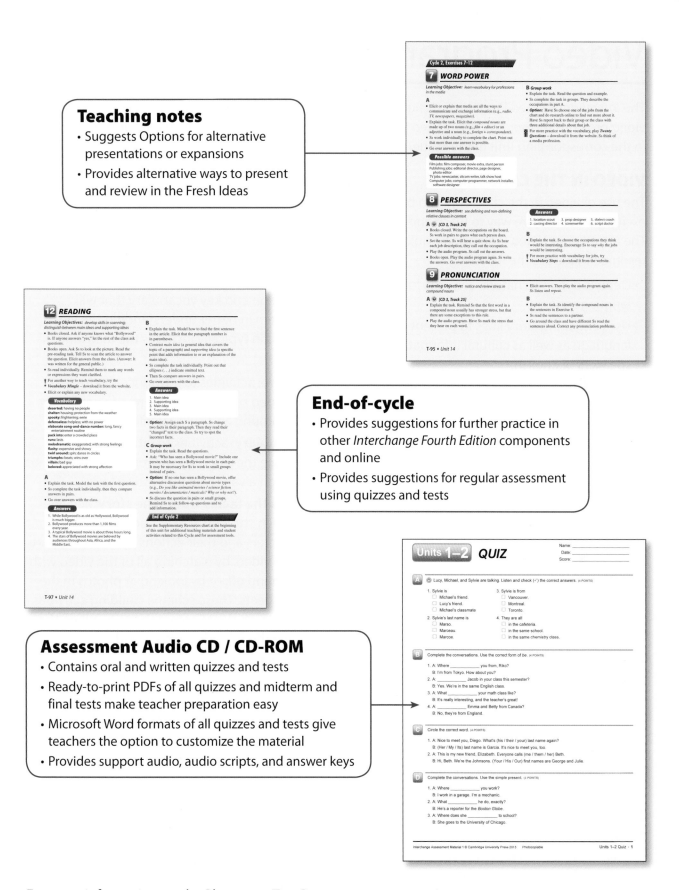

Teaching notes

- Suggests Options for alternative presentations or expansions
- Provides alternative ways to present and review in the Fresh Ideas

End-of-cycle

- Provides suggestions for further practice in other *Interchange Fourth Edition* components and online
- Provides suggestions for regular assessment using quizzes and tests

Assessment Audio CD / CD-ROM

- Contains oral and written quizzes and tests
- Ready-to-print PDFs of all quizzes and midterm and final tests make teacher preparation easy
- Microsoft Word formats of all quizzes and tests give teachers the option to customize the material
- Provides support audio, audio scripts, and answer keys

For more information on the Placement Test Program see page xxvi.

Video Program overview

The *Interchange* Video Program is designed to complement the Student's Books. Each video provides further practice related to the topics, language, and vocabulary introduced in the corresponding unit of the Student's Book.

VIDEO IN THE CLASSROOM

The use of video in the classroom can be an exciting and effective way to teach and learn. The *Interchange* Video Program is a unique resource that does the following:

- Depicts dynamic, natural contexts for language use.
- Uses engaging story lines to present authentic language as well as cultural information about speakers of English.
- Enables learners to use visual information to enhance comprehension.
- Allows learners to observe the gestures, facial expressions, and other aspects of body language that accompany speech.

PROGRAM COMPONENTS

Video

The sixteen videos in each level's video program complement Units 1 through 16 of the corresponding Student's Book. There are a variety of genres: dramatized stories, documentaries, interviews, profiles, and travelogues.

Video Resource Book

The Video Resource Book contains the following:

- engaging **photocopiable worksheets** for students
- detailed **teaching notes** for teachers
- **answer keys** for the student worksheets
- complete **video transcripts**

TEACHING A TYPICAL VIDEO SEQUENCE

The **worksheets** and **teaching notes** for each video are organized into four sections: *Preview, Watch the video, Follow-up,* and *Language*

close-up. The unit-by-unit teaching notes in the Video Resource Book give detailed suggestions for teaching each unit.

Preview

The *Preview* activities build on each other to provide students with relevant background information and key vocabulary that will assist them in better understanding the video. This section typically includes the following elements.

- **Culture**: activities to introduce the topics of the video sequences and provide important background and cultural information
- **Vocabulary**: activities to introduce and practice the essential vocabulary of the videos through a variety of interesting tasks
- **Guess the facts / Guess the story**: activities in which students make predictions about characters and their actions by watching part of the video, by watching all of the video with the sound off, or by looking at photos in the worksheets. These schema-building activities improve students' comprehension when they watch the full video with sound.

Watch the video

The carefully sequenced Watch the video activities first help students focus on gist and then guide them in identifying important details and language. These tasks also prepare them for *Follow-up* speaking activities.

- **Get the picture:** initial viewing activities first help students gain a global understanding of the videos by focusing on gist. Activity types vary from unit to unit, but typically involve watching for key information needed to complete a chart, answer questions, or arrange events in sequential order.

- **Watch for details**: activities in which students focus on more detailed meaning by watching and listening for specific information to complete the tasks
- **What's your opinion?**: activities in which students make inferences about the characters' actions, feelings, and motivations, or state their own opinions about topics in the video

Follow-up

The *Follow-up* speaking activities encourage students to extend and personalize information by voicing their opinions or carrying out communicative tasks.

- **Role play, interview, and other expansion activities**: communicative activities based on the videos in which students extend and personalize what they have learned. Students can use new language to talk about themselves and their ideas as they complete the tasks.

Language close-up

Students finish with the *Language close-up*, examining and practicing the particular language structures and functions presented in the video.

- **What did they say?**: cloze activities that aim to develop bottom-up listening skills by having students focus on the specific language in the videos and then fill in missing words.
- **Grammar and functional activities**: activities which reflect the structural and functional focus of a particular unit as presented in the videos.

OPTIONS FOR THE CLASSROOM

Once teachers feel comfortable with the basic course procedures, they can try other classroom techniques for presenting and working with the videos. Here are several proven techniques.

Fast-forward viewing For activities in which students watch the video with the sound off, play the entire sequence on fast-forward and have students list all of the things they see. Nearly all of the activities designed to be completed with the sound off can be done in this manner.

Information gap Play approximately the first half of a video, and then have students work in pairs or groups to predict what will happen next. Play the rest of the sequence so that students can check their predictions.

Act it out All of the videos provide an excellent basis for role plays and drama activities. Select a short scene, and have students watch it several times. Then have pairs or groups act out the scene, staying as close as possible to the actions and expressions of the characters. Have pairs or groups act out their scenes in front of the class.

What are they saying? Have students watch a short segment of a video in which two people are talking, but without sound. Then have pairs use the context to predict what the people might be saying to each other. Have pairs write out sample dialogs and share their work with the class.

Freeze-frame Freeze a frame of a video and have students call out information about the scene: the objects they can see, what the people are doing, the time and place – whatever is appropriate to the scene or the learning situation.

Teacher Support Site overview

This website offers a variety of materials to assist with your teaching of the series. It includes practical articles, author video and audio casts on methodology, correlations, language summaries, overviews of supplementary materials, ideas for games and extra activities, as well as a number of downloadable worksheets for projects and extra practice of vocabulary, grammar, listening, writing, and speaking.

Author videocasts
Provide useful information on methodology and practical tips

Supplementary Resources Overviews
Indicate all the activities available in the various ancillary components that can be used after each exercise in the Student's Book units for extra practice, review, and assessment

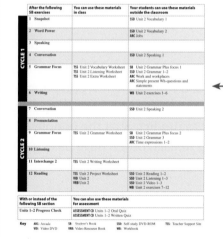

Downloadable worksheets
- Offer extra speaking opportunities
- Provide guidance for projects and extra practice of grammar, vocabulary, listening, and writing

Classroom Presentation Software overview

Interchange Classroom Presentation Software combines the contents of the Student's Book, the class audio, and the video program for each level of the series into a convenient one-stop presentation solution. It can be used with all types of interactive whiteboards or with just a projector and a computer to present *Interchange* core materials in the classroom in a lively and engaging way.

The software provides an effective medium to focus students' attention on the content being presented and practiced. It can also help promote their participation and interaction with the material in a more dynamic way.

This component simplifies several of the teaching tasks that take place in the classroom. You can use the software to play audio or video without having to use a separate CD or DVD player, display the answers for the exercises in an uncomplicated way, zoom in on a page to more efficiently focus students' attention on an activity or image, and even annotate pages for future lessons.

Animated Presentations overview

The *Interchange Fourth Edition* Animated Presentations contain the digitally reproduced Student's Book pages in PowerPoint format, allowing teachers to display answers in the classroom using only a computer and a projector. Please contact your local Cambridge University Press representative for more details.

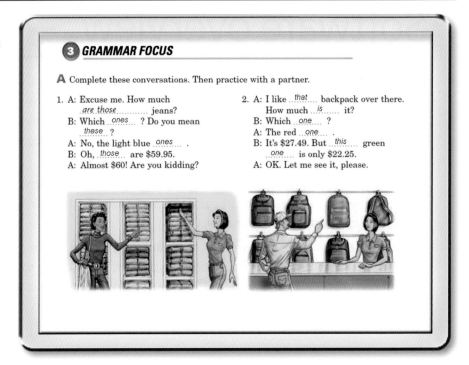

Placement Test Program overview

The *Interchange* and *Passages* Placement Test Program provides three versions of an Objective Placement Test with Listening, three versions of a Placement Essay Test, and Placement Speaking Assessment. An audio program, audio scripts, answer keys, and guidelines for administering the tests are included. Please contact your local Cambridge University Press representative for more details.

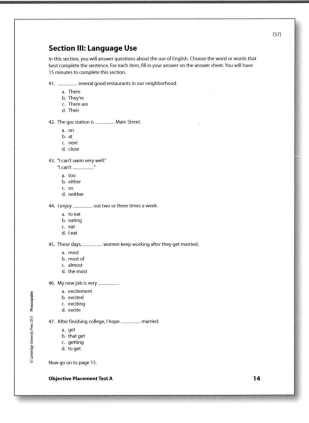

Introduction to the CEFR

Introduction to the Common European Framework of Reference (CEFR)

The overall aim of the Council of Europe's Common European Framework of Reference (CEFR) is to provide objective criteria for describing and assessing language proficiency in an internationally comparable manner. The Council of Europe's work on the definition of appropriate learning objectives for adult language learners dates back to the '70s. The influential Threshold series (J. A. van Ek and J. L. M. Trim, Cambridge University Press, 1991) provides a detailed description in functional, notional, grammatical, and sociocultural terms, of what a language user needs to be able to do in order to communicate effectively in the sort of situations commonly encountered in everyday life. Three levels of proficiency are identified, called Waystage, Threshold, and Vantage (roughly corresponding to Elementary, Intermediate, and Upper Intermediate).

The Threshold series was followed in 2001 by the publication of the Common European Framework of Reference, which describes six levels of communicative ability in terms of competences or "can do" statements: A1 (Breakthrough), A2 (Waystage), B1 (Threshold), B2 (Vantage), C1 (Effective Operational Proficiency), and C2 (Mastery). Based on the CEFR descriptors, the Council of Europe also developed the European Language Portfolio, a document that enables learners to assess their language ability and to keep an internationally recognized record of their language learning experience.

Interchange Fourth Edition and the Common European Framework of Reference

The table below shows how *Interchange Fourth Edition* correlates with the Council of Europe's levels and with some major international examinations.

	CEFR	Council of Europe	Cambridge ESOL	IELTS	TOEFL iBT	TOEIC
Interchange						
Level Intro	A1	Breakthrough				120+
Level 1	A2	Waystage				225+
Level 2						
Level 3	B1	Threshold	KET (Key English Test)	4.0–5.0	57–86	550+
			PET (Preliminary English Test)			
Passages						
Level 1	B2	Vantage	FCE (First Certificate in English)	5.5–6.5	87–109	785+
Level 2	C1	Effective Operational Efficiency	CAE (Certificate in Advanced English)	7.0–8.0	110–120	490+ (Listening) 445+ (Reading)

Sources: http://www.cambridgeesol.org/about/standards/cefr.html
http://www.ets.org/Media/Research/pdf/CEFR_Mapping_Study_Interim_Report.pdf
http://www.sprachenmarkt.de/fi leadmin/sprachenmarkt/ets_images/TOEIC_Can-do-table_CEFR_2008.pdf

Essential teaching tips

Classroom management

Error correction

- During controlled practice accuracy activities, correct students' wrong use of the target language right away, either by correcting the error yourself or, whenever possible, having the student identify and / or correct the error. This way, the focus is on accuracy, and students can internalize the correct forms, meaning, and use of the language.
- During oral fluency activities, go around the room and take notes on errors you hear. Do not interrupt students. Instead, take notes of their errors in the use of target language and write these errors on the board. Encourage students to correct them first. Be sure to point out and praise students for language used correctly as well.

Grouping students

It is good to have students work in a variety of settings: individually, in pairs, in groups and as a class. This creates a more student-centered environment and increases student talking time.

- The easiest and quickest way to put students in pairs is to have two students sitting close to one another work together. This is good for when students need to have a quick discussion or check answers.
- To ensure students don't always work with the same partner and / or for longer activities, pair students by name, e.g., Maria, work with Javier.
- One way to put students in groups is to give them a number from 1 to 4, and then have all number 1s work together, all number 2s work together, and so forth.

Instructions

- Give short instructions and model the activity for the students.
- Check your instructions, but avoid asking, *Do you understand*? Instead ask concept questions such as, *Are you going to speak or write when you do this activity?*

Monitoring

- Make sure you go around the room and check that the students are doing the activity and offer help as necessary.
- Monitor closely during controlled practice, but don't make yourself too accessible during fluency activities; otherwise, students may rely on you to answer questions rather than focus on communicating their ideas to their partner or group.

Teaching multi-level classes

- Teach the Classroom Language on page xxix and put useful language up in the classroom, so the students get used to using English.
- Don't rush. Make sure all the students have had enough time to practice the material.
- Do a lot of repetition and drilling of the new target language.
- Encourage students to practice and review target language by doing activities in the Workbook, and Self-study DVD-ROM.
- Elicit answers from your students and involve them in the learning process. Find out what they already know by asking them questions.
- Use the optional activities within the Teaching Notes and the Supplementary Resources Overview charts at the beginning of each unit in this Teacher's Edition to add variety to your lessons.

Teaching reading and listening

- Reading and Listening texts are meant to help the students become better readers / listeners, not to test them. Explain to your students why they need to read or listen to a text several times.
- Adapt the reading speed to the purpose of the reading. When the students read for gist, encourage them to read quickly. When students read for detail, give them more time.

Unit 1 Supplementary Resources Overview

	After the following SB exercises	You can use these materials in class	Your students can use these materials outside the classroom
CYCLE 1	1 Snapshot		
	2 Conversation		SSD Unit 1 Speaking 1–2
	3 Grammar Focus		SB Unit 1 Grammar Plus focus 1 SSD Unit 1 Grammar 1 ARC Relative pronouns
	4 Word Power	TSS Unit 1 Vocabulary Worksheet TSS Unit 1 Extra Worksheet	SSD Unit 1 Vocabulary 1–2 ARC Relative pronouns and Personalities ARC Personalities
	5 Listening	TSS Unit 1 Listening Worksheet	
	6 Discussion		
	7 Writing		WB Unit 1 exercises 1–5
CYCLE 2	8 Perspectives		
	9 Pronunciation		
	10 Grammar Focus	TSS Unit 1 Grammar Worksheet TSS Unit 1 Writing Worksheet	SB Unit 1 Grammar Plus focus 2 SSD Unit 1 Grammar 2 ARC Relative pronouns, Personalities, and Clauses ARC *It* clauses + adverbial clauses with *when*
	11 Interchange 1		
	12 Reading	TSS Unit 1 Project Worksheet VID Unit 1 VRB Unit 1	SSD Unit 1 Reading 1–2 SSD Unit 1 Listening 1–3 SSD Unit 1 Video 1–3 WB Unit 1 exercises 6–10

Key **ARC:** Arcade   **SB:** Student's Book   **SSD:** Self-study DVD-ROM   **TSS:** Teacher Support Site
      VID: Video DVD   **VRB:** Video Resource Book   **WB:** Workbook

My Plan for Unit 1

Use the space below to customize a plan that fits your needs.

With the following SB exercises	I am using these materials in class	My students are using these materials outside the classroom

With or instead of the following SB section	I am using these materials for assessment

1 That's what friends are for!

1 SNAPSHOT

Love and Marriage in North America

What women look for in a partner

1. love
2. understanding
3. conversation
4. time together
5. a positive attitude
6. a good listener
7. affection
8. responsibility at home
9. free time
10. good health

What men look for in a partner

1. belief in his capabilities
2. understanding
3. compliments
4. acceptance
5. direct conversation
6. affection
7. respect
8. free time
9. trust
10. companionship

Source: http://marriage.about.com

What qualities do both men and women look for in their partners?
In your opinion, which of the things above are most important to look for in a partner?
Are there other important qualities missing from the lists?

2 CONVERSATION *I like guys who . . .*

A  Listen and practice.

Chris: Do you have a date for your friend's wedding yet?
Kim: Actually, no, I don't. . . . Do you know anyone I could go with?
Chris: Hmm. What kind of guys do you like?
Kim: Oh, I like guys who aren't too serious and who have a good sense of humor. You know, someone like you.
Chris: OK. Uh, what else?
Kim: Well, I'd prefer someone I have something in common with – who I can talk to easily.
Chris: I think I know just the guy for you. Bob Branson. Do you know him?
Kim: No, I don't think so.
Chris: OK, I'll ask him to meet us for coffee, and you can tell me what you think.

B  Listen to Chris and Kim discuss Bob after they met for coffee. How did Kim like him?

That's what friends are for!

> In this unit, students practice talking about personalities and qualities of friends, parents, partners, and roommates. In Cycle 1, students discuss ideal friends and partners using relative pronouns. In Cycle 2, they talk about things they like and don't like with clauses containing *it* and adverbial clauses with *when*.

Option: Brainstorm questions Ss might ask to find out about classmates. Write Ss' ideas on the board:

<u>Wh-questions</u>
Where do you live? What do you do?
Why are you studying English?

<u>Yes/No questions</u>
Do you speak any other languages?
Are you married? Do you have any children?

- Ss work in pairs (preferably with someone they don't know). They take turns interviewing each other. Remind Ss to use the questions on the board and others of their own.
- After ten minutes, stop the activity. Pairs take turns introducing their partners to the class.

 SNAPSHOT

Learning Objective: *learn vocabulary for relationships*

- Books closed. Ask: "What do you think women look for most in a partner? What do men look for most in a partner?"
- Ss discuss these questions in pairs. Elicit ideas and write them on the board.
- Books open. Ss read the Snapshot individually. Answer vocabulary questions, or allow Ss to use their dictionaries.
- Ask Ss to look carefully at the information in the Snapshot. Ask: "What are some important differences between men and women?" Elicit ideas.

- Read the questions. Discuss the questions as a class, or ask Ss to discuss them in pairs or small groups.
- **Option:** Ask Ss to copy this chart into their vocabulary notebook:

Adjective		Noun	
conversational	positive	conversation	_____
affectionate	healthy	_____	_____
responsible	accepting	_____	_____
trusting	loving	_____	_____

Tell them to complete the *Noun* column by finding the information in the Snapshot.

 CONVERSATION

Learning Objectives: *practice a conversation between two friends about dating preferences; see relative pronouns* who *and* that *in context*

A ▶ **[CD 1, Track 1]**

- As a warm-up, ask: "What do you think of 'matchmaking'? Does it work?" Elicit ideas.
- Books closed. Write these focus questions on the board:
  1. What is Kim's problem?
  2. Who does Chris suggest?
  3. How will Kim meet Chris's friend?
- Play the audio program and elicit Ss' answers. (Answers: 1. Kim has no one to go to the party with. 2. Chris suggests Bob Branson. 3. They will all meet for coffee.)
- Write on the board:
  Kim likes guys who . . .
  1. are serious
  2. have a good sense of humor

  3. are sensitive
  4. she has something in common with
- Explain that *guys* is an informal word for *men*. Ask Ss to listen to find out which guys Kim likes.
- Play the audio program again. Elicit answers. (Answers: 2 and 4)
- Books open. Play the audio program again. Ss listen and read silently.
- Ss practice the conversation in pairs.
- ! For a new way to teach this Conversation, try **Look Up and Speak!** – download it from the website.

B ▶ **[CD 1, Track 2]**

- Read the focus question aloud.
- Play the audio program once or twice. Ss listen for the answer to the question. (Answer: She liked him a lot.)

AudioScript

See page T-165.

GRAMMAR FOCUS

Learning Objective: *practice relative pronouns* who
and that *as subjects and objects*

 [CD 1, Track 3]

Relative pronouns

- Focus Ss' attention on the Grammar Focus box.
  Explain that relative pronouns *(who and that)* do two
  jobs at the same time. They enable us to:
  1. join two ideas (e.g., *Kim likes guys*, and *they aren't
     too serious*).
  2. add information (e.g., *Kim likes guys*. What kind of
     guys? *Guys who aren't too serious.*).

Relative pronouns as subjects and objects

- Point to *I like guys who/that aren't too serious.*
  Tell Ss to underline the relative clause. (Answer:
  who/that aren't too serious) Ask: "What's the subject
  in the relative clause? Who or what 'aren't too
  serious'?" (Answer: who/that, guys) Explain that the
  relative pronoun is the subject here. Repeat for the
  second sentence.

- Point to *I'd prefer someone (who/that) I can talk
  to easily.* Tell Ss to underline the relative clause.
  (Answer: *(who/that) I can talk to easily*) Ask: "What's
  the subject in this relative clause? Who 'can talk to
  easily'?" (Answer: I) Explain that the relative pronoun
  is the object here. Repeat for the last sentence.

- Explain that a relative pronoun *who* or *that* is
  necessary when the relative pronoun is a subject.
  When the relative pronoun is an object, we can omit it.

- Focus Ss' attention on the Conversation on page 2.
  Ask Ss to find four examples of relative clauses.

- Play the audio program for the Grammar Focus box.
  Ss listen and repeat.

A

- Explain the task. Model the first item. Point out that
  more than one answer is possible.
- Ss complete the task individually. Then they compare
  answers in pairs. Go over answers with the class.

Possible answers

1. d. I don't want to have a partner who/that I have
   nothing in common with.
2. g. I'd prefer a roommate who/that is quiet,
   considerate, and neat.
3. f. I don't like to be with people who/that I don't feel
   comfortable around.
4. e. I discuss my problems with friends who/that can
   give me good advice.
5. b. I'd like to have a boss who/that I respect as
   a leader.
6. a. I enjoy teachers who/that help me understand
   things easily.
7. c. I'd like to meet people who/that have a good
   sense of humor.

B

- Ss complete the task individually. Then they compare
  answers in pairs. Go over answers with the class.

Answers

Who/that are optional in sentences 1, 4, and 6.

C Pair work

- Model with your own information (e.g., *I don't want a
  partner who doesn't like to talk.*).

- Ss complete the sentences individually. Encourage Ss
  to be creative and use their own ideas.

- Ss work in pairs. They take turns reading their
  sentences to each other. The goal is to find where they
  have similar opinions.

WORD POWER

Learning Objectives: *learn adjectives that describe
personal characteristics; practice giving definitions*

A

- Ss do the matching individually or in pairs. When
  finished, Ss can check a dictionary.

Answers

1. h, P	3. a, N	5. f, P	7. d, P	9. e, N
2. c, N	4. i, P	6. b, N	8. g, N	

B Pair work

- Tell Ss to cover the definitions. Read the example
  sentence. Ask a S to complete it.

- Explain the task. Ss work in pairs. They take turns
  asking about the adjectives.

C Pair work

- Model the task by using some adjectives to describe
  yourself.

- Ss work individually to write down adjectives to
  describe themselves. Go around the class and give
  help as needed.

- Then Ss work in pairs. Ss take turns sharing their
  descriptions.

- For more practice with vocabulary from Exercises 1-4,
  play ***Prediction Bingo*** – download it from the website.
  Read aloud the definitions, not the adjectives.

T-3 ▪ *Unit 1*

3 GRAMMAR FOCUS

> **Relative pronouns** ⊙
>
> **As the subject of a clause**
> I like guys **who/that** aren't too serious.
> I like guys **who/that** have a good sense of humor.
>
> **As the object of a clause**
> I'd prefer someone **(who/that)** I have fun with.
> I'd prefer someone **(who/that)** I can talk to easily.

A Match the information in columns A and B. Then compare with a partner.

A

1. I don't want to have a partner who/that ....d....
2. I enjoy teachers who/that ....
3. I'd prefer a roommate who/that ....
4. I don't like to be with people who/that ....
5. I discuss my problems with friends who/that ....
6. I'd like to have a boss who/that ....
7. I like to meet people who/that ....

B

a. help me understand things easily.
b. I respect as a leader.
c. have a good sense of humor.
d. I have nothing in common with.
e. can give me good advice.
f. I don't feel comfortable around.
g. is quiet, considerate, and neat.

B Put a line through *who/that* in part A if it's optional. Then compare with a partner.

C PAIR WORK Complete the sentences in column A with your own information.
Do you and your partner have similar opinions?

A: I don't want to have a partner who isn't a good listener.
B: Neither do I. I don't want to have a partner who doesn't have a positive attitude either.

4 WORD POWER *Personalities*

A Match the words with the definitions. Then decide whether the words are
positive (**P**) or negative (**N**). Write **P** or **N** after each word.

.....h.... 1. easygoing ....P....
.... 2. egotistical ....
.... 3. inflexible ....
.... 4. modest ....
.... 5. sociable ....
.... 6. stingy ....
.... 7. supportive ....
.... 8. temperamental ....
.... 9. unreliable ....

a. a person who doesn't change easily and is stubborn
b. someone who doesn't like sharing
c. someone who has a very high opinion of him- or herself
d. someone who is helpful and encouraging
e. a person who doesn't do what he or she promised
f. a person who enjoys being with other people
g. a person who has unpredictable or irregular moods
h. a person who doesn't worry much or get angry easily
i. someone who doesn't brag about his or her accomplishments

B PAIR WORK Cover the definitions. Take turns talking about the adjectives in your own words.

"An easygoing person is someone who . . ."

C PAIR WORK Think of at least two adjectives to describe yourself. Then tell a partner.

5 LISTENING What are they like?

A ▶ Listen to conversations that describe three people. Are the descriptions positive (**P**) or negative (**N**)? Check (✓) the box.

1.	Andrea	☐ P	☑ N	*getting on my nerves, brags.*
2.	James	☐ P	☐ N	....
3.	Mr. Johnson	☐ P	☐ N	....

B ▶ Listen again. Write two adjectives that describe each person in the chart.

6 DISCUSSION Ideal people

A What is the ideal parent, friend, or partner like? What is one quality each should have and one quality each should *not* have? Complete the chart.

	This person is . . .	This person is not . . .
The ideal parent	....	....
The ideal friend	....	....
The ideal partner	....	....

B GROUP WORK Take turns describing your ideal people. Try to agree on the two most important qualities for a parent, a friend, and a partner.

A: I think the ideal parent is someone who is easygoing and who . . .
B: I agree. The ideal parent is someone that doesn't get upset easily and who isn't temperamental.
C: Oh, I'm not sure I agree. . . .

7 WRITING About a best friend

A Think about your best friend. Answer the questions. Then write a paragraph.

What is your best friend like?
How long have you been friends?
How did you meet?
How are you similar?
How are you different?

> My best friend is someone who is friendly and easygoing. She's a reliable friend and someone who I can call anytime. We've been friends for about five years, but we didn't become friends right away. We . . .

B PAIR WORK Exchange paragraphs. How are your best friends similar? How are they different?

5 LISTENING

Learning Objective: *develop skills in making inferences*

A ▶ *[CD 1, Track 4]*

- Books closed. Divide the class into teams. Each team brainstorms positive and negative adjectives to describe personalities.
- Set a time limit of three minutes. Call on different Ss from each team to write the adjectives in two columns on the board.
- Books open. Set the scene. Ss will listen to descriptions of three people. After listening to each conversation, Ss decide if the general feeling is positive (P) or negative (N).
- Play the audio program. Ss listen and check (✓) the positive or negative box.

AudioScript

See page T-165.

- Go over answers with the class.

Answers

1. Andrea, N
2. James, P
3. Mr. Johnson, N

B ▶ *[CD 1, Track 5]*

- Play the audio program again. Pause after each conversation. Ss write two adjectives that describe each person.
- Elicit answers from the class. Ask Ss to explain why they chose those words (e.g., *Andrea is egotistical because she talks about herself.*).

Possible answers

1. Andrea: egotistical, stingy
2. James: sociable, easygoing
3. Mr. Johnson: temperamental, unreliable

6 DISCUSSION

Learning Objectives: *develop the skill of describing qualities in other people; develop the skill of agreeing and disagreeing*

A

- Focus Ss' attention on the picture. Ask: "What is happening? What kind of parent do you think the man is?"
- Explain the task. Read the discussion questions, and go over the chart.
- Ss work in small groups to complete the chart.

B Group work

- Explain the task. Have three Ss model the conversation.
- Ss work in small groups. Ss take turns describing their "ideal people" using information from their chart in part A. Go around the class and give help as needed.
- **Option:** Ss discuss other ideal people (e.g., the ideal boss/employee/teacher/student/brother/sister).

❗ For a new way to practice discussion, try the *Onion-Ring* technique – download it from the website.

7 WRITING

Learning Objectives: *write a paragraph using relative pronouns; write a description of a best friend*

A

- Explain the task. Go over the example paragraph.
- Read the questions. Ask Ss to find the answers to the first two questions in the paragraph.
- Ask Ss to identify the two relative clauses in the paragraph.
- Have Ss think about their best friend and write answers to the questions.
- Ss write the first draft of their paragraph. Write one paragraph, focusing on three areas:
  (1) content, (2) organization, (3) grammar.

- **Option:** Ss write the paragraph for homework.

B Pair work

- Ss work in pairs to complete the task.
- Call on pairs to explain how their best friends are similar and different.
- Ss make final revisions. Then they turn in their work for checking.

End of Cycle 1

See the Supplementary Resources chart at the beginning of this unit for additional teaching materials and student activities related to this Cycle.

8 PERSPECTIVES

Learning Objectives: *complete a fun quiz; see clauses with* it *and adverbial clauses with* when *in context*

A ▶ [CD 1, Track 6]

- Ss cover the text and look only at the picture. Ask Ss to discuss these questions in pairs:
  What is happening?
  How do you think the man feels?
  Would this annoy you? Why?
- While Ss are talking, write the left-hand column on the board (answers are on the right).

Common complaints - topics

cell phones in the classroom	(2)
people who talk with their mouths full	(4)
teachers forgetting names	(3)
an early morning phone call	(7)
loud talking during a movie	(6)
children who scream in restaurants	(1)
friends who forget birthdays	(5)
doctors who are late	(8)

- Books closed. Set the scene. Ss will hear eight common complaints. They are written on the board but in the wrong order.
- Tell Ss to listen and number the complaints in the order they hear them. Play the audio program. Then Ss open their books and check their own answers.

- Next, Ss complete the quiz individually. Then Ss count the things that annoy them and check their score.
- **Option:** Ss find out who is similar to them by going around the class and asking people what their score was. When they find someone with the same score, they work with that person to do part B.

B

- Explain the task. Ss read the quiz again. This time, they circle *one* complaint that bothers them most.
- Call on Ss to read each complaint in turn. Ask Ss to raise their hand if they chose that complaint. Note how many people chose each complaint, and count the score. Which one bothers people the most?
- **Option:** Ss with the same complaint work in groups. They discuss these questions:
  Why does that situation annoy you so much?
  When did it last happen? What did you do about it?
- **Option:** Tell Ss to look at the sentences in the quiz. Elicit four ways of saying *I don't like it.* Write Ss' answers on the board. (Answers: I hate it. It bothers me. I can't stand it. It upsets me.)

9 PRONUNCIATION

Learning Objective: *notice and use linked sounds*

A ▶ [CD 1, Track 7]

- Explain that English speakers often link words together. They often link a final consonant to the vowel sound that follows it (e.g., *It upsets me. I can't stand it.*).
- Point out that we link *sounds* together, not letters. Write some examples on the board:
  I ha**te it** = /tI/   I lo**ve it** = /vI/
- Give Ss time to read the two example sentences and to study the examples of consonant + vowel links in each sentence.
- Play the audio program. Ss practice the sentences.

B ▶ [CD 1, Track 8]

- Explain the task. Ss read the sentences and decide which sounds are linked. They mark the linked sounds.

- Play the audio program. Ss listen and check their answers.
- Go over answers with the class. Write the sentences on the board. Call on Ss to mark the linked sounds.

Answers

I can't stand it when someone is late for an appointment.
Does it bother you when a friend is unreliable?
I hate it when a cell phone goes off in class.

C

- Explain the task. Model the first sentence in the quiz.
- Ss work in pairs. They take turns saying the sentences. Go around the class and listen for linking.
- Play the audio program again if needed.
- **Option:** Ss practice reading the statements in the Perspectives.

8 PERSPECTIVES Quiz

A ▶ Listen to some common complaints. Check (✓) the ones you agree with.

Do you get annoyed easily?

- ☐ I can't stand it when a child screams in a restaurant.
- ☐ I don't like it when a cell phone rings in the classroom.
- ☐ It bothers me when a teacher forgets my name.
- ☐ I hate it when people talk with their mouths full.
- ☐ It upsets me when a close friend forgets my birthday.
- ☐ I can't stand it when people talk loudly to each other during a movie.
- ☐ I don't like it when people call me early in the morning.
- ☐ It bothers me when my doctor arrives late for an appointment.

Score: If you checked . . .
1–2 complaints: Wow! You don't get annoyed very easily.
3–4 complaints: You're fairly easygoing.
5–6 complaints: You get annoyed pretty easily.
7–8 complaints: Relax! You get annoyed too easily.

B Calculate your score. Do you get annoyed easily? Tell the class what bothers you the most.

9 PRONUNCIATION Linked sounds

A ▶ Listen and practice. Final consonant sounds are often linked to the vowel sounds that follow them.

It upsets me when a person is unreliable.

I love it when a friend is supportive and kind.

B ▶ Mark the linked sounds in the sentences below. Listen and check. Then practice saying the sentences.

1. I can't stand it when someone is late for an appointment.

2. Does it bother you when a friend is unreliable?

3. I hate it when a cell phone goes off in class.

C Take turns saying the sentences in Exercise 8. Pay attention to linked sounds.

It *clauses + adverbial clauses with* when ▶

I like **it**	**when** a teacher is helpful and supportive.
I don't mind **it**	**when** a friend visits without calling me first.
I can't stand **it**	**when** a child screams in a restaurant.
It makes me happy	**when** people do nice things for no reason.
It bothers me	**when** my doctor arrives late for an appointment.
It upsets me	**when** a close friend forgets my birthday.

A How do you feel about these situations? Complete the sentences with *it* clauses from the list. Then take turns reading your sentences with a partner.

I love it	I don't mind it	I don't like it
I like it	It doesn't bother me	It really upsets me
It makes me happy	It annoys me	I can't stand it

1. .... when someone gives me a compliment.
2. .... when I get phone calls on my birthday.
3. .... when a stranger asks me for money.
4. .... when people call me late at night.
5. .... when teachers are temperamental.
6. .... when people are direct and say what's on their mind.
7. .... when someone corrects my English in front of others.
8. .... when a friend is sensitive and supportive.
9. .... when people throw trash on the ground.
10. .... when a friend treats me to dinner.

B GROUP WORK Do you ever get annoyed by a certain type of person or situation? Write down five things that annoy you the most. Then compare in groups.

A: I can't stand it when someone puts me on hold.
B: I feel the same way.
C: Yeah, but it bothers me more when . . .

11 *INTERCHANGE 1* *Personality types*

Interview a classmate to find out about his or her personality.
Go to Interchange 1 on page 114.

GRAMMAR FOCUS

Learning Objective: *practice clauses with* it *and adverbial clauses with* when

 [CD 1, Track 9]

Clauses with **it** *and* **when**

- Focus Ss' attention on the Perspectives on page 5. Ask Ss to find examples of sentences that begin with *I*. Write the sentences on the board like this:

1	2	3	4	5
I	don't like	it	when	a cell phone rings . . .
I	hate	it	when	people talk . . .
I	can't stand	it	when	people talk loudly . . .

- Ask Ss what is in each column to elicit the rule:

<u>Clause with *it*</u>   <u>Adverbial clause with *when*</u>
subject + verb + it + when + subject + verb

- Point out that we use *it when* in this structure.

Sentences beginning with **it** **and adverbial clauses with** **when**

- In the same Perspectives, ask Ss to find two examples of sentences that begin with the word *it*. Write the sentences on the board. Also add the phrase *it embarrasses me.*

1	2	3	4	5
It	bothers	me	when	a teacher forgets . . .
It	upsets	me	when	a close friend . . .
It	bothers	me	when	my doctor . . .

- Ask Ss what is in each column to elicit the rule:

<u>Clause with *it*</u>   <u>Adverbial clause with *when*</u>
It + verb + object   +   when + subject + verb

- Play the audio program.

- **Option:** For additional practice, write these cues on the board and ask Ss to complete them orally:

I like it when . . .   It bothers me when . . .
I don't like it when . . .   It really upsets me when . . .

A

- Focus Ss' attention on the picture. Ask: "What is happening? How do you feel when you have to wait for something?" Elicit ideas from the class.

- Ss read the expressions and clauses silently.

- Explain any new vocabulary. Elicit which phrases are positive (e.g., *I love it.*), neutral (e.g., *I don't mind it.*), and negative (e.g., *It really upsets me.*).

- Explain the task. Model the first one by eliciting suggestions.

- Ss complete the task individually. Go around the class and give help as needed.

- **Option:** Tell Ss to use each expression only once and to add their own expression for number 10.

- Ss work in pairs. They take turns reading their sentences aloud to compare responses. Remind Ss to focus on linking the words.

- Elicit Ss' responses. Accept any sentences that are logical and grammatically correct. Let Ss self-correct before you correct them.

> **TIP** To deal with common errors, write the word on a note card (e.g., the word *when* or *it*). Each time Ss make the error, show the card.

For more practice with the expressions, play *Tic-Tac-Toe* – download it from the website.

B *Group work*

- Explain the task. Have three Ss model the conversation.

- Ss work individually to write down five things that annoy them. Go around the class and give help as needed.

- Write some useful phrases on the board. Point out that these are ways to agree with someone:

I feel the same way.   Absolutely!
I know what you mean!   Me too./Me neither.
You can say that again.

- Ss work in small groups and compare what annoys them.

- Encourage Ss to use some of the phrases on the board. Remind them to ask follow-up questions and to give their own opinions. Set a time limit of about ten minutes.

 INTERCHANGE 1

See page T-114 for teaching notes.

That's what friends are for! ▪ **T-6**

Learning Objective: *develop skills in identifying main ideas and understanding vocabulary in context*

- Books closed. Read the pre-reading questions aloud, or write them on the board. Ask Ss to discuss the questions in pairs.

- Ss predict what kind of information they will read in the article.

- Books open. Ss read the article silently. Ss should read the article without stopping to ask questions or use a dictionary.

- Then tell Ss to go back through the text and circle words they can't guess from context. Ss work in pairs to figure out unfamiliar vocabulary.

- Elicit or explain any remaining new vocabulary.

Vocabulary

cyberfriends: people you interact with online
get rid of: remove
endlessly: constantly; without stopping
status updates: information posted online about what someone is doing or thinking
nasty: mean; cruel
phenomenon: event; trend

❗ For a good way to find the meaning of unknown words, try **Vocabulary Mingle** – download it from the website.

A

- Explain the task. Ss decide what is true or false based on the article. Explain that *Not given* means the article has no information on that topic.

- Ss reread the article individually and answer the questions.

- **Option:** Ss compare answers in pairs. Ss show their partners where answers are in the article.

- Go over answers with the class.

Answers

1. True	3. True	5. True
2. False	4. Not given	6. Not given

TIP Two or three smaller, purposeful readings can be more productive than one long, detailed reading.

B

- Explain the task. Ask Ss to find the first phrase. (Answer: paragraph 1, sentence 4.) Read the sentence aloud. Elicit context clues that help Ss figure out the meaning. (Answer: the word *close* suggests people in a personal relationship know each other well.)

- Read the first sentence in part B. Elicit the answer. (Answer: know)

- Ss work individually or in pairs to find the phrases and choose the meanings.

- Go over answers with the class.

Answers

1. know	4. remove
2. unfriend	5. the same
3. strongly	

- **Option:** Write these punctuation marks and their names on the board:

  " " quotation marks
  —   dash
  :   colon

- Ss work in pairs to find this these punctuation marks in the article. Ask Ss to figure out the function. Elicit answers. (Answers: quotation marks around "to remove someone as a 'friend' from a social networking site" for a definition, and quotation marks around "friend" for a special use of a word; dash before *unfriend* follows an explanation; colon after *this* introduces a definition)

C *Pair work*

- Explain the task. Read the questions.

- Ss discuss the questions in pairs.

- Play **Just One Minute** – download it from the website. Ask Ss to talk about the article or a specific friend or loved one.

End of Cycle 2

See the Supplementary Resources chart at the beginning of this unit for additional teaching materials and student activities related to this Cycle.

To Friend or Unfriend?

**How do you choose your friends online?
What qualities do you look for in cyberfriends?**

Social networking makes it very easy to have friends – lots and lots of friends. Hundreds of millions of people have joined Facebook, Orkut, and other sites so that they can communicate with their friends online. However, the meaning of the word "friend" seems to have changed. In the past, a friend was someone you had a close personal relationship with. Now, anyone in the world can be your friend online! Some people have thousands of cyberfriends, but what do you do if you don't want so many friends?

Easy! You can dump an unwanted friend with just one click of your mouse. In recent years, it has become so common to get rid of friends in this way that there is a new word to describe it – to "unfriend." The *New Oxford American Dictionary* named it Word of the Year in 2009 and defined it like this: "to remove someone as a 'friend' from a social networking site." But why would you want to do such a drastic thing as unfriend someone?

The most common reason for unfriending someone is to eliminate annoying people from your social life. For example, some friends post messages much too frequently – and those messages can be extremely boring. They endlessly post status updates that say things like "I'm cooking dinner" or "I'm doing my homework." Another reason for unfriending someone is disagreement about world issues. A third reason is to get rid of people who write nasty things on social websites.

Although dumping friends is not just an Internet phenomenon, far more online friendships end suddenly than off-line ones. Even in this computer age, it remains true that many people prefer spending time together face-to-face. After all, that's what friends are for!

A Read the article. Then for each statement, check (✓) True, False, or Not given.

	True	False	Not given
1. Social networking has changed the way many people make friends.	☐	☐	☐
2. It's not easy to remove cyberfriends.	☐	☐	☐
3. The word "unfriend" became popular in 2009.	☐	☐	☐
4. People who are unfriended may feel upset.	☐	☐	☐
5. Some people write unpleasant things on websites.	☐	☐	☐
6. Sometimes family members are unfriended from websites.	☐	☐	☐

B Find the words and phrases in *italics* in the text. Then choose the meaning for each one.

1. When you have a *personal relationship*, you **know / don't know** someone well.
2. If you *dump* people you know, you **friend / unfriend** them.
3. You might do something *drastic* when you feel **easygoing / strongly** about it.
4. When you *eliminate* someone from your life, you **add / remove** them.
5. If you are *face-to-face* with someone, you are in **the same / a different** location.

C **PAIR WORK** Have you ever unfriended anyone? Why? Have you ever been unfriended? How did you feel?

Unit 2 Supplementary Resources Overview

	After the following SB exercises	You can use these materials in class	Your students can use these materials outside the classroom
CYCLE 1	1 Snapshot		
	2 Perspectives		
	3 Grammar Focus		**SB** Unit 2 Grammar Plus focus 1 **SSD** Unit 2 Grammar 1
	4 Word Power		**SSD** Unit 2 Vocabulary 1–2
	5 Speaking	**TSS** Unit 2 Writing Worksheet	**ARC** Gerund phrases 1–2
	6 Writing		**ARC** Expressions for describing pros and cons **WB** Unit 2 exercises 1–4
CYCLE 2	7 Conversation		**SSD** Unit 2 Speaking 1–2
	8 Grammar Focus	**TSS** Unit 2 Vocabulary Worksheet **TSS** Unit 2 Grammar Worksheet	**SB** Unit 2 Grammar Plus focus 2 **SSD** Unit 2 Grammar 2 **ARC** Comparisons
	9 Pronunciation	**TSS** Unit 2 Listening Worksheet	
	10 Listening		
	11 Role Play	**TSS** Unit 2 Extra Worksheet	
	12 Interchange 2		
	13 Reading	**TSS** Unit 2 Project Worksheet **VID** Unit 2 **VRB** Unit 2	**SSD** Unit 2 Reading 1–2 **SSD** Unit 2 Listening 1–3 **SSD** Unit 2 Video 1–3 **WB** Unit 2 exercises 5–8

With or instead of the following SB section	You can also use these materials for assessment
Units 1–2 Progress Check	**ASSESSMENT CD** Units 1–2 Oral Quiz **ASSESSMENT CD** Units 1–2 Written Quiz

Key

ARC: Arcade	**SB:** Student's Book	**SSD:** Self-study DVD-ROM	**TSS:** Teacher Support Site
VID: Video DVD	**VRB:** Video Resource Book	**WB:** Workbook	

My Plan for Unit 2

Use the space below to customize a plan that fits your needs.

With the following SB exercises	I am using these materials in class	My students are using these materials outside the classroom

With or instead of the following SB section	I am using these materials for assessment

2 Career moves

HOT JOBS ➤ In-demand careers of the future

☐ **Simulation engineer** You develop different kinds of simulators, such as flight simulators for training pilots or virtual patients for training medical students.

☐ **Health informatics technician** You use computer systems to update patients' files, which helps doctors diagnose and treat patients.

☐ **Green researcher** You research new environmentally friendly technologies for fields such as transportation, energy, and recycling.

☐ **Organic food farmer** You grow healthy food in a sustainable way, without using harmful pesticides or chemicals.

☐ **Social media manager** You control the representation of a company's brand online on sites like Facebook, Twitter, and others.

Source: www.careerbuilder.com

Rank the careers from 1 (most interesting) to 5 (least interesting). Compare with a partner.
Can you think of any other careers that will be in demand in the future?
What jobs do you think will not be in demand? Why?

2 PERSPECTIVES *Career debate*

A ⊙ Listen to the people talk about jobs. Do you agree or disagree?
Check (✓) the speaker you agree with more.

"Being a flight attendant sounds very exciting. Flying all the time would be fun." ☐	"But flight attendants get tired of traveling. They spend most of their time in airports!" ☐	"Designing clothes is not a man's job. Women are much more fascinated by fashion." ☐	"That's not true! Many great clothing designers are men. Just look at Calvin Klein!" ☐
"I'd enjoy working with animals. I think working as a veterinarian could be rewarding." ☐	"I'm not so sure. Animals can be very unpredictable. Getting a dog bite would be scary!" ☐	"I'd like to work in the television industry. Directing a TV show would be really interesting." ☐	"I disagree! Working in front of the camera as an actor would be much more satisfying." ☐

B Compare your responses with your classmates. Give more reasons to support your opinions.

Career moves

Cycle 1, Exercises 1–6

1 SNAPSHOT

Learning Objective: *learn vocabulary for discussing jobs*

- Books closed. Introduce the topic of *in-demand careers* or *hot jobs* by writing the phrases on the board.

- Explain that some jobs or careers will be more "in demand" in the future. Explain that "in demand means something that is strongly needed, and "hot" means popular.

- With the class, brainstorm hot jobs of the future (e.g., social media manager). Write Ss' ideas on the board. Ask Ss to guess which ones will be mentioned in the Snapshot.

- Books open. Give Ss several minutes to read the Snapshot on their own. Allow Ss to use a dictionary after they finish reading, if they wish.

- Elicit or explain any new vocabulary.

Vocabulary

simulation: something that looks or behaves like something real, but is not
simulator: a machine on which people can practice operating a vehicle or aircraft without driving or flying
virtual: using computer images and sounds that make you think an imagined situation is real

informatics: the field of information processing; information science
diagnose: to say what is wrong with someone who is ill
green: good for the environment
organic: growing plants or keeping animals for food without using artificial chemicals
sustainable: able to continue over a period of time
pesticides: chemicals used to kill insects
representation: the way someone or something is shown
brand: a product that is made by a particular company

- Read the questions aloud. Then Ss discuss the questions in pairs.

- ***Option:*** Ask Ss to discuss jobs that will not be in demand in the future or that are already outdated. (e.g., telephone operator). Write Ss' ideas on the board.

- For a new way to review the five hot jobs, try *Vocabulary Steps* – download it from the website.

- To practice jobs, play **Hot Potato** – download it from the website. Ask Ss to brainstorm one job beginning with each letter of the alphabet.

2 PERSPECTIVES

Learning Objectives: *listen to people talking about jobs; see gerunds in context; practice the skill of agreeing and disagreeing*

A ▶ [CD 1, Track 10]

- Books closed. Set the scene. Ss will hear people talking about four jobs. Two people give different opinions about each job.

- Play the audio program. Ss listen and write down the four jobs. (Answers: fashion designer, flight attendant, TV director, veterinarian)

- Books open. Tell Ss to read the Perspectives to check their answers.

- Elicit or explain any new vocabulary. Elicit that Calvin Klein is one of the most successful male fashion designers in the world.

- Explain the task. Ss read and check which of the two speakers they agree with more.

B

- Explain the task. Go over the language used by the speakers in part A to agree or disagree (e.g., *That's not true! I disagree! I'm not so sure.*).

- Ss compare their answers in pairs. Encourage Ss to ask follow-up questions.

- Play the audio program again. Tell Ss to focus on the intonation used for disagreeing and presenting opinions.

- Ss practice the conversations in pairs. Tell Ss to try to imitate the original speakers' intonation.

Learning Objective: *practice gerund phrases as subjects and as objects*

▶ *[CD 1, Track 11]*

- Elicit or explain that a gerund is formed by adding *-ing* to a verb (e.g., *designing, being*). This is the same form as the present continuous. However, a gerund is a noun, so it can be a subject or an object in a sentence.

> **TIP** To help Ss remember the structure, encourage them to try to work out rules themselves. Training Ss in this skill will help them deal with new structures in the future.

- Write on the board:

  <u>Gerund phrases</u>
  1. *As the subject of a sentence:*
     <u>Being a flight attendant</u> sounds exciting.
  2. *As the object of the verb:*
     He'd love <u>being a flight attendant.</u>
  3. *As the object of a preposition:*
     I'm interested in <u>being a flight attendant.</u>

- Play the audio program.
- Focus Ss' attention on the Perspectives on page 8. Tell Ss to underline the gerunds. Call on Ss to write the gerunds on the board. (Answers: designing, being, flying, traveling, writing, working, getting, directing) Note: *Clothing designer* is a noun phrase; *exciting* and *rewarding* are participial adjectives.
- **Option:** Ask Ss to use the gerunds on the board as subjects. Then ask Ss to use the gerunds as objects (e.g., *Designing clothes is a job for men and women. Calvin Klein is great at designing clothes.*).

A

- Explain the task. Use the example sentence to model the task. Have Ss read the gerund phrases in column A. Explain any new vocabulary.

- **Option:** Review or present other adverbs that Ss can use with the adjectives in column C (e.g., *pretty, kind of, really, very, extremely, so, quite, incredibly*).
- Ss work individually to write their opinions of each job. Go around the class and give help as needed.
- Go over answers with the class. Accept any answers that are logical and grammatically correct.

> **TIP** Let Ss correct problems themselves. Then explain those errors that Ss can't correct.

B *Pair work*

- Explain the task. Model the task with several Ss using the example conversation in the book.
- Ss work in pairs to compare their opinions about the jobs in part A. Go around the class and give help as needed. Make notes of errors with gerund phrases.
- When pairs finish, write some of the errors on the board. Elicit corrections from the class.

C *Group work*

- Explain the task. Ss complete the sentences with gerund phrases as objects. Ask a S to read the example sentence.
- Ss work individually to complete the task. Go around the class and give help as needed.
- Then Ss work in small groups, taking turns reading their sentences. Encourage Ss to ask follow-up questions and to give more information.
- Ask each group to choose the three most interesting sentences. Different Ss read them aloud to the class.
- **Option:** Ss go around and exchange their information with classmates.

For more practice with gerund phrases, play ***True or False?*** – download it from the website.

Gerund phrases ▶

Gerund phrases as subjects	Gerund phrases as objects
Being a flight attendant sounds exciting.	He'd love **being a flight attendant**.
Designing clothes is not a man's job.	He wouldn't like **being a fashion designer**.
Working as a veterinarian could be rewarding.	She'd enjoy **working with animals**.
Directing a TV show would be interesting.	She'd be good at **directing a TV show**.

A Look at the gerund phrases in column A. Write your opinion of each job by choosing information from columns B and C. Then add two more gerund phrases and write similar sentences.

A	B	C
1. working as an accountant	seems	awful
2. taking care of children	sounds	stressful
3. being a farmer	could be	fantastic
4. designing clothes	would be	fascinating
5. working on a movie set	must be	pretty difficult
6. making a living as an artist		kind of boring
7. doing volunteer work overseas		really rewarding
8. retiring at age 40		very challenging
9.		
10.		

> 1. Working as an accountant would be kind of boring.

B PAIR WORK Give reasons for your opinions about the jobs in part A.

A: In my opinion, working as an accountant would be kind of boring.
B: Really? Why is that?
A: Because you work in an office and do the same thing every day.
B: I'm not sure that's true. For me, working as an accountant could be . . .

C GROUP WORK Complete the sentences with gerund phrases. Then take turns reading your sentences. Share the three most interesting sentences with the class.

1. I'd be interested in . . .
2. I'd get tired of . . .
3. I'd be very excited about . . .
4. I'd enjoy . . .
5. I think I'd be good at . . .
6. I wouldn't be very good at . . .

"I'd be interested in working with children."

4 WORD POWER Suffixes

A Add the suffixes *-er, -or, -ist,* or *-ian* to form the names of these jobs.
Write the words in the chart and add one more example to each column.

computer technic...ian...   gossip column............   politic...........   TV report...........
factory supervis...........   guidance counsel...........   psychiatr...........   zookeep...........

-er	-or	-ist	-ian
....	....	....	*computer technician*
....	....	....	....
....	....	....	....

B PAIR WORK Can you give a definition for each job?

"A computer technician is someone who fixes computers."

5 SPEAKING Possible careers

GROUP WORK Talk about a career you would
like to have. Use information from Exercises 1–4 or your
own ideas. Other students ask follow-up questions.

A: I'd enjoy doing TV interviews with famous people.
B: Why is that?
A: Asking people about their lives would be fascinating.
C: Who would you interview?
A: Well, I think I'd be good at talking to politicians.

6 WRITING Describing pros and cons

A Choose a job and make a list of its advantages. Then use the list to
write a paragraph about the job. Add a title.

> Being a comedian: It's fun to be funny
> Working as a comedian seems exciting.
> First of all, making people laugh would be a
> lot of fun because you'd be laughing all the
> time, too. In addition, . . .

useful expressions

First of all, . . .
In addition, . . .
Furthermore, . . .
For example, . . .
However, . . .
On the other hand, . . .
In conclusion, . . .

B PAIR WORK Read your partner's paragraph. Then write a paragraph
about the disadvantages of your partner's job. Add a title.

C PAIR WORK Read your partner's paragraph about your job's
disadvantages. Do you agree or disagree? Why or why not?

4 WORD POWER

Learning Objective: *learn suffixes for jobs*

A

- Explain the task. Ask a S to read the example.
- Ss complete the task individually or in pairs. First, Ss add suffixes to form names of jobs. Then Ss write the words in the chart. Remind Ss to add one more example to each column.
- To check answers, draw the chart on the board. Ask Ss to come up to complete it.

Answers

-er	**-or**
TV report**er**	factory supervis**or**
zookeep**er**	guidance counsel**or**
*Web design**er***	*invent**or***
*child-care work**er***	*decorat**or***
*photograph**er***	*investigat**or***
-ist	**-ian**
gossip column**ist**	computer techni**cian**
psychiat**rist**	politi**cian**
*dent**ist***	*musi**cian***
*chem**ist***	*electri**cian***

*pharmac**ist***   *veterinar**ian***
*art**ist***

(Note: Additional examples are italicized.)

- Pronounce the words. Explain that the *p* is silent in words beginning with *psy*.
- **Option:** Ask Ss to name jobs where the verb and noun are the same (e.g., *coach, cook, guide, TV host*).
- **Option:** Ask Ss to talk about the jobs in the chart, using gerunds as subjects or objects.

B *Pair work*

- Ask a S to read the example definition.
- Ss work in pairs and take turns making definitions. Remind Ss to use *someone who* or *someone that*.

 For a new way to practice jobs and their suffixes, try *Mime* – download it from the website.

5 SPEAKING

Learning Objective: *talk about possible careers*

Group work

- Ask three Ss to model the conversation. Point out the follow-up questions.

- Ss work in small groups. Set a time limit of about ten minutes. Ss take turns talking about possible careers. Tell Ss to ask two follow-up questions each per discussion. Go around the class and give help as needed.

6 WRITING

Learning Objective: *write about the advantages and disadvantages of a particular job*

A

- Explain the task. Ask a S to read the model paragraph aloud. Discuss the title. Go over the useful expressions. Elicit other expressions (e.g., *One advantage/disadvantage is . . .*).
- Ss work individually. Ss choose one of the jobs they talked about in Exercise 5 (or another job). Ss make a list of advantages and write a paragraph.
- Encourage Ss to write about at least *three* advantages. Remind Ss to add a title. Go around the class and give help as needed.

B *Pair work*

- Ss work in pairs. They read each other's paragraphs.

- Ss write a paragraph about the disadvantages of their partner's job. Encourage Ss to write about at least *three* disadvantages. Remind Ss to add a title.
- **Option:** Ss do this step for homework.

C *Pair work*

- Ss exchange and read each other's paragraphs about job disadvantages. Partners say if they agree or disagree.

End of Cycle 1

See the Supplementary Resources chart at the beginning of this unit for additional teaching materials and student activities related to this Cycle.

7 CONVERSATION

Learning Objectives: *practice a conversation about summer jobs; see comparisons in context*

A ⊚ *[CD 1, Track 12]*

- Books closed. Set the scene. Tracy and Mark are talking about summer jobs. Explain that in the United States, young people often get a job during summer vacation to pay for their studies or to gain experience.
- Ask: "What job has Tracy found?" Tell Ss to listen for the answer.
- Books open. Play the first five lines of the audio program. Elicit the answer. (Answer: working at an amusement park)
- Ss cover the text and look at the picture. Explain that these are Mark's two leads, or possible jobs.

  Elicit that an intern is a person working to gain experience, usually for little or no pay.
- Books closed. Play the audio program.
- Ss compare Mark's two job leads in pairs. Ask Ss to discuss the advantages of each.

- Books open. Play the audio program again. Ss listen and read. Ask different Ss to read each line aloud.
- Ss practice the conversation in pairs.

B ⊚ *[CD 1, Track 13]*

- Read the focus question aloud. Ss listen for the answer to the question.
- Play the second part of the audio program. Encourage Ss to take notes.

AudioScript

See page T-165.

Answers

Tracy is going to work at Children's World at the amusement park, where she'll teach young kids interesting games and educational activities. She'll also wear a costume and greet people around the park.

8 GRAMMAR FOCUS

Learning Objective: *practice comparisons with adjectives, verbs, nouns, and past participles*

⊚ *[CD 1, Track 14]*

- Play the audio program. Ask Ss to underline the adjectives, verbs, nouns, and past participles.
- Point out that all the comparisons are based on the same few structures. Write them on the board:

  more . . . than   better . . . than   as . . . as

  less . . . than   worse . . . than   not as . . . as
- Give a few examples with familiar occupations. Elicit other examples.

A

- Explain the task.
- Ss work individually to complete the sentences with the words in parentheses. Remind Ss that there are several correct answers for each item.
- Ss go over their answers in pairs. Then go over answers with the class.

Possible answers

1. Being a fashion designer is **more interesting than** being an accountant.
2. A TV reporter's job is **less dangerous than** a firefighter's job.

3. A police officer **travels less than** a flight attendant.
4. A factory supervisor **earns more than** a volunteer teacher.
5. Long-distance truck drivers have **worse hours than** bank tellers.
6. Pilots usually have **more education than** airport security guards.
7. A doctor is **better trained than** a medical assistant.
8. A social worker isn't **as well paid as** a pharmacist.

B Group work

- Ask a S to read the first sentence in Part A. Ask Ss to make another comparison between the two jobs. They do not need to use the words in parentheses. (e.g., *Being a fashion designer is harder than being an accountant. Being a fashion designer is more exciting than being an accountant.*).
- Ss work in small groups. They think of one more comparison for each pair of jobs. They take turns making up sentences. They can change the comparative word, the sentence structure, or both. Go around the class and give help as needed.
- Go over answers with the class. Elicit Ss' responses around the class.

7 CONVERSATION *You get a great tan!*

A ▶ Listen and practice.

Tracy: Guess what. . . . I've found a summer job!
Mark: That's great! Anything interesting?
Tracy: Yes, working at an amusement park.
Mark: Wow, that sounds fantastic!
Tracy: So, have *you* found anything?
Mark: Nothing yet, but I have a couple of leads.
One is working as an intern for a record
company – mostly answering phones.
Or I can get a landscaping job again.
Tracy: Being an intern sounds more interesting
than landscaping. You'd have better hours,
and it's probably not as much work.
Mark: Yeah, but a landscaper earns more than
an intern. And you get a great tan!

B ▶ Listen to the rest of the conversation.
What is Tracy going to do at the amusement park?

8 GRAMMAR FOCUS

Comparisons ▶

with adjectives
. . . is **more/less** interesting **than** . . .
. . . is hard**er than** . . .
. . . is **not as** hard **as** . . .

with verbs
. . . earns **more/less than** . . .
. . . earns **as much as** . . .
. . . doesn**'t** earn **as much as** . . .

with nouns
. . . has **better/worse** hours **than** . . .
. . . has **more** education **than** . . .
. . . is**n't as much** work **as** . . .

with past participles
. . . is **better** paid **than** . . .
. . . is **as** well paid **as** . . .
. . . is**n't as** well paid **as** . . .

A Complete the sentences using the words in parentheses. Compare
with a partner. (More than one answer is possible.)

1. Being a fashion designer is .... (interesting) being an accountant.
2. A TV reporter's job is .... (dangerous) a firefighter's job.
3. A police officer .... (travel) a flight attendant.
4. A factory supervisor .... (earn) a volunteer teacher.
5. Long-distance truck drivers have .... (hours) bank tellers.
6. Pilots usually have .... (education) airport security guards.
7. A doctor is .... (trained) a medical assistant.
8. A social worker isn't .... (paid) a pharmacist.

B GROUP WORK Make one more comparison for each pair of jobs in part A.

9 PRONUNCIATION *Stress with compound nouns*

A ▶ Listen and practice. Notice that the first word in these compound nouns has more stress. Then add two more compound nouns to the chart.

⬤	⬤	⬤	⬤
zookeeper firefighter	bank teller truck driver	gossip columnist guidance counselor	....

B **GROUP WORK** Which job in each column would be more interesting? Why? Tell the group. Pay attention to stress.

10 LISTENING *Summer jobs*

A ▶ Listen to three people talk about their summer jobs. Number the pictures from 1 to 3.

B ▶ Listen again. Do they like their jobs? Why or why not?

11 ROLE PLAY *My job is the worst!*

A Choose a job from the unit. Make a list of all the reasons why you *wouldn't* like it. Think about what is negative, difficult, or boring about it – the salary, the hours, the location, etc.

B **GROUP WORK** Role-play a discussion. Explain why your job is the worst!

A: I'm a teacher, and my salary is terrible!
B: I'm a doctor. I have a higher salary than a teacher, but a teacher has better hours.
C: Well, I'm a taxi driver. My hours aren't as bad as a doctor's, but . . .

12 INTERCHANGE 2 *The dinner party*

Would you be a good party planner? Go to Interchange 2 on page 115.

9 PRONUNCIATION

Learning Objective: *notice and use stress in compound nouns*

A [CD 1, Track 15]

- Books closed. Write the following jobs on the board. Ask: "What do these nouns have in common?"

  truck driver   gossip columnist   zookeeper

- Elicit that these are all compound nouns (two-word nouns). In compound nouns, the main stress falls on the first word.
- Play the audio program. Signal stressed words by tapping a pencil or clapping.
- Books open. Play the audio program again. Ss listen and repeat, tapping or clapping on each stressed word.

- Ss work individually to add two more compound nouns to the chart. Ss can look back through Unit 2 for ideas.
- Write Ss' answers on the board. Ss practice pronouncing the words.

B Group work

- Dictate this sentence, or write it on the board:

  Being a bank teller would be more interesting than being a bus driver, because . . .

- Ask Ss to complete the sentence. Then ask pairs to compare answers.
- Elicit a few answers. Remind Ss to use the correct stress.
- Explain the task.
- Ss work in small groups.

10 LISTENING

Learning Objective: *develop skills in listening to descriptions*

A [CD 1, Track 16]

- Ask Ss to identify the workplace in each picture. (Answers: an office, a school, a restaurant)
- Play the audio program. Ss listen to find out who works in each place.

AudioScript

See page T-165.

Answers

3. (Julia)   1. (Carlos)   2. (Paul)

B [CD 1, Track 17]

- Explain the task. Read the focus question.
- Play the audio program again. This time Ss take notes.

Answers

Carlos likes his job because the kids are fun to work with, and he gets to choose his own hours.
Paul doesn't like his job because it's really hard work, and it's really hot in the kitchen.
Julia likes her job because she works with many other students, and they have fun when they're not making calls. It's really easy, too, and she gets to sleep late.

11 ROLE PLAY

Learning Objectives: *practice making comparisons among various jobs; take part in a role play*

A

- Explain the task. Ss choose a job from the unit. Give Ss time to think about the criteria for the job they chose. The goal is to explain why each S thinks his or her job is the worst.

B Group work

- Three students model the conversation.
- Ss role-play in small groups. Go around the class and listen in. Take notes on problems.
- Set a time limit of eight to ten minutes. When time is up, call on groups to say who has the worst job and why. Encourage Ss to ask follow-up questions.
- Write some problems you heard on the board. Elicit Ss' suggestions on how to correct them.

12 INTERCHANGE 2

See page T-115 for teaching notes.

Learning Objective: *develop skills in scanning for specific information and making inferences*

- Books closed. To introduce the topic, ask: "Who has a job now? How did you find your job?"
- Ask Ss to work in pairs to brainstorm how people should look for a job, or go *job-hunting*. Ask each pair to share some of their ideas with the class.
- Books open. Ask a S to read the title of the article. Explain that a job-hunter (username riley18) has posted a problem on a message board. Five people have responded with job-hunting advice.
- Ask Ss to read the pre-reading task. Ss scan the article to see if riley18 used any of their ideas.
- Elicit or explain any new vocabulary.

Vocabulary

figure: guess; suppose
aim too high: have unrealistic expectations or goals
be too proud: feel you are more important than you really are
modest: not proud
specialize: develop a skill or knowledge in a specific area
suited to: appropriate; fitting
hit the streets: go from door to door; go to real places of business to look for opportunities

A

- Explain the task. Ask different Ss to read the sentences aloud. Say that the comments express opinions of people on the message board, in different words.
- Ss work individually to match the comments to the usernames. Allow Ss to consult with others near them if they want help.
- *Option:* Explain that we can infer or guess people's opinions based on other opinions that they state directly.

- Go over answers with the class. Ask: "Who would probably say 'Do something that others can't do!'?" (maggie_ks). Alternatively, ask an early finisher to write the answers on the board.

Answers

1. maggie_ks	3. luis005	5. jackie_s
2. erikjones	4. table9_5	

! For a new way to practice scanning for specific
• information, try **Reading Race** – download it from the website.

B

- Explain the task. Point out that Ss are imagining other situations for riley18. They must imagine the kind of advice that the message board posters would give.
- Ss work individually to write the usernames by each situation.
- Go over answers with the class.

Answers

1. luis005	3. maggie_ks	5. erikjones
2. jackie_s	4. table9_5	

C Group work

- Read the discussion question.
- Ss discuss the question in small groups. Tell the groups to ask one person to write down any new advice they think of for riley18's job search.
- Ask the groups to share any new strategies. Write them on the board. Also ask the groups to share other interesting ideas from the discussions.

End of Cycle 2

See the Supplementary Resources chart at the beginning of this unit for additional teaching materials and student activities related to this Cycle and for assessment tools.

Help! How can I find a job?

*Make a short list of things people should do to find a job.
Then scan the message board. Has riley18 done any of these things?*

 I've been job-hunting for a year with no luck. I've done all the right things. I graduated with a degree in information technology – everybody says you can't go wrong with IT! I've sent my résumé to lots of local companies. I dress professionally and answer interview questions well. But I haven't gotten a single job offer! Other applicants have work experience. How can I get experience if no one offers me a job? Help!
riley18

 What kinds of jobs are you applying for? I figure you're aiming too high. Don't be too proud! Entering the job market for the first time requires you to be modest. Good luck!
erikjones

 The thing about IT is you need to specialize. I work in medicine. Diagnostic imaging – stuff like PET and MRI scanning – uses complex software that can only be operated by highly specialized people.
maggie_ks

 I had the same problem as you. I graduated in IT, too! Then I went to a career counselor. She made me realize I'm more suited to a job with people than one with computers. I'm a really sociable person. I applied for work in telesales and got a job immediately. I love it! I talk to people on the phone all day!
jackie_s

 Don't just sit there and expect a job to come to you! When job-hunting, the three most important things to remember are location, location, location! Hit the streets and go where the jobs are!
luis005

 There are so many more interesting jobs than working with computers! Why does everyone think IT is so special? Everyone has to eat and drink! Why don't you open a coffee shop or restaurant?
table9_5

A Read the message board. Where do these sentences belong?
Write the username of the person who probably made each comment.

 1. Do something that others can't do!
.... 2. The key thing is to get a job and then work your way up.
.... 3. If you're prepared to relocate, you'll easily find a job in IT.
.... 4. Have you thought about being self-employed?
.... 5. Working alone all day on a computer isn't much fun for me!

B Whose advice would riley18 *most* likely follow in each of these situations?
Write the username.

.... 1. if he can move to a new place easily
.... 2. if he is happy to seek professional advice
.... 3. if he is prepared to study for another degree
.... 4. if he has some money to invest in a small business
.... 5. if he is patient enough to wait for promotion

C **GROUP WORK** Whose comment do you think is the most helpful to riley18? Why?
What advice or comment would you offer?

Units 1–2 Progress check

SELF-ASSESSMENT

How well can you do these things? Check (✓) the boxes.

I can	Very well	OK	A little
Describe personalities (Ex. 1)	☐	☐	☐
Ask about and express preferences (Ex. 1)	☐	☐	☐
Understand and express complaints (Ex. 2)	☐	☐	☐
Give opinions about jobs (Ex. 3)	☐	☐	☐
Describe and compare different jobs (Ex. 4)	☐	☐	☐

1 SPEAKING *People preferences*

A What two qualities would you like someone to have for these situations?

A person to . . .
1. go on vacation with   ....
2. share an apartment with   ....
3. work on a class project with   ....

B CLASS ACTIVITY Find someone you could do each thing with.

A: What kind of person would you like to go on vacation with?
B: I'd prefer someone who is fairly independent.
A: Me, too! And I like to travel with someone who I can . . .

2 LISTENING *Our biggest complaints*

A ▶ Listen to Ann and John discuss these topics. Complete the chart.

	John's biggest complaint	Ann's biggest complaint
1. taxi drivers	....	....
2. people with dogs	....	....
3. TV commercials	....	....
4. store clerks	....	....

B PAIR WORK What is your biggest complaint about the topics in part A?

"I can't stand it when taxi drivers don't have change. . . ."

Units 1–2 Progress check

SELF-ASSESSMENT

Learning Objectives: *reflect on one's learning; identify areas that need improvement*

- Ask: "What did you learn in Units 1 and 2?" Elicit Ss' answers.
- Ss complete the Self-assessment. Encourage them to be honest, and point out they will not get a bad grade if they check (✓) "a little."

- Ss move on to the Progress check exercises. You can have Ss complete them in class or for homework, using one of these techniques:
  1. Ask Ss to complete all the exercises.
  2. Ask Ss: "What do you need to practice?" Then assign exercises based on their answers.
  3. Ask Ss to choose and complete exercises based on their Self-assessment.

1 SPEAKING

Learning Objective: *assess one's ability to use relative clauses*

A
- Explain the task. Model with an example of your own. Say: "Let's see. I'd like to go on vacation with someone who is organized, so I'll write *organized* here. And I'd also like someone who is calm, so I'll write *calm*."

- Ss complete the task individually. Remind them to write two qualities for each situation. Go around the class and give help as needed.

B *Class activity*
- Explain the task. Ask two Ss to model the conversation.
- Ss go around the class to find someone they could do each thing with.

2 LISTENING

Learning Objective: *assess one's ability to express likes and dislikes with* it *clauses*

A ▶ *[CD 1, Track 18]*
- Explain the task. Ask a S to read the chart.
- Ask Ss to predict complaints they might hear.
- Tell Ss to listen for the complaints. Play the audio program once or twice. Ss complete the chart. Remind Ss to use their own words.
- Play the audio program again for Ss to check their answers.
- Go over answers with the class.

| 3. when they interrupt a ball game at the most exciting moment | when they're louder than the programs |
| 4. when they're rude | when they try too hard to sell you something |

B *Pair work* ▶ *[CD 1, Track 19]*
- Explain the task. Read the question. Ask a S to read the example.
- **Option:** Elicit verbs for expressing likes and dislikes (e.g., *can't stand, hate, love*). Write them on the board.
- **Option:** Play the audio again. Have Ss listen for verbs to express likes and dislikes and write them down. Elicit examples and write them on the board.
- Ss discuss complaints in pairs. Remind them to use clauses with *it* and *when*.
- Ask Ss to share complaints with the class. Write each new complaint on the board. See which complaint was mentioned most often.

> **AudioScript**
>
> See page T-166.

> **Possible answers**

Ann's biggest complaint	John's biggest complaint
1. when they have their radios turned up	when they drive too fast
2. when they take their dogs into a park and let them make messes	when they go out and leave their dogs at home all day, barking

3 SURVEY

Learning Objective: *assess one's ability to express likes and dislikes using gerund phrases*

A Group work

- Explain the task. Ask four Ss to model the conversation.
- Ss work in groups of four to ask and answer questions about jobs. Each S completes the chart.

B Group work

- Explain the task. Read the questions.

- Ss work in the same group or a different one. Point out that Ss can talk about other aspects.
- Ask one S from each group to share the most unusual, the best, and the worst jobs from the group.
- **Option:** Each S writes a short paragraph about the job he or she chose and the job one of the group members chose.

4 ROLE PLAY

Learning Objective: *assess one's ability to make comparisons to talk about jobs*

- Elicit or explain that a *headhunter* is a person who finds new employees for companies. Explain the task.
- Divide the class into pairs, and assign A/B roles. Student As are the headhunters. Student Bs are the job seekers. Ask two Ss to model the conversation. Read the questions.
- Give Ss time to plan what they are going to say.
- Ss role-play in pairs. Encourage Ss to ask as many questions as possible, rather than choosing a job quickly.

- Ss change roles and repeat the role play.
- **Option:** Divide the class in half. Half of the Ss are headhunters, and the other half are job hunters. The headhunters sit at the front of the class and tell the class which two jobs each has. The job hunters then come up and talk to any of the headhunters. Set a time limit of five to ten minutes. When time is up, each S chooses a job.

WHAT'S NEXT?

Learning Objective: *become more involved in one's learning*

- Focus Ss' attention on the Self-assessment again. Ask: "How well can you do these things now?"

- Ask Ss to underline one thing they need to review. Ask: "What did you underline? How can you review it?"
- If needed, plan additional activities or reviews based on Ss' answers.

3 SURVEY Good and bad points

A **GROUP WORK** What job would you like to have? Ask and answer questions in groups to complete the chart.

Name	Job	Good points	Bad points
1.			
2.			
3.			
4.			

A: What job would you like to have?
B: I'd like to be a chef.
C: What would be the good points?
B: Well, thinking of menus would be fun.
D: Would there be any bad points?
B: Oh, sure. I'd dislike working long hours. . . .

useful expressions

I would(n't) be good at . . .
I would enjoy/dislike . . .
I would(n't) be interested in . . .
I would(n't) be excited about . . .

B **GROUP WORK** Who thought of the most unusual job? the best job? the worst job?

4 ROLE PLAY Job headhunter

Student A: Imagine you're a headhunter. You find jobs for people. Based on Student B's opinions about jobs in Exercise 3, offer two other jobs that Student B might enjoy.

Student B: Imagine you are looking for a job. Student A suggests two jobs for you. Discuss the questions below. Then choose one of the jobs.

Which one is more interesting? harder?
Which one has better hours? better pay?
Which job would you rather have?

A: I have two jobs for you. You could be a high school basketball coach or a veterinarian.
B: Hmm. Which job is more interesting?
A: Well, a veterinarian's job is more interesting than a job as a basketball coach, but . . .

Change roles and try the role play again.

WHAT'S NEXT?

Look at your Self-assessment again. Do you need to review anything?

Unit 3 Supplementary Resources Overview

	After the following SB exercises	You can use these materials in class	Your students can use these materials outside the classroom
CYCLE 1	1 Snapshot		
	2 Conversation		**SSD** Unit 3 Speaking 1–2
	3 Grammar Focus		**SB** Unit 3 Grammar Plus focus 1 **SSD** Unit 3 Grammar 1 **ARC** Requests with modals, *if* clauses, and gerunds 1–2
	4 Pronunciation		
	5 Listening		
	6 Writing	**TSS** Unit 3 Writing Worksheet	
	7 Interchange 3		**WB** Unit 3 exercises 1–4
CYCLE 2	8 Word Power	**TSS** Unit 3 Vocabulary Worksheet	**SSD** Unit 3 Vocabulary 1–2 **ARC** Collocations
	9 Perspectives		
	10 Grammar Focus	**TSS** Unit 3 Grammar Worksheet **TSS** Unit 3 Listening Worksheet **TSS** Unit 3 Extra Worksheet	**SB** Unit 3 Grammar Plus focus 2 **SSD** Unit 3 Grammar 2 **ARC** Indirect requests 1–2
	11 Speaking		
	12 Reading	**TSS** Unit 3 Project Worksheet **VID** Unit 3 **VRB** Unit 3	**SSD** Unit 3 Reading 1–2 **SSD** Unit 3 Listening 1–3 **SSD** Unit 3 Video 1–3 **WB** Unit 3 exercises 5–9

Key
ARC: Arcade	**SB:** Student's Book	**SSD:** Self-study DVD-ROM	**TSS:** Teacher Support Site
VID: Video DVD	**VRB:** Video Resource Book	**WB:** Workbook	

My Plan for Unit 3

Use the space below to customize a plan that fits your needs.

With the following SB exercises	I am using these materials in class	My students are using these materials outside the classroom

With or instead of the following SB section	I am using these materials for assessment

3 Could you do me a favor?

1 SNAPSHOT

Favors People Dislike Being Asked

Could you...?

- buy me a coffee
- treat me to a movie
- fix my computer
- babysit my kids
- lend me some money
- help me move to a new apartment
- pick up some groceries
- donate to my favorite charity

Source: http://answers.yahoo.com

Imagine that a close friend asked you each of these favors. Which would you agree to do? What are three other favors that you dislike being asked?

2 CONVERSATION *Would you mind...?*

A ● Listen and practice.

Min-gu: Hello?

Jana: Hi, Min-gu. This is Jana.

Min-gu: Oh, hi, Jana. What's up?

Jana: My best friend is in a band, and I'm going to one of his concerts this weekend. I'd love to take some pictures for his website. Would you mind if I borrowed your new camera?

Min-gu: Um, no. That's OK, I guess. I don't think I'll need it for anything.

Jana: Thanks a million.

Min-gu: Sure. Uh, have you used a camera like mine before? It's sort of complicated.

Jana: Uh-huh, sure, a couple of times. Would it be OK if I picked it up on Friday night?

Min-gu: Yeah, I guess so.

B ● Listen to two more calls Jana makes. What else does she want to borrow? Do her friends agree?

Could you do me a favor?

> *In this unit, students discuss favors, messages, and requests. In Cycle 1, they talk about favors, borrowing, and lending with modals,* if *clauses, and gerunds. In Cycle 2, students practice leaving messages using indirect requests.*

1 SNAPSHOT

Learning Objective: *learn about favors*

- ***Option:*** Books closed. Introduce a well-known proverb: "A friend in need is a friend indeed." Elicit the meaning. (Answer: A friend who helps you when you need it is a true friend.) Then ask: "Should you always say 'yes' to a friend? What would you do if your friend asked you a favor you didn't feel good about?"

- Explain that people were interviewed about favors they dislike being asked. Elicit that *a favor* is something you do to help someone else.

- With the class, brainstorm the favors the people might have mentioned (e.g., *Can you lend me some money?*). Write Ss' ideas on the board. Ask Ss to guess what the top three were.

- Books open. Tell Ss to read the Snapshot. Did Ss guess any of the favors people dislike being asked?

- Read the questions. Ss discuss the questions in pairs. Go around the class and give help as needed.

- Then each pair joins another pair to compare their answers.

- ***Option:*** Clarify the difference between *lend* and *borrow. To lend* is to give; *to borrow* is to take. If helpful, ask an artistic S to draw a picture on the board that shows the difference between the two verbs.

- ***Option:*** Clarify the expression *buy me a coffee.* Explain that it means buying a cup of coffee for someone, either loaning them money for it or treating them to a cup of coffee.

2 CONVERSATION

Learning Objectives: *practice a conversation about borrowing; see requests with modals,* if *clauses, and gerunds in context*

A [CD 1, Track 19]

- Ask Ss to cover the text and look at the picture. Ask: "What are they doing? What are they talking about? What does Jana want to borrow? Does her friend Min-gu want to lend it? How do you know?" Elicit ideas.

- Tell Ss to listen to find out if their predictions are correct. Play the audio program.

- Write this incorrect summary on the board:
  This weekend Jana is going to her cousin's concert. She wants to take photos for a photo album. Jana has used a digital camera many times before. She would like to pick the camera up tonight.

- Ask Ss to listen and correct four mistakes. Play the audio program again. Go over Ss' answers. (Answers: She's going to her <u>best friend's</u> concert. She wants the photos for <u>his website</u>. She has used a digital camera <u>a couple of times</u>. She'll pick it up on <u>Friday</u> night.)

- Ss read the conversation silently.

- Elicit or explain any new vocabulary.

Vocabulary

What's up?: How are you? *or* Is there a problem?
I guess: used to answer yes but not with certainty

Thanks a million.: Thank you very much.
complicated: difficult to understand
a couple of times: one or two times

- Play the audio program again. Ss listen and read. Ask Ss to focus on how Min-gu agrees to Jana's request (e.g., *That's OK, I guess. I guess so.*).

- Ss practice the conversation in pairs.

- For a new way to practice this conversation, try ***Moving Dialog*** – download it from the website.

B [CD 1, Track 20]

- Read the focus questions aloud.

- Play the second part of the audio program. Pause after each conversation. Ss take notes.

- Ss compare answers in pairs. Elicit Ss' responses around the class.

AudioScript

See page T-166.

Answers

Jana wants to borrow Carrie's shirt.
Carrie agrees.
Jana wants to borrow Andy's car.
Andy doesn't agree to because a friend is coming to visit.

3 GRAMMAR FOCUS

Learning Objective: *practice making requests with modals, if clauses, and gerunds*

⏵ **[CD 1, Track 21]**

Requests with modals, **if** *clauses, and gerunds*

- Books closed. Ask a few favors around the class, using modals *can* and *could*. Write them on the board:

  <u>Can I borrow</u> your pen, please?
  <u>Could you lend me</u> your cell phone?

- Books open. Focus Ss' attention on the Conversation on page 16. Ask Ss to find two examples of requests beginning with *would*. Ask a S to write them on the board:

  <u>Would you mind if</u> I borrowed . . . ?
  <u>Would it be OK if</u> I picked it up . . . ?

- Explain that there are many ways to ask favors. They also vary in degrees of formality.

- Point out that we use *can* and *could* for informal requests. Elicit that the structures with *would* are more formal. We use them with people we don't know well or with friends if the request is very demanding.

- Play the audio program. Point out the continuum.

- Elicit or explain the structures used in requests.

  1. Requests with *if* clauses and the present tense
     Is it OK if . . . ? and *Do you mind if . . . ?* are followed by the present tense:
     Is it OK if I borrow your phone?
     Do you mind if I use your CD burner?
     Note: *Is it OK if . . .* is answered with "yes" if the request is granted. "No" means the person denies the request. *Do you mind if . . .* is answered with "no" if the request is granted. "Yes" means the person denies the request.

  2. Requests with *if* clauses and the past tense
     Would it be OK if . . . ? and *Would you mind if . . . ?* are followed by the past tense:
     Would it be OK if I picked it up on Friday?
     Would you mind if I borrowed your new digital camera?
     Note: *Would you mind* is answered with "no" if the request is granted. "Yes" means the person denies the request.

  3. Requests with gerunds (*-ing*)
     Would you mind (without *if*) is followed by a gerund:
     Would you mind letting me use your laptop?
     Note: *Would you mind* + gerund is answered with "no" if the request is granted. "Yes" means the person denies the request.

  4. Requests with *if* clauses and modals
     Wonder + *if* is followed by a modal:
     I wonder if I could borrow some money.

I was wondering if you would mind letting me use your car.
Note: *wonder* + *if* is a statement, not a question. Possible responses if the request is granted: "Sure, that's fine."/ "Of course." / "No problem." Possible response if the request is denied: "Sorry" + explanation.

- For more practice with requests, play **Run For It!** - download it from the website. Assign a structure to each wall: Present tense, past tense, modals and gerunds.

- Tell Ss to make their own requests and ask favors around the class.

A

- Read the first conversation. Elicit the correct form of *help* to complete the question (*helping*). Then ask a S to read the first conversation with you.

- Ss complete the task individually. Elicit Ss' responses to check answers. Then Ss practice the conversations in pairs.

Answers

1. Would you mind **helping** me paint on Saturday?
2. I was wondering **if I could** borrow your gold earrings.
3. **Is it OK if** I use your cell phone?
4. Would you mind if I **used** your car to pick up some groceries?
5. Could you **lend** me your suit for a wedding?
6. **Can** you buy me a snack from the vending machine, please?

B

- Explain the task. Model the first example.

- Elicit more examples. Write them on the board:
  I wonder if I could borrow some money for . . .
  I was wondering if you'd mind lending me some money for . . .
  Would it be OK if I borrowed some money for . . . ?

- Ss complete the task individually.

- Ask different Ss to read their formal requests aloud. Model accepting some and declining others.
  S1: Would you mind if I borrowed some money for a soda?
  T: No. Not at all. Here you go./I'm really sorry. All I have is a dollar.

- Tell Ss to look at part A for more examples of ways to accept and decline.

- Ss work in pairs. They take turns making requests and responding. Go around the class and check for logical and grammatical responses.

3 GRAMMAR FOCUS

Requests with modals, if clauses, and gerunds ▶

Less formal	**Can I** borrow your pen, please?
	Could you lend me a jacket, please?
↓	**Is it OK if** I use your phone?
	Do you mind if I use your laptop for a minute?
	Would it be all right if I compar**ed** our homework?
	Would you mind if I borrow**ed** your new camera?
	Would you mind babysitt**ing** my kids on Saturday night?
More formal	**I was wondering if** I **could** borrow some money.

A Circle the correct answers. Then practice with a partner.

1. A: Would you mind **help** / **helped** / **helping** me paint on Saturday?
   B: No, I don't mind. I'm not doing anything then.

2. A: I was wondering **I could** / **if I could** / **if I would** borrow your gold earrings.
   B: Sure, that's fine. Just don't lose them!

3. A: **Is it OK if** / **Would** / **Do you mind** I use your cell phone?
   B: No problem, but can you keep it short?

4. A: Would you mind if I **use** / **using** / **used** your car to pick up some groceries?
   B: Sorry, but it's not working. It's at the mechanic's.

5. A: Could you **lend** / **lending** / **lent** me your suit for a wedding?
   B: Of course. But you should dry-clean it first.

6. A: **Would you mind** / **Can** / **Is it OK if** you buy me a snack from the vending machine, please?
   B: Sorry, I don't have any change.

B Rewrite these sentences to make them more formal requests. Then practice making your requests with a partner. Accept or decline each request.

1. Lend me some money for a soda.
2. Return these books to the library for me.
3. Let me borrow your math homework.
4. I'd like to borrow your cell phone to call my friend in London.
5. Can I look at that magazine when you've finished reading it?
6. Help me clean the house before Mom and Dad get home.

> 1. Would you mind lending me some money for a soda?

4 PRONUNCIATION *Unreleased consonants*

A 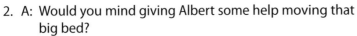 Listen and practice. Notice that when /t/, /d/, /k/, /g/, /p/, and /b/ are followed by other consonant sounds, they are unreleased.

Coul**d** **D**oug ta**ke** care of my pe**t** spider?
Can you as**k** Bo**b** to hel**p** me?

B 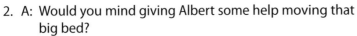 Circle the unreleased consonants in the conversations. Listen and check. Then practice the conversations with a partner.

1. A: I was wondering if I could borrow that book.
   B: Yes, but can you take it back to Greg tomorrow?

2. A: Would you mind giving Albert some help moving that big bed?
   B: Sorry, but my doctor said my back needs rest.

5 LISTENING *Favors*

A 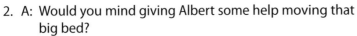 Listen to three telephone conversations. Write down what each caller requests. Does the other person agree to the request? Check (✓) Yes or No.

Request	Yes	No
1. Tina	☐	☐
2. Kyle	☐	☐
3. Phil	☐	☐

B **PAIR WORK** Use the chart to act out each conversation in your own words.

6 WRITING *An email request*

A Write an email to a classmate asking for several favors. Explain why you need help.

B **PAIR WORK** Exchange emails. Write a reply accepting or declining the requests.

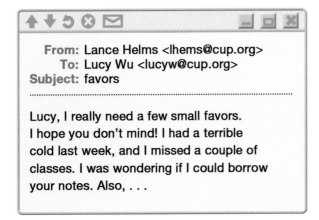

From: Lance Helms <lhems@cup.org>
To: Lucy Wu <lucyw@cup.org>
Subject: favors

Lucy, I really need a few small favors. I hope you don't mind! I had a terrible cold last week, and I missed a couple of classes. I was wondering if I could borrow your notes. Also, . . .

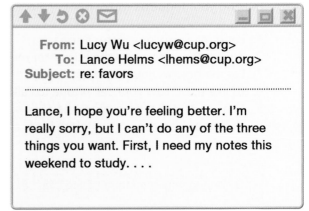

From: Lucy Wu <lucyw@cup.org>
To: Lance Helms <lhems@cup.org>
Subject: re: favors

Lance, I hope you're feeling better. I'm really sorry, but I can't do any of the three things you want. First, I need my notes this weekend to study. . . .

4 PRONUNCIATION

Learning Objective: *learn to sound natural using unreleased consonants*

A *[CD 1, Track 22]*

- Read the explanation. Tell Ss to compare /d/ in a fully released form (e.g., *did*) with /d/ in the phrase "could Doug" in an unreleased form.
- Play the first part of the audio program once or twice. Pause to allow Ss to repeat. Encourage Ss to say the unreleased consonants softly, blending them with the next word.
- Explain that it is easier to blend these consonants than it is to pronounce them separately.

B ⏵ *[CD 1, Track 23]*

- Explain the task. Ss work individually.

> **Answers**
>
> A: I was wondering if I coul**d** borrow tha**t** book.
> B: Yes, bu**t** can you take i**t** ba**ck** to Gre**g** tomorrow?
> A: Would you min**d** giving Alber**t** some hel**p** moving tha**t** bi**g** bed?
> B: Sorry, bu**t** my doctor sai**d** my ba**ck** needs rest.

- Play the second part of the audio program. Ss listen and check their answers.
- Then Ss practice the conversations in pairs.

5 LISTENING

Learning Objectives: *develop skills in listening for specific information; listen to requests; listen to telephone conversations*

A *[CD 1, Track 24]*

- Explain the task. Ss listen first for what each caller requests.
- Play the audio program. Pause briefly after each conversation for Ss to write down the requests.

> **AudioScript**
>
> See page T-166.

- Play the audio program again. Ss listen to find out whether the other person agrees to the request.
- Ss work in pairs to compare information. Elicit responses around the class to check answers.

> **Answers**
>
> 1. Tina wants to borrow Robert's camera. yes
> 2. Kyle wants to borrow Maggie's bread maker. no
> 3. Phil wants Li-ling to take care of his bird while he's away. yes

❗ To practice recognizing different types of requests, try *Stand Up, Sit Down* - download it from the website.

B *Pair work*

- Model the task by role-playing the phone conversations with Ss. Write phrases on the board to help Ss begin and end the conversations:
  Hello/Hi, . . . This is . . .
  What's up?
  Well, actually, would you mind . . . ?
  No problem.
  Thanks a million! See you in class tomorrow.
  Yeah, see you then. Bye!
- Remind Ss to use their own words. Tell Ss to role-play accepting and declining each request.
- Ss work in pairs. Tell Ss to sit back-to-back to role-play. Go around the class and note any problem areas. Go over the problems with the class after the role play.

6 WRITING

Learning Objective: *write an informal email request*

A

- Explain the task. Ask a S to read the first email.
- Ss work individually. They write an email to a classmate asking several favors. Remind Ss to include reasons for their requests. Set a time limit of about five minutes. Go around the class and give help as needed.

B *Pair work*

- Explain the task. Ask a S to read the second email.
- Ss exchange emails and write replies accepting or declining requests.
- Tell Ss to give reasons for declining requests.
- Set a time limit of five minutes. When time is up, Ss exchange their replies again and read them.

7 INTERCHANGE 3

See page T-116 for teaching notes.

End of Cycle 1

See the Supplementary Resources chart at the beginning of this unit for additional teaching materials and student activities related to this Cycle.

Cycle 2, Exercises 8–12

8 WORD POWER

Learning Objective: *learn collocations of words used for making requests and responding*

A

- Focus Ss' attention on the example and explain why *do* is crossed out.
- Ss complete the task individually or in pairs. Challenge Ss to do it without checking a dictionary.
- Ss compare answers in pairs. Then elicit responses.

Answers

1. do   3. do   5. offer   7. do
2. do   4. make   6. offer

B *Pair work*

- Read the questions. Ask Ss to underline the collocations. Elicit the answers (received a gift,

accepted someone's apology, return phone calls).

- Elicit questions Ss can use to add to the list. Write them on the board:

  When was the last time you . . . ?
  How often do you . . . ?
  How would you feel if . . . ?
  What would you say if . . . ?

- Ss work in pairs. Ss choose two collocations from part A to write two more questions. Then they take turns asking and answering all five questions.

 Practice the collocations with ***Vocabulary Tennis*** – download it from the website (e.g., Team A – return; Team B – a compliment; Team B – a gift; Team A – refuse).

9 PERSPECTIVES

Learning Objectives: *practice leaving messages; listen to indirect requests made in context*

A ▶ *[CD 1, Track 25]*

- Books closed. Set the scene. While Jeff was at lunch today, six people left messages.
- Write the topic of each message in random order on the board:

  class   last night's date   party
  report   birthday present   basketball

- Play the audio program. Pause after the first message. Ss listen and decide what the message was about. (Answer: a party)
- Play the rest of the audio program. Pause after each message. Ss listen. Elicit what the message was about.
- Books open. Ss read the messages and work individually to complete them with *ask* or *tell.*
- Play the audio program again. Have Ss listen and check their answers.

Answers

tell / ask / tell / tell / ask / ask

- Elicit or explain any new vocabulary.

B

- Explain the task. Ask a S to read the list of people. Explain that more than one answer is possible.
- Ss work individually to decide *who* left each message.
- Ss go over their answers in pairs. Answer any questions Ss may have.

Possible answers

Could you tell Jeff that Tony is having a party on Friday night? his friend
Could you ask Jeff what he would like me to get him for his birthday? his mother
Jeff is picking me up after basketball practice. Can you tell him not to be late? his younger sister
Please tell Jeff I owe him an apology—I forgot about our date last night. his girlfriend
Can you ask Jeff to return my call? I need to know when his report will be ready. his boss
Could you ask Jeff whether he can come to class on Friday night instead of Thursday? his teacher

INTERCHANGE 3 *Borrowers and lenders*

Find out how generous you are. Go to Interchange 3 on page 116.

8 ## WORD POWER *Collocations*

A Which verb is *not* usually paired with each noun? Put a line through the verb. Then compare with a partner.

1. (~~do~~ / receive / give / accept)   a gift
2. (owe / offer / do / accept)   an apology
3. (do / return / make / receive)   a phone call
4. (return / do / ask for / make)   a favor
5. (receive / accept / turn down / offer)   an invitation
6. (accept / make / decline / offer)   a request
7. (receive / return / do / give)   a compliment

B **PAIR WORK** Add two questions to the list using the collocations in part A. Then take turns asking and answering the questions.

1. When was the last time you received a gift from someone? What was it?
2. Have you ever *not* accepted someone's apology? Why not?
3. Do you usually return phone calls that you miss? Why or why not?
4. ....
5. ....

9 ## PERSPECTIVES *Could you tell Jeff . . . ?*

A ▶ Listen to the messages Jeff's assistant received while Jeff was away at lunch today. Complete each request with *ask* or *tell*.

1. Could you .... Jeff that Tony is having a party on Friday night?

2. Could you .... Jeff what he would like me to get him for his birthday?

3. Jeff is picking me up after basketball practice. Can you .... him not to be late?

4. Please .... Jeff that I owe him an apology – I forgot about our date last night.

5. Can you .... Jeff to return my call? I need to know when his report will be ready.

6. Could you .... Jeff whether he can come to class on Friday night instead of Thursday?

B Who do you think left each message?

his boss   his friend   his girlfriend   his mother   his teacher   his younger sister

10 GRAMMAR FOCUS

Indirect requests ▶

Statements	**Indirect requests introduced by that**
Jeff, Tony is having a party. →	Could you tell Jeff (**that**) **Tony is having a party**?

Imperatives	**Indirect requests using infinitives**
Jeff, don't be late. →	Can you tell Jeff **not to be late**?

Yes/No questions	**Indirect requests introduced by if or whether**
Sofia, are you free on Friday? →	Can you ask Sofia **if she's free on Friday**?
Sofia, do you have my number? →	Could you ask her **whether or not she has my number**?

Wh-questions	**Indirect requests introduced by a question word**
Jeff, when does the party start? →	Can you ask Jeff **when the party starts**?
Sofia, what time should I pick you up? →	Could you ask Sofia **what time I should pick her up**?

Rewrite these sentences as indirect requests. In other words, ask someone to deliver the message for you. Then compare with a partner.

1. Nina, will you drive us to the party on Friday?
2. Tony, how many friends can I bring to your party?
3. Sofia, are you going to the party with Jeff?
4. Kevin, did you accept the invitation to Tony's party?
5. Mario, are you going to give Tony a gift?
6. Anne-Marie, please return my phone call.
7. Dan, where is the best place to park?
8. Kimberly, I have to turn down your invitation to the movies.

> 1. Could you ask Nina if she'll drive us to the party on Friday?

11 SPEAKING Pass it on.

A Write five unusual requests for your partner to pass on to classmates.

> Would you ask Jin-sook if she could lend me $100?

B CLASS ACTIVITY Ask your partner to pass on your requests. Go around the class and make your partner's requests. Then tell your partner how people responded.

A: Would you ask Jin-sook if she could lend me $100?
B: Sure. . . . Jin-sook, could you lend Isam $100?
C: I'm sorry, but I can't! Could you tell Isam I'm broke?
B: Isam, Jin-sook says that she's broke.

10 GRAMMAR FOCUS

Learning Objective: *practice indirect requests with statements, imperatives, and yes/no and wh-questions*

▶ **[CD 1, Track 26]**

- Books closed. To explain an indirect request, draw a picture on the board of Jeff's boss passing a message to Jeff via Jeff's assistant:

Jeff's boss   Jeff's assistant   Jeff

Could you tell Jeff that Tony is having a party?

- Tell Ss that we use indirect requests when we want someone to give a message to someone else.

- Books open. Present the direct requests on the left and the indirect requests on the right. Ask Ss to (a) work out the rule and (b) find examples in the Perspectives on page 19.

  1. Statements
  Can/Could you (*or* Please) tell + (Jeff) + (that) + original statement?
  (Examples from the Perspectives: messages 1, 4)
  Note: *That* is optional. Indirect requests can also use *would*.

  2. Imperatives
  Can/Could you tell/ask + (Jeff) + (not) + infinitive?
  (Examples from the Perspectives: messages 2 and 5)

  3. *Yes/No* questions
  Can/Could you ask + (Sophia) + if/whether + SVO statement?
  (Example from the Perspectives: message 6)

  4. *Wh*-questions
  Can/Could you ask (Sophia) + *wh*-word + SVO statement?
  (Example from the Perspectives: message 2)

- Point out to students that the last example in the grammar box shows a change in the indirect object pronoun. The direct question uses *pick you up* because the speaker is talking directly to the person; but in the indirect form, *you* changes to *her* since the speaker is now talking about a third person.

- Play the audio program. Remind Ss that direct requests are on the left and indirect requests on the right.

- **Option:** Point out that most indirect requests have rising intonation. Play the audio program again. Ask Ss to focus on the rising intonation. Ss practice.

- **Option:** Write indirect sentences on the board in the wrong order (e.g., *not tell to could Jeff be call you me?*). Ss put them in the correct order.

- Explain the task. Use the first sentence as an example. Ask a S to read the example answer.

- Ss complete the task individually. Ss change the direct requests to indirect requests. Go around the class and give help as needed.

- Check some early finishers' answers. Tell the Ss to write their answers on the board.

Possible answers

1. Can/Could you ask Nina if/whether or not she'll drive us to the party on Friday?
2. Can/Could you ask Tony how many friends I can bring to his party?
3. Can/Could you ask Sofia if/whether or not she's going to the party with Jeff?
4. Can/Could you ask Kevin if/whether or not he accepted the invitation to Tony's party?
5. Can/Could you ask Mario if/whether or not he is going to give Tony a gift?
6. Can/Could you ask/tell Anne-Marie to please return my phone call?
7. Can/Could you ask Dan where the best place to park is?
8. Can/Could you tell Kimberly (that) I have to turn down her invitation to the movies?

11 SPEAKING

Learning Objective: *practice passing on and responding to indirect requests*

A

- Explain the task. Read the example request.
- Ss complete the task individually. They write five unusual requests. Go around the class and give help as needed.

B *Class activity*

- Explain the task. Ask three Ss to model the conversation. Elicit or explain that "I'm broke" means "I don't have any money."

- First, Ss work in pairs. They exchange requests from part A.

- Then Ss go around the class and make their partner's requests. They note how each person responds. Set a time limit of about ten minutes. Go around the class and listen in.

- Ss return to their partners and tell how each person responded.

- **Option:** Add one more person to the chain. Ss 2 and 3 are both messengers.

- Ask Ss to share some interesting requests they received and how they responded.

12 READING

Learning Objectives: *read about cultural differences; develop skills in scanning, reading for main ideas and details, and recognizing referents*

Note: You may want to bring a world map to class to help Ss locate the places mentioned in the article.

- Books closed. Ask the class to brainstorm different ways to indicate "yes" or "no" without speaking. If Ss are from different countries, elicit answers for each country. Summarize similarities and differences.

- Books open. Read the title. Tell Ss the article is about communication difficulties in different countries.

- Read the pre-reading question. Ask: "What kinds of words will you look for?" (Answer: names of countries, therefore, words beginning with a capital letter)

- Tell Ss to raise their hands when they find the answers. Elicit answers. (Answers: Micronesia, Bulgaria, India) Make sure Ss know where these places are.

- Ss read the article individually. Remind Ss to mark words they can't guess from context and continue reading.

- Elicit or explain any new vocabulary.

Vocabulary

miscommunications: problems communicating
were ignoring: weren't paying any attention to
rephrased: expressed in different words
gave up: stopped trying to do something
nodded: moved the head up and down
shakes: movements from side to side

! For an alternate way to present this Reading, try
• *Jigsaw Learning* – download it from the website.

A

- Ss read the article again.

- Ss complete the task individually. Ask Ss to mark the lines in the text where they find the answers to the questions.

- Ss go over their answers in pairs. Remind Ss to show each other where they found the answers. Go around the class to resolve any problems, or ask Ss to raise their hands if they have a question.

Answers

1. They were teaching English.
2. She was trying to buy a cold drink.
3. They raise their eyebrows.
4. She was talking to a waiter.
5. A head nod means "no."
6. His students nodded and shook their heads in different ways to indicate "yes."

B

- Explain the task. Elicit that words like *it, their, her,* and *that* are pronouns. Pronouns refer to a previous noun. Other phrases can also refer to earlier information.

- Ss work individually. Ss find referents for nouns and noun phrases. Go around the class and give help as needed.

- *Option:* If Ss are having difficulty, they can work in pairs or small groups.

- Ss go over their answers in pairs. Then go over answers with the class.

Answers

1. living in a foreign culture
2. the group of Americans
3. Lisa
4. Bulgaria
5 responded with different nods and shakes of the head

C *Group work*

- Explain the task. Read the questions.

- Ss work in pairs. Ss talk about communication problems. They can talk about problems with *yes* and *no,* other gestures, vocabulary, or something else.

- Ask Ss to tell the rest of the class some of the more interesting problems they discussed.

- *Option:* Ss can work in small groups, or this can be done with the whole class.

> **TIP** Ask Ss how they are progressing with their self-study listening. Encourage Ss to share useful strategies and offer advice.

End of Cycle 2

See the Supplementary Resources chart at the beginning of this unit for additional teaching materials and student activities related to this Cycle.

YES or NO?

Scan the article. Where did the three events occur?

1 Living in a foreign culture can be exciting, but it can also be confusing. A group of Americans who taught English in other countries recently discussed their experiences. They decided that miscommunications were always possible, even over something as simple as "yes" and "no."

2 On her first day in Micronesia, Lisa thought people were ignoring her requests. The day was hot, and she needed a cold drink. She went into a store and asked, "Do you have cold drinks?" The woman there didn't say anything. Lisa rephrased the question. Still the woman said nothing. Lisa gave up and left the store. She later learned that the woman had answered her: She had raised her eyebrows, which in Micronesia means "yes."

3 This reminded Jan of an experience she had in Bulgaria. She had gone to a restaurant that was known for its stuffed cabbage. She asked the waiter, "Do you have stuffed cabbage today?" He nodded his head. Jan eagerly waited, but the cabbage never came. In that country, a nod means "no."

4 Tom had a similar problem when he arrived in India. After explaining something in class, he asked his students if they understood. They responded with many different nods and shakes of the head. He assumed some people had not understood, so he explained again. When he asked again if they understood, they did the same thing. He soon found out that his students did understand. In India, people nod and shake their heads in different ways depending on where they come from. You have to know where a person is from to understand if they are indicating "yes" or "no."

A Read the article. Then answer the questions.

1. What were these Americans doing in other countries? ....
2. What was Lisa trying to buy? ....
3. How do people show "yes" in Micronesia? ....
4. Who was Jan talking to? ....
5. What does a head nod mean in Bulgaria? ....
6. Why did Tom misunderstand his class? ....

B What or who do these words refer to? Write the correct word(s).

1. it (par. 1, line 2) ....
2. their (par. 1, line 4) ....
3. her (par. 2, line 14, first word) ....
4. that country (par. 3, line 6) ....
5. the same thing (par. 4, line 10) ....

C GROUP WORK Have you ever had a similar communication problem, or do you know someone who has? What happened?

Unit 4 Supplementary Resources Overview

	After the following SB exercises	You can use these materials in class	Your students can use these materials outside the classroom
CYCLE 1	1 Snapshot		**ARC** Newspaper categories
	2 Perspectives		
	3 Grammar Focus		**SB** Unit 4 Grammar Plus focus 1 **SSD** Unit 4 Grammar 1 **ARC** Past continuous vs. simple past
	4 Pronunciation		
	5 Listening		
	6 Writing		**WB** Unit 4 exercises 1–4
CYCLE 2	7 Conversation		**SSD** Unit 4 Speaking 1–2
	8 Grammar Focus	**TSS** Unit 4 Grammar Worksheet **TSS** Unit 4 Writing Worksheet	**SB** Unit 4 Grammar Plus focus 2 **SSD** Unit 4 Grammar 2 **ARC** Past continuous vs. simple past and Past perfect
	9 Word Power	**TSS** Unit 4 Vocabulary Worksheet **TSS** Unit 4 Listening Worksheet **TSS** Unit 4 Extra Worksheet	**SSD** Unit 4 Vocabulary 1–2 **ARC** Events
	10 Speaking		
	11 Interchange 4		
	12 Reading	**TSS** Unit 4 Project Worksheet **VID** Unit 4 **VRB** Unit 4	**SSD** Unit 4 Reading 1–2 **SSD** Unit 4 Listening 1–3 **SSD** Unit 4 Video 1–3 **WB** Unit 4 exercises 5–9

With or instead of the following SB section	You can also use these materials for assessment
Units 3–4 Progress Check	**ASSESSMENT CD** Units 3–4 Oral Quiz **ASSESSMENT CD** Units 3–4 Written Quiz

Key **ARC:** Arcade **SB:** Student's Book **SSD:** Self-study DVD-ROM **TSS:** Teacher Support Site
VID: Video DVD **VRB:** Video Resource Book **WB:** Workbook

My Plan for Unit 4

Use the space below to customize a plan that fits your needs.

With the following SB exercises	I am using these materials in class	My students are using these materials outside the classroom

With or instead of the following SB section	I am using these materials for assessment

4 What a story!

1 SNAPSHOT

Popular Online News Categories
Search

| Top Stories | Entertainment | Sports | Art | Travel | Opinion |

World
Politics
Business
Technology
Science
Health
Odd News

New Species of Frog Discovered in Amazon

Source: http://news.yahoo.com

In your opinion, which sections contain the most interesting news? the least interesting news?
Choose five categories. Give an example of a possible type of story for each one.
Where do you get your news? What's happening in the news today?

2 PERSPECTIVES *Surprise endings*

A Listen to the news stories. In which news category from Exercise 1 do you think each story belongs?

PODCASTS

"An attempted robbery took place at Eastern Bank today. A man was trying to rob the bank, but he wasn't very lucky! While he was escaping from the bank, the robber got caught in the revolving door. The police arrived and took the man to jail."

"It was a strange soccer match last night. The Bears won the game, but the Lions scored the winning goal for them! As Jake Walters was running toward the ball, he tripped and accidentally kicked it into the wrong goal. The score was Bears 1, Lions 0."

"An electrical problem at Pax Arena interrupted a Planets concert last night. The Planets were performing a new song when the lights went out – but the show went on! The Planets continued to play in the dark, and the lights came back on an hour later."

B **PAIR WORK** What happened in each story that was surprising?

What a story!

Cycle 1, Exercises 1–6

In this unit, students focus on storytelling. In Cycle 1, students describe past events using the simple past and the past continuous tenses. In Cycle 2, students tell stories using the past perfect tense

 ## SNAPSHOT

Learning Objective: *learn about the different sections of newspapers*

- **Option:** Hold a brief discussion about news. Ask: "Who follows the news? How do you get your news? What news do you find interesting? How important is it to keep up-to-date?"
- Books closed. Brainstorm with Ss about online newspapers. Ask what sections, or categories, they contain. Ask Ss to write their ideas on the board.

> **TIP** To introduce a new unit, ask Ss motivating questions and elicit information related to the unit topic. If possible, bring – or ask Ss to bring – realia to class (e.g., for this unit, printouts or screen shots of online newspapers, local and/ or international).

- Books open. Say that this Snapshot lists popular categories of online news. Read the categories. Ss circle categories that match the ones they brainstormed.
- Elicit or explain any new vocabulary.

> **Vocabulary**
>
> **top:** the most important
> **odd:** unusual

- **Option:** Ss look through printouts of online newspapers or view them online. Ask Ss to find the categories listed in the Snapshot. Encourage Ss to note any others they find.
- Read the questions.
- Ss discuss the focus questions in pairs or small groups. Set a time limit of about five minutes.

 ## PERSPECTIVES

Learning Objectives: *listen to news stories; see the past continuous and simple past tenses in context*

A ⊙ *[CD 1, Track 27]*

- Books closed. Explain the task. Elicit more types of stories (e.g., local, main/top, arts, entertainment).
- Play the audio program. Ss listen to three news stories. Ss decide what type of story each one is. Pause after each story to give Ss time to write down the type of story.
- Elicit answers from the class. For each news story, ask: "Which words told you the answer?"

> **Answers**
>
> 1. local/main/top   2. Sports   3. main

- Books open. Play the audio program again. Ss listen and read. Explain that a thief robs a person or a place, but steals an object.
- Elicit or explain any new vocabulary.

> **Vocabulary**
>
> **attempted:** tried but did not succeed
> **got caught in:** was trapped in something
> **revolving door:** a door that turns around
> **tripped:** lost his balance when his foot hit something
> **lights went out:** the electricity stopped working
> **show went on:** the performance continued
> **lights came back on:** the electricity returned

B *Pair work*

- Focus Ss' attention on the title of the exercise: "Surprise endings." Explain that all these stories had surprise endings.
- Explain the task. Ask a S to read the first story aloud. Elicit what happened to change the ending. (Answer: The robber got stuck in the revolving door.)
- Ss work in pairs. They discuss the remaining three stories.

3 GRAMMAR FOCUS

Learning Objective: *practice the past continuous and the simple past*

▶ [CD 1, Track 28]

Past continuous vs. simple past

- Draw two pictures on the board. One picture shows a man running. The second shows the man tripping.

1.   2.

- Focus Ss' attention on the Perspectives on page 22. Ask Ss to find the sentence that fits the pictures. Write it on the board. Underline and label the sentence like this:

  As Jake <u>was running</u> toward the ball, he <u>tripped</u>...
      past continuous   simple past

- To help Ss see the relationship between the tenses, ask questions like these:
  1. [*point to first picture*] What was Jake doing here? Is *running* a "continued" action that lasted for some time?
  2. Was the action of *running* interrupted by another action?

- Say that the past continuous (*was running*) describes an ongoing action in the past. The simple past (*tripped*) is a shorter complete action. It takes place at one moment and interrupts the ongoing action.

- Ask Ss to look for past continuous and simple past verbs in the Perspectives on page 22. Tell Ss to underline past continuous verbs and put a circle around simple past verbs.

- Focus Ss' attention on the Grammar Focus box. Point out the adverb clauses with *while* and *as*. Say that these clauses cannot stand alone as a sentence. When an adverb clause comes before the main clause, it has a comma.

- Next, point out the clause with *when* in the second column. When an adverb clause comes after the main clause, it does not have a comma.

- Play the audio program. Ss listen and read or repeat.

- To practice the sentences, try the activity **Split Sentences** – download it from the website.

A

- Explain the task.

- Ss complete the task individually. Tell Ss to read each story once before filling in the blanks. This will help Ss understand which action was ongoing and which action interrupted it.

- Elicit or explain any new vocabulary (e.g., a *daily round-up* is a summary of events in the news; *hit the jackpot* means to win money or something worth a lot of money).

- To help Ss with vocabulary in this exercise, try the **Vocabulary Mingle** – download it from the website.

- Ss work in pairs to compare answers.

> ### Answers
>
> 1. While divers **were working** off the coast of Florida, they **discovered** a shipwreck containing gold worth $2 million. The divers **were filming** a show about the coral reef when they **found** the gold.
> 2. One windy day, a woman **was walking** her pet poodle down the street. A hairstylist **saw** the dog through a window and **noticed** its crazy hair! Later, while the stylist **was creating** a new line of hair care products for dogs and cats, he **came up with** a new slogan: "Even animals have bad hair days!"
> 3. An ambulance driver **was having** breakfast in a coffee shop when a woman **hopped** into his ambulance and **drove** away. The driver **grabbed** his cell phone and **alerted** the police. The carjacker **was going** over 90 miles an hour when the highway patrol finally **caught up with** her.

B *Group work*

- Explain the task.

- Ss work in groups of three. Ask each S to reread a different story and note four or five key words or phrases. Ss use their notes to retell the story. Remind Ss to add new information or a new ending.

4 PRONUNCIATION

Learning Objective: *notice and use correct intonation in complex sentences*

A ▶ [CD 1, Track 29]

- Point out that each clause has a falling intonation pattern. This helps the listener follow the two groups of ideas in a long sentence.

- Play the audio program. Ss listen and repeat.

B *Pair work*

- Explain the task. Ss work in pairs to make complex sentences with *while* or *as* and the past continuous. Ss take turns starting and finishing the sentences, using falling intonation.

3 GRAMMAR FOCUS

Past continuous vs. simple past ▶

Use the past continuous for an ongoing action in the past.
Use the simple past for an event that interrupts that action.

Past continuous	Simple past
While he **was escaping** from the bank,	the robber **got caught** in the revolving door.
As Jake **was running** toward the ball,	he **tripped** and **kicked** it into the wrong goal.
The Planets **were performing** a song	when the lights **went** out.

A Complete the news stories using the past continuous or simple past forms of the verbs. Then compare with a partner.

DAILY ROUNDUP

A Golden Find

While divers _____ (work) off the coast of Florida, they _____ (discover) a shipwreck containing gold worth $2 million. The divers _____ (film) a show about the coral reef when they _____ (find) the gold.

Four-legged Customers

One windy day, a woman _____ (walk) her pet poodle down the street. A hairstylist _____ (see) the dog through a window and _____ (notice) its crazy hair! Later, while the stylist _____ (create) a new line of hair care products for dogs and cats, he _____ (come up with) a new slogan: "Even animals have bad hair days!"

Rescue...the Ambulance!

An ambulance driver _____ (have) breakfast in a coffee shop when a woman _____ (hop) into his ambulance and _____ (drive) away. The driver _____ (grab) his cell phone and _____ (alert) the police. The carjacker _____ (go) over 90 miles an hour when the highway patrol finally _____ (catch up with) her.

B GROUP WORK Take turns retelling the stories in part A. Add your own ideas and details to make the stories more interesting!

4 PRONUNCIATION Intonation in complex sentences

A ▶ Listen and practice. Notice how each clause in a complex sentence has its own intonation pattern.

While divers were working off the coast of Florida, they discovered a shipwreck.

As Jake was running toward the ball, he tripped and kicked it into the wrong goal.

B PAIR WORK Use your imagination to make complex sentences. Take turns starting and finishing the sentences. Pay attention to intonation.

A: While Sam was traveling in South America . . .
B: . . . he ran into an old friend in Lima.

5 LISTENING *In the news*

A ▶ Listen to three news stories. Number the pictures from 1 to 3. (There is one extra picture.)

B ▶ Listen again. Take notes on each story.

	Where did it happen?	When did it happen?	What happened?
1.			
2.			
3.			

6 WRITING *A news story*

A Match each headline with the beginning of a news story.

1._____	2._____	3._____	4._____
Lucky Discovery for French Girl	*Social Network Engagement*	**Man Receives Letter Mailed 50 Years Ago**	Job Applicant's Life Saved by Being 5 Minutes Late

a. Rick Jones got a surprise when he went to his mailbox last week.

b. Sophie Denis was playing in her yard when she found 30 Roman coins.

c. Lisa Miller is lucky. As she was hurrying to a job interview, she missed her bus.

d. Derek Adams didn't propose to his longtime girlfriend in the traditional way. He did it online.

B Complete one of the news stories from part A, or write a news story using your own idea. First, answer these questions. Then write your article.

Who was involved?   Where did it happen?
When did it happen?   What happened?

C **GROUP WORK** Take turns telling your stories. Other students ask questions. Who has the best story?

5 LISTENING

Learning Objectives: *develop skills in listening for details; develop note-taking skills; listen to news stories*

A 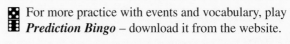 [CD 1, Track 30]

- Ask: "Who watched the news on TV today or yesterday?" Encourage the class to tell any interesting stories they heard.
- Have Ss look at the pictures and describe what they see.
- Explain the task. Ss will listen to the audio and number the pictures in the order that they hear the matching news stories in the audio. Make sure Ss understand that there is one extra picture.
- Play the audio program. Ss complete the task individually.
- Allow pairs to compare answers. Then go over answers with the class.

> **Answers**
>
> 2, 3, X, 1

B [CD 1, Track 31]

- Read the questions in the chart aloud.
- Explain the task. Ss will listen to the audio and answer the questions in the chart for each news story.
- Play the audio program. Pause after each news event. Give Ss time to complete the chart. Ask Ss to write their answers on the board.
- **Option:** Ask: "Which story did you find most interesting? Why?" Elicit Ss' ideas.

> **AudioScript**
>
> See page T-167.

> **Answers**
>
> 1. in Thailand; on Sunday; a man was almost strangled to death by a snake
> 2. in Australia; on Friday; two teenage girls who disappeared were found
> 3. in California; early Tuesday morning; two police officers were rescued by the thief they were chasing

For more practice with events and vocabulary, play *Prediction Bingo* – download it from the website.

6 WRITING

Learning Objective: *write a newspaper article*

A

- Explain the task. Go over the headlines.
- Ss work in small groups. They match each headline to the correct story. Go over answers with the class.

> **Answers**
>
> 1. b   2. d   3. a   4. c

B

- Model the task. Ask a S to read the first headline and story beginning. Write a next line on the board:

  She was digging when her shovel hit a box.

  Then elicit a possible next sentence from Ss and write that on the board, too.

- Ss work individually to write their news stories. Ask them to write one or two paragraphs and to come up with an interesting ending.

> **TIP** If Ss struggle to find ideas, remind them of the *5 Ws* and *H* questions used by journalists: *who, what, where, when, why,* and *how.*

C Group work

- Ss read or tell their stories in small groups.
- The group votes on the best story.

End of Cycle 1

See the Supplementary Resources chart at the beginning of this unit for additional teaching materials and student activities related to this Cycle.

7 CONVERSATION

Learning Objectives: *practice a conversation about something unlucky that happened; see the past perfect in context*

A *[CD 1, Track 32]*

- Play the audio program. Ss take notes.
- Ss compare notes in pairs. Then Ss use their notes to write three comprehension questions.
- Each pair joins another pair. They take turns asking and answering their questions.
- Tell Ss to uncover the text. Play the audio program. Ss listen and read. Then they practice the conversation in pairs.

B ▶ *[CD 1, Track 33]*

- Read the focus questions. Play the second part of the audio program. Elicit Ss' answers.

AudioScript

See page T-167.

Answers

Kathy once had her purse stolen. She was in Belgium. A bunch of guys asked her if they could help her, and when they left, her purse was gone. She called her credit card company, and they assisted her.

8 GRAMMAR FOCUS

Learning Objective: *practice the past perfect*

▶ *[CD 1, Track 34]*

Past perfect

- Explain that the past perfect is *had* + past participle. Focus Ss' attention on the Conversation. Elicit sentences with the past perfect. Write them on the board in a chart:

1	2	3	4
I	had	put	my stuff in my locker.
Someone	had	stolen	my wallet.
I	'd	forgotten	to lock the locker.

- Explain that when we are talking about *two* events in the past, we use the past perfect to express the earlier one. Write an example on the board:

from 7–8 p.m.   at 6:45 p.m.

I was working out, and I <u>had put</u> my stuff in my locker.

- Next, write these sentences on the board:

I came back.   Someone stole my wallet.

- Ask: "Which event happened 'earlier'?" (Answer: Someone stole my wallet.) Elicit a sentence with the cues and the past perfect. (Answer: When I came back, someone had stolen my wallet.)
- Play the audio program.

A

- Ss complete the task for Columns A and B individually.

- Allow pairs to compare answers. Then go over answers with the class.

Answers

1. 1. A thief **broke into** our house last night while my sister and I **were picking up** a pizza for dinner.
2. I **was shopping** with some friends yesterday, and I **lost** my keys.
3. I **was driving/drove** around with my friends all day on Sunday, and I **ran out** of gas on the freeway.
4. I **was trying** to visit my parents last night when I **got** stuck in the elevator in their apartment building.
   a. Luckily, I **had given** a friend a copy of them, and she **came over** and let me into my apartment.
   b. It **had reached** the fifth floor when it **stopped**. After I **had been** stuck for an hour, someone **started** it again.
   c. I guess we **had left** the door unlocked, because that's how the thief **got** into the house.
   d. Fortunately, I **had brought** my cell phone with me, so I **called** my brother for help.

❗ To practice this tense, use a *Disappearing Dialog* – download it from the website (with the Conversation in Exercise 7).

B *Pair work*

- Ss work in pairs to complete the task.
- Allow pairs to compare answers with another pair. Then go over the answers with the class.

Answers

1. c   2. a   3. d   4. b

A ▶ Listen and practice.

Brian: Guess what! Someone stole my wallet last night!
Kathy: Oh, no! What happened?
Brian: Well, I was working out, and I had put my stuff in my locker, just like I always do. When I came back, someone had stolen my wallet. I guess I'd forgotten to lock the locker.
Kathy: That's terrible! Did you lose much money?
Brian: Only about $15. But I lost my credit card and my driver's license. What a pain!

B ▶ Listen to the rest of the conversation. What did Kathy have stolen once? Where was she?

8 **GRAMMAR FOCUS**

> **Past perfect** ▶
>
> **Use the past perfect for an event that occurred before another event in the past.**
>
> | **Past event** | **Past perfect event** |
> |---|---|
> | I **was working out,** | and I **had put** my stuff in my locker. |
> | When I **came back,** | someone **had stolen** my wallet. |
> | They **were able** to steal it | because I **had forgotten** to lock the locker. |

A Complete the sentences in column A with the simple past or past continuous forms of the verbs. Complete the sentences in column B with the simple past or past perfect forms of the verbs.

A

1. A thief .... (break into) our house last night while my sister and I .... (pick up) a pizza for dinner.
2. I .... (shop) with some friends yesterday, and I .... (lose) my keys.
3. I .... (drive) around with friends all day on Sunday, and I .... (run out) of gas on the freeway.
4. I .... (try) to visit my parents last night when I .... (get) stuck in the elevator in their apartment building.

B

a. Luckily, I .... (give) a friend a copy of them, and she .... (come over) and let me into my apartment.
b. It .... (reach) the fifth floor when it .... (stop). After I .... (be) stuck for an hour, someone .... (start) it again.
c. I guess we .... (leave) the door unlocked because that's how the thief .... (get) into the house.
d. Fortunately, I .... (bring) my cell phone with me, so I .... (call) my brother for help.

B **PAIR WORK** Match the sentences in parts A and B to make complete stories. Read them aloud.

1. ....   2. ....   3. ....   4. ....

9 WORD POWER *Events*

A Match the words in column A with the definitions in column B.

A

1. coincidence ....
2. dilemma ....
3. disaster ....
4. emergency ....
5. lucky break ....
6. misfortune ....
7. mystery ....
8. triumph ....

B

a. an unexpected event that brings good fortune
b. a situation that involves a difficult choice
c. something puzzling or unexplained
d. an event that causes suffering or destruction
e. a great success or achievement
f. unexpected events that seem to be connected
g. a sudden, dangerous event that requires quick action
h. an unlucky event, or bad luck

B **PAIR WORK** Choose one kind of event from part A. Write a situation for it.

> Two people were traveling separately in China when they met at a
> restaurant in Shanghai. They both lived in the same town their whole
> lives, but they had never met before. (coincidence)

C **GROUP WORK** Read your situation. Can others guess
which kind of event it describes?

10 SPEAKING *Tell me more.*

GROUP WORK Have you ever had any of these experiences? Tell your
group about it. Answer any questions.

I . . .
faced a dilemma
had an emergency
was unable to solve a mystery
had a lucky break
had a personal triumph

A: I faced a dilemma last week.
B: Really? What was it?
A: I got two job offers. I could take either
a job with a large, successful company for
a low salary or one with a smaller, less successful
company for more pay.
C: So what did you decide to do?

11 INTERCHANGE 4 *A double ending*

Solve a mystery! Go to Interchange 4 on page 117.

9 WORD POWER

Learning Objective: *learn vocabulary for discussing events*

A

- Explain the task. Model the first word as an example.
- **Option:** Model the word stress of each noun. Ss listen and repeat.
- Ss work individually or in pairs. Ss match words with definitions. Tell Ss to check their dictionaries only after they finish.
- Go over answers with the class.

Answers

1. f	3. d	5. a	7. c
2. b	4. g	6. h	8. e

B Pair work

- Explain the task. Read aloud the example for *coincidence*.
- Ss work in pairs. Ss choose one event from part A. Then they write a situation for it. Go around the class and briefly check sentences.

C Group work

- Explain the task. Two or three pairs work in a group. Ss take turns reading their situations without saying the kind of event. Others in the group guess the event.

10 SPEAKING

Learning Objective: *tell stories using various past tenses*

Group work

- Read the question and situations. Ask three Ss to model the conversation.
- Explain the task. Give Ss time to think of a situation they would like to talk about.
- **Option:** If Ss appear reluctant or embarrassed to talk about a personal situation, allow them to tell a story about a friend or someone they heard about in the news.
- Ss work in small groups. They take turns talking about the situations. Tell Ss to talk about the events in any order. Encourage Ss to ask follow-up questions.

> **TIP** A fluency activity is designed to challenge Ss to do their best with whatever language abilities they have. It's best to give help only if asked directly.

> **TIP** To ensure that all Ss ask four follow-up questions, ask each S to take out four small coins (or paper clips) and put them in a pile. As they ask a follow-up question, they can remove a coin from the pile.

- **Option:** As a follow-up, two groups form a large group to swap stories, or do this as a whole class activity.
- For a different way to use this activity, try the **Chain Game** – download it from the website.

11 INTERCHANGE 4

See page T-117 for teaching notes.

12 READING

Learning Objectives: *read news stories; develop skills in understanding vocabulary in context, reading for specific information, and summarizing*

Note: If possible, bring several print-outs of blogs to class (such as an individual/personal blog, a corporate blog, and a celebrity blog) and pass them around.

- Books closed. Ask: "What are blogs? Have you ever written a blog, or would you like to write a blog? Why or why not?"
- Books open. Ask a S to read the title of the reading. Elicit or explain that a blog is an online log or diary.
- Explain the pre-reading task. Read the questions.
- Give Ss time to scan the article themselves. Ss work individually to find answers to the pre-reading task.
- Elicit the answers from the class.

! To introduce new vocabulary and have Ss predict the stories, try **Cloud Prediction** – download it from the website.

> ### Answers
>
> Anyone can blog (if they have access to an Internet connection).
> Many people are moving from blogging to social networking; blogging can now include video, which is sometimes called "vlogging."

- Ss read the article individually.

> **TIP** Tell Ss not to look up any words as they read. Instead, they should underline or circle words they don't know and keep reading.

- Then Ss work in small groups. Each S shares words he or she underlined. If group members know the word, they explain it. If no one in the group knows the word, Ss look at the context and as a group write one or two guesses about its meaning.
- **Option:** Each group says what words they chose and what their guesses were. Each group gets one point for making a guess and two points for a correct guess.
- Elicit or explain any new vocabulary.

> ### Vocabulary
>
> **yesterday's news:** outdated information or news; not current
> **revolution:** a very important change in the way people think or do things
> **interactive:** involving communication between people
> **e-publish:** publish or post something online
> **in any case:** regardless, anyway
> **camcorder:** a hand-held video recording device

A

- Explain the task.
- Ss complete the task individually or in pairs. Ss scan the article to find the words. Then they guess the meaning. Point out that this exercise will help Ss confirm their previous guesses and remember the words.
- Ss go over answers in pairs. Ss may use their dictionaries to check the meaning of words to be matched to the ones in italics.
- Go over answers with the class.

> ### Answers
>
> 1. doing something new
> 2. disappear
> 3. whole
> 4. TV or radio news reporters
> 5. replaced
> 6. buying and selling online

B Pair work

- Ask a S to read the questions out loud.
- Ss work in pairs to discuss the questions. Encourage Ss to share opinions about blogs and blogging. Go around the class and listen.

C Group work

- Read the focus questions.
- Ss work in groups. Ss discuss the questions. Encourage Ss to give specific examples and to ask each other follow-up questions.
- **Option:** Groups share one particularly interesting thing they talked about.

End of Cycle 2

See the Supplementary Resources chart at the beginning of this unit for additional teaching materials and student activities related to this Cycle and for assessment tools.

The changing world of blogging

Scan the article. Who blogs? How is blogging changing?

Only a few years ago, blogging seemed new and exciting. Now, some people are saying it is yesterday's news and that the Internet revolution is moving on. The word "blog" comes from "web log," which means an online log or diary. Blogging is interactive, and bloggers hope that their readers will respond with interesting posts. In turn, they can respond to these posts. Some blogs continue like this for years whereas others simply vanish overnight. Blogs are usually started by one person for personal or professional reasons.

Anyone is free to blog: individuals, celebrities, companies, journalists. When blogging started, it was the first time ordinary people could write whatever they wanted and then e-publish it for the entire online world to see. Some people have become famous as bloggers, such as Julie Powell. Some celebrities have blogs, such as John Mayer and TV chef Jamie Oliver. Some companies, such as Microsoft and Boeing, use blogs to communicate with their employees. Journalists and broadcasters also write blogs. These are often on news websites, such as those for the *New York Times* and CNN.

However, things change fast with information technology. For many people, especially young people, social networking sites like Facebook have superseded blogging. In any case, there have always been far more blog readers than blog writers,

Julie Powell

perhaps because some people don't like writing. But developments in technology have changed blogging, too. With a videophone, camera, or camcorder plus a computer with video-editing software, bloggers can turn their blogs into video logs, or "vlogs." Some people think vlogging will replace blogging. Others disagree, saying that television didn't replace radio and that e-commerce hasn't stopped people from going shopping. What do *you* think?

A Read the article. Find the words in *italics* in the article.
Then check (✓) the meaning of each word.

1. *moving on* ☐ going backward ☐ doing something new
2. *vanish* ☐ continue to grow ☐ disappear
3. *entire* ☐ whole ☐ international
4. *broadcasters* ☐ TV or radio news reporters ☐ people who write news stories
5. *superseded* ☐ replaced ☐ became more exciting than
6. *e-commerce* ☐ electronic communication ☐ buying and selling online

B **PAIR WORK** Discuss these questions.

Why do some people think that blogging is no longer exciting?
What are some ways to maintain a blog successfully?
Do you think blogs are a good way to sell things? Why or why not?
Why have some people switched from blogging to social networking sites?

C **GROUP WORK** Do you read any blogs? Have you ever posted a message on one?
Why or why not?

Units 3–4 Progress check

How well can you do these things? Check (✓) the boxes.

I can	Very well	OK	A little
Make and respond to requests (Ex. 1)	☐	☐	☐
Pass on messages (Ex. 2)	☐	☐	☐
Tell a story, making clear the sequence of events (Ex. 3, 5)	☐	☐	☐
Understand the sequence of events in a story (Ex. 4)	☐	☐	☐

1 ROLE PLAY Planning a party

Student A: You are planning a class party at your house. Think of three things you need help with. Then call a classmate and ask for help.

Student B: Student A is planning a party. Agree to help with some things, but not everything.

"Hi, Dave. I'm calling about the party. Would you mind . . . ?"

Change roles and try the role play again.

2 DISCUSSION Mystery messages

A GROUP WORK Take turns reading each request. Then discuss the questions and come up with possible answers.

I'm sorry to bother you, but if Mr. Wall in Apartment 213 uses my space again, I'll have to complain to the manager.

I'd really like to borrow it for the match on Friday. Please tell Tom to let me know soon if it's OK.

Tell your officers that she's brown and has a red collar but no tag. She answers to the name "Lady." Call if you find her.

1. What is the situation?
2. Who is the request for? Who do you think received the request and passed it on?
3. Give an indirect request for each situation.

"Please tell Mr. Wall . . ."

B CLASS ACTIVITY Compare your answers. Which group has the most interesting answers for each message?

Units 3–4 Progress check

SELF-ASSESSMENT

Learning Objectives: *reflect on one's learning; identify areas that need improvement*

- Ask: "What did you learn in Units 3 and 4?" Elicit Ss' answers.
- Ss complete the Self-assessment. Encourage them to be honest, and point out they will not get a bad grade if they check (✓) "a little."

- Ss move on to the Progress check exercises. You can have Ss complete them in class or for homework, using one of these techniques:
  1. Ask Ss to complete all the exercises.
  2. Ask Ss: "What do you need to practice?" Then assign exercises based on their answers.
  3. Ask Ss to choose and complete exercises based on their Self-assessment.

1 ROLE PLAY

Learning Objective: *assess one's ability to make requests with modals,* if *clauses, and gerunds*

- Explain the task.
- Divide the class into pairs, and assign A/B roles. Student As are planning a party. Student Bs are asked to help. Ask a S to model the request.

- Ss role-play in pairs. To set the scene for a telephone conversation, ask Ss to sit back-to-back. Remind Student Bs to agree to some things, but not others.
- Ss change roles and repeat the role play.

2 DISCUSSION

Learning Objective: *assess one's ability to make indirect requests*

A Group work

- Explain the task. Ask different Ss to read the requests and focus questions.
- Ss work in groups of three. Ss take turns reading aloud a request and discussing the questions. Then Ss write an indirect request for each situation.

- Go around the class and give help as needed.

B Class activity

- Explain the task. Ask a S to share each group's answers with the class.
- Take a vote to see who has the most interesting answers.

SPEAKING

Learning Objective: *assess one's ability to tell a story using the past continuous and simple past*

A *Pair work*

- Explain the task. Ask a S to read the types of events in the box.
- Ss work in pairs. Remind Ss to choose only the type of event and write a title.

B *Pair work*

- Explain the task. Ask a S to read the example story. Elicit *who, what, where, when, why,* and *how* questions and answers for the example.
- Pairs exchange titles with another pair. Then pairs discuss how to answer the questions about the other

pair's title. Point out that the stories do not have to be true.

- Pairs can take notes on their ideas or write out the story. Only one S needs to write, but both Ss should contribute equally. Ask the S who didn't write to check for errors.

C

- Explain the task. Ss tell their stories to the pair who wrote the title.
- Ask: "Were you surprised at the way the story turned out?"
- Ask some Ss to tell their stories to the class.

4 LISTENING

Learning Objective: *assess one's ability to listen to and understand sequence in the past*

⊙ **[CD 1, Track 35]**

- Explain the task. Give Ss time to read all of the sentences.
- Tell Ss to listen and number the events in each situation from 1 to 3. Play the audio program. Pause after each event.
- Play the audio program as many times as needed. Elicit answers.

AudioScript

See page T-167.

Answers

1. She was running. She hurt her ankle. She went to work. [2, 1, 3]
2. I moved away. John wrote to me. I didn't get the letter. [2, 3, 1]
3. I was very scared. The plane landed. I was relieved. [1, 2, 3]
4. I was watching a movie. My cousin stopped by. We went out. [2, 1, 3]

 ## DISCUSSION

Learning Objective: *assess one's ability to describe events using the past perfect*

Group work

- Explain the task. Read the beginnings and endings. Ask four Ss to model the example story chain.
- Ss work in small groups. Ss choose any beginning and any ending. They discuss events that could link the two. Point out that Ss can decide the story as they do the task.

- The first S reads the sentence the group chose and then adds a sentence of his or her own. Ss take turns adding sentences to the story. Remind Ss to keep the ending in mind when they add a sentence.
- The story ends when a S is able to use the group's ending.
- **Option:** Ss change groups and repeat the exercise. This time Ss write the story. Ss pass a sheet of paper around the group. Each S adds a sentence to the story.

WHAT'S NEXT?

Learning Objective: *become more involved in one's learning*

- Focus Ss' attention on the Self-assessment again. Ask: "How well can you do these things now?"

- Ask Ss to underline one thing they need to review. Ask: "What did you underline? How can you review it?"
- If needed, plan additional activities or reviews based on Ss' answers.

3 SPEAKING *What happened?*

A **PAIR WORK** Choose a type of event from the box. Then make up a title for a story about it. Write the title on a piece of paper.

| disaster | emergency | lucky break | mystery | triumph |

B **PAIR WORK** Exchange titles with another pair. Discuss the questions *who, what, where, when, why,* and *how* about the other pair's title. Then make up a story.

C Share your story with the pair who wrote the title.

> <u>Dog Show Disaster</u>
> My brother recently entered his pet, Poofi, in a dog show. But Poofi is a cat! He was bringing Poofi into the show when . . .

4 LISTENING *What comes first?*

 Listen to each situation. Number the events from 1 to 3.

1. ☐ She hurt her ankle.　　☐ She was running.　　☐ She went to work.
2. ☐ John wrote to me.　　☐ I didn't get the letter.　　☐ I moved away.
3. ☐ I was very scared.　　☐ The plane landed.　　☐ I was relieved.
4. ☐ We went out.　　☐ My cousin stopped by.　　☐ I was watching a movie.

5 DISCUSSION *From A to B*

GROUP WORK Choose the beginning of a story from column A and an ending from column B. Discuss interesting or unusual events that could link A to B. Then make up a story.

A

Once, I . . .

received an unexpected phone call.
was asked to do an unusual favor.
accepted an interesting invitation.
owed someone a big apology.

B

Believe it or not, . . .

I opened the door, and a horse was standing there!
when I got there, everyone had left.
he didn't even remember what I had done.
it was the star of my favorite TV show!

A: Once, I received an unexpected phone call.
B: Let's see. . . . I was making coffee when the phone rang.
C: It was early in the morning, and I had just gotten up.
D: I had not completely woken up yet, but . . .

WHAT'S NEXT?

Look at your Self-assessment again. Do you need to review anything?

Unit 5 Supplementary Resources Overview

	After the following SB exercises	You can use these materials in class	Your students can use these materials outside the classroom
CYCLE 1	1 Perspectives		
	2 Word Power	**TSS** Unit 5 Vocabulary Worksheet	**SSD** Unit 5 Vocabulary 1–3 **ARC** Culture shock
	3 Grammar Focus	**TSS** Unit 5 Listening Worksheet	**SB** Unit 5 Grammar Plus focus 1 **SSD** Unit 5 Grammar 1 **ARC** Noun phrases containing relative clauses
	4 Pronunciation		
	5 Discussion	**TSS** Unit 5 Extra Worksheet	**WB** Unit 5 exercises 1–3
CYCLE 2	6 Snapshot		
	7 Conversation		**SSD** Unit 5 Speaking 1–2
	8 Grammar Focus	**TSS** Unit 5 Grammar Worksheet	**SB** Unit 5 Grammar Plus focus 2 **SSD** Unit 5 Grammar 2 **ARC** Expectations 1–2
	9 Listening		
	10 Speaking		
	11 Writing	**TSS** Unit 5 Writing Worksheet	
	12 Interchange 5		
	13 Reading	**TSS** Unit 5 Project Worksheet **VID** Unit 5 **VRB** Unit 5	**SSD** Unit 5 Reading 1–2 **SSD** Unit 5 Listening 1–3 **SSD** Unit 5 Video 1–3 **WB** Unit 5 exercises 4–7

Key
ARC: Arcade	**SB:** Student's Book	**SSD:** Self-study DVD-ROM	**TSS:** Teacher Support Site
VID: Video DVD	**VRB:** Video Resource Book	**WB:** Workbook	

My Plan for Unit 5

Use the space below to customize a plan that fits your needs.

With the following SB exercises	I am using these materials in class	My students are using these materials outside the classroom

With or instead of the following SB section	I am using these materials for assessment

5 Crossing cultures

1 PERSPECTIVES *If I moved to a foreign country...*

A ▶ Listen to the people talk about moving to a foreign country. Would you have any of the same concerns?

.... "One thing I'd really miss is my mom's cooking."

.... "I'd be worried about the local food. I might not like it."

.... "Getting used to different customs might be difficult at first."

.... "My room at home is the thing that I'd miss the most."

.... "Not knowing the prices of things is something I'd be concerned about."

.... "Moving to a country with a very different climate could be a challenge."

.... "I'd be worried about getting sick and not knowing how to find a good doctor."

.... "Something I'd be nervous about is communicating in a new language."

B Rate each concern from 1 (not worried at all) to 5 (really worried). What would be your biggest concern? Why?

2 WORD POWER *Culture shock*

A These words are used to describe how people sometimes feel when they live in a foreign country. Which are positive (**P**)? Which are negative (**N**)?

anxious	embarrassed	insecure ....
comfortable	enthusiastic	nervous ....
confident	excited	uncertain ....
curious	fascinated	uncomfortable ....
depressed	homesick	worried ....

curious

B **GROUP WORK** Tell your group about other situations in which you experienced the feelings in part A. What made you feel that way? How do you feel about the situations now?

A: I felt anxious yesterday. I had to give an important presentation at work.
B: How did the presentation go?
A: I was nervous and uncomfortable at first. I don't like speaking in public.
C: How did you feel after the presentation?
A: Actually, I felt pretty confident. I think it went really well!

Crossing cultures

In this unit, Ss discuss differences among customs and the joys and difficulties of living in a foreign country. In Cycle 1, students talk about living abroad using noun phrases and relative clauses. In Cycle 2, they describe expectations using when and if clauses.

1 PERSPECTIVES

Learning Objective: *see noun phrases containing relative clauses in context*

A ▶ *[CD 1, Track 36]*

- Books closed. Explain that Ss will hear people talking about concerns they would have about living abroad.
- Ask Ss to brainstorm concerns they would have about living abroad and things they would miss. Write Ss' ideas on the board like this:

  I'd worry about: the food, the climate, getting sick . . .

  I'd miss: my mom's cooking, my friends, my dog . . .

- Books open. Play the audio program.

- **Option:** Books closed. Ss listen and write the sentences they hear, like a dictation. Books open. Ss check their answers.
- ! For an alternative dictation, try the **Running Dictation** – download it from the website.
- Ss compare their ideas on the board with those in the book.

B

- Explain the task. Read the first sentence in part A aloud. Model the task by rating the concern as it is appropriate for you.
- Ss work individually to rate the concerns.
- Ask several Ss to tell the class their biggest concerns. Ask: "Does anyone agree?" Take a class vote.

2 WORD POWER

Learning Objective: *learn adjectives to describe a person's positive and negative feelings about living abroad*

A

- Read the exercise title aloud. Elicit that *culture shock* describes the feelings that people have when they live in a foreign country or visit for the first time.
- Explain the task. Focus Ss' attention on the photograph and caption. Ask: "How does the woman feel? Is *curious* a positive or negative feeling?" (Answer: positive) Model the task by writing *P* next to *curious*.
- Ss complete the task individually or in pairs. Ask Ss to try the task first without a dictionary. Go around the class and give help as needed.
- Elicit or explain any new vocabulary.

Vocabulary

anxious: feeling nervous
confident: certain about the ability to do things well
curious: wanting to know or learn about something
depressed: low in spirits; sad
enthusiastic: energetically interested in something
fascinated: being completely interested; showing complete attention to something
homesick: longing for home and family while absent from them
insecure: not confident or sure
uncertain: lacking clear knowledge or a definite opinion

- To check answers, write two columns on the board: negative and positive. Ss come up to the board and write their answers in the correct column.

Answers

anxious,	N	embarrassed,	N	insecure,	N
comfortable,	P	enthusiastic,	P	nervous,	N
confident,	P	excited,	P	uncertain,	N
curious,	P	fascinated,	P	uncomfortable,	N
depressed,	N	homesick,	N	worried,	N

- **Option:** Model the pronunciation of the adjectives on the list. Ss practice.

B Group work

- Explain the task. Read the focus questions aloud. Read the example with two Ss.
- Ss work in small groups. Ss take turns talking about their feelings. Remind Ss to use the adjectives in part A.
- When time is up, ask: "What did you have in common with other Ss in your group?" Elicit ideas.
- To practice the new vocabulary, play **Tic-Tac-Toe** – download it from the website.

3 GRAMMAR FOCUS

Learning Objective: *practice noun phrases containing relative clauses*

 [CD 1, Track 37]

- Write these four phrases on cards:

  one thing   I'd really miss

  is   my mom's cooking

- Write *one thing* and *is* in another color.

- Ask two Ss to come to the front of the class. Ask them to hold up these two cards: *I'd really miss* and *my mom's cooking.*

- Explain that we can say the same thing in a different way. Ask two more Ss to come to the front. Give them the other two cards.

- Now the four Ss stand facing the class, holding up their cards in this order:

  S1: *one thing*   S2: *I'd really miss*   S3: *is*
  S4: *my mom's cooking*

- Say that *one thing I'd really miss* is a noun phrase. It is made up of a noun *(one thing)* and a relative clause *(I'd really miss).* The noun phrase can go before or after *be.* Here it is before the verb *be.* It is the subject.

- Next, show the noun phrase after *be.* Ss rearrange themselves so that they are holding up this sentence:

  S4: *my mom's cooking*   S3: *is*   S1: *one thing*
  S2: *I'd really miss*

- Point out that the noun phrase is now the object. It is after the verb *be.*

- Finally, explain that all three example sentences have the same meaning. Note: If needed, ask Ss to show the class the three sentences again.

- Play the audio program. Point out that the pronouns in parentheses can be omitted. Remind Ss to use *who* with people.

A

- Ask Ss to read the list of phrases. Use the picture to model the first sentence.

- Ss work individually. Tell Ss to write their sentences on a separate piece of paper. Ss will use these sentences again in part B of Exercise 4.

- Go around the class and give help as needed. Ask Ss to write their answers on the board.

> **Possible answers**
>
> 1. trying new foods
> 2. My room at home
> 3. my friends and my family
> 4. Getting sick and getting lost in a new city
> 5. being away from home
> 6. Not understanding people
> 7. getting sick
> 8. My family and my friends
> 9. speaking a new language
> 10. Making new friends and trying new foods

B

- Explain the task. Ss complete the sentences in part A with their own information. Encourage Ss to use their own ideas and feelings.

C *Group work*

- Explain the task. Ss work individually to change the order of each sentence in part A. Read the example answer for number 1.

- Ss work in groups. They take turns reading their sentences. After about five minutes, ask groups to share the sentences that most of them agreed with.

4 PRONUNCIATION

Learning Objective: *notice and use word stress in sentences*

A **[CD 1, Track 38]**

- Write a sentence like this on the board:

  Argentina is a country that I'd like to live in.

- Explain that we stress the key words in a sentence.

- Elicit the three key words in the sentence. Underline them. (Answer: Argentina, country, live) Read the sentence aloud, stressing those words. Ss repeat.

- Play the audio program. Ss listen and notice which words are stressed.

- Play the audio program again. Ss listen and repeat.

- **Option:** Ss tap their desk with a pencil each time they hear a stressed word.

B *Pair work*

- Explain the task. Ss mark the key words in the sentences they wrote in part A of Exercise 3.

- Then pairs take turns reading their sentences aloud. Remind Ss to pay attention to the stress on key words. Go around the class and help with stress as needed.

❗ To practice word stress in a fun and useful way, use *Walking Stress* – download it from the website.

3 GRAMMAR FOCUS

Noun phrases containing relative clauses ▶

One thing (that) I'd really miss is my mom's cooking.

Something (that) I'd be nervous about is communicating in a new language.

Two people (who/that) I'd call every week are my parents.

My mom's cooking is **one thing (that) I'd really miss**.

Communicatng in a new language is **something (that) I'd be nervous about**.

My parents are **two people (who/that) I'd call every week**.

A Complete the sentences about living in a foreign country. Use the phrases below. Then compare with a partner.

my friends	trying new foods	making new friends	getting lost in a new city
my family	my favorite food	being away from home	not understanding people
getting sick	my room at home	speaking a new language	getting used to a different culture

1. One thing I'd definitely be excited about is . . .
2. . . . is something I'd really miss.
3. Two things I'd be homesick for are . . .
4. . . . are two things I'd be anxious about.
5. Something I'd get depressed about is . . .
6. . . . is one thing that I might be embarrassed about.
7. The thing I'd feel most uncomfortable about would be . . .
8. . . . are the people who I'd miss the most.
9. One thing I'd be insecure about is . . .
10. . . . are two things I'd be very enthusiastic about.

B Now complete three sentences in part A with your own information.

C GROUP WORK Rewrite your sentences from part B in another way. Then compare. Do others feel the same way?

1. One thing I'd definitely be excited about is taking pictures as I go sightseeing.

4 PRONUNCIATION Word stress in sentences

A ▶ Listen and practice. Notice that the important words in a sentence have more stress.

Argentina is a country that I'd like to live in.

Speaking a new language is something I'd be anxious about.

Trying new foods is something I'd be curious about.

B PAIR WORK Mark the stress in the sentences you wrote in Exercise 3, part A. Then practice the sentences. Pay attention to word stress.

5 **DISCUSSION** *Going abroad*

GROUP WORK Read the questions. Think of two more questions to add to the list. Then take turns asking and answering the questions in groups.

What country would you like to live in? Why?
What country wouldn't you like to live in? Why?
Who is the person you would most like to go
    abroad with?
What is something you would never travel without?
Who is the person you would email first after
    arriving somewhere new?
What would be your two greatest concerns
    about living abroad?
What is the thing you would enjoy the most
    about living abroad?

A: What country would you like to live in?
B: The country I'd most like to live in is Italy.
C: Why is that?
B: Well, I've always wanted to study art.

6 **SNAPSHOT**

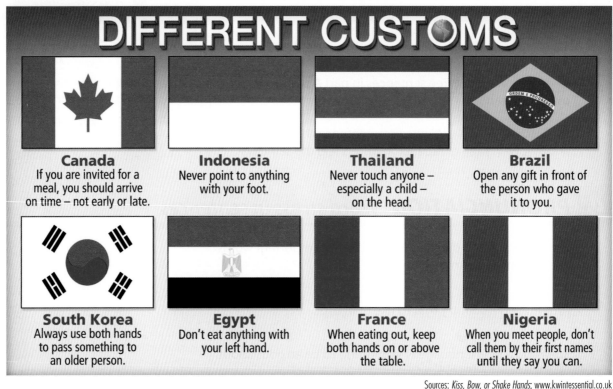

DIFFERENT CUSTOMS

Canada
If you are invited for a meal, you should arrive on time – not early or late.

Indonesia
Never point to anything with your foot.

Thailand
Never touch anyone – especially a child – on the head.

Brazil
Open any gift in front of the person who gave it to you.

South Korea
Always use both hands to pass something to an older person.

Egypt
Don't eat anything with your left hand.

France
When eating out, keep both hands on or above the table.

Nigeria
When you meet people, don't call them by their first names until they say you can.

Sources: *Kiss, Bow, or Shake Hands*; www.kwintessential.co.uk

Does your culture follow any of these customs?
Do any of these customs seem unusual to you? Explain.
What other interesting customs do you know?

DISCUSSION

Learning Objective: *discuss living in a foreign country*

Group work

- Explain the task. Ask different Ss to read each question aloud. Ask three Ss to model the conversation.

- **Option:** Use the questions to practice pronunciation, intonation, and word stress. Read each question. Ss listen and repeat.

- Ss work individually to write two more questions. Go around the class and give help as needed.

- Ss work in small groups.

> **TIP** To form groups, go around the class and assign each S an adjective (e.g., *confident, curious, enthusiastic*, etc.). Ask all the "confident" Ss to form a group together, all the "curious" Ss together, etc.

- Ss take turns asking and answering the questions. Remind Ss that one-word answers are not allowed!

Cycle 2, Exercises 6–13

 SNAPSHOT

Learning Objective: *learn information about the topic of the second cycle – customs from various countries*

- Books closed. To introduce the topic of countries and customs, brainstorm with the class. Write Ss' ideas on the board:

  -U.S.: Say "Excuse me" if you bump into or touch someone accidentally.

  -Indonesia: Wear proper clothes when visiting temples.

- Write this chart on the board. Ask Ss to guess the answers and match the country and custom:

Custom	Country
Arrive on time for a meal.	Thailand
Never touch anyone on the head.	Indonesia
Never point to anything with your foot.	Canada

> **TIP** To increase student talking time, introduce challenging rules (e.g., answers must have more than three words; each S must ask three follow-up questions) and rewards (e.g., Ss earn one point for each question they ask).

- Set a time limit of about ten minutes. Go around the class and listen in discreetly. Make note of problems, especially with noun phrases and relative clauses.

- When time is up, write some of the problems on the board. Elicit Ss' suggestions on how to correct them.

! Try the discussion activity in a different way, using the
• *Onion Ring* technique – download it from the website.

> **End of Cycle 1**

See the Supplementary Resources chart at the beginning of this unit for additional teaching materials and student activities related to this Cycle.

- Books open. Ss read the information in the Snapshot and check their answers. Encourage Ss to use a dictionary to check unfamiliar words.

- Read the questions.

- Ss discuss the questions in small groups. (Try to put Ss from different countries or regions together in each group.)

- **Option:** Play *Earthlings have some strange customs!* Ss imagine they are from another planet and have just landed on Earth. Pairs describe five strange customs on Earth (e.g., *The human female species around 14 years old - called "girls" - start to paint their lips red or pink. The males don't do this at any age.*). Ss share their observations.

7 CONVERSATION

Learning Objectives: *practice a conversation about customs; see clauses with* when *and* if *in context*

A ▶ *[CD 1, Track 39]*

- Tell Ss to cover the text and look only at the picture.
- Ss discuss the picture in pairs and create a story about it. Tell Ss there is no correct answer.
- Set the scene. A foreign student, Marta, is asking her friend Karen for advice about visiting someone's home. Tell Ss to listen to find out who invited Marta to dinner.
- Play the opening line of the audio program. Elicit the answer. (Answer: Marta's teacher)
- Write these statements on the board:

  Marta asks Karen:

  -what kind of gift she should take to her teacher's house

  - what time she should arrive

  - whether it's all right to bring a friend along

- Tell Ss to listen to find out which question Marta does *not* ask Karen.
- Play the rest of the audio program. Elicit Ss' answers. (Answer: Marta doesn't ask the second question.)
- Play the audio program again. Ss listen and read. Elicit the customs that Karen mentions. (Answers: It's the custom to bring a small gift. If you want to bring someone, you're expected to call first and ask if it's OK.)
- Ss practice the conversation in pairs.
- ❗ For a new way to practice this Conversation, try the *Disappearing Dialog* – download it from the website.

B ▶ *[CD 1, Track 40]*

- Explain the task. Read the focus question aloud. Use it to elicit Ss' responses around the class.

> **AudioScript**

See page T-168.

8 GRAMMAR FOCUS

Learning Objective: *practice using clauses with* when *and* if *for expectations*

▶ *[CD 1, Track 41]*

- Point out that there are several ways to describe expectations. Play the audio program for the Grammar Focus box. Ss listen, read, and repeat.
- Elicit or explain any new vocabulary.

> **Vocabulary**
>
> **expectations:** feelings or beliefs about the way something should be or how someone should behave
> **be supposed to:** should
> **host:** the person giving a party or dinner
> **be acceptable:** considered to be socially correct

- Explain that statements with *when* and *if* clauses can be used to describe a custom or something that is expected or normally done.
- Write these sentences on the board:

  I'm going to Brazil this summer. _____ I go to Brazil, I'll visit my family there.
  I might go to Brazil this summer. _____ I go to Brazil, I'll visit my family there.

- Elicit which set of sentences should use *when* and which should use *if*. (Answer: The first set should use *when*. The second should use *if*).
- Explain that we use *when* for things that are sure to happen and *if* for things that will possibly happen.

A

- Explain the task. Ss match up information about some customs in the United States and Canada. Ask a S to model the first one.
- Ss complete the task individually. Then Ss compare answers in pairs. Go around the class and give help as needed. Ask early finishers to write their answers on the board.

> **Answers**
>
> 1. a   2. e   3. d   4. f   5. b   6. c

B *Group work*

- Read the question aloud.
- Ss work in groups to discuss the customs in part A.

C

- Explain the task. Ask one or more Ss to complete the first sentence.
- Ss work individually. Encourage Ss to be creative.
- To practice sentences with *if* and *when*, Ss play *Sculptures* – download it from the website.
- Ss work in pairs. They take turns reading their sentences aloud.
- Ask Ss to share some of their sentences with the class.

7 CONVERSATION *What's the custom?*

A ▶ Listen and practice.

Marta: I just got invited to my teacher's house for dinner.
Karen: Oh, how nice!
Marta: Yes, but what do you do here when you're invited to someone's house?
Karen: Well, here in the U.S., it's the custom to bring a small gift.
Marta: Like what?
Karen: Oh, maybe some flowers or chocolates.
Marta: And is it all right to bring a friend along?
Karen: Well, if you want to bring someone, you're expected to call first and ask if it's OK.

B ▶ Listen to the rest of the conversation. If you are invited to someone's house in Germany, when are you expected to arrive? What can you bring as a gift?

8 GRAMMAR FOCUS

Expectations ▶

When you visit someone,	it**'s the custom to** bring a small gift.
	you **aren't supposed to** arrive early.
If you want to bring someone,	you**'re expected to** call first and ask.
	you**'re supposed to** check with the host.
	it**'s not acceptable to** arrive without calling first.

A Match information in columns A and B to make sentences about customs in the United States and Canada. Then compare with a partner.

A

1. If you plan to visit someone at home, ...
2. If you've been to a friend's home for dinner, ...
3. When you have been invited to a wedding, ...
4. When you go out on a date, ...
5. If the service in a restaurant is acceptable, ...
6. When you meet someone for the first time, ...

B

a. you're supposed to call first.
b. you're expected to leave a tip.
c. you aren't supposed to kiss him or her.
d. you're expected to respond in writing.
e. it's the custom to thank him or her.
f. it's acceptable to share the expenses.

B GROUP WORK How are the customs in part A different in your country?

C Complete these sentences with information about your country or a country you know well. Then compare with a partner.

1. In . . . , if people invite you to their home, . . .
2. When you go out with friends for dinner, . . .
3. If a friend gets engaged to be married, . . .
4. When a relative has a birthday, . . .
5. If a friend is in the hospital, . . .
6. When someone is going to have a baby, . . .

9 LISTENING Unique customs

 Listen to people describe customs they observed abroad. Complete the chart.

	Where was the person?	What was the custom?	How did the person react?
1. Alice			
2. John			
3. Susan			

10 SPEAKING Things to remember

A **PAIR WORK** What should a visitor to your country know about local customs? Make a list. Include these points.

greeting someone
eating in public
taking photographs
shopping

dressing appropriately
visiting someone's home
traveling by bus or train
tipping

B **GROUP WORK** Compare your lists with another pair. Then share experiences in which you (or someone you know) *didn't* follow the appropriate cultural behavior. What happened?

A: On my last vacation, I tried to bargain for something in a store.
B: What happened?
A: I was told that the prices were fixed. It was a little embarrassing because . . .

11 WRITING A tourist pamphlet

A **GROUP WORK** Choose five points from the list you made in Exercise 10. Use them to write and design a tourist pamphlet for your country.

 **Tips for Travelers**

When you visit Indonesia, there are some important things you should know. For example, if you are visiting a mosque or temple, it's not acceptable to take photographs. Also, you are supposed to . . .

B **CLASS ACTIVITY** Present your pamphlets. Would a visitor to your country have all the information he or she needed?

12 INTERCHANGE 5 Culture check

Compare customs in different countries. Go to Interchange 5 on page 118.

LISTENING

Learning Objectives: *listen to the experiences of people who have lived abroad; identify key information*

 [CD 1, Track 42]

- Write this famous saying on the board:

  When in Rome, do as the Romans do.

- Ask: "What do you think this means? Should a person living abroad follow *all* the customs of the country? Would you celebrate different holidays? Wear different clothes?" Elicit Ss' ideas.

- Explain the task. Ask Ss to read the questions and the names in the chart.

- Play the audio program once or twice. Ss listen and complete the chart.

AudioScript

See page T-168.

- Ss compare answers in groups of three.

Answers

1. South Korea; people make noise when they drink soup; it bothered her at first, but she got used to it
2. Spain; people eat late in the evening and stay out very late; he found it difficult
3. Saudi Arabia; women wear something to cover the head and a dress that covers the whole body; she found it a nuisance at first but then started to like it

- Ss discuss their reactions to the Listening. How would they feel about each of those customs?

SPEAKING

Learning Objective: *talk about local customs*

A Pair work

- Explain the task. Read the focus question aloud. Then read the points. Elicit other situations Ss could give advice on. Write Ss' suggestions on the board.

- Show how to set up a "do's and don'ts" list on the board:

  Some do's and don'ts when visiting my country
  Do's
  When you visit . . . , you're supposed to . . .
  It's the custom to . . .
  You're also expected to . . .
  Don'ts
  In . . . , it's not acceptable for foreign visitors to . . .

You aren't expected to . . .
People aren't supposed to . . .

- Ss work in pairs. Try to match up Ss from the same country or from similar ethnic or cultural areas. Set a time limit of about ten minutes. Go around the class and give help as needed.

B Group work

- Explain the task. Read the example with a S. Explain or elicit that *the prices were fixed* means the seller will not bargain or change the price.

- Tell pairs to select three customs from their lists and present them to the rest of the class. Note: Tell Ss to keep their lists for use in Exercise 11.

WRITING

Learning Objective: *write a tourist pamphlet*

A Group work

- Explain the task. Ask a S to read the model paragraph.

- Ss work individually. Remind Ss to include at least five points. Encourage Ss to write two or three paragraphs.

B Class activity

- Explain the task. Read the focus question aloud.

- Ss present their pamphlets to the class. Ss discuss anything they feel is missing from each other's pamphlets.

- Ss revise their pamphlets, incorporating the suggestions (as they wish) and their own ideas. Then they present them to the class.

 ## INTERCHANGE 5

See page T-118 for teaching notes.

13 ■ READING

Learning Objectives: *read a blog; develop skills in reading for main ideas and details*

- Books closed. Ask: "Do you ever read travel blogs? Why or why not? What kind of information do you get from a travel blog?" Elicit Ss' responses around the class.
- Books open. Read the question. Ask Ss to scan the text quickly to determine the kinds of culture shock the writer experienced.
- Elicit answers. (She was surprised by: (i) the short business hours; (ii) American students' behavior in class; and (iii) people's behavior with strangers.)
- *Option:* Elicit the similarities and differences between a personal travel journal (or diary) and a travel blog. Ask: "Why do some travelers like to write about their experiences online?"
- *Option:* Ask if anyone writes a travel blog or keeps a travel journal. If someone says yes, let the class ask that S questions (e.g., *How often do you write in it or post entries? How long have you had it? What kinds of things do you write about?*). If many Ss keep blogs or journals, this can be done in small groups.
- *Option:* If your class has students from Southeast Asia, ask them to predict what differences the Taiwanese student found between Taipei and Chicago. Write Ss' guesses on the board.
- Elicit or explain any new vocabulary.

Vocabulary

window-shopping: wandering around shopping areas and looking in store windows
interrupt: to begin talking before someone else has finished
ended up: resulted in something unplanned
chatting: talking informally about topics

- Ss read the article individually. Ask them to notice where vocabulary they just learned occurs.

A

- Explain the task. Point out that the three titles express the main ideas of the paragraphs. Explain that *24/7* means all day, seven days a week (all the time, around the clock).
- Ss reread the blog individually. Then Ss match the entries to the titles.
- Go over answers with the class.

Answers

August 31: Less than 24/7
September 5: Just say it!
October 6: Café etiquette

B

- Explain the task. Ask Ss to read the questions in the chart. Explain that Ss need to find the same information about each city.
- Ss complete the chart individually. Ss can write notes instead of complete sentences.
- Ask Ss to compare answers in pairs.
- Go over answers by asking Ss the questions.

Answers

1. Chicago: It shuts down in the evening.; Taipei: It doesn't shut down.
2. Chicago: Students answer questions almost immediately; some interrupt the teacher. Taipei: Students are silent in class.
3. Chicago: Students leave the class as soon as the class ends. Taipei: Students ask the teacher questions after class.
4. Chicago: People are friendly to strangers. Taipei: People don't start conversations with strangers.

C *Pair work*

- Read the questions. Ss work in pairs. (Mix nationalities if possible.) First tell Ss to answer the questions in part B about their own cities.
- Ss compare their cities to Taipei and Chicago. Encourage Ss to discuss other differences as well. Ss can work orally or can take notes about differences.
- *Option:* Ss talk about differences between their cities and other cities they know about, not just Taipei and Chicago.
- Call on Ss to tell the whole class some of the interesting or surprising things they learned from their partner.
- *Option:* Ss role-play. S1 interviews the person who wrote the journal (played by S2) about his or her experiences living abroad.
- ! To recycle information Ss have learned from the Reading and the unit, play *True or False?* – download it from the website.

End of Cycle 2

See the Supplementary Resources chart at the beginning of this unit for additional teaching materials and student activities related to this Cycle.

CULTURE SHOCK

Scan the blog. What kinds of culture shock did the writer experience?

Kit-ken Lim, a student from Taipei, Taiwan, is studying in Chicago. The following entries are taken from her blog during her first three months in the United States.

August 31

People often refer to Taipei as "The Sleepless City," but I didn't understand why until I got to Chicago. I was window-shopping with another student this evening. Suddenly, the store owners started pulling down their gates and locking their doors. Soon the whole street was closed. And it wasn't even dark yet! I'd never seen this in Taiwan. Back home, the busiest streets "stay awake" all night. You can go out to restaurants, stores, and movies even long after midnight.   MORE

September 5

After the first week of class, I've found some differences between Taiwanese students and American students. Whenever a teacher asks a question, my classmates immediately shout out their answers. And some of them interrupt the teacher. In Taiwan, we're usually quiet in class so that the teacher can finish on time. We usually ask the teacher questions afterward. American students seem to leave the room as soon as the class ends.   MORE

October 6

I met an interesting girl at an Internet café today. I was writing an email to my mother, and she asked me what language I was using. We ended up talking for about an hour! People in Chicago seem very comfortable with each other. It's very natural for two people to start talking in a café. This is something that doesn't happen in Taipei. At home, I'd never just start chatting with a stranger. I like that it's easy to meet new people here.   MORE

A Read the blog. Then add the correct title to each blog entry.

Café etiquette   Less than 24/7   Just say it!

B Complete the chart.

	Chicago	Taipei
1. When does the city shut down?		
2. How do students behave in class?		
3. How do students behave after class?		
4. How do people act toward strangers?		

C **PAIR WORK** How do things in your city compare with Taipei? with Chicago?

Unit 6 Supplementary Resources Overview

	After the following SB exercises	You can use these materials in class	Your students can use these materials outside the classroom
CYCLE 1	1 Snapshot		
	2 Perspectives	**TSS** Unit 6 Extra Worksheet	
	3 Grammar Focus		**SB** Unit 6 Grammar Plus focus 1 **SSD** Unit 6 Grammar 1
	4 Listening		
	5 Role Play		**WB** Unit 6 exercises 1–2
CYCLE 2	6 Conversation		**SSD** Unit 6 Speaking 1–2
	7 Grammar Focus	**TSS** Unit 6 Grammar Worksheet **TSS** Unit 6 Listening Worksheet	**SB** Unit 6 Grammar Plus focus 2 **SSD** Unit 6 Grammar 2 **ARC** Describing problems 1–5
	8 Word Power	**TSS** Unit 6 Vocabulary Worksheet	**SSD** Unit 6 Vocabulary 1–2
	9 Pronunciation		
	10 Listening		
	11 Writing	**TSS** Unit 6 Writing Worksheet	
	12 Interchange 6		
	13 Reading	**TSS** Unit 6 Project Worksheet **VID** Unit 6 **VRB** Unit 6	**SSD** Unit 6 Reading 1–2 **SSD** Unit 6 Listening 1–3 **SSD** Unit 6 Video 1–3 **WB** Unit 6 exercises 3–7

With or instead of the following SB section	You can also use these materials for assessment
Units 5–6 Progress Check	**ASSESSMENT CD** Units 5–6 Oral Quiz **ASSESSMENT CD** Units 5–6 Written Quiz

Key
ARC: Arcade **SB:** Student's Book **SSD:** Self-study DVD-ROM **TSS:** Teacher Support Site
VID: Video DVD **VRB:** Video Resource Book **WB:** Workbook

My Plan for Unit 6

Use the space below to customize a plan that fits your needs.

With the following SB exercises	I am using these materials in class	My students are using these materials outside the classroom

With or instead of the following SB section	I am using these materials for assessment

6 What's wrong with it?

1 SNAPSHOT

Some Common Complaints

Wireless service
There is no signal, so you can't get online.

Hotels
The bathroom sink is leaking.

Cleaners
The dry cleaner shrinks your favorite sweater.

Taxis
The driver tries to charge you too much.

Doctors
You have to wait a long time for your appointment.

Restaurants
Your food is undercooked.

Source: Based on information from *The Great American Gripe Book*

Have you ever had any of these complaints? Which ones?
What would you do in each of these situations?
What other complaints have you had?

2 PERSPECTIVES

A ⊙ Listen to people describe complaints on a call-in radio show.
Check (✓) what you think each person should do.

Ask Priscilla *the Problem Solver!*

❶ "I ordered a jacket online, but when it arrived, I found the lining was torn."
☐ ask for a refund   ☐ send it back and get a new one

❷ "I bought a new table from a store, but when they delivered it, I noticed it was damaged on the top."
☐ ask for a discount   ☐ ask the store to replace it

❸ "A friend sent me a vase for my birthday, but when it arrived, it was chipped."
☐ tell her about it   ☐ say nothing and repair it yourself

❹ "I lent a friend my sunglasses, and now there are scratches on the lenses."
☐ say nothing   ☐ ask him to replace them

❺ "I took some pants to the cleaners, and when they came back, they had a stain on them."
☐ wash them by hand   ☐ ask the cleaners to wash them again for free

B Have you ever had similar complaints? What happened? What did you do?

What's wrong with it?

Cycle 1, Exercises 1–5

In this unit, students practice making complaints and describing problems. In Cycle 1, students describe problems using nouns and past participles as adjectives. In Cycle 2, they discuss what needs fixing using need with passive infinitives and gerunds, and keep with gerunds.

1 SNAPSHOT

Learning Objective: *talk about common complaints*

- To introduce the topic of complaints, write this well-known joke on the board:

  Customer: Waiter, waiter! There's a fly in my soup!
  Waiter: Well, don't shout about it, or the other customers will want one, too.

- Elicit the meaning of *complaint*. (Answer: a criticism about a problem) Ask Ss to brainstorm typical complaints about restaurants (e.g., *The waiter was rude. The food was cold.*).

- **Option:** Label each of six sheets of paper with a business from the Snapshot. Put the sheets around the classroom walls. Ss write typical complaints on each sheet.

- Tell Ss to skim through the list of businesses and complaints in the Snapshot.

- Elicit or explain any new vocabulary.

  Vocabulary

  undercooked: not cooked enough
  dry cleaners: a business that cleans clothing
  shrink: to make a piece of clothing smaller by accident
  leaking: (water or gas) coming from a hole
  charge: to ask for money (for a service)

- Read the questions. Ss discuss the questions in pairs or small groups.

- **Option:** Have a class discussion about services and complaints in the Ss' country(ies). Recycle language from Unit 5 by asking questions such as: "Is it the custom to complain in writing? Is it acceptable to ask to see the manager?" etc.

2 PERSPECTIVES

Learning Objectives: *listen to people describing complaints; see past participles as adjectives in context*

A ▶ [CD 1, Track 43]

- Books closed. Set the scene. People are calling a radio show called *Ask Priscilla the Problem Solver!* to ask for advice about complaints.

- Tell Ss to listen first for what *item* each of the six callers is talking about. Ask Ss to write down the items.

- Play the audio program. Elicit the answers. (Answers: 1. a jacket 2. a table 3. a vase 4. sunglasses 5. pants)

- Books open. Play the audio program again. Ss listen and read or repeat.

- Elicit or explain any new vocabulary.

  Vocabulary

  lining: the inside material in a jacket
  torn: having a hole or a rip in fabric
  damaged: not in good condition
  chipped: with a small piece broken off
  scratches: small cuts from something rough
  stain: a mark from something

TIP To help Ss remember the new vocabulary, ask Ss to draw each item and problem in their vocabulary notebook.

- Model the task. Read the first complaint. Ask a S to read the two possible solutions. If necessary, elicit or explain the meaning of *refund*.

- Ask Ss what advice they would give. Make sure Ss understand that both answers are possible. Ss check (✓) the option they prefer.

- Find out which options are most popular. Ss put up their hands if they checked the option.

B

- Explain the task.

- In pairs or small groups, Ss discuss similar complaints of their own. Ss share what their complaint was, what they did to try to resolve it, and what the result was.

- Ss share their responses with the class.

3 GRAMMAR FOCUS

Learning Objective: *practice describing problems with past participles as adjectives and with nouns*

▶ **[CD 1, Track 44]**

- Explain that the two sets of sentences have more or less the same meaning (e.g., *We can say that something is torn or has a tear in it.*).

- Focus Ss' attention on the sentences on the left of the Grammar Focus box. Elicit the rule:
  subject + *be* + past participle as adjective
  Note: *Is leaking* is the present continuous form.

- Then do the same with the right column: subject + *have* + noun OR *there is/there are* + noun

- Play the audio program to present the sentences in the Grammar Focus box. Ss listen and read or repeat.

- **Option:** Write this chart on the board. Ask Ss to complete the chart with the verbs *stain, scratch,* and *leak.* Tell Ss to copy the chart into their notebooks. As Ss learn new words in part B, add them to the chart:

Verb	Participle/Adjective	Noun
tear	torn	a tear
damage	damaged	some damage
chip	chipped	a chip

A

- Explain the task. Model the first item with *It's stained./It has a stain on it.*

- Ss work individually to complete each sentence two ways. Go around the class and give help as needed.

- Ss go over their answers in pairs or small groups.

- Draw two columns on the board. Label them *Past participles* and *Nouns.* Ask Ss to write examples for each item on the board.

Possible answers

1. This tablecloth isn't very clean. It's **stained.**/It **has a stain (on it).**
2. Could we have another water pitcher? This one **is leaking.**/This one **has a leak (in it).**
3. The table looks pretty dirty. The wood **is scratched,** too./The wood **has a lot of scratches,** too.
4. The waiter needs a new shirt. The one he's wearing **is torn.**/The one he's wearing **has a tear (in it).**
5. Could you bring me another cup of coffee? This cup **is chipped.**/This cup **has a chip (in it).**
6. The walls really need paint. And the ceiling **is damaged.**/And the ceiling **has some damage.**

B Pair work

- **Option:** Explain the words in the box. Show how the words are collocated, using a chart like this on the board:

	chip	dent	crack	scratch	stain	tear	leak	break
Glass, china	✓		✓	✓				✓
Paper, cloth					✓	✓		
Plastic			✓	✓			✓	✓
Wood	✓		✓	✓	✓			✓
Metal		✓	✓	✓			✓	✓

- Explain the task. Read the words in the box. Focus Ss' attention on the pictures.

- Ask two Ss to model the conversation.

- Ss work in pairs and take turns making two different sentences about each picture. Ask Ss to write down their answers. Go around the class and give help as needed.

- Ask a few Ss to read their answers for the class. Ask if anyone has a different answer (e.g., *The mug has a chip in it.*).

Possible answers

1. The car is dented. The paint is scratched.
2. The mug has a crack in it. It is leaking.
3. The jeans are torn. They have stains on them.
4. The glasses are cracked. The frames are broken.

C Group work

- Explain the task. Read the example sentence. Ss find problems in the classroom.

- Ss work individually. Set a time limit of about ten minutes. Ss move around the room if necessary.

- Then in groups of three, Ss compare notes. They take turns describing the problems they found. Ask which group found the most problems.

▦ To practice the new language, play **Picture It!** – download it from the website.

3 GRAMMAR FOCUS

Describing problems 1 ▶

With past participles as adjectives

The jacket lining is **torn**.
The tabletop is **damaged**.
That vase is **chipped**.
My pants are **stained**.
Her sunglasses are a little **scratched**.
The sink **is leaking**.*

With nouns

It has **a tear** in it./There's **a hole** in it.
There is **some damage** on the top.
There is **a chip** in it.
They have **a stain** on them.
There are **a few scratches** on them.
It has **a leak**.

*Exception: is leaking is a present continuous form.

A Read the comments from customers in a restaurant. Write sentences in two different ways using forms of the word in parentheses. Then compare with a partner.

1. This tablecloth isn't very clean. It . . . (stain)
2. Could we have another water pitcher? This one . . . (leak)
3. The table looks pretty dirty. The wood . . . , too. (scratch)
4. The waiter needs a new shirt. The one he's wearing . . . (tear)
5. Could you bring me another cup of coffee? This cup . . . (chip)
6. The walls really need paint. And the ceiling . . . (damage)

> 1. It's stained.
>   It has a stain on it.

B **PAIR WORK** Describe two problems with each thing below. Use forms of the words in the box. You may use the same word more than once.

break	crack	damage	dent	leak	scratch	stain	tear

1 2 3 4

A: The car is dented.
B: Yes. And the paint is scratched.

C **GROUP WORK** Look around your classroom. How many problems can you describe?

"The floor is scratched, and the window is cracked. The desks are . . ."

4 LISTENING *Fair exchange?*

A ▶ Listen to three customers return an item they purchased.
What's the problem? Take notes. Then complete the chart.

Item	Problem	Will the store exchange it?	
		Yes	**No**
1.	....	☐	☐
2.	....	☐	☐
3.	....	☐	☐

B Were the solutions fair? Why or why not?

5 ROLE PLAY *What's the problem?*

Student A: You are returning an item to a store. Decide what
the item is and explain why you are returning it.

Student B: You are a salesperson. A customer is returning
an item to the store. Ask these questions:

What exactly is the problem?   When did you buy it?
Can you show it to me?   Do you have the receipt?
Was it like this when you   Would you like a refund or
  bought it?   a store credit?

Change roles and try the role play again.

6 CONVERSATION *It keeps burning!*

A ▶ Listen and practice.

Ms. Lock: Hello?
 Mr. Burr: Hello, Ms. Lock. This is Jack Burr.
Ms. Lock: Uh, Mr. Burr . . .
 Mr. Burr: In Apartment 305.
Ms. Lock: Oh, yes. What can I do for you? Does your
    refrigerator need fixing again?
 Mr. Burr: No, it's the oven this time.
Ms. Lock: Oh, so what's wrong with it?
 Mr. Burr: Well, I think the temperature control needs
    to be adjusted. The oven keeps burning
    everything I try to cook.
Ms. Lock: Really? OK, I'll have someone look at it right away.
 Mr. Burr: Thanks a lot, Ms. Lock.
Ms. Lock: Uh, by the way, Mr. Burr, are you sure it's
    the oven and not your cooking?

B ▶ Listen to another tenant calling Ms. Lock. What's the tenant's problem?

4 LISTENING

Learning Objectives: *listen to customer complaints; develop skills in listening for main ideas and details*

A [CD 1, Track 45]

- Books closed. Ask: "Have you ever returned anything to a store? What happened? Did you get a refund or an exchange?" Encourage discussion.
- Books open. Explain the task.
- Play the audio program. Ss listen to find out what each person is returning and what the problem is. They complete the first two columns of the chart.
- Play the audio program again. Ss listen to find out if the store will exchange the item. Ss complete the chart.

AudioScript

See page T-168.

- Elicit answers.

Answers

1. briefcase;   the lock doesn't work;   yes
2. shoes;   falling apart;   yes
3. shirt;   the color changed;   no

B

- Read the questions. Ss discuss who got a fair deal and who didn't, in their opinion.

5 ROLE PLAY

Learning Objective: *role-play a conversation describing problems between a customer and a store clerk*

- Focus Ss' attention on the picture. Ask: "What is the woman returning? Does the salesperson trust her? How do you know?"
- Assign A/B roles. Explain the task. Student A is the customer who is returning something to the store. Student B is the salesperson.
- Students As work in pairs. Tell them to brainstorm some items they could return and the problems each item might have (e.g., *a pair of jeans - too big, stained, torn*).

- Students Bs work in pairs. They read the questions a salesperson might ask. Ss add questions to the list.
- Divide the class into A/B pairs. Set a time limit of three or four minutes. Tell Student Bs to begin. Encourage Ss to use humor and have fun!
- Ss change roles and try the role play again.
- To carry out the Role Play in a new way, try *Time Out!* – download it from the website.

End of Cycle 1

See the Supplementary Resources chart at the beginning of this unit for additional teaching materials and student activities related to this Cycle.

Cycle 2, Exercises 6–13

6 CONVERSATION

Learning Objectives: *practice a conversation about problems; see* keep *and* need *with gerunds and* need *with passive infinitives in context*

A [CD 1, Track 46]

- Focus Ss' attention on the picture. Ss describe the picture in pairs.
- Books closed. Set the scene. A tenant, Jack Burr, is calling the building manager, Ms. Lock. Write focus questions like these on the board:

  Which household appliance isn't working? (the oven)
  What is the problem? (Everything gets burned.)
  What does Ms. Lock think the real problem is? (his cooking)

- Play the audio program. Ss listen and answer the focus questions.

- Books open. Play the audio program again. Ss listen and read.
- Then Ss practice the conversation in pairs.

B [CD 1, Track 47]

- Explain the task. Read the focus question.
- Play the second part of the audio program. Ss listen. Elicit answers.

AudioScript

See page T-168.

Answers

The lights keep going off and coming back on again.

GRAMMAR FOCUS

Learning Objectives: *practice* keep *and* need *with gerunds; practice* need + *passive infinitives*

▶ *[CD 1, Track 48]*

Keep + *gerund*

- Focus Ss' attention on the Conversation on page 38. Ask: "What's the problem with the oven?" Elicit the answer and write it on the board:

  The oven <u>keeps</u> bur<u>ning</u> everything.

- Explain that a gerund follows the verb *keep* when it refers to a repetitive action. Write sentence stems like these on the board:

  My coffee mug keeps . . . (leaking)
  My jeans keep . . . (shrinking)
  My parents keep . . . (telling me to get married)

- Ask Ss to complete the sentences with their own ideas.

Need + *gerund or passive infinitive*

- Explain that a gerund also follows the verb *need* (e.g., *The oven needs fixing.*).

- Say that need with a passive infinitive (e.g., *to be fixed*) means the same thing. Write on the board:

  The oven needs fixing. = The oven needs to be fixed.

- Ask Ss to look around the classroom and make sentences using the two structures with need (e.g., *These chairs need fixing. This desk needs to be repaired.*).

- Play the audio program. Ss listen and read or repeat.

A

- Explain the task. Focus Ss' attention on the picture. Ask different Ss to read the eight items and the example sentences.

- Elicit or explain any new vocabulary.

Vocabulary

pick up: put away
replace: change for something new
adjust: make a change so that something works better

- Ss complete the task individually or in pairs.

- Draw two columns on the board: (1) *need* + gerund, (2) *need* + passive infinitive. Ask Ss to write one sentence in either column. Then go over answers.

Answers

1. The walls **need to be painted/need painting**.
2. The rug **needs to be cleaned/needs cleaning**.
3. The windows **need to be washed/need washing**.
4. The clothes **need to be picked up/need picking up**.
5. The lamp shade **needs to be replaced/needs replacing**.
6. The wastebasket **needs to be emptied/needs emptying**.
7. The ceiling fan **needs to be adjusted/needs adjusting**.
8. The plant **needs to be watered/needs watering**.

B *Pair work*

- Explain the task. Read the questions. Model the activity with improvements you would like to make.

- Ss discuss their plans in pairs.

---

8 WORD POWER

Learning Objective: *learn vocabulary for discussing things that can go wrong with electronic items*

A

- Explain the task. Read the verbs in bold. Model the task with the first sentence.

- Ss complete the task individually.

- Elicit or explain any new vocabulary.

Vocabulary

flickering: flashing on and off
sticking: won't move
jumps: moves suddenly
crashing: failing, used for computers
skipping: moving from one place to another suddenly
freezing: stopping completely
dying: suddenly no longer working
jamming: not moving

- Ss compare answers in pairs.

Possible answers

1. flickering	4. sticking	7. freezing
2. skipping	5. crashing	8. dropping
3. dying	6. jamming	

B *Group work*

- Explain the task. Read the example sentences.

- Ss work in small groups. Ss take turns describing their problems. Remind Ss not to say what the item is! The rest of the group guesses the item.

- For more practice with this vocabulary, try *Tic-Tac-Toe* – download it from the website. Add one more verb, e.g., *getting stuck*.

7 GRAMMAR FOCUS

Describing problems 2 ▶

Need + *gerund*	Need + *passive infinitive*	Keep + *gerund*
The oven **needs adjusting**.	It **needs to be adjusted**.	Everything **keeps burning**.
The alarm **needs fixing**.	It **needs to be fixed**.	The alarm **keeps going off**.

A What needs to be done in this apartment? Write sentences about these items using *need* with gerunds or passive infinitives.

1. the walls (paint)
2. the rug (clean)
3. the windows (wash)
4. the clothes (pick up)
5. the lamp shade (replace)
6. the wastebasket (empty)
7. the ceiling fan (adjust)
8. the plant (water)

> 1. The walls need painting.
>
> OR
>
> 1. The walls need to be painted.

B **PAIR WORK** Think of five improvements you would like to make in your home. Which improvements will you most likely make? Which won't you make?

"First, the smoke alarm in the kitchen needs replacing. It keeps going off. . . ."

8 WORD POWER *Electronics*

A Circle the correct gerund to complete the sentences. Then compare with a partner.

1. My TV screen goes on and off all the time. It keeps **flickering / sticking**.
2. That old DVD player often jumps to another scene. It keeps **crashing / skipping**.
3. The battery in my new camera doesn't last long. It keeps **freezing / dying**.
4. The buttons on the remote control don't work well. They keep **skipping / sticking**.
5. Something is very wrong with my computer! It keeps **jamming / crashing**.
6. This printer isn't making all the copies I want. It keeps **jamming / flickering**.
7. My computer screen needs to be replaced. It keeps **dropping / freezing**.
8. I can't make long calls on my new phone. They keep **dying / dropping**.

B **GROUP WORK** Describe a problem with an electronic item you own. Don't identify it! Others will try to guess the item.

"Something I own keeps jamming. It happens when I'm driving. . . ."

9 PRONUNCIATION *Contrastive stress*

A ▶ Listen and practice. Notice how a change in stress changes the meaning of each question and elicits a different response.

Is the **bedroom** window cracked?   (No, the kitchen window is cracked.)

Is the bedroom **window** cracked?   (No, the bedroom door is cracked.)

Is the bedroom window **cracked**?   (No, it's broken.)

B ▶ Listen to the questions. Check (✓) the correct response.

1. a. Are my jeans torn?
⬜ No, they're stained.
⬜ No, your shirt is torn.

  b. Are my jeans torn?
⬜ No, they're stained.
⬜ No, your shirt is torn.

2. a. Is the computer screen flickering?
⬜ No, it's freezing.
⬜ No, the TV screen is flickering.

  b. Is the computer screen flickering?
⬜ No, it's freezing.
⬜ No, the TV screen is flickering.

10 LISTENING *Repair jobs*

▶ Listen to three people talk about their jobs. Complete the chart.

	What does this person repair?	What is the typical problem?
1. Joe		
2. Louise		
3. Sam		

11 WRITING *A critical online review*

A Imagine that you ordered a product online, but when you received it, you were unhappy with it. Write a critical online review. Explain all of the problems with the product and why you think others shouldn't buy it.

B GROUP WORK Read your classmates' reviews. What would you do if you read this critical online review and worked for the company that sold the product?

DON'T BUY
from **Games and Things!**

Last month I ordered a new joystick for my video game system online. First, it took way too long for the company to send it to me. Then, after using it for a few weeks, I discovered it was damaged. It keeps sticking and . . . READ MORE

12 INTERCHANGE 6 *Fixer-upper*

Do you have an eye for detail? Student A, go to Interchange 6A on page 119; Student B, go to Interchange 6B on page 120.

9 PRONUNCIATION

Learning Objective: *practice using contrastive stress*

A *[CD 1, Track 49]*

- Explain the concept of contrastive stress. If we want to call attention to a word or contrast it with something said earlier, we give it stronger stress. Give Ss these examples:
  A: Do you want to borrow a **pen**?
  B: No, I want to borrow a **pencil**.
  A: Do you want to **borrow** a pen?
  B: No, I want to **buy** a pen.
- Play the audio program to present the three sentences. Point out the different responses.

B ▶ *[CD 1, Track 50]*

- Explain the task.
- Play the audio program. Ss listen and check (✓) the correct answer to the questions.

> **Answers**
>
> 1. a. No, your shirt is torn.
>   b. No, they're stained.
> 2. a. No, it's freezing.
>   b. No, the TV screen is flickering.

- Ss work in pairs. S1 reads the questions in part B, stressing a different word each time. S2 chooses the correct response.

▣ Using the picture on page 35, Ss write *True or False?* statements – download it from the website.

10 LISTENING

Learning Objectives: *listen to job descriptions; develop skills in listening for main ideas and details*

[CD 1, Track 51]

- Books closed. Ask: "What kinds of things have you had repaired at home in the past year? What kinds of things have you taken to a repair shop?"
- Books open. Explain the task. Ask Ss to read the questions in the chart.
- Next, ask Ss to listen and find out what each person repairs. Play the audio program. Elicit answers.
- Ask Ss to predict what problems each person faces. Write Ss' ideas on the board.

- Now tell Ss to find out the typical problem. Tell Ss to take notes rather than write full sentences.
- Play the audio program once or twice. Pause after each speaker. Then elicit Ss' responses.

> **AudioScript**
>
> See page T-168.

> **Answers**
>
> 1. watches; need a new battery
> 2. luggage; the wheels
> 3. household appliances; garbage disposal gets jammed

11 WRITING

Learning Objective: *write a critical online review*

A

- Read the scenario. Then read the example review.
- Ss choose a product and make notes individually.
- They use their notes to write a critical online review. Remind Ss to include: (a) the problem with the item (and possibly with the online store), and (b) why they think others shouldn't buy the item.
- Ss revise their letters.

❗ For a new way to do the Writing activity, try *Mind Mapping* – download it from the website.

B Group work

- Explain the task. Ss read letters and discuss what they could do about the critical review.
- Ss pass around their letters and read as many as possible in about five minutes.
- Ss talk about letters they read. Each S should say what the classmate bought, what happened, and why others shouldn't buy it.
- Ask Ss to pretend that they work for the company that sold the product and say what they would do about the critical review.

12 INTERCHANGE 6

See page T-120 for teaching notes.

Learning Objectives: *read an article about reusing materials to make things of greater value; develop skills in scanning, and reading for main ideas and specific information*

- Read the pre-reading questions aloud. Remind Ss that scanning means reading quickly just to find the answer, not carefully concentrating on each word.
- Ss scan individually for the answer. Ss should raise their hands to let you know they are finished.

> **TIP** Seeing their classmates' hands raised will remind others to scan quickly instead of reading slowly.

- Elicit answers. (Answers: Upcycling is reusing waste materials so that they have a greater value. Its promoters feel there are problems with waste that is not reused and that products with upcycled material can be profitable.) Praise any correct answers.
- Ss read the article individually. Ask Ss to underline vocabulary they are not sure about but not to look up words in the dictionary.
- **Option:** Play *I know, I think I know*.
  1. Write vocabulary from the box below on the board (without definitions). Tell each S to organize the vocabulary into three lists: *I know, I think I know*, and *I don't know*. Ss should also add words they underlined to the appropriate list.
  2. Ss work in small groups to share their words. If other Ss can explain unknown words, the S moves the words to the *I think I know* or *I know* columns. Ss change groups at least once and repeat.
- Elicit or explain any remaining new vocabulary.
- Point out that *value* has two meanings in this article. Elicit the difference between *value* in the title and *value* in sentence 3.

Vocabulary

value: how useful or important something is; how much money something could be sold for
promote: encourage something to happen
waste materials: garbage
huge: very big
dump: put something somewhere to get rid of it (especially in a place where it should not be put)
pollute: to make water, air, or soil harmful
evidence: proof, signs
adopt: accept or start using something new
profitably: in a way that makes money
asset: something of value
element: a part of something
mosaic: a picture made with small pieces of colored stones, glass, tiles, etc.

A

- Explain the task. Elicit that *Not given* means the information does not appear in the article.
- Ss complete the task individually.
- Then Ss work in pairs to compare answers. Ss should be able to show their partners where they found the answers.
- Go over answers with the class.

Answers

1. False	3. False	5. True
2. Not given	4. Not given	6. False

B

- Explain the task.
- Ss complete the task individually.
- Elicit answers from different Ss.

Answers

1. wooden boards
2. chopsticks
3. pants
4. safety pins
5. car parts

- **Option:** Have Ss work in pairs to role-play a conversation between a shopper and a salesclerk. The salesclerk chooses three of the products and tries to sell them to the shopper.

C *Group work*

- Read the questions aloud. Ss work in groups to discuss the questions. Encourage Ss to ask follow-up questions and give additional information.
- **Option:** Ss work in pairs or small groups to plan a remodel of the classroom using upcycled materials. Ss can draw pictures if they wish. Then ask each pair or group to explain their ideas to the whole class.
- To recycle vocabulary from Units 5 and 6, play *Vocabulary Tennis* – download it from the website. Use categories (e.g., Adjectives) to describe broken things, and adjectives (e.g., anxious) to describe feelings.

End of Cycle 2

See the Supplementary Resources chart at the beginning of this unit for additional teaching materials and student activities related to this Cycle and for assessment tools.

THE VALUE OF UPCYCLING

Scan the article. What is "upcycling"? Why are some people trying to promote it?

Recycling is a well-known idea that refers to reusing waste materials in any way possible. But what about "upcycling"? It's a new word, even though it's something that has been going on since human civilization began. It means reusing waste materials so that they have greater value. Throughout history, people have always done creative things with "trash." For example, they've used straw and dead leaves to make roofs, skin from dead animals to make leather goods, and wood from fallen trees to make boats. So why is there a new word for it now?

One answer to this question is that we reuse fewer and fewer things, and so we have become a "throwaway" society. This has raised huge questions about waste: Where can we dump it all? Will it pollute the environment? Could it endanger our health? The evidence is everywhere – even in the Pacific Ocean, where billions of bits of broken plastic float near the surface. Fish eat them, and then we eat the fish.

So upcyclers have adopted this new word to focus people's attention on how waste cannot simply be reused, but be reused profitably. In fact, upcyclers don't like the idea of waste and prefer to call it an "asset," something of value. Nowadays, there are lots of organizations that market products with upcycled material. Some artists and designers have upcycled things like denim from old jeans to make rugs, and wood from old houses to make furniture. Others have even used old magazines to make stools, and candy wrappers to make handbags! Sometimes they'll add a stylish element to their products, such as a beautiful mosaic made with chipped or broken dishes. With an endless supply of "assets," it seems that upcycling has a great future.

A Read the article. Then for each statement, check (✓) True, False, or Not given.

	True	False	Not given
1. Upcycling is a new kind of recycling.	☐	☐	☐
2. People have always used wood to build houses.	☐	☐	☐
3. A "throwaway" society is careful to reuse things.	☐	☐	☐
4. The Atlantic Ocean is full of pieces of broken plastic.	☐	☐	☐
5. Some people make money by upcycling.	☐	☐	☐
6. Artists are not interested in upcycling.	☐	☐	☐

B Look at the photos. What do you think each product is made of?

car parts	chopsticks	pants	safety pins	wooden boards

1. .... 2. .... 3. .... 4. .... 5. ....

C GROUP WORK Do you own anything that is made from upcycled material? If so, what is it? What do you think of the idea of upcycling? Explain your opinion.

Units 5–6 Progress check

SELF-ASSESSMENT

How well can you do these things? Check (✓) the boxes.

I can	Very well	OK	A little
Describe a range of emotions (Ex. 1)	☐	☐	☐
Give opinions about behavior (Ex. 2)	☐	☐	☐
Understand problems and complaints (Ex. 3)	☐	☐	☐
Describe problems with physical objects (e.g., a car) (Ex. 4)	☐	☐	☐
Describe problematic situations (e.g., in a school) (Ex. 5)	☐	☐	☐

 SPEAKING *How would you feel?*

PAIR WORK Choose a situation. Then ask your partner
questions about it using the words in the box. Take turns.

getting married   starting a new job
meeting your hero   going to a new school

anxious	excited
curious	insecure
embarrassed	nervous
enthusiastic	worried

A: If you were getting married tomorrow, what would you be anxious about?
B: One thing I'd be anxious about is the vows. I'd be worried about saying the wrong thing!

2 SURVEY *What's acceptable?*

A What do you think of these behaviors? Complete the survey.

Is it acceptable to . . . ?	Yes	No	It depends
kiss in public	☐	☐	☐
ask how old someone is	☐	☐	☐
call your parents by their first names	☐	☐	☐
use a cell phone in a restaurant	☐	☐	☐
put your feet on the furniture	☐	☐	☐

B GROUP WORK Compare your opinions. When are these behaviors acceptable?
When are they unacceptable? What behaviors are never acceptable?

A: It's not acceptable to kiss in public.
B: Oh, I think it depends. In my country, if you're greeting someone, it's the
custom to kiss on the cheek.

Units 5–6 Progress check

SELF-ASSESSMENT

Learning Objectives: *reflect on one's learning; identify areas that need improvement*

- Ask: "What did you learn in Units 5 and 6?" Elicit Ss' answers.
- Ss complete the Self-assessment. Encourage them to be honest, and point out they will not get a bad grade if they check (✓) "a little."

- Ss move on to the Progress check exercises. You can have Ss complete them in class or for homework, using one of these techniques:
  1. Ask Ss to complete all the exercises.
  2. Ask Ss: "What do you need to practice?" Then assign exercises based on their answers.
  3. Ask Ss to choose and complete exercises based on their Self-assessment.

 ## SPEAKING

Learning Objective: *assess one's ability to describe emotions using noun phrases containing relative clauses*

Pair work

- Explain the task. Read the situations. Ask two Ss to model the conversation.

- Ss work in pairs. They take turns interviewing each other.
- Then Ss change partners and repeat the exercise.

 ## SURVEY

Learning Objective: *assess one's ability to talk about customs and expectations*

A

- Explain the task. Ask different Ss to read the survey items.
- Ss complete the survey individually. Ss can answer with what's acceptable to them, in their family, or in their country.

B Group work

- Explain the task. Read the questions. Ask two Ss to model the conversation.
- Ss work in small groups. Try to mix nationalities, ages, and genders. Ss take turns offering opinions. Set a time limit of five minutes.
- When time is up, read each survey item. Ask Ss to raise hands to show their responses.
- If time allows, ask some Ss to explain their answers.

3 LISTENING

Learning Objective: *assess one's ability to listen to and understand complaints*

A [CD 1, Track 52]

- Explain the task. Elicit or explain *tenant* (someone who rents a house or apartment) and *building manager* (someone who takes care of an apartment building for the owner).
- Play the audio program two or three times. Pause after each conversation. Ss listen and complete the chart. Ss may compare answers in pairs.

AudioScript

See page T-169.

- Go over answers with the class.

Answers

Tenant's complaints	How the problems are solved
1. light bulb out front needs changing	building manager gives a light bulb; tenant changes bulb herself
2. neighbor's dog has been barking all night	building manager will call the neighbor and ask if he can keep his dog quiet
3. kitchen window has jammed shut; it won't open	tenant will call cousin, who's a weightlifter, and ask him to open it

B Group work

- Explain the task. Read the questions.
- Ss work in small groups to discuss solutions.
- Ask a S from each group to share some of the solutions.

4 ROLE PLAY

Learning Objective: *assess one's ability to describe problems using nouns and past participles as adjectives*

- Explain the task. Elicit or explain that *haggling* means "bargaining."
- Divide the class into pairs, and assign A/B roles. Student As are the car buyers. Students Bs are the car sellers. Ask two Ss to model the conversation.
- Student As work in small groups to discuss problems with the car. Student Bs work in small groups to discuss a price and good features of the car.

- Ss role-play in A/B pairs. Ss negotiate the price of the car. Encourage Ss to find a price they can both agree on.
- Ss change roles and repeat the role play. If needed, Student As and Bs can work in small groups again to prepare.
- Take a class poll: Who paid the most for the car? Which car was in the best condition? Which car was in the worst condition?

5 DISCUSSION

Learning Objective: *assess one's ability to describe problems with gerunds and passive infinitives*

A Group work

- Explain the task. Elicit or explain that a *school council* is a group of elected student leaders that makes suggestions to the school administrators. Ask two Ss to model the conversation.
- Ss work in small groups. Remind Ss to decide on five improvements.

B Class activity

- Explain the task. Ask the secretaries to read their group's lists.
- Write all the ideas on the board. Then ask the class to vote on the three most important.
- Ask the class to suggest ways to make the improvements.
- **Option:** Ss can first discuss how to make the improvements in their groups.

WHAT'S NEXT?

Learning Objective: *become more involved in one's learning*

- Focus Ss' attention on the Self-assessment again. Ask: "How well can you do these things now?"

- Ask Ss to underline one thing they need to review. Ask: "What did you underline? How can you review it?"
- If needed, plan additional activities or reviews based on Ss' answers.

3 LISTENING Complaints

A ▶ Listen to three tenants complain to their building manager. Complete the chart.

Tenants' complaints	How the problems are solved
1.	....
2.	....
3.	....

B GROUP WORK Do you agree with the solutions? How would you solve the problems?

4 ROLE PLAY Haggling

Student A: Imagine you are buying this car from Student B, but it's too expensive. Describe the problems you see to get a better price.

Student B: You are trying to sell this car, but it has some problems. Make excuses for the problems to get the most money.

A: I want to buy this car, but the body has a few scratches. I'll give you $ . . . for it.
B: That's no big deal. You can't really see them, anyway. How about $ . . . ?
A: Well, what about the seat? It's . . .
B: You can fix that easily. . . .

Change roles and try the role play again.

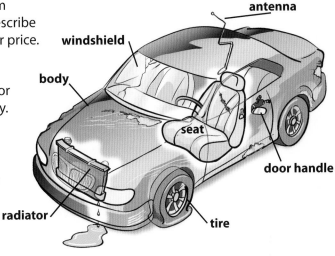

5 DISCUSSION School council meeting

A GROUP WORK Imagine you are on the school council. You are discussing improvements to your school. Decide on the five biggest issues.

A: The cafeteria food needs to be improved.
B: Yes, but it's more important to fix the computer in the lounge. It keeps crashing.

B CLASS ACTIVITY Share your list with the class. What are the three most needed improvements? Can you think of how to accomplish them?

WHAT'S NEXT?

Look at your Self-assessment again. Do you need to review anything?

Unit 7 Supplementary Resources Overview

	After the following SB exercises	You can use these materials in class	Your students can use these materials outside the classroom
CYCLE 1	1 Snapshot		
	2 Perspectives		
	3 Grammar Focus	**TSS** Unit 7 Extra Worksheet	**SB** Unit 7 Grammar Plus focus 1 **SSD** Unit 7 Grammar 1 **ARC** Passive with prepositions
	4 Pronunciation		**ARC** Reduction of auxiliary verbs
	5 Listening		
	6 Word Power	**TSS** Unit 7 Vocabulary Worksheet	**SSD** Unit 7 Vocabulary 1–2 **ARC** World problems **WB** Unit 7 exercises 1–4
CYCLE 2	7 Conversation		**SSD** Unit 7 Speaking 1–2
	8 Grammar Focus	**TSS** Unit 7 Grammar Worksheet **TSS** Unit 7 Listening Worksheet	**SB** Unit 7 Grammar Plus focus 2 **SSD** Unit 7 Grammar 2 **ARC** Infinitive clauses and phrases
	9 Discussion	**TSS** Unit 7 Writing Worksheet	
	10 Interchange 7		
	11 Writing		
	12 Reading	**TSS** Unit 7 Project Worksheet **VID** Unit 7 **VRB** Unit 7	**SSD** Unit 7 Reading 1–2 **SSD** Unit 7 Listening 1–3 **SSD** Unit 7 Video 1–3 **WB** Unit 7 exercises 5–8

Key

ARC: Arcade	**SB:** Student's Book	**SSD:** Self-study DVD-ROM	**TSS:** Teacher Support Site
VID: Video DVD	**VRB:** Video Resource Book	**WB:** Workbook	

My Plan for Unit 7

Use the space below to customize a plan that fits your needs.

With the following SB exercises	I am using these materials in class	My students are using these materials outside the classroom

With or instead of the following SB section	I am using these materials for assessment

 # The world we live in

1 SNAPSHOT

Waste Not, Want Not

~Some alarming facts~

Americans . . . .

- make **750,000** *photocopies every minute*
- throw away **2.5 million** *plastic bottles every hour*
- get rid of **30,000** *cars every day*
- dispose of **49 million** *baby diapers every day*
- receive **4 million** *tons of junk mail every year*
- use **65 billion** *aluminum cans every year*
- throw out **270 million** *tires every year*

Source: www.cleanair.org

Which of the things above seem the most wasteful?
What do you throw away? What do you tend to recycle?
What are two other environmental problems that concern you?

2 PERSPECTIVES *Clean up our city!*

A ▶ Listen to an announcement from an election campaign.
What kinds of problems does Roberta Chang want to fix?

VOTE FOR ROBERTA CHANG CITY COUNCIL

Roberta Chang will clean up Cradville!
Have you noticed these problems in our city?

★ The air is being polluted by fumes from cars and trucks.

★ Potholes aren't being repaired due to a lack of funding.

★ The homeless have been displaced from city shelters because of overcrowding.

★ Many parks have been lost through overbuilding.

★ Our city streets are being damaged as a result of heavy traffic.

★ Our fresh water supply is being depleted through overuse by people who don't conserve.

☆ *A vote for Roberta Chang is a vote for solutions!* ☆

B Which of these problems affect your city? Can you give specific examples?

The world we live in

> In this unit, students discuss social problems and environmental concerns. In Cycle 1, they talk about environmental problems using the present continuous and present perfect passive tenses, as well as prepositions of cause. In Cycle 2, students discuss what they can do about problems using infinitive clauses and phrases.

SNAPSHOT

Learning Objective: *talk about the environment*

- Books closed. Write the word *environment* on the board. Elicit the meaning. (Answer: the land, water, and air in which people, animals, and plants live)
- Books open. Ask: "How much trash did you see on the way to class today? What kind of things? Where?"

- Ss read the Snapshot individually. Ask: "Which fact was the most surprising to you?" Elicit answers through a show of hands.
- Read the questions aloud.
- Ss discuss the questions in pairs or small groups.

PERSPECTIVES

Learning Objectives: *discuss a campaign announcement; see the passive with prepositions in context*

A ▶ [CD 2, Track 1]

- Books closed. Set the scene. Roberta Chang wants to be elected to the city council. In her campaign announcement, she describes problems in her city. Elicit or explain the meaning of *election campaign* (an organized series of activities to get people to vote someone into an official position).
- Write questions like these on the board. Ask Ss to listen for the answers.

  In the city of Cradville, what or who is . . .
  polluted?   lost?
  not repaired?   displaced?
  damaged?   depleted?

- Explain any vocabulary that Ss don't know (without giving away the answers!).
- Show Ss how to predict an answer (e.g., *Polluted? Let's see. That could be water or air.*). Ss predict the others. Write Ss' ideas on the board.
- Play the audio program. Ss listen for the answers.
- Books open. Ss go over their answers in pairs. (Answers: air, potholes, streets, parks, the homeless, water) Discuss how accurate Ss' predictions were.

- Point out that Roberta Chang also talked about the *cause* of each problem. Elicit the words she used to describe the cause (e.g., *by, due to, as a result of, through, because of*).
- Ask Ss to read and underline the cause of each problem. Model the first sentence with the class. Tell Ss to underline <u>by fumes from cars and trucks</u>.
- Ss complete the task in pairs.
- Elicit or explain any new vocabulary.

> **Vocabulary**
>
> **displaced:** forced out
> **depleted:** reduced in amount
> **conserve:** use something so that it's not wasted

- Play the audio program again. Ss listen and read.
- For a new way to teach this vocabulary, try **Vocabulary Mingle** – download it from the website.

B *Group work*

- Explain the task. Read the questions.
- Ss discuss the questions in small groups. Set a time limit. Then elicit examples of how these problems affect their city.
- **Option:** Ss discuss these questions: *If you were mayor of your city, which of the problems would you try to fix first? How would you solve them?*

3 GRAMMAR FOCUS

Learning Objectives: *practice the present continuous passive and the present perfect passive; describe causes with* by, because of, due to, through, *and* as a result of

▶ **[CD 2, Track 2]**

Present continuous passive

- Focus Ss' attention on the Perspectives on page 44. Ask Ss to find examples with *is being* or *are being*. Write the examples on the board, in columns, like this:

1	2	3
The air	is being	polluted
Our city streets	are being	damaged
Our water supply	is being	depleted

- Elicit or explain how to form the present continuous passive:

  subject + *is/are being* + past participle

- Point out that the present continuous passive describes an action that is in progress right now. Write an example on the board:

  Too many trees <u>are being cut down</u> right now/these days.

- Focus Ss' attention on the examples in the Grammar Focus box. Elicit a few more sentences from the class.

Present perfect passive

- Focus Ss' attention on the Perspectives on page 44. Ask Ss to find examples with *has been* or *have been*. Write them on the board in columns.

- Elicit or explain how to form the present perfect passive:

  subject + *has/have been* + past participle

- Point out that the present perfect passive describes something that started before the present (the exact time isn't important). Write an example on the board:

  Too many trees <u>have been cut down</u> recently/in the last few years.

- Play the audio program. Ss listen and repeat.

- Remind Ss to use *by, because of, due to, through,* and *as a result of* before the cause. Explain that these words have similar meanings.

A *Pair work*

- Books open. Tell Ss to look at the six photos. Elicit words to describe the pictures (*e.g., sheep, farm, livestock*). Write Ss' ideas on the board.

- Explain the task. Model the task with the first photo.

- Ss complete the task in pairs. They match the photos with the sentences. Elicit Ss' responses to check answers.

B

- Explain the task. Show Ss how to change an active sentence into a passive sentence. Model it on the board. Use different colors if possible.

  (a) Write the cause, the verb, and the object. Underline them and number them:

      1   2

  <u>Air pollution</u> is threatening <u>the health of people.</u>

  (b) Exchange 1 and 2 (the object and the cause). Then write a preposition (e.g., *by*) before the cause:

      2   1

  <u>The health of people</u> (verb) <u>by air pollution.</u>

  (c) Identify the original tense (present continuous) and write the verb *be* in that tense (e.g., *is/are being*). Take the original verb (e.g., *threaten*) and make it a past participle:

  present continuous: <u>is/are being + threatened</u>

- Repeat the above steps with a present perfect passive sentence.

- Ss complete the task individually. Go around the class and give help as needed. Tell Ss to keep their sentences to use in Exercise 4.

> **TIP** If Ss finish early, check their work and ask them to join other Ss. Tell early finishers to help the slower Ss by giving them clues, not by telling them the answers.

Answers

1. The health of people in urban areas is being threatened by air pollution.
2. Soil and underground water have been contaminated because of livestock farms.
3. Statues and buildings have been eroded as a result of acid rain.
4. Birds, fish, and other marine life are being harmed through oil spills.
5. Huge amounts of farmland have been eaten up due to the growth of suburbs.
6. The extinction of plants and wildlife is being accelerated by the destruction of rain forests.

C *Pair work*

- Explain the task. Model the activity with a S.

- Ss work in pairs to take turns describing and guessing pictures. Go around the room and take notes on errors with passives. Write any errors you hear on the board. Elicit corrections from Ss.

Passive with prepositions ▶

Present continuous passive

The air is **being polluted**	**by** fumes from cars and trucks.
City streets **are being damaged**	**as a result of** heavy traffic.
Potholes **aren't being repaired**	**due to** a lack of funding.

Present perfect passive

Many parks **have been lost**	**through** overbuilding.
The homeless **have been displaced**	**because of** overcrowding in city shelters.

A **PAIR WORK** Match the photos of environmental problems with the sentences below.

1. Air pollution is threatening the health of people in urban areas. (by)
2. Livestock farms have contaminated soil and underground water. (because of)
3. Acid rain has eroded statues and buildings. (as a result of)
4. Oil spills are harming birds, fish, and other marine life. (through)
5. The growth of suburbs has eaten up huge amounts of farmland. (due to)
6. The destruction of rain forests is accelerating the extinction of plants and wildlife. (by)

B Rewrite the sentences in part A using the passive and the prepositions given. Then compare with a partner.

> 1. The health of people in urban areas is being threatened by air pollution.

C **PAIR WORK** Cover the sentences in part A above. Take turns describing the environmental problems in the pictures in your own words.

4 PRONUNCIATION Reduction of auxiliary verbs

A ⊙ Listen and practice. Notice how the auxiliary verb forms **is**, **are**, **has**, and **have** are reduced in conversation.

Fresh water ~~is~~ being wasted.
Newspapers ~~are~~ being thrown away.

Too much trash ~~has~~ been created.
Parks ~~have~~ been lost.

B **PAIR WORK** Practice the sentences you wrote in Exercise 3, part B. Pay attention to the reduction of **is**, **are**, **has**, and **have**.

5 LISTENING Environmental solutions

A ⊙ Listen to three people describe some serious environmental problems. Check (✓) the problem each person talks about.

	Problem			What can be done about it?
1. Jenny	☐ landfills	☐ poor farmland		....
2. Adam	☐ electricity	☐ e-waste		....
3. Katy	☐ air pollution	☐ water pollution		....

B ⊙ Listen again. What can be done to solve each problem? Complete the chart.

6 WORD POWER World problems

A **PAIR WORK** How concerned is your partner about these problems? Check (✓) his or her answers.

Problems	Very concerned	Fairly concerned	Not concerned
cancer	☐	☐	☐
drug trafficking	☐	☐	☐
famine	☐	☐	☐
global warming	☐	☐	☐
government corruption	☐	☐	☐
inflation	☐	☐	☐
overpopulation	☐	☐	☐
political unrest	☐	☐	☐
poverty	☐	☐	☐

B **GROUP WORK** Share your partner's answers with another pair. Which problems concern your group the most? What will happen if the problem isn't solved?

A: Many lives have been lost to due to cancer.
B: We need to find ways to raise money for more research.
C: I agree. If we don't, the disease will continue to spread.

4 PRONUNCIATION

Learning Objective: *notice and use reduced auxiliary verbs*

A ▶ [CD 2, Track 3]

- Ask Ss to listen for the auxiliaries. Play the audio program. Model the difference between the full auxiliaries and the reductions.
- Play the audio program again. Pause after each sentence. Ss practice.

- **Option:** Ask Ss to stand in a line, facing the class. Each S represents a word in the example sentence. If the word is unstressed, the S sits or crouches down. Then they say their sentence aloud.

B *Pair work*

- Explain the task.
- Ss work in pairs. They take turns reading the sentences from part B of Exercise 3 on page 45.
- Go around the class and listen for reductions.

5 LISTENING

Learning Objectives: *develop skills in listening for main ideas and note taking; listen to environmental problems*

A ▶ [CD 2, Track 4]

- Explain the task. Go over the information in the chart. Elicit or explain *e-waste* (electronic or electrical devices that people have thrown away).
- Tell Ss to listen and put a check next to the environmental problems that the speakers talk about. Remind Ss to listen for key phrases.
- Play the audio program. Pause after each description to give Ss time to write their answers. Then check Ss' responses.

AudioScript

See page T-169.

Answers

1. landfill
2. e-waste
3. water pollution

B ▶ [CD 2, Track 5]

- Explain the task. Read the question.
- Tell Ss to listen and write down the solutions. Remind Ss to listen for key phrases.
- Play the audio program. Pause after each description to give Ss time to write their answers.
- Then elicit Ss' answers.

Answers

1. do more recycling
2. dispose of it responsibly; take products to e-waste processing centers and reuse parts
3. treat all waste products more carefully

6 WORD POWER

Learning Objective: *learn vocabulary for discussing world problems*

A *Pair work*

- Explain the task. Read the question and the chart headings. Point out that there are no right or wrong answers.
- Model the task with a S:
  - T: What does *drug trafficking* mean?
  - S: Isn't it when people buy or sell illegal drugs?
  - T: Yes, that's right. How concerned are you about it?
  - S: Oh, I worry about it a lot! What about you? Are you concerned about it?
- Ss work in pairs. Set a time limit of about ten minutes. Go around the class and give help as needed.
- Go over any unfamiliar vocabulary.

B *Group work*

- Read the questions. Ask three Ss to model the conversation.
- Each pair from part A joins another pair to discuss the problems.

End of Cycle 1

See the Supplementary Resources chart at the beginning of this unit for additional teaching materials and student activities related to this Cycle.

7 CONVERSATION

Learning Objectives: *talk about solutions to problems; see infinitive clauses and phrases in context*

A *[CD 2, Track 6]*

- Tell Ss to cover the text and look only at the picture. Ask Ss to make notes about the problems they can see in the picture.
- Ask: "What environmental issue do you think Carla and Andy are talking about?" Write Ss' suggestions on the board.
- Play the audio program. Then ask the class which topics on the board were "correct guesses." Circle them.
- Elicit any additional problems Ss heard. Add them to the board.
- Give Ss a few minutes to read the conversation. Then ask Ss to compare the conversation with their notes.
- Elicit or explain any new vocabulary.

Vocabulary

pumping: moving liquid from one place to another with a machine (a pump)

against the law: illegal

ignore: not pay attention to someone or something; disregard

management: the people who are in charge of a company

run a story: report about a recent event in a newspaper, on TV, or on the radio

bad publicity: negative attention that someone or something gets from a news story

top executives: the highest level of managers in a company

- Play the audio program again. Ask Ss to pay attention to the intonation. Then Ss practice the conversation in pairs.
- ! For fun and good intonation, encourage Ss to use the activity *Say It With Feeling!* – download it from the website.

B *Class activity*

- Explain the task. Read the question. Have a brief class discussion about the question. Write Ss' suggestions on the board.

C *[CD 2, Track 7]*

- Read the focus question aloud.
- Play the second part of the audio program. Ss listen and take notes.

AudioScript

See page T-170.

- Check answers. Find out if Ss' suggestions in part B match what Andy and Carla decide to do.

Answers

They decide to monitor the situation by taking pictures of the river and taking water samples (to see how bad the situation is).

8 GRAMMAR FOCUS

Learning Objective: *practice infinitive clauses and phrases*

▶ *[CD 2, Track 8]*

- Play the audio program.
- Elicit how to form the sentences:
  (One way/Another way) + infinitive + *is/are* + infinitive
- Ask Ss to generate more example sentences. Write their sentences on the board. Make corrections with the class.

A

- Explain the task. Ss match problems and solutions individually or in pairs.
- Ss go over their answers in pairs. Then go over answers with the class.

Possible answers

1. b/h	3. f	5. c/h
2. d	4. g	6. a/c/h

B *Group work*

- Explain the task. Read the question.
- Ss work in small groups. Tell Ss to first take turns giving their opinion on each solution in part A. Then Ss discuss new solutions. Set a time limit of about five minutes. Go around the class and give help as needed.
- Groups share one or two of their more interesting ideas with the rest of the class.

7 CONVERSATION *What can we do?*

A  Listen and practice.

Carla: Look at all those dead fish! What do you think happened?
Andy: Well, there's a factory outside town that's pumping chemicals into the river.
Carla: How can they do that? Isn't that against the law?
Andy: Yes, it is. But a lot of companies ignore those laws.
Carla: That's terrible! What can we do about it?
Andy: Well, one way to change things is to talk to the company's management.
Carla: What if that doesn't work?
Andy: Well, then another way to stop them is to get a TV station to run a story on it.
Carla: Yes! Companies hate bad publicity. By the way, what's the name of this company?
Andy: It's called Avox Industries.
Carla: Really? My uncle is one of their top executives.

B **CLASS ACTIVITY** What else could Andy and Carla do?

C Listen to the rest of the conversation. What do Andy and Carla decide to do?

8 GRAMMAR FOCUS

> ### Infinitive clauses and phrases
>
> | | |
> |---|---|
> | One way **to change** things is | **to talk** to the company's management. |
> | Another way **to stop** them is | **to get** a TV station to run a story. |
> | The best ways **to fight** cancer are | **to do** more research and educate people. |

A Find one or more solutions for each problem. Then compare with a partner.

Problems

1. One way to reduce famine is ....
2. The best way to fight cancer is ....
3. One way to stop political unrest is ....
4. One way to improve air quality is ....
5. The best way to reduce poverty is ....
6. One way to help the homeless is ....

Solutions

a. to build more public housing.
b. to train people in modern farming methods.
c. to start free vocational training programs.
d. to educate people on healthy lifestyle choices.
e. to have more police on the streets.
f. to provide ways for people to voice their concerns.
g. to develop cleaner public transportation.
h. to create more jobs for the unemployed.

B **GROUP WORK** Can you think of two more solutions for each problem in part A? Agree on the best solution for each.

9 DISCUSSION Problems and solutions

A PAIR WORK Describe the problems shown in the photos.
Then make suggestions about how to solve these problems.

What can be done . . . ?

1. to stop drug trafficking
2. to improve children's health
3. to keep our parks clean
4. to reduce unemployment

A: Our economy is being ruined by drug trafficking.
B: Well, one way to stop it is . . .

B CLASS ACTIVITY Share your solutions. Which ones are the most innovative?
Which ones are most likely to solve the problems?

10 INTERCHANGE 7 Make your voices heard!

Brainstorm solutions to some local problems. Go to Interchange 7 on page 121.

11 WRITING A message on a community website

A Choose a problem from the unit or use one of your own ideas. Write a message
to post on a local community website.

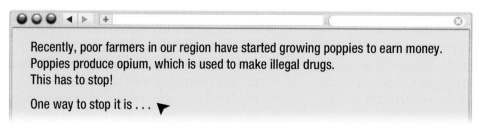

> Recently, poor farmers in our region have started growing poppies to earn money.
> Poppies produce opium, which is used to make illegal drugs.
> This has to stop!
>
> One way to stop it is . . . ▶

B PAIR WORK Exchange messages with a partner. Imagine you live in the same community.
Write a response suggesting another solution.

9 DISCUSSION

Learning Objectives: *discuss problems and solutions; develop the skill of giving opinions*

A Pair work

- Focus Ss' attention on the pictures. Ask Ss to describe the pictures.
- Explain the task. Ask a S to read the question and the cues. Ask two Ss to model the conversation. Encourage them to continue with additional suggestions and follow-up questions.
- **Option:** Ss earn one point for every follow-up question they ask or for every solution they suggest.

> **TIP** To provide variety and challenge, make sure Ss work with different partners. If possible, put Ss of a similar ability together for oral fluency activities.

- Ss work in pairs. Remind Ss to make suggestions for each problem. Set a time limit of about five minutes. Go around the class and discreetly listen in. Make note of grammar or vocabulary problems.

- When time is up, write the common errors you noticed on the board. Elicit corrections from Ss.

 For a new way to develop oral fluency, play **Just One Minute** – download it from the website.

B Class activity

- Explain the task. Read the question. Elicit that *innovative* refers to something that is new or different (e.g., an idea, a method, a solution).
- Act as the discussion monitor. Present each problem. Elicit each pair's solutions. Ask a S to record solutions on the board, using key phrases.
- Take a class vote (through a show of hands) on which solutions were the most innovative.
- **Option:** Follow up with a class debate. Elicit topics for the debate. Show Ss how to debate in teams.

> **TIP** To give Ss of all levels confidence that they are progressing, remind them regularly of what they have learned in the last few exercises. For example, say "Now you know how to talk about problems and give solutions."

10 INTERCHANGE 7

See page T-119 for teaching notes.

11 WRITING

Learning Objective: *write a message to a community website describing a problem and offering solutions*

A

- Explain the task. Ask a S to read the model message. Point out that the first paragraph should present the problem. Later paragraphs should outline solutions.
- Ask Ss to brainstorm and make notes.

> **TIP** To help Ss brainstorm, set a time limit and ask them to write continuously for that time. "Free writing" is a useful way of writing fluently to generate ideas.

- Ss organize their ideas and draft their messages.
- **Option:** Step 3 can be done for homework.
- **Option:** Ss can take turns coming up to you for a mini-conference on their organization and content. If there is time, point out vocabulary or grammar problems Ss need to correct.

> **TIP** Use a correction code rather than correct Ss' work yourself. Write symbols on the page to indicate what needs fixing (e.g., *P* = punctuation, *Sp* = spelling, *WO* = word order, *Aux* = auxiliary, *WW* = wrong word, *MW* = missing word). Ss correct their own work.

B Pair work

- Explain the task. Ss work in pairs. Set a time limit of about ten minutes for this task.
- Ss read each other's messages. Then Ss pretend to be a reader of the community website and write back to their partner proposing another solution to the problem.
- Ss exchange messages again. Ss read the messages and comment on the alternate solutions. They can comment in writing or discuss the solutions together.
- **Option:** Display the messages on the bulletin board or around the room, with a piece of blank paper beneath each one. Ss read the messages on the board or around the room and choose three to respond to. They write their responses and alternative solutions beneath the message, as if responding to posts on a discussion forum.

Learning Objective: *develop skills in scanning, reading for main ideas, and identifying causes and results*

Note: You might want to bring a world map to show the location and size of Apo Island, and a picture of a coral reef.

- Books closed. Ask: "What do you know about coral reefs? What do you know about commercial fishing?" Elicit ideas. If a S seems to know quite a bit, put him or her on the "hot seat." The rest of the class asks questions to get more information.
- Books open. Read the pre-reading question aloud.
- Ask Ss to skim the first two paragraphs to find out the problem for the people of Apo Island. (Answer: The problem was that there were almost no fish in the local coral reef and fishermen had to go far out to sea to find enough fish. OR: New fishing methods were destructive; they depleted the fish supply in their coral reef).

A

- Explain the task. Point out the flow charts and read the sentences. Say that flow charts can help us to organize information to show causes and effects. Ss will add information from the article to complete the flow charts.
- Ss read the article individually. Remind Ss to mark words or phrases they can't guess from context. When Ss finish, they can use their dictionaries to check words they marked.
- Elicit or explain any new vocabulary.

Vocabulary

coral reef: a line of rocks or sand near the surface of the sea; the home to many forms of sea life
coral: a hard, rock-like substance in the ocean produced by vast numbers of very small animals
eco: relating to the environment
tipping point: the time when a big change happens
alarming: causing fear or great concern
inevitably: is to be expected
rich in: have a lot of something
explosives: substances or pieces of equipment that cause explosions
cyanide: very strong poison
marine: related to the sea
zone: an area where a particular thing happens
sanctuary: a place that provides protection
destructive: causing damage
curriculum: all the subjects taught in a school
model: positive example

- Ss work individually or in pairs to complete the flow chart. Point out that the cause (reason) makes the effect (result) happen. These sentences could be joined with *so*.
- Ss go over their answers with a partner or another pair. Ss should show where they found their answers.
- Go over answers with the class.

Possible answers

Apo Island's negative eco tipping point
Local fishermen adopted destructive fishing methods in the reef.
▼
They caught more fish.
▼
They increased their use of destructive fishing methods.
▼
There were almost no fish in the reef.
▼
The fishermen had to go far out to sea to find enough fish.

Apo Island's positive eco tipping point
The fishermen created a fish sanctuary in the reef.
▼
There were more fish in and near the sanctuary.
▼
The fishermen could find enough fish in the reef.
▼
They banned destructive fishing methods.
▼
Marine ecosystem management was included in education.

- **Option:** Ss work in groups of three or four. Each group writes at least five comprehension questions with *how, what, why, where,* or *when*. Groups exchange questions and answer the other group's questions – if possible, from memory!

B

- Explain the task. Read the question.
- Ss work in small groups. Ss take turns giving their opinions.

End of Cycle 2

See the Supplementary Resources chart at the beginning of this unit for additional teaching materials and student activities related to this Cycle.

Saving a Coral Reef

An Eco Tipping Point

Scan the first two paragraphs. What was the problem for the people of Apo Island?

Nowadays, there seems to be so much bad news about the environment. Scientists have predicted all kinds of alarming ecological "tipping points." These are times when, for some reason, big changes happen suddenly, such as when farmland turns to desert due to climate change. But do tipping points inevitably go in the wrong direction?

Apo Island is nine kilometers off the coast of Negros in the Philippines, an area rich in coral reefs. Until the 1950s, local fishermen used traditional fishing methods and there were always lots of fish in the island's reef. Then the fishermen adopted new techniques. They used explosives to scare the fish out of their hiding places, cyanide to poison the fish, and fine nets to catch even very small fish. As a result, they caught more fish. So they increased their use of these techniques. Then there was a tipping point – almost no fish in the reef! So the fishermen had to go further out to sea to find enough fish.

In the 1980s, Dr. Angel Alcala, a marine scientist, visited Apo Island to help the fishermen solve the problem. One way to reverse the tipping point, he explained, was to create a no-fishing zone. The fishermen decided that almost 10 percent of the island's reef should become a

The Philippines

★Manila

Apo Island

sanctuary. After three years, the sanctuary was full of fish and the fishermen were able to catch lots of fish near its edge.

The fishermen were so impressed by this positive eco tipping point that they decided to stop all destructive fishing methods around the entire island. This ecological lesson is now part of the curriculum in the local school, and income from tourism is used to fund scholarships for local students to study marine ecosystem management. Moreover, Apo Island has become a model fishing community – 700 villages in the Philippines now have marine sanctuaries.

A Read the article. Then complete the chart with information from the article.

APO ISLAND'S NEGATIVE ECO TIPPING POINT
Local fishermen adopted destructive fishing methods in the reef.
_____
They increased their use of destructive fishing methods.
_____
The fishermen had to go far out to sea to find enough fish.

APO ISLAND'S POSITIVE ECO TIPPING POINT
The fishermen created a fish sanctuary in the reef.
_____
The fishermen could find enough fish in the reef.
_____
Marine ecosystem management was included in education.

B What can other communities with ecological problems learn from Apo Island?

	After the following SB exercises	You can use these materials in class	Your students can use these materials outside the classroom
CYCLE 1	1 Snapshot		**ARC** Popular college majors
	2 Perspectives		
	3 Pronunciation		**ARC** Intonation in questions of choice
	4 Grammar Focus	**TSS** Unit 8 Writing Worksheet	**SB** Unit 8 Grammar Plus focus 1 **SSD** Unit 8 Grammar 1 **ARC** *Would rather* and *would prefer*
	5 Listening	**TSS** Unit 8 Listening Worksheet	
	6 Role Play	**TSS** Unit 8 Extra Worksheet	
	7 Interchange 8		**WB** Unit 8 exercises 1–5
CYCLE 2	8 Conversation		**SSD** Unit 8 Speaking 1–2
	9 Grammar Focus	**TSS** Unit 8 Grammar Worksheet	**SB** Unit 8 Grammar Plus focus 2 **SSD** Unit 8 Grammar 2 **ARC** *By* + gerund to describe how to do things
	10 Discussion		
	11 Word Power	**TSS** Unit 8 Vocabulary Worksheet	**SSD** Unit 8 Vocabulary 1–2 **ARC** Personal qualities
	12 Writing		
	13 Reading	**TSS** Unit 8 Project Worksheet **VID** Unit 8 **VRB** Unit 8	**SSD** Unit 8 Reading 1–2 **SSD** Unit 8 Listening 1–2 **SSD** Unit 8 Video 1–3 **WB** Unit 8 exercises 6–9

With or instead of the following SB section	You can also use these materials for assessment
Units 7–8 Progress Check	**ASSESSMENT CD** Units 7–8 Oral Quiz **ASSESSMENT CD** Units 7–8 Written Quiz **ASSESSMENT CD** Units 1–8 Test

Key **ARC:** Arcade **SB:** Student's Book **SSD:** Self-study DVD-ROM **TSS:** Teacher Support Site
VID: Video DVD **VRB:** Video Resource Book **WB:** Workbook

My Plan for Unit 8

Use the space below to customize a plan that fits your needs.

With the following SB exercises	I am using these materials in class	My students are using these materials outside the classroom

With or instead of the following SB section	I am using these materials for assessment

Lifelong learning

1 SNAPSHOT

THE TEN MOST POPULAR COLLEGE MAJORS

1. **Business:** Learn about commerce, finance, marketing, and accounting.
2. **Social Sciences and History:** Study economics, geography, and sociology.
3. **Education:** Study how people learn and how best to teach them.
4. **Psychology:** Learn about human mental processes and behavior.
5. **Nursing:** Acquire the skills needed to take care of sick people.
6. **Communications:** Learn about journalism, new media, and human interaction.
7. **Biology:** Learn the fundamentals of life science.
8. **Engineering:** Study the application of math and science to practical ends.
9. **English:** Analyze works of literature written in the English language.
10. **Computer Science:** Study the theoretical foundations of computation and its applications.

Source: www.campusgrotto.com

Which of these majors would be good for people who like technology?
like to work with others? like to be outside? like to solve problems?
Which ones sound the most interesting to you? Why?

2 PERSPECTIVES

A ▶ Listen to the survey. Who is the survey targeting? What does the survey want to know?

Pick a subject!

We are expanding the school curriculum next year. What kinds of classes should we add? Please take a moment to answer a few questions.

1 Would you rather take a business class or a communications class?
- ○ I'd rather take a business class. (Go to question 2a.)
- ○ I'd rather take a communications class. (Go to question 2b.)
- ○ I'd rather take another type of course. (Go to question 3.)

2a Would you prefer to study commerce or marketing?
- ○ I'd prefer to study commerce.
- ○ I'd prefer to study marketing.
- ○ I'd prefer not to study either. I'd prefer another business course: _____

2b Would you rather study journalism or new media?
- ○ I'd rather study journalism.
- ○ I'd rather study new media.
- ○ I'd rather not study either. I'd prefer another communications course: _____

3 What other types of courses would you add to the curriculum? _____

B Take the survey. Be sure to fill in the blanks if necessary.

Lifelong learning

Cycle 1, Exercises 1–7

 In this unit, students talk about learning preferences and types of learning styles. In Cycle 1, students discuss personal preferences using *would rather* and *would prefer*. In Cycle 2, students discuss ways to learn and personal qualities using *by* + gerund for manner.

1 SNAPSHOT

Learning Objective: *talk about popular college majors*

- Ask: "What are the most important universities in your country? Are they private or public? What subjects do Ss study? Do many people go on to college? Why or why not?"
- Explain that Ss who go to college in the U.S. have to choose a major subject in addition to other courses.
- Encourage Ss to use their dictionaries to check any unfamiliar words or expressions.
- Elicit or explain any remaining new vocabulary.

Vocabulary

commerce: activities involved in buying and selling things
marketing: advertising or selling products
accounting: the field of study that involves keeping or examining the financial records of a company or organization
sociology: the study of society and the relationships between people in society

mental: related to the mind
acquire: get
media: newspapers, magazines, radio, and television, as a group
new media: online forms of media, such as blogging, podcasting, and social networking
fundamentals: basics; basic principles
application: use
practical ends: uses in the "real world"
theoretical: not practical; an idea
foundations: basic principles on which to build further study or knowledge

- Read the questions. Ss work in pairs or small groups to discuss the questions. Then ask Ss to share ideas around the class.
- To introduce the topic of learning, give the class a fun warm-up activity using *Vocabulary Tennis* – download it from the website. Ss name as many school subjects as they can.

2 PERSPECTIVES

Learning Objectives: *discuss a campus survey; see examples of* rather *and* prefer *in context*

A [CD 2, Track 9]

- Explain that a college is offering new courses and is asking Ss to complete a survey.
- Explain the task. Ask Ss to listen and find out which group of people the survey is targeting and what it wants to know.
- Play the audio program. Ss listen and read. Check answers. (Answers: They are targeting students; they want to know students' preferences for types of new classes.)

B

- Explain the task. To help Ss complete question 3, ask Ss to brainstorm some classes they would add to the curriculum.
- Make sure Ss understand what to do after they answer number 1. Remind Ss to fill in the blanks if they answer "c."

- Ss complete the survey individually. Then Ss discuss their answers in pairs.
- Tally the survey results as a class. Draw this chart on the board:

New Classes
Media | Health | Other

1. film studies   3. exercise science   5._____
2. broadcasting 4. nutritional science 6._____

- Ask a S to come to the board. The S names each course and counts the number of Ss who raise their hand to add the course. Remind Ss to vote for only one course. The S writes the totals on the board.
- The S asks classmates to name other courses they would like and repeats the process.

3 PRONUNCIATION

Learning Objective: *notice and use rising and falling intonation in questions of choice*

 [CD 2, Track 10]

- Play the audio program. Point out the intonation patterns. Explain that when we ask someone to choose between two things, we use rising intonation on the word before *or* and falling intonation on the word after it. Also, point out the slight pause before *or*.
- Play the audio program again. Pause after each question to let Ss practice several times.

TIP To demonstrate rising and falling intonation, ask Ss to stand up and rise or fall with their bodies. Alternatively, Ss can hum and use their hands to indicate rising and falling.

- Ss work in pairs. They take turns asking each other the questions. Ask Ss to answer with real information.
- **Option:** Ss practice reading the questions of choice in the Perspectives on page 50.

4 GRAMMAR FOCUS

Learning Objective: *practice* would rather (not) *and* would prefer (not) to

 [CD 2, Track 11]

- Focus Ss' attention on the Perspectives on page 50. Ask Ss to find examples of *I'd rather* and *I'd prefer*. Elicit that *I'd* is the contraction of *I would*.
- Point out *would rather* and *would prefer* mean the same thing. Both are used with choices.
- Ask Ss to look at the examples in the Perspectives. Ask Ss to find one difference between *would rather* and *would prefer*. Elicit the answer. (Answer: *Would prefer* takes the infinitive; *would rather* takes the base form.)
- Write the following on the board:
  1. would rather + (not) + base form of verb:
     I'd rather learn . . .
     I'd rather (not) study . . .
  2. would prefer + (not) + infinitive:
     I'd prefer to learn . . .
     I'd prefer (not) to study . . .
- Focus Ss' attention on the right-hand column and ask: "How do you form a short answer?" (Answer: I'd rather [not]; I'd prefer [not] to.)
- Play the audio program. Ss listen and practice.
- **Option:** Elicit additional examples of questions and responses from around the class.

A

- Explain the task. Model the task with the first conversation. Ask different Ss to complete the answers.
- Ss complete the task individually. Go around the class and give help as needed. Check Ss' responses.

Answers

1. A: **Would** you prefer **to sign up for** a course in biology or geography?
   B: I'm not really interested in geography, so I'd prefer **to take** a biology course.
2. A: **Would** you rather **learn** English in England or Canada?
   B: To tell you the truth, I'd prefer **not to study** in either place. I'd rather **go** to Australia because it's warmer there.
3. A: If you needed to learn a new skill, **would** you prefer **to attend** a class or **have** a private tutor?
   B: I'd rather **take** a class than **hire** a tutor.
4. A: **Would** you rather **have** a job in an office or **work** outdoors?
   B: I'd definitely rather **have** a job where I'm outdoors.

- Ss practice the conversations in pairs. Remind Ss to pay attention to intonation.

TIP To keep working on a specific pronunciation feature, make it the "pattern (or sound) of the week" and focus on it for the next few classes.

B Pair work

- Explain the task. Ask two Ss to model the first conversation in part A.
- Ss work in pairs. They take turns asking the questions in part A. Remind Ss to give their own information and to pay attention to intonation. Go around the class and give help as needed.
- **Option:** Ss write a survey like the one in the Perspectives. They use their own information and a different setting if they wish (e.g., *English classes*).

! For more practice, try **Question Exchange** – download it from the website. Ss write their own questions.

Listen and practice. Notice the intonation in questions of choice.

Would you prefer to study nursing or education?   Would you rather be a psychologist or an engineer?

4 *GRAMMAR FOCUS*

> **Would rather *and* would prefer**
>
> **Would rather *takes the base form of the verb*. Would prefer *usually* *takes an infinitive*. Both are followed by not *in the negative*.**
>
> **Would** you **rather take** a business or communications class?
>   I**'d rather take** a communications class.
>   I**'d rather not take** either.
>   I**'d rather take** another course **than study** business or
>   communications.
>
> Would you **prefer to study** business or communications?
>   I**'d prefer to study** business.   I**'d prefer not to study** either.
>
> Let's join a club.
>   I**'d rather not join** a club.
>   I**'d rather not**.
>   I**'d prefer not to join** a club.
>   I**'d prefer not to**.

A Complete the conversations with *would* and the appropriate form of the verbs in parentheses. Then practice with a partner.

1. A: .... you prefer .... (sign up) for a course in
   biology or geography?
   B: I'm not really interested in geography, so I'd prefer ....
   (take) a biology course.

2. A: .... you rather .... (learn) English in England or
   Canada?
   B: To tell you the truth, I'd prefer .... (not study) in either
   place. I'd rather .... (go) to Australia because it's warmer
   there.

3. A: If you needed to learn a new skill, ... you prefer
   .... (attend) a class or .... (have) a private tutor?
   B: I'd rather .... (take) a class than .... (hire) a tutor.

4. A: .... you rather .... (have) a job in an office or
   .... (work) outdoors?
   B: I'd definitely rather .... (have) a job where I'm outdoors.

B **PAIR WORK** Take turns asking the questions in part A. Pay
attention to intonation. Give your own information when responding.

5 LISTENING *Just for fun*

A ▶ Listen to three people talk about the part-time courses they took recently. What course did each person take?

	What course each person took	What each person learned
1. Linda	....	....
2. Rich	....	....
3. Gwen	....	....

B ▶ Listen again. What additional information did each person learn?

6 ROLE PLAY *Choose a major.*

Student A: Choose a major from the Snapshot on page 50 or use your own idea. Explain to Student B, your guidance counselor, why the major is the right choice for your future career.

Student B: You are Student A's guidance counselor. Convince Student A that he or she has chosen the wrong major. Give reasons why the major isn't right for him or her.

Change roles and try the role play again.

7 INTERCHANGE 8 *Learning curves*

What would your classmates like to learn? Take a survey. Go to Interchange 8 on page 122.

8 CONVERSATION *Maybe I should try that!*

A ▶ Listen and practice.

Won-gyu: So how's your French class going?
Kelly: Not bad, but I'm finding the pronunciation difficult.
Won-gyu: Well, I imagine it takes a while to get it right. You know, you could improve your accent by listening to language CDs.
Kelly: That's a good idea. But how do you learn new vocabulary? I always seem to forget new words.
Won-gyu: I learn new English words best by writing them on pieces of paper and sticking them on things in my room. I look at them every night before I go to sleep.
Kelly: Hmm. Maybe I should try something like that!

B ▶ Listen to two other people explain how they learn new words in a foreign language. What techniques do they use?

C CLASS ACTIVITY How do you learn new words in a foreign language?

5 LISTENING

Learning Objectives: *develop skills in listening for main ideas and details; listen to people's experiences*

A *[CD 2, Track 12]*

- Explain the task. Tell Ss to write down only key words and phrases.
- Play the audio program, pausing after each conversation. Ss listen and complete the chart.
- Elicit the answers.

Answers

1. African dance and samba
2. vegetarian cooking
3. how to run a small business

AudioScript

See page T-170.

B *[CD 2, Track 13]*

- Explain the task. Read the focus question. Tell Ss to listen for what each person learned in addition to the focus of the course.
- Play the audio program.
- Ss go over their answers in pairs.

Answers

1. how to be more confident and interact better with people
2. the health value of foods
3. investing and managing money

6 ROLE PLAY

Learning Objective: *talk about choosing a major*

- Explain the task. Tell Ss to choose a major from the Snapshot on page 50. Then they decide which specialization they prefer.

- Ss work in pairs. Student A tells Student B about the major. Student B is Student A's counselor and has to convince Student A to choose a different major.
- Have students change roles and do the role play again.

7 INTERCHANGE 8

See page T-122 for teaching notes.

End of Cycle 1

Cycle 2, Exercises 8–13

See the Supplementary Resources chart at the beginning of this unit for additional teaching materials and student activities related to this Cycle.

8 CONVERSATION

Learning Objectives: *practice giving advice on language learning; see* by + *gerund in context*

A *[CD 2, Track 14]*

- Set the scene. Two students, Won-gyu and Kelly, are talking about ways to improve language learning.
- Write these focus questions on the board:
  Who is taking French classes? (Kelly)
  . . . finds pronunciation difficult? (Kelly)
  . . . writes new words on pieces of paper? (Won-gyu)
- Play the audio program. Ss listen for the answers.

B *[CD 2, Track 15]*

- Explain the task. Read the focus question.
- Play the second part of the audio program. Elicit Ss' responses.

AudioScript

See page T-170.

Answers

1. keeps a record of new words and then makes and reviews study cards of them
2. keeps an electronic vocabulary list with key information about the words

C *Class activity*

- Read the question. Discuss the question with the class. Give extra suggestions if possible.

9 GRAMMAR FOCUS

Learning Objective: *practice* by + gerund *to describe how to do things*

 [CD 2, Track 16]

- Write the following on the board. Focus Ss' attention on the Conversation on page 52. Ask Ss to complete these sentences from the conversation.

  You could improve your accent by . . . (listening to language CDs.)

  I learn new English words best by . . . (writing them on pieces of paper and sticking them on things.)

- Point out the *by* + gerund structure in each sentence. Explain that *by* + gerund is used:

  1. to say how something can happen: You can improve your English by doing a lot of reading.

  2. to describe how something was done: I learned a lot of idioms by watching TV.

  3. to describe how something could be done: One way of becoming fluent is by talking a lot in class.

- Explain the negative form *not . . . but* (e.g., *The best way to learn slang is* **not** *by reading newspapers* **but** *by watching movies.*).

- Play the audio program. Ss listen and read or repeat.

- Elicit additional ways to complete Won-gyu's advice using *by* + gerund. Write Ss' ideas on the board.

A

- Explain the task. Point out that more than one answer is possible.

- Ss complete the task individually. Then Ss compare answers in pairs. Check Ss' answers.

Possible answers

1. You can improve your accent **by mimicking native speakers**.
2. A good way to learn idioms is **by watching** videos online.
3. Students can become better writers **by getting** a private tutor.
4. A good way to learn new vocabulary is **by accessing** a "learner's dictionary."
5. People can become faster readers **by skimming** magazines in English.
6. One way of practicing conversation is **by role-playing** with a partner in class.
7. You can learn to use grammar correctly **by utilizing** self-study materials.
8. The best way to develop self-confidence in speaking English is **by conversing** with native English speakers.

B *Group work*

- Explain the task. Ss complete the statements in part A with their own ideas. Have two Ss read the example dialog.

- Ss work individually. Ask Ss to write down at least eight statements.

- Ss work in small groups and take turns sharing their suggestions. The group chooses the best suggestion for each item. Set a time limit of about ten minutes.

- Ss change groups and share their best suggestion for each item with the new group.

10 DISCUSSION

Learning Objective: *discuss learning*

A **[CD 2, Track 17]**

- Explain the task. Ask a S to read the two skills listed in the chart. Explain that a good *conversationalist* is someone skilled at talking with people.

- Tell Ss they are going to hear two people discussing these skills. Tell Ss to write down key words and phrases in note form in the chart.

- Play the audio program.

AudioScript

See page T-170.

Answers

1. Todd: "how to" video and free video lessons online; Lucy: private lessons with a teacher
2. Todd: working as a flight attendant and talking to passengers; Lucy: took an acting class

B *Group work*

- Explain the task. Write some useful phrases on the board:

  I think a good way to learn a musical instrument is by . . . Another way I try to learn a musical instrument is by . . . The best way to learn an instrument is by . . .

- Ss discuss their ideas in small groups.

C *Group work*

- Explain the task and read the list of skills. Model the task with a S.

- Ss work in small groups. They take turns discussing the best way to learn each skill.

9 GRAMMAR FOCUS

> ### By + gerund to describe how to do things ⊙
>
> You could improve your accent **by listening** to language CDs.
> I learn new words best **by writing** them on pieces of paper and **sticking** them on things.
> The best way to learn slang is not **by watching** the news but **by watching** movies.

A How can you improve your English? Complete the sentences with *by* and the gerund forms of the verbs. Then compare with a partner.

1. You can improve your accent .... (mimic) native speakers.
2. A good way to learn idioms is .... (watch) videos online.
3. Students can become better writers .... (get) a private tutor.
4. A good way to learn new vocabulary is .... (access) a "learner's dictionary."
5. People can become faster readers .... (skim) magazines in English.
6. One way of practicing conversation is .... (role-play) with a partner in class.
7. You can learn to use grammar correctly .... (utilize) self-study materials.
8. The best way to develop self-confidence in speaking is .... (converse) with native speakers.

B GROUP WORK Complete the sentences in part A with your own ideas.
What's the best suggestion for each item?

A: In my opinion, a good way to improve your accent is by watching sitcoms.
B: I think the best way is not by watching TV but by talking to native speakers.

10 DISCUSSION *Ways of learning*

A ⊙ Listen to Todd and Lucy describe how they developed two skills.
How did they learn? Complete the chart.

	Todd	Lucy
1. learn to play a musical instrument	....	....
2. become a good conversationalist	....	....

B GROUP WORK How would *you* learn to do the things in the chart?

C GROUP WORK Talk about different ways to learn to do each of these activities. Then agree on the most effective method.

ride a motorcycle
learn ballroom dancing
write a short story
use a new computer program
be a good public speaker
create, edit, and post videos

Lifelong learning ▪ 53

11 WORD POWER *Personal qualities*

A PAIR WORK How do we learn each of these things? Check (✓) your opinions.

	From parents	From school	On our own
artistic appreciation	☐	☐	☐
communication skills	☐	☐	☐
competitiveness	☐	☐	☐
concern for others	☐	☐	☐
cooperation	☐	☐	☐
courtesy	☐	☐	☐
creativity	☐	☐	☐
perseverance	☐	☐	☐
self-confidence	☐	☐	☐
tolerance	☐	☐	☐

B GROUP WORK How can you develop the personal qualities in part A? Use the activities in the box or your own ideas.

A: You can learn artistic appreciation by going to museums.
B: You can also learn it by studying painting or drawing.

some activities

studying world religions
volunteering in a hospital
taking a public speaking class
performing in a play
going to museums
learning a martial art
playing a team sport

12 WRITING *Something I learned*

A Think of a skill or a hobby you have learned. Read these questions and take notes. Then use your notes to write about what you learned.

What is required to be successful at it?
What are some ways people learn to do it?
How did you learn it?
What was difficult about learning it?

> I enjoy making jewelry, and many people say I am very talented at it. To make interesting jewelry, you need creativity. You have to use simple things and combine them in different ways to make beautiful pieces of jewelry.
>
> Some people learn to make jewelry by taking classes or by following instructions in a book. I first learned how to make a necklace by watching my aunt make . . .

B GROUP WORK Share your writing. Have any of your classmates' experiences inspired you to learn a new skill?

11 WORD POWER

Learning Objectives: *learn nouns to describe personal qualities; discuss what can be learned from doing specific activities*

A *Pair work*

- Ask Ss to read the list of personal qualities.
- Give Ss some time to work in pairs to discuss the meanings of any new words in the list. If needed, let Ss check their dictionaries.
- Elicit or explain any remaining new vocabulary.

> **Vocabulary**
>
> **artistic appreciation:** awareness and knowledge of art and/or artists
> **competitiveness:** the desire to win contests of skill
> **concern for others:** caring feelings for other people
> **cooperation:** the act of working together to achieve a common goal
> **courtesy:** polite or considerate behavior
> **perseverance:** steady or continued action or belief
> **self-confidence:** strong belief in one's powers and abilities
> **tolerance:** the state of accepting differences in other people and/or their opinions

> **TIP** Create a Vocabulary Box, using a transparent container (so that Ss can see how many words they have learned) or a shoe box. As new words are taught, ask a S to write each one on a slip of paper and put it in the box.

- Explain the task. Model one or two items in the chart. Tell Ss how you learned each thing.

- Ss work in pairs. They take turns talking about each quality. Tell Ss that there are no right or wrong answers. Also remind Ss to check (✓) the appropriate boxes in their charts.
- Ss think of three more things we learn from parents, from school, and on our own.

B *Group work*

- Explain the task. Ask a S to read the activities in the box. Ask two Ss to model the conversation. Elicit additional suggestions from Ss.
- Ss work in small groups. Ss take turns sharing their opinions and ideas. Set a time limit of about ten minutes. Go around the class and give help as needed. Make note of difficulties Ss have with grammar or vocabulary.
- When time is up, share some of the problems with the class. Elicit Ss' solutions.
- *Option:* Ss work in pairs to write a conversation. Tell Ss to model their conversation after the one on page 52 and to include suggestions using *by* + gerund.

> **TIP** To review vocabulary, pull out words from your Vocabulary Box. Write a check (✓) on the slip of paper if Ss were able to recall the word. When a slip has three checks, take it out of the box.

 For more practice, play **Bingo** – download it from the website.

12 WRITING

Learning Objective: *write about a skill or hobby*

A

- Explain the task. Ask different Ss to read the four questions and the model paragraphs. Elicit the focus of each of the model paragraphs. (Answers: Paragraph one explains how to do the hobby; paragraph two explains how the writer learned it.).
- First, ask Ss to brainstorm skills and hobbies learned in recent years. Write Ss' suggestions on the board:
  <u>Skills</u>: *cooking, playing golf, speaking English*
  <u>Hobbies</u>: *playing chess, baking, making origami*
- Then Ss work individually to choose a topic. Ss use the questions to make notes. Go around the class and give help as needed.

- Then Ss use their notes to write at least two paragraphs.
- *Option:* Step 4 can be completed for homework.

B *Group work*

- Explain the task. Ss share their writing in small groups. They can read aloud or sit in a circle and take turns passing their writing to another person.
- Encourage Ss to ask each other follow-up questions about their group members' skills.
- Groups discuss whether they feel inspired to learn a new skill.

For another way to practice giving a speech, try **Look Up and Speak!** – download it from the website.

13 *READING*

Learning Objectives: *develop skills in understanding vocabulary in context, reading for specific information, and summarizing; develop discussion skills; read a magazine article*

- Books closed. Use the pre-reading questions for a discussion about learning styles.
- **Option:** Ask Ss to brainstorm about learning styles. Write Ss' ideas on the board.
- Books open. Ss read the article individually. Ask Ss to read without dictionaries because they will be working with vocabulary in part A.
- Ask Ss to summarize in one or two sentences what they read.
- **Option:** Ss work in pairs or small groups to write a short summary of the main ideas of the article. Then Ss present their summaries to the class.

A

- Explain the task. Use the first word to model the task.
- Ss work individually or in pairs. Ss scan the article for the words in italics and match the words with their meanings. Remind Ss to use the other words in the sentence and the sentences before and after as clues.
- Go over answers with the class.

Answers

1. b	2. f	3. e	4. a	5. c	6. d

- **Option:** To reinforce new vocabulary, ask each pair or group to write one original sentence with each word. Ask Ss to read their sentences aloud or write them on the board. Correct as needed.
- Ss work on additional vocabulary from the article. Ss can check their dictionaries at this time, if needed.
- Elicit or explain any remaining new vocabulary.

Vocabulary

presentation: the way something is shown, said, or taught to others
formulas: series of numbers or letters that represent mathematical or scientific rules
principles: basic truths that explain how something works
kinesthetic: related to movement of parts of the body
intrapersonal: existing within a person's mind or self
interpersonal: involving relationships among people
encounter: meet or experience

B

- Explain the task. Ss correct false statements. Point out that there may be more than one way to make a statement true.
- Ss complete the task individually. Then Ss compare answers in pairs.
- Go over answers by asking Ss to read the corrected sentences aloud. Ask if other Ss corrected them in a different way.

Possible answers

1. If you can't understand something, maybe the presentation didn't fit your learning style. / If you can't understand something, knowing your learning style may help.
2. Linguistic learners will comprehend written information. / Linguistic learners may have trouble with visual information.
3. A visual learner will probably learn best by seeing. / A visual learner may learn well by using charts and graphs.
4. A musical learner learns well when information is presented through music. / A musical learner may have a good understanding of patterns.
5. Interpersonal learners generally work well with other people. / Intrapersonal learners learn best by connecting new information with their own experiences.

C *Group work*

- Explain the task. Read the questions.
- Ss discuss their learning styles in small groups. Encourage Ss to ask follow-up questions and add information.
- Ask the class: "How many people are (linguistic) learners?" Write the results for each learning style on the board.
- **Option:** Ss decide which learning styles they feel work best for them. Tell Ss to choose a maximum of two. Ss go around the class, asking other Ss what their preferred styles are until they find someone with the same styles.

> **TIP** Make a note of your Ss' preferred learning styles, so you can adapt future classes to their needs.

End of Cycle 2

See the Supplementary Resources chart at the beginning of this unit for additional teaching materials and student activities related to this Cycle and for assessment tools.

Learning Styles

Have you ever had trouble learning something? Did you overcome the problem? How?

Have you ever sat in class wondering if you would ever grasp the information that was being taught? Maybe the presentation didn't fit your learning style.

Our minds and bodies gather information in different ways and from all around us: seeing, hearing, and doing. Then our brains process that information, organizing it and making connections to things we already know. This process can also work in different ways: Do we think in pictures or words? Do we remember details or the big picture?

When we're trying to learn, it helps to know how our brain works. How do we best gather and organize information? Different people have different learning styles. For example, one person might struggle with written information but understand it immediately in an illustration. Another person might have problems with the picture, but not the written text.

Psychologists have identified seven basic learning styles:

Linguistic: These people learn by using language – listening, reading, speaking, and writing.
Logical: These people learn by applying formulas and scientific principles.
Visual: These people learn by seeing what they are learning.
Musical: Insted of finding music a distraction, these people learn well when information is presented through music.
Kinesthetic: Movement and physical activities help these people learn.
Intrapersonal: These people learn best if they associate new information directly with their own experiences.
Interpersonal: These people learn well by working with others.

You will often encounter situations that do not match your strongest learning style. If you know what your strengths are, you can develop strategies to balance your weaknesses for a more successful learning experience.

A Read the article. Find the words in *italics* in the article. Then match each word with its meaning.

.... 1. *grasp*   a. try hard to do something
.... 2. *gather*   b. understand
.... 3. *the big picture*   c. something that takes attention away
.... 4. *struggle*   d. show one thing is connected to another
.... 5. *distraction*   e. a general view of a situation
.... 6. *associate*   f. pick up or collect

B These sentences are false. Correct each one to make it true.

1. If you can't understand something, you aren't concentrating hard enough.
2. Linguistic learners will not comprehend written information.
3. A visual learner will probably learn best by listening and speaking.
4. A musical learner needs peace and quiet to focus on something.
5. Intrapersonal learners generally work well with other people.

C **GROUP WORK** Which learning styles do you think work best for you? Why?

Units 7–8 Progress check

How well can you do these things? Check (✓) the boxes.

I can	Very well	OK	A little
Describe environmental problems (Ex. 1)	☐	☐	☐
Suggest solutions to problems (Ex. 2)	☐	☐	☐
Understand examples of personal qualities (Ex. 3)	☐	☐	☐
Ask about and express preferences (Ex. 4)	☐	☐	☐

 1 GAME *What's the cause?*

CLASS ACTIVITY Go around the room and make sentences. Check (✓) each phrase after it is used. The students who check the most items win.

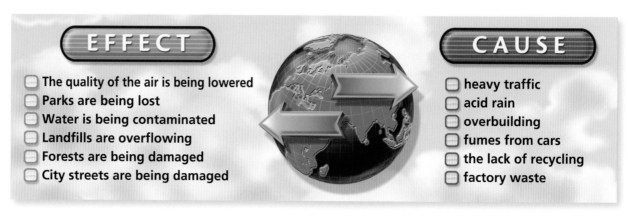

EFFECT

- ☐ **The quality of the air is being lowered**
- ☐ **Parks are being lost**
- ☐ **Water is being contaminated**
- ☐ **Landfills are overflowing**
- ☐ **Forests are being damaged**
- ☐ **City streets are being damaged**

CAUSE

- ☐ **heavy traffic**
- ☐ **acid rain**
- ☐ **overbuilding**
- ☐ **fumes from cars**
- ☐ **the lack of recycling**
- ☐ **factory waste**

A: The quality of the air is being lowered . . .
B: . . . due to fumes from cars.

2 DISCUSSION *Social disasters*

A PAIR WORK Read these problems that friends sometimes have with each other. Suggest solutions for each problem.

A friend is having a party and you weren't invited.
Your roommate keeps damaging your things.
Your friend always keeps you on the phone too long.

useful expressions
One thing to do is to . . .
Another way to help is to . . .
The best thing to do is . . .

B GROUP WORK Agree on the best solution for each problem.

"One thing to do is to ask another friend to talk to your friend, to find out if it was a mistake."

Units 7–8 Progress check

SELF-ASSESSMENT

Learning Objectives: *reflect on one's learning; identify areas that need improvement*

- Ask: "What did you learn in Units 7 and 8?" Elicit Ss' answers.
- Ss complete the Self-assessment. Encourage them to be honest, and point out they will not get a bad grade if they check (✓) "a little."

- Ss move on to the Progress check exercises. You can have Ss complete them in class or for homework, using one of these techniques:
  1. Ask Ss to complete all the exercises.
  2. Ask Ss: "What do you need to practice?" Then assign exercises based on their answers.
  3. Ask Ss to choose and complete exercises based on their Self-assessment.

 GAME

Learning Objective: *assess one's ability to describe problems using the passive with prepositions*

Class activity
- Explain the task. Ask Ss to read the chart. Elicit or explain any new vocabulary.
- Ask two Ss to model the conversation. Student A checks "The quality of the air is being lowered," and Student B checks "fumes from cars." Ss should not use the same phrase again. Remind Ss that sentences must be logical.

- Ss go around the class, talking to classmates. Ask Ss to switch partners after every sentence. In a smaller class, Ss may later speak to the same partner again.
- Ss try to check all the boxes to "win." When Ss "win," tell them to sit down. Let other Ss continue for a few more minutes.
- Spot-check by asking different Ss to read complete sentences.

 DISCUSSION

Learning Objectives: *assess one's ability to offer solutions with infinitive clauses and phrases*

A Pair work
- Explain the task. Ask Ss to read the problems and useful expressions.
- Give Ss time to think of some solutions.
- Ss work in pairs to discuss solutions.
- **Option:** For added practice, ask one S to write down the solutions.

B Group work
- Explain the task. Ask a S to read the example sentence.
- Each pair joins another pair, or Ss work in new small groups. Ss take turns sharing their solutions.
- Next, the group discusses and chooses the best solution. One S in each group should write down the best solution.
- Ask each group to share their best solutions.

3 LISTENING

Learning Objective: *assess one's ability to listen to and understand the meaning of personal qualities*

 [CD 2, Track 18]

- Explain the task. Tell Ss to listen first for the event or activity.
- Play the audio program once or twice. Pause after each speaker for Ss to write. Remind Ss to write notes, not full sentences.
- Then read the qualities. Make sure Ss remember what each one means. If needed, ask other class members to explain or act out the meaning.
- Tell Ss to listen again for the quality the speakers demonstrate.

- Play the audio program again. Ss check (✓) the boxes.
- Ss compare answers in pairs. If there are any disagreements, play the audio program again.
- Go over answers with the class.

AudioScript

See page T-171.

Answers

1. losing a soccer game; competitiveness
2. auditioning for a dance company; perseverance
3. painting; creativity

4 QUESTIONNAIRE

Learning Objective: *assess one's ability to ask about preferences using* would rather *and* would prefer; *assess one's ability to talk about learning preferences with* by + gerund

A Pair work

- Explain the task. Ask Ss to read the interview questions. Elicit or explain any new vocabulary. Ask a S to read the example answer.
- Ss interview each other in pairs. Encourage Ss to give reasons for their answers.

B Group work

- Explain the task. Ask three Ss to model the conversation.
- Each pair joins another pair. Tell Ss to discuss both options, even if all Ss chose the same option. Ask Ss to discuss other options.
- Ask each group to share their other options with the class.

WHAT'S NEXT?

Learning Objective: *become more involved in one's learning*

- Focus Ss' attention on the Self-assessment again. Ask: "How well can you do these things now?"

- Ask Ss to underline one thing they need to review. Ask: "What did you underline? How can you review it?"
- If needed, plan additional activities or reviews based on Ss' answers.

3 LISTENING *I could just kick myself.*

Listen to people talk about recent events and activities in their lives. What events and activities are they talking about? What quality does each person's behavior demonstrate? Complete the chart.

Event or activity	Quality	
1. Mark	☐ competitiveness	☐ cooperation
2. Joan	☐ perseverance	☐ tolerance
3. Kim	☐ self-confidence	☐ creativity

4 QUESTIONNAIRE *What works?*

A **PAIR WORK** Interview your partner. Circle the ways your partner prefers to improve his or her English.

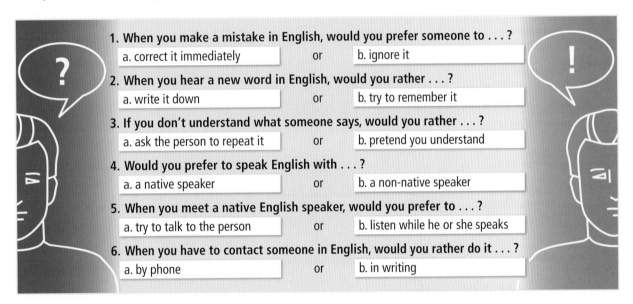

1. **When you make a mistake in English, would you prefer someone to . . . ?**
   a. correct it immediately   or   b. ignore it

2. **When you hear a new word in English, would you rather . . . ?**
   a. write it down   or   b. try to remember it

3. **If you don't understand what someone says, would you rather . . . ?**
   a. ask the person to repeat it   or   b. pretend you understand

4. **Would you prefer to speak English with . . . ?**
   a. a native speaker   or   b. a non-native speaker

5. **When you meet a native English speaker, would you prefer to . . . ?**
   a. try to talk to the person   or   b. listen while he or she speaks

6. **When you have to contact someone in English, would you rather do it . . . ?**
   a. by phone   or   b. in writing

"I'd prefer someone to correct my mistakes immediately."

B **GROUP WORK** Discuss the advantages and disadvantages of each option in part A. Are there better options for each situation?

A: When someone corrects me immediately, I get irritated.
B: Yes, but when someone ignores the mistake, you don't know that you've made one.
C: I think the best way someone can help you is by correcting you at the end of a conversation.

WHAT'S NEXT?

Look at your Self-assessment again. Do you need to review anything?

Unit 9 Supplementary Resources Overview

	After the following SB exercises	You can use these materials in class	Your students can use these materials outside the classroom
CYCLE 1	1 Snapshot	**TSS** Unit 9 Vocabulary Worksheet	
	2 Perspectives		
	3 Grammar Focus	**TSS** Unit 9 Extra Worksheet	**SB** Unit 9 Grammar Plus focus 1 **SSD** Unit 9 Grammar 1–2 **ARC** *Get* or *have* something done
	4 Pronunciation		
	5 Discussion		
	6 Interchange 9		**WB** Unit 9 exercises 1–4
CYCLE 2	7 Word Power		**SSD** Unit 9 Vocabulary 1–2 **ARC** Three-word phrasal verbs 1–2
	8 Conversation		**SSD** Unit 9 Speaking 1
	9 Grammar Focus	**TSS** Unit 9 Grammar Worksheet	**SB** Unit 9 Grammar Plus focus 2 **SSD** Unit 9 Grammar 3 **ARC** Making suggestions 1–2
	10 Listening	**TSS** Unit 9 Listening Worksheet	
	11 Speaking		
	12 Writing	**TSS** Unit 9 Writing Worksheet	
	13 Reading	**TSS** Unit 9 Project Worksheet **VID** Unit 9 **VRB** Unit 9	**SSD** Unit 9 Reading 1–2 **SSD** Unit 9 Listening 1–3 **SSD** Unit 9 Video 1–3 **WB** Unit 9 exercises 5–6

Key

ARC: Arcade	**SB:** Student's Book	**SSD:** Self-study DVD-ROM	**TSS:** Teacher Support Site
VID: Video DVD	**VRB:** Video Resource Book	**WB:** Workbook	

My Plan for Unit 9

Use the space below to customize a plan that fits your needs.

With the following SB exercises	I am using these materials in class	My students are using these materials outside the classroom

With or instead of the following SB section	I am using these materials for assessment

Improvements

1 SNAPSHOT

Nine commonly offered services

Language tutoring ▷	Computer services ▷	House cleaning ▷
Home repairs ▷	Moving services ▷	Financial services ▷
Music lessons ▷	Pet-sitting ▷	Clothing alterations ▷

Source: Based on information from the community bulletin board at the Coffee Pot, New York City

Why would someone need these services? Have you ever used any of them?
What are some other common services and skills people offer?

2 PERSPECTIVES

A ▶ Listen to an advertisement. Would you use a service like this? Why or why not?

Hazel's Personal Services

Don't have time to do all the things you need to do? Call Hazel's Personal Services!

- Get your apartment cleaned.
- Have your car washed.
- Get your computer fixed.
- And much more . . . all for a very low price!

Call Hazel! (646) 555-2121
If Hazel doesn't offer the service you need, she'll find someone who does. Guaranteed!

Hazel offers:
- Computer support
- Repairs
- Beauty services
- Financial services
- Laundry and dry cleaning
- Pet-sitting

B What services do you need or want? What questions would you ask Hazel?

Improvements

> *In this unit, students discuss several contemporary topics, such as professional services and dating. In Cycle 1, students talk about services, using causatives. In Cycle 2, students use three-word phrasal verbs and make suggestions with a variety of structures.*

1 SNAPSHOT

Learning Objective: *talk about commonly offered services*

- To explain the concept of services, ask Ss about their haircuts. Ask: "Where do you get your hair cut? When you go to a hair salon or barber shop, do you leave with a product or a service?"
- Go over the information in the Snapshot. Point out that these are eight services that people commonly offer in the U.S.
- Elicit or explain any new vocabulary.

Vocabulary

tutoring: working with one person to give extra help in a school subject
pet-sitting: taking care of someone's pet

- Read the first two questions. Ss discuss the questions in small groups.
- ! Ss rank the usefulness of each service in the Snapshot using ***Vocabulary Steps*** – download it from the website.
- Read the last question. Then ask Ss to list eight common services offered in their own country. To get Ss started, elicit suggestions. Write Ss' ideas on the board:

Common Services in My Country
photocopying   translating   beauty treatments

- Ask Ss to compare services in the United States and other countries.

2 PERSPECTIVES

Learning Objectives: *discuss problems; see* have *or* get something done *in context*

A ⊙ [CD 2, Track 19]

- Books closed. Write on the board:
  (a) a survey   (b) an interview   (c) an ad
- Explain the task. Ss listen and guess what they are listening to (e.g., *a survey, an ad, or an interview*).
- Play the first few lines of the audio program. Elicit the answer. (Answer: an ad) Explain that some people offer a variety of services. You can find similar ads in the newspaper or the yellow pages of the phone book.
- Write these services on the board:

  Music lessons   Laundry and dry cleaning
  Computer support   Financial services
  Beauty services   Repairs
  Tutoring   Pet-sitting

- Tell Ss to listen to find out which services are mentioned. Play the audio program. (Answer: All except Music lessons and Tutoring, but Hazel can find someone to offer these services, too.)
- Books open. Play the audio program again. Ss listen and read.

B

- Explain the task. Introduce *have something done* with questions like these: "What can you have done in a beauty salon? at a computer store? by a handyman? by an optician?" Write ideas on the board:

  have your hair cut   have your house painted
  have your computer fixed   have your eyes tested

- Read the first question. Write a model conversation on the board:

  A: What do you need to have done?
  B: Well, I need to have my eyes tested, and
     I want to have my computer upgraded.
     What about you?

- Model the conversation with a S. Tell Ss to think of at least five things they need to have done.
- Ss discuss the question in pairs. Go around the class and give help as needed. Then ask Ss to share ideas with the class.
- Read the second question. Elicit Ss' ideas (e.g., *How much do you charge for _____? What beauty services do you offer? Do you pick up and drop off the laundry? Where can I get my car repaired?*).

Learning Objective: *practice* have *or* get *something done*

▶ **[CD 2, Track 20]**

Active

- Write these words on nine cards:

you can	get	have
a repair shop	your computer	at
to fix	fix	fixed

- Ask five Ss to come to the front of the class. Give each S a card. Ask Ss to face the class, holding up their cards in this order:

  S1: *you can*   S2: *have*   S3: *a repair shop*   S4: *fix*
  S5: *your computer*

- Explain that we can say the same sentence another way. Give S2 and S4 new cards. Now all five Ss face the class, holding up their cards in this order:

  S1: *you can*   S2: *get*   S3: *a repair shop*   S4: *to fix*
  S5: *your computer*

- Elicit the rules and write them on the board:

  Active

  You can have a repair shop fix your computer.

      have + someone + base form verb

  You can get a repair shop to fix your computer.

      get + someone + infinitive verb

- Write two cues on the board. Elicit examples about Hazel's Personal Services:

  You can have Hazel's . . .   *You can get Hazel's to . . .*

Passive

- Ask six Ss to hold up cards:

  S1: *you can*   S2: *have*   S3: *your computer*
  S4: *fixed*   S5: *at*   S6: *a repair shop*

- Explain that we can say the same thing another way. Replace S2's card. Then ask Ss to hold up cards:

  S1: *you can*   S2: *get*   S3: *your computer*
  S4: *fixed*   S5: *at*   S6: *a repair shop*

- Elicit the rules and write them on the board:

  Passive

  You can have/get your computer fixed (at/by a shop).

     have/get + object + past participle (at/by)

- Focus Ss' attention on the Perspectives on page 58. Ask Ss to underline the active examples and circle the passive examples. Remind Ss that questions with *Do you know where . . .* have subject/verb/object order in the second clause.

- Play the audio program. Ss listen and practice.

A

- Explain the task. Ask a S to read the first item.
- Ss complete the task individually.

Answers

1. Luis didn't mow the lawn in front of his house. He **had it mowed**.
2. Samantha isn't cutting her own hair. She**'s getting it cut**.
3. Barbara doesn't clean her apartment. She **has it cleaned**.
4. JoAnn and John didn't paint their house. They **got it painted**.
5. Doug isn't repairing his bike. He**'s having it repaired**.

B *Pair work*

- Explain the task. Read the example. Ask Ss which picture it describes.
- Ss work in pairs. Ss take turns describing the services in the pictures with the passive of *have* or *get*.

C *Pair work*

- Explain the task. Model the activity by saying something you've had done for you recently and asking a S what he or she has had done. Ask one or two follow-up questions.
- Ss work in pairs to discuss recent services they've had. Go around the room and listen for the passive of *have* or *get*. Take notes on errors you hear.
- Write any errors on the board. Elicit corrections from the class.

 PRONUNCIATION

Learning Objective: *notice and use sentence stress*

A ▶ **[CD 2, Track 21]**

- Play the audio program. Ss listen. Elicit that stressed words carry the most important information. Point out that we don't usually stress pronouns.
- Play the audio program again. Ss practice both chorally and individually.

! To practice sentence stress, try the activity *Walking Stress* – download it from the website.

B *Group work*

- Explain the task. Each S decides on three things he or she wants to have done.
- Ss work in small groups and take turns asking and answering questions.

GRAMMAR FOCUS

Get or have something done

*Use **get** or **have**, the object, and the past participle of the verb to describe a service performed for you by someone else.*

Do something yourself	**Get/have something done for you**
I **clean** my apartment every week.	I **get** my apartment **cleaned** (by Hazel) every week.
He **is washing** his car.	He **is having** his car **washed**.
They **fixed** their computer.	They **got** their computer **fixed**.
Did you **repair** your watch?	Did you **have** your watch **repaired**?
Where can I **print** these pictures?	Where can I **get** these pictures **printed**?

A   Complete the sentences to express that the services are performed by someone else.

1. Luis didn't mow the lawn in front of his house. He <u>had it mowed</u> . (have)
2. Samantha isn't cutting her own hair. She .... (get)
3. Barbara doesn't clean her apartment. She .... (have)
4. JoAnn and John didn't paint their house. They .... (get)
5. Doug isn't repairing his bike. He .... (have)

B   **PAIR WORK**   Take turns describing the services in the pictures.

1. Mei-ling

2. Rodrigo

3. Maggie

4. Simon

"Mei-ling is getting her skirt shortened."

C   **PAIR WORK**   Tell your partner about three things you've had done for you recently. Ask and answer questions for more information.

4   **PRONUNCIATION** *Sentence stress*

A   ⏵ Listen and practice. Notice that when the object becomes a pronoun (sentence B), it is no longer stressed.

A: Where can I get my **watch fixed**?

B: You can get it **fixed** at the **Time** Shop.

A: Where can I have my **shoes shined**?

B: You can have them **shined** at **Sunshine** Shoes.

B   **GROUP WORK**   Ask questions about three things you want to have done. Pay attention to sentence stress. Other students give answers.

DISCUSSION *Different places, different ways*

GROUP WORK Are these services available in your country? For those that aren't, do you think they would be a good idea?

Can you . . . ?

have your portrait drawn by a street artist
get your blood pressure checked at a pharmacy
have your clothes dry-cleaned at work
get library books delivered to your home
have your shoes shined on the street
get your car washed for less than $15
have a suit made in under 24 hours
get your teeth whitened
have pizza delivered after midnight

A: Can you have your portrait drawn by a street artist?
B: Sure! You can have it done at . . .

6 **INTERCHANGE 9** *Put yourself in my shoes!*

What do teenagers worry about? Go to Interchange 9 on page 123.

7 **WORD POWER** *Three-word phrasal verbs*

A Match each phrasal verb in these sentences with its meaning. Then compare with a partner.

Phrasal verbs

1. Jennifer has **broken up with** her boyfriend – again! ....
2. Kevin **came up with** a great idea for our class reunion. ....
3. I'm not **looking forward to** watching my neighbor's dogs. They're not very friendly. ....
4. My doctor says I'm overweight. I should **cut down on** fatty foods. ....
5. Rob can't **keep up with** the students in his Mandarin class. He should get a tutor. ....
6. I can't **put up with** the noise on my street! I'll have to move. ....
7. My girlfriend doesn't **get along with** her roommate. They're always fighting. ....
8. Bill can't **take care of** his own finances. He has an accountant manage his money. ....

Meanings

a. be excited for
b. end a romantic relationship with
c. stay in pace with
d. tolerate
e. reduce the quantity of
f. have a good relationship with
g. be responsible for
h. think of; develop

B **PAIR WORK** Take turns making sentences with each phrasal verb in part A.

5 DISCUSSION

Learning Objective: *develop the skill of asking where to find services*

Group work

- Explain the task. Focus Ss' attention on the picture and the first question. Have two Ss model the conversation.
- Give Ss some time to read the situations.
- Elicit or explain any new vocabulary.

Vocabulary

portrait: a painting of a person or group of people

- Ss discuss the questions in small groups. If possible, form groups with Ss from different countries.
- Encourage Ss to give opinions. For services that aren't available, Ss should discuss whether the service would be a good idea. Set a time limit of about ten minutes.

TIP As you walk around the class, make note of any grammar problems. When time is up, write representative problems on the board and elicit corrections from Ss.

! For another way to practice the Discussion, try the *Onion Ring* technique – download it from the website.

6 INTERCHANGE 9

See page T-123 for teaching notes.

End of Cycle 1

See the Supplementary Resources chart at the beginning of this unit for additional teaching materials and student activities related to this Cycle.

Cycle 2, Exercises 7–13

7 WORD POWER

Learning Objective: *learn three-word phrasal verbs to talk about services and dating*

A

- Read the first sentence. Ask Ss to find the meaning of *break up with* in the meanings column.
- Elicit that these are three-word phrasal verbs. Point out that Ss already know a lot of two-word phrasal verbs. Elicit examples and write them on the board.
- Explain that the meaning of the three parts together is different from the individual parts:
  base verb + adverb particle + preposition
    break   *up*   *with*
- Ss complete the task individually.
- Then Ss compare answers in pairs. Ask Ss to write the answers on the board. Ss check their own work.

Answers

1. b 2. h 3. a 4. e 5. c 6. d 7. f 8. g

- **Option:** Show Ss ways to organize and store new vocabulary in their notebooks (e.g., *break up with* can be recorded as a diagram or a picture):

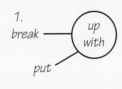

B *Pair work*

- Explain the task. Ask a S to model the first phrasal verb in a sentence.
- Ss work in pairs. They take turns making sentences, preferably about their own lives.
- **Option:** Ask Ss to write a conversation or short story using the new vocabulary.

To review the phrasal verbs, try the game *Sculptures* – download it from the website.

8 CONVERSATION

Learning Objectives: *practice a conversation about dating; see ways of making suggestions in context*

A [CD 2, Track 22]

- Books closed. To introduce the topic, ask: "How, when, and where did you meet your friend/partner?"

- Ss discuss the questions in pairs. Then elicit some interesting stories (e.g., *She was my next-door neighbor. One day . . .*).

- Books open. Ask Ss to cover the text and look only at the picture. Ask questions to set the scene (e.g., *How old are the two men? What have they been doing? Are they friends?*).

- Ask Ss to listen to find out what James is upset about. Play the first line of the audio program. Elicit the answer. (Answer: He hasn't had a date for a long time.)

- Next, ask Ss to take notes as they listen. Remind Ss to write down key words or phrases. Play the audio program once or twice.

- Ss compare notes in pairs. Ask Ss to share some of the things they heard discussed.

- Play the audio program again. Ss listen and read.

Vocabulary

dating service: a company that matches people up for a fee
I have two left feet: I'm not a good dancer; I'm clumsy.

❗ Pairs can practice the conversation using *Say It With Feeling!* – download it from the website.

B Class activity

- Read the question. Use the question to stimulate a short class discussion.

- **Option:** Tell Ss to imagine it is three weeks later and James has been to the dance class. Ss write a follow-up conversation between James and Mike.

9 GRAMMAR FOCUS

Learning Objective: *practice making suggestions with gerunds, infinitives, modals plus verbs, and negative questions*

▶ [CD 2, Track 23]

- Focus Ss' attention on the previous Conversation. Ask Ss to underline examples of suggestions Mike makes.

- Point out the ways to make suggestions in the Grammar Focus box.

- Play the audio program. Ss listen and read or repeat.

- Go over the examples in the box again. Clarify which forms go together by writing this information on the board:

Making suggestions or giving advice

1. What about/Have you thought about + gerund . . . ?

2. It might be a good idea/One thing you could do is + infinitive . . .

3. Maybe you could + base form verb . . .

4. Why don't you + base form verb . . . ?

- Give Ss some additional situations. Elicit suggestions:
  T: I'd like to lose some weight.
  S1: One thing you could do is to walk everywhere.
  S2: Have you thought about going on a diet?
  S3: Why don't you join a health club?

A

- Explain the task. Ask Ss to read each problem and suggestion. Elicit or explain any new vocabulary.

- To model the task, read the first problem and suggestion. Elicit the answer. Elicit that *why don't you* is incorrect because that phrase cannot be followed by a gerund.

- Ss complete the task individually.

- Have Ss work in pairs to compare answers. Then go over the answers with the class.

Answers

1. A: How can I build self-confidence?
   B: **What about** participating in more social activities?
2. A: What could help me be happier?
   B: **Maybe** you could try not to get annoyed about little things.
3. A: How can I get better grades?
   B: **It might be a good idea** to join a study group.
4. A: What can I do to save money?
   B: **Why don't you** come up with a budget?
5. A: How can I get along with my roommate better?
   B: **Have you thought about** planning fun activities to look forward to every week?

B Group work

- Explain the task. Ask two or three Ss to model the activity by making suggestions for the first problem in part A.

- Ss work in small groups. Set a time limit of about five minutes. Go around the class and give help as needed.

- **Option:** Ask one S in each group to disagree with everything (e.g., *No, that doesn't work! I've already tried it!*).

8 CONVERSATION *I have two left feet!*

A ▶ Listen and practice.

James: This is so depressing! I haven't had a date since
         Angela broke up with me. What can I do?

Mike: Why don't you join an online dating service?
         That's how I met Amy.

James: Actually, I've tried that. But the people you meet
         are always different from what you expect.

Mike: Well, what about taking a dance class? A friend
         of mine met his wife that way.

James: A dance class? Are you serious?

Mike: Sure, why not? They offer them here at the gym.

James: I don't think that's a very good idea. Have you
         ever seen me dance? I have two left feet!

B CLASS ACTIVITY What are some other good ways to
meet people?

9 GRAMMAR FOCUS

> ### Making suggestions ▶
>
> **With modals + verbs**
> **Maybe you could go** to a chat room.
>
> **With gerunds**
> **What about taking** a dance class?
> **Have you thought about asking** your friends
>   to introduce you to their other friends?
>
> **With negative questions**
> **Why don't you join** an online dating service?
>
> **With infinitives**
> **One option is to join** a club.
> **It might be a good idea to check out** those
>   discussion groups at the bookstore.

A Circle the correct answers. Then practice with a partner.

1. A: How can I build self-confidence?
   B: **What about** / **Why don't you** participating in more social activities?

2. A: What could help me be happier?
   B: **Maybe** / **One option** you could try not to get annoyed about little things.

3. A: How can I get better grades?
   B: **Have you thought about** / **It might be a good idea** to join a study group.

4. A: What can I do to save money?
   B: **Why don't you** / **What about** come up with a budget?

5. A: How can I get along with my roommate better?
   B: **Why don't you** / **Have you thought about** planning fun activities to look forward
      to every week?

B GROUP WORK Take turns asking and answering the questions in part A.
Answer with your own suggestions.

10 LISTENING All you have to do is ...

A ▶ Listen to people give different suggestions for each problem. Put a line through the suggestion that was *not* given.

1. How to overcome shyness:
   a. read a self-help book
   b. join a club
   c. see a therapist
   d. take medication

2. How to stop biting your fingernails:
   a. count instead
   b. wear gloves
   c. paint your nails
   d. figure out why you're nervous

3. How to organize your busy schedule:
   a. program your phone
   b. make a list of priorities
   c. cancel appointments
   d. talk to a consultant

B PAIR WORK Look at the suggestions. Which one seems the most helpful? Why?

11 SPEAKING Bad habits

GROUP WORK Make three suggestions for how to break each of these bad habits. Then share your ideas with the class. Which ideas are the most creative?

How can I stop ... ?

buying things I don't need

eating junk food at night

cracking my knuckles

"One thing you could do is cut up your credit cards. And why don't you ... ?"

12 WRITING A letter of advice

A Imagine you are an advice columnist at a magazine. Choose one of the letters below and make a list of suggestions. Then write a reply.

> My best friend seems anxious a lot. She bites her fingernails and always looks tired. I don't think she's eating right, either. How can I convince her to take better care of herself?
> – *Worried*

> I argue with my girlfriend all the time. I try to do nice things for her, but we always end up in a fight. I can't put up with this much longer – what can I do?
> – *Frustrated*

B GROUP WORK Take turns reading your advice. Whose advice do you think will work? Why?

10 LISTENING

Learning Objectives: *listen to problems and suggestions; develop skills in listening to detail*

A [CD 2, Track 24]

- Read the three problems in the chart. Ask: "Do you know people who have these problems? What have they done about them?" Elicit ideas.

- For more practice with predicting content, play **Prediction Bingo** – download it from the website.

- Explain the task. Ss will put a line through the suggestion that was not mentioned in the audio.

- Play the audio program. Pause after each speaker for Ss to write. Ss listen and choose the best suggestion for each problem.

- Have Ss compare answers. Go over the answers with the class.

- **Option:** Have Ss think of one more suggestion for each problem.

B Pair work

- Explain the task.

- Ss work in pairs to discuss which suggestion seems most helpful for each problem.

11 SPEAKING

Learning Objective: *make suggestions on how to break bad habits*

Group work

- Explain the task. Ask Ss to read the caption for each picture. Ss think of three suggestions for each habit. Ss should be able to explain why they are making the suggestion.

- Ss work individually to write down ideas.

- Then Ss work in groups. Ss take turns sharing suggestions. Remind Ss to ask follow-up questions.

TIP To increase student talking time, introduce challenging rules (e.g., fewer than three-word answers are not acceptable, each S must ask three follow-up questions, or use at least three phrasal verbs).

- Go around the class and listen in. Note any problems and go over them later with the class.

- **Option:** Ss role-play one of the problems.

- For a new way to practice this exercise, try the **Substitution Dialog** with the Conversation on page 61 – download it from the website. Ss think of a new problem to discuss.

12 WRITING

Learning Objective: *write a letter of advice*

A

- Explain the task. Ss imagine they are advice columnists.

- Give Ss a few minutes to read the letters and choose one. Set a time limit of about five minutes.

- Then Ss write a reply. Encourage Ss to give more than one suggestion for solving the problem.

TIP To make writing assignments more challenging for higher-level Ss, increase the length of the assignment. You can also encourage them to use more new vocabulary and grammar.

B Group work

- Collect the replies and shuffle them. Hand one letter to each S. Give Ss a few minutes to read the letter. Go around the class and give help as needed.

- Explain the task. Ss imagine they are the person who wrote asking for advice. They decide if the advice columnist gave good advice.

- Ss work in groups to discuss the letters. Ss tell the rest of the group what kind of advice they received.

- Ss decide who has the best advice for each letter. They should try to agree on why they chose the letters as best.

- **Option:** Ss change groups. Then Ss share their information with the new group.

Learning Objective: *develop skills in summarizing, identifying main ideas and details, and identifying examples*

- Books closed. Read the pre-reading questions. Use the questions for a class discussion on thinking before speaking.

> **TIP** Asking Ss a personal question related to a challenging or theoretical reading helps them to connect to the topic and encourages intrapersonal learning.

- Books open. Ss read the article. Tell Ss to mark any words they are unable to guess from context. Afterward, Ss can check their dictionaries for the meanings of any words they marked.
- Elicit or explain any new vocabulary.

Vocabulary

regret: feel sorry about a situation, especially something you wish you had not done
sufficient: as much as is necessary
see things in terms of black and white: see only an either/or situation; not considering all possibilities
consequences: results
rely on: depend
objectively: only influenced by facts, not feelings
biases: personal opinions that influence how you see a situation
prejudices: biases; dislikes
subjectively: influenced only by feelings, not facts
interpretations: explanations or opinions of what something means
blind spots: areas you cannot see; things you do not think about or consider
automatically: without planning
serve you well: benefit you

A

- Explain the task. Ss will identify the main idea of each paragraph. Point out that the other sentences in the paragraph all support the main idea.

- Ss complete the task individually. Then they compare their answers in pairs.
- Go over answers with the class.

Answers

3, 4, 1, 2

B

- Explain the task. Point out that although these three people are not mentioned in the article, they are examples of three characteristics of critical thinking.
- Ss work individually to match the three people to the characteristics of critical thinking. Remind Ss that more than one characteristic may be possible.
- Then Ss compare their answers in pairs. Ask Ss to explain their reasons to their partner.
- Elicit answers from pairs.

Possible answers

1. c   2. a   3. b/c

C *Group work*

- Explain the task. To model the task, say how good you are at critical thinking and give an example of a time when critical thinking has helped you. Encourage Ss to ask you follow-up questions.
- Ss work in small groups to discuss the questions. Remind Ss to ask follow-up questions and give additional suggestions.
- ***Option:*** Ask Ss to summarize their group members' experiences for the class.

End of Cycle 2

See the Supplementary Resources chart at the beginning of this unit for additional teaching materials and student activities related to this Cycle.

Critical Thinking

Have you ever said something – and then regretted that you didn't think carefully before opening your mouth? What happened?

1 "Think before you speak!" Has anyone ever said that to you? It's only human to react quickly and perhaps emotionally to things that happen. But without giving ourselves sufficient thinking time, we may see things in terms of black and white instead of considering various shades of gray or other colors. Also, it's all too easy to ignore connections and consequences.

2 At one level, thinking is fairly simple. For instance, it might simply involve making a shopping list. However, there is a deeper and more complex level of thinking. This is often called "critical thinking," and it has several characteristics. First, it requires that you rely on reason rather than emotion. This means you have to look objectively at all available

evidence and decide if it is true, false, or perhaps partly true. Second, you have to be self-aware and recognize your biases and prejudices because these may cause you to think subjectively. A third characteristic is that you need to be open to new ideas and interpretations.

3 Critical thinking can help you in just about everything you do. One of the most important things it helps you do is solve problems. This has always been an asset in many traditional fields, such as education, research, business and management. But it's also very useful to help people keep up with the new, fast-moving knowledge economy, which is driven by information and technology. Modern workers often have to analyze and integrate information from many different sources in order to solve problems.

4 We all sometimes speak before we think, and we all have blind spots. Nevertheless, while thinking critically doesn't always happen automatically, it will certainly serve you well whatever you do in life.

A Read the article. Then write the number of each paragraph next to its main idea.

.... For many people, critical thinking is useful in the workplace.
.... It's worth the effort to think critically.
.... We often don't allow ourselves enough time to think.
.... Critical thinking has three important aspects.

B Read about these people. Which of the three characteristics of critical thinking did they need to apply? Explain your answers.

a = Check if the evidence is true.   b = Recognize your prejudices.   c = Be open to new ideas.

.... 1. Jane worked as a bank teller for ten years. She never considered doing anything else. When she was offered a promotion, she refused it.
.... 2. Bella received an email from someone she didn't know. The email said she had won $1 million in the lottery. She immediately bought a new car.
.... 3. Ian thinks our new neighbors are loud, but I disagree. I think he's just more sensitive to the noise because they play music and watch TV shows that aren't in English.

C **GROUP WORK** How good are you at critical thinking? How has it helped you?

Unit 10 Supplementary Resources Overview

	After the following SB exercises	You can use these materials in class	Your students can use these materials outside the classroom
CYCLE 1	1 Snapshot		
	2 Conversation		**SSD** Unit 10 Speaking 1–2
	3 Grammar Focus	**TSS** Unit 10 Listening Worksheet	**SB** Unit 10 Grammar Plus focus 1 **SSD** Unit 10 Grammar 1 **ARC** Referring to time in the past
	4 Pronunciation	**TSS** Unit 10 Extra Worksheet	**ARC** Syllable stress
	5 Word Power	**TSS** Unit 10 Vocabulary Worksheet	**SSD** Unit 10 Vocabulary 1–2 **ARC** Historic events
	6 Discussion		
	7 Writing		
	8 Interchange 10		**WB** Unit 10 exercises 1–4
CYCLE 2	9 Perspectives		
	10 Grammar Focus	**TSS** Unit 10 Grammar Worksheet **TSS** Unit 10 Writing Worksheet	**SB** Unit 10 Grammar Plus focus 2 **SSD** Unit 10 Grammar 2 **ARC** Predicting the future with *will*
	11 Listening		
	12 Discussion		
	13 Reading	**TSS** Unit 10 Project Worksheet **VID** Unit 10 **VRB** Unit 10	**SSD** Unit 10 Reading 1–2 **SSD** Unit 10 Listening 1–4 **SSD** Unit 10 Video 1–3 **WB** Unit 10 exercises 5–8

With or instead of the following SB section	You can also use these materials for assessment
Units 9–10 Progress Check	**ASSESSMENT CD** Units 9–10 Oral Quiz **ASSESSMENT CD** Units 9–10 Written Quiz

Key

ARC: Arcade	**SB:** Student's Book	**SSD:** Self-study DVD-ROM	**TSS:** Teacher Support Site
VID: Video DVD	**VRB:** Video Resource Book	**WB:** Workbook	

My Plan for Unit 10

Use the space below to customize a plan that fits your needs.

With the following SB exercises	I am using these materials in class	My students are using these materials outside the classroom

With or instead of the following SB section	I am using these materials for assessment

10 The past and the future

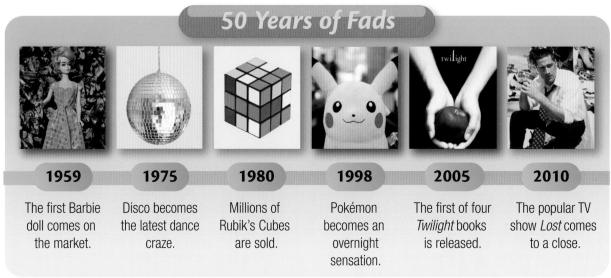

50 Years of Fads

1959	1975	1980	1998	2005	2010
The first Barbie doll comes on the market.	Disco becomes the latest dance craze.	Millions of Rubik's Cubes are sold.	Pokémon becomes an overnight sensation.	The first of four *Twilight* books is released.	The popular TV show *Lost* comes to a close.

Sources: *New York Public Library Book of Chronologies*; http://answers.yahoo.com

Have any of these fads ever been popular in your country?
Can you think of four other fads from the past or present?
Is there anything popular right now that could be a fad?

2 CONVERSATION *I'm good at history.*

A ▶ Listen and practice.

Emma: Look. Here's a quiz on events of the twentieth century.
Steve: Oh, let me give it a try. I'm good at history.
Emma: All right. First question: When did World War I begin?
Steve: I think it began in 1917.
Emma: Huh. And how long has the United Nations been in existence?
Steve: Uh, since Kennedy became president in 1961.
Emma: Hmm. Next question: How long were the Beatles together?
Steve: Well, they started in 1965, and broke up in 1980, so they were together for 15 years. So, how am I doing so far?
Emma: Not very well. Not one of your answers is correct!

B ▶ Do you know the answers to the three questions in part A? Listen to the rest of the conversation. What are the correct answers?

The past and the future

> In this unit, students talk about significant historic events around the world and predictions. In Cycle 1, students talk about important past events using time references. In Cycle 2, students discuss the future with a variety of structures.

1 SNAPSHOT

Learning Objective: *talk about 50 years of fads*

- Books closed. Write the following on the board. Elicit what each is. Ask Ss to match these things with the date they became popular:

Lost ends	*1975*
Pokémon	*2005*
Disco	*2010*
Twilight book	*1998*

- Books open. Point out that the Snapshot contains six fads in the U.S. from the last 50 years. Elicit or explain that a *fad* is something that becomes very popular for a short time.

- Ss check their answers.

- Discuss the pictures. Give Ss a few minutes to read the Snapshot.

- Explain that these sentences are written in the present tense, but they refer to past events. This is sometimes called the *historical present*: it's occasionally used for special effect (as in newspaper headlines) or in informal conversation when narrating a past event.

- Elicit or explain any new vocabulary.

Vocabulary

comes on the market: becomes available for purchase
craze: a fashion that is popular for a short time
overnight sensation: a sudden success
is released: is published or put on the market for sale
comes to a close: ends

- Read the questions. Ss discuss the questions in small groups.

2 CONVERSATION

Learning Objectives: *practice a conversation about a world history quiz; see time references in context*

A ▶ [CD 2, Track 25]

- Write the title on the board. Ask Ss: "Are you good at history? Did you like it at school? Why or why not?"

- Ss cover the text and look only at the picture. Elicit Ss' ideas about the picture.

- Ss study the picture for one minute. Then Ss close their books. In pairs, Ss discuss all they can remember about the picture, including small details.

- Set the scene. Emma is quizzing Steve on some historical events in the twentieth century.

- Divide the class into A and B groups. Tell Group A to listen and take notes on Emma's three questions. Tell Group B to listen and make note of Steve's answers.

- Play the audio program.

- Text uncovered. Ss read the conversation and check the accuracy of their notes. Ask: "Is Steve good at history? How many answers does he get right?" (Answer: none)

- Play the audio program again. Ss listen and read.

- Ss practice the conversation in pairs.

B ▶ [CD 2, Track 26]

- Explain the task. Ask Ss to find and read the quiz questions in part A. Elicit Ss' guesses for each one and ask them to write their ideas on the board.

> **TIP** To keep activity lively at the board, have several Ss work at the same time. Assign each S a section of the board and give each a marker. When Ss are finished, they pass their marker to another S.

- Play the second part of the audio program. Ss listen for the correct answers.

AudioScript

See page T-172.

- Discuss the correct answers.

Answers

World War I began in 1914.
The United Nations has been in existence since the end of World War II/since 1945.
The Beatles were together for ten years, from 1960 to 1970.

⚑ For another way to practice speaking, try the ***Substitution Dialog*** – download it from the website. Ss substitute the original quiz with their own. Then they practice the conversation in pairs.

3 GRAMMAR FOCUS

Learning Objective: *practice referring to time in the past*

▶ **[CD 2, Track 27]**

- Write the following on the board. Ask Ss to complete the blanks with the time references:

  ago   during   for   from . . . to   in   since

  1. World War I began . . .
     ___ 1914 / ___ the 1900s / over 70 years ___
  2. The United Nations has been in existence . . .
     ___ 1945 / ___ the last 60 years
  3. The Beatles were together . . .
     ___ 10 years / ___ 1960 ___ 1970

> **TIP** Let Ss try a task first, and then teach them what they don't know.

- Write the answers on the board. (Answers: 1. in, in/during, ago 2. since, for/during 3. for, from . . . to)

A point of time in the past (in, ago, during)

Rock 'n' roll became popular about 60 years **ago**.
Disco became a craze **in** 1975.
Rubik's Cubes were popular during the 1980s.

A period of time that continues into the present (since, for)

The United Nations has existed **since** 1945.
The United Nations has existed **for** over 60 years.
since + a point of time (e.g., *since last year/Tuesday*)
for + a length of time (e.g., *for two weeks/three hours*)

A period of time in the past (from . . . to, for)

World War I lasted **from** 1914 **to** 1918.
World War I lasted **for** four years.

- Play the audio program. Ss listen and read or repeat.

A

- Focus Ss' attention on the pictures. Elicit what Ss know about Pluto and about dinosaurs.
- Explain the task. Ss use time words to complete the paragraphs. List the time words on the board.
- Ss complete the task individually.
- Ss compare answers in pairs.

Possible answers

1. The planet Pluto was discovered **in** 1930. Scientists accepted this **for** many years but **during/in** the 1970s, some began to question if Pluto was indeed a planet. **In** 2008, after a long debate, Pluto was downgraded to a new category called a "dwarf planet." **Since** that time, our solar system has had only eight planets.
2. Scientists found a new species of dinosaur in the U.S. state of Utah **in** 2007. Like some other species of dinosaur, it ate plants. Unlike other species, however, it had 15 giant horns on its head. These dinosaurs lived **for** over 30 million years **during** the Cretaceous period. Scientists believe they lived **from** about 68 **to** 99 million years **ago**.

B Group work

- Explain the task. Ask two Ss to model the conversation.
- Ss work individually. They write two true and two false statements about world events.
- Then Ss present their questions to the group. Others listen and correct the false statements.

4 PRONUNCIATION

Learning Objective: *notice and use syllable stress*

A ▶ **[CD 2, Track 28]**

- Explain that in longer words, one syllable carries the main stress while another syllable carries the secondary stress.
- Tell Ss to focus on the main and secondary stress. Play the audio program. Ask Ss to tap or clap in time to the stress. Point out that the syllable before *tion* is always stressed.

B ▶ **[CD 2, Track 29]**

- Explain the task.
- Play the second part of the audio program.
- Play the audio program again. Go over answers.

Answers

(main stress in boldface, secondary in italics)		
i**dent**ify	*dis*ad**van**tage	communi**ca**tion
ca**tas**trophe	*re*vo**lu**tion	as*sas*si**na**tion
ap**pre**ciate	*con*ver**sa**tion	consider**a**tion

3 GRAMMAR FOCUS

Referring to time in the past

A point or period of time in the past

When did World War II take place?
During the 1940s. **In** the 1940s. Over 70 years **ago**.

How long were the Beatles together?
From 1960 **to** 1970. **For** ten years.

A period of time that continues into the present

How long has the United Nations been in existence?
Since 1945. **Since** World War II ended. **For** about the last 70 years.

A Complete the paragraphs with the **boldface** words from the grammar box. Then compare with a partner.

1. The planet Pluto was discovered .... 1930. Scientists accepted this .... many years but .... the 1970s, some began to question if Pluto was indeed a planet. .... 2008, after a long debate, Pluto was downgraded to a new category called "dwarf planet." .... that time, our solar system has had only eight planets.

2. Scientists found a new species of dinosaur in the U.S. state of Utah .... 2007. Like some other species of dinosaur, it ate plants. Unlike other species, however, it had 15 giant horns on its head. These dinosaurs lived .... over 30 million years .... the Cretaceous period. Scientists believe they lived .... about 68 .... 99 million years ....

B **GROUP WORK** Write two true and two false statements about world events. Then take turns reading your statements. Others give correct information for the false statements.

A: Bill Clinton was president of the U.S. for four years.
B: That's false. He was president for eight years.

4 PRONUNCIATION *Syllable stress*

A Listen and practice. Notice which syllable has the main stress in these four- and five-syllable words. Notice the secondary stress.

○ ● ○ ○
identify

○ ○ ● ○
disadvantage

○ ● ○ ● ○
communication

appreciate
assassination
catastrophe
consideration
conversation
revolution

B 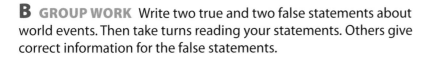 Listen to the words in the box. Which syllable has the main stress? Write the words in the correct column in part A.

The past and the future ■ 65

5 WORD POWER Historic events

A Match each word with the best example. Then compare with a partner.

1. achievement ....
2. assassination ....
3. discovery ....
4. election ....
5. epidemic ....
6. natural disaster ....
7. revolution ....
8. terrorist act ....

a. The eruption of Mount St. Helens in 1980 destroyed over 250 homes.
b. In the late 18th century, 13 American colonies broke free of British rule.
c. Four planes were hijacked in the United States on September 11, 2001.
d. In 2003, a dinosaur with feathers and four wings was found in China.
e. Since the late 1970s, HIV has infected more than 60 million people.
f. In 2008, Barack Obama beat John McCain to become U.S. president.
g. U.S. president John F. Kennedy was shot to death in 1963.
h. In 1953, Sir Edmund Hillary and the Sherpa Tenzing Norgay were the first to reach the summit of Mount Everest.

B PAIR WORK Give another example for each kind of historic event in part A.

"The exploration of Mars is an amazing achievement."

6 DISCUSSION It made a difference.

GROUP WORK Choose two or three historic events (an election, an epidemic, an achievement, etc.) that had an impact on your country. Discuss the questions.

What happened (or what was achieved)? When did it happen?
What was the immediate effect on your country? the world? your family?
Did it change things permanently? How is life different now?

"Recently a large oil field was discovered off the coast of Brazil. . . ."

7 WRITING A biography

A Find information about a person who has had a major influence on the world or your country. Answer these questions. Then write a biography.

What is this person famous for?
How and when did he or she become famous?
What are his or her important achievements?

B PAIR WORK Exchange biographies. What additional details can your partner add?

Kim Dae-jung (1925–2009)

Kim Dae-jung became famous during the 1960s, when he was first elected to government. He became an opposition leader and spent many years in the 1970s and 1980s in prison.

He was president of South Korea from 1998 to 2003. He was awarded the Nobel Peace Prize in 2000 for his efforts toward peace, democracy, and human rights. Kim Dae-jung died . . .

8 INTERCHANGE 10 History buff

Find out how good you are at history.
Student A, go to Interchange 10A on page 124; Student B, go to Interchange 10B on page 126.

5 WORD POWER

Learning Objective: *learn vocabulary for discussing historic events*

A

- Explain the task. Model the task with the first word.
- Ss complete the task individually. Ss match words with definitions. Go around the class and give help as needed.
- Ss go over their answers in pairs. Then elicit Ss' answers. As you go over answers, help Ss with pronunciation and stress.

Answers

1. h   2. g   3. d   4. f   5. e   6. a   7. b   8. c

B *Pair work*

- Elicit two or three examples for each word or phrase.
- Explain the task. Ask a S to read the example sentence.
- Ss work in pairs to use the words from Part A in complete sentences.
- Then ask several pairs to write their best sentences on the board.
- **Option:** Ss write a story instead of sentences.
- To practice the vocabulary, play *Tic-Tac-Toe* – download it from the website. Add two more words from the unit.

6 DISCUSSION

Learning Objectives: *discuss historic events using prepositions of time; develop the skill of talking about cause and effect in the past*

Group work

- Explain the task. Elicit the meaning of *had an impact on* (changed or greatly affected; the result could be either positive or negative).
- Read the questions aloud. Read the beginning of the example sentence aloud. Finish the sentence by explaining that the oil field was found 114 miles off shore from Rio de Janiero and it could contain more

than 8 billion barrels of oil. This could double Brazil's oil reserves.

- Ss work in small groups. First, they choose two or three historic events. Then they discuss the questions. Set a time limit of about ten minutes.
- Go around the class and give help as needed. Note any common errors.
- Elicit corrections orally to the common errors.
- When time is up, have one S from each group choose one event and tell the class what his or her group discussed.

7 WRITING

Learning Objectives: *research a famous person's life and achievements; learn how to write a biography*

A

Note: Ss will need to do research ahead of time. This task can also be done for homework.

- Explain the task. Ask Ss to read the questions. Then read aloud the entry about Kim Dae-jung.
- Ask Ss to find the answers to the prewriting questions in the model paragraphs. Elicit the answers.
- Then Ss work individually to chose an influential person and write a biography. Allow time for Ss to do research to find out answers to the prewriting questions.

B *Pair work*

- Explain the task. Ss work in pairs to exchange biographies and suggest details to add.
- **Option:** Have pairs check each other's biographies for the correct use of time phrases.
- Have Ss revise their paragraphs to include new details, if possible, or make changes to time phrases, if necessary. Collect the biographies.
- **Option:** Post the biographies around the room or on a bulletin board and have Ss read them. Ask Ss which influential people and achievements were most memorable or interesting to them.

8 INTERCHANGE 10

See page T-124 for teaching notes.

End of Cycle 1

See the Supplementary Resources chart at the beginning of this unit for additional teaching materials and student activities related to this Cycle.

9 PERSPECTIVES

Learning Objectives: *discuss a survey about the future; see examples of future tenses with* will

A ▶ *[CD 2, Track 30]*

- Ask Ss to cover the text and look only at the picture. Ask what is happening in the picture. (Answer: The woman is talking to her computer by voice command; she has no keyboard.)

- Write this prediction on the board:

  Computers <u>will</u> recognize any voice command. You <u>won't</u> need a keyboard.

- Now write these topics on the board. Ss discuss the topics in pairs. Ask Ss to make predictions about the future.

  A cure for baldness   Where people will live
  Terrorism   Robots   Mars   Alzheimer's

- Ask Ss to come to the board and write one prediction for each topic. Remind Ss to use *will*, not *be going to*, for predictions.

- Tell Ss to listen to find out if their predictions are mentioned. If their predictions aren't mentioned, elicit what they heard about each topic. Play the audio program.

- Text uncovered. Ask Ss to read the predictions.

- Elicit or explain any new vocabulary.

Vocabulary

baldness: loss of hair on the head
eliminated: stopped
cure: a treatment that corrects or relieves a medical problem

- Tell Ss to check (✓) the predictions they think will happen. Play the audio program again. Ss listen and answer.

- Take a vote for each prediction. Ask for a show of hands.

B

- Read the question. Ss discuss the question in pairs or small groups. Elicit ideas around the class.

10 GRAMMAR FOCUS

Learning Objectives: *use* will, *the future continuous, and the future perfect for future events*

▶ *[CD 2, Track 31]*

- Explain that there are many ways to describe the future in English. Write the three future tenses on the board. Ask Ss to find examples in the previous Perspectives. Write the examples on the board:

  1. <u>will/won't + base verb</u>
     Computers <u>will recognize</u> any voice command. You <u>won't need</u> a keyboard.

  2. <u>future continuous: will be + present participle</u>
     People <u>will be living</u> in cities under the ocean. Robots <u>will be performing</u> most factory jobs.

  3. <u>future perfect: will have + past participle</u>
     Within 20 years, scientists <u>will have discovered</u> a cure for baldness. By 2050, we <u>will have set up</u> human communities on Mars.

- Elicit or explain the differences among the structures. Ask: "Which describes an ongoing action? Which describes something that will be completed by a specific time?" Point out that the future perfect needs a date or time of completion (e.g., *within 20 years, by 2050).*

- Play the audio program. Ss listen and read or repeat.

A

- Explain the task. Model the first sentence.

- Ss complete the task individually.

- Ss go over their answers in pairs. Then elicit Ss' responses around the class.

Answers

1. In ten years, flights from New York to Tokyo **will take** less than two hours.
2. Soon, they **will sell/will be selling** computers that can translate perfectly from one language to another.
3. By the middle of the twenty-first century, scientists **will have discovered** a way to prevent aging.
4. Sometime in the future, scientists **will invent** a machine that transmits our thoughts.
5. In the future, people **will live/will be living** on the moon.
6. In less than a decade, the polar ice caps **will have melted/will melt** and many islands **will have disappeared/will disappear.**

9 PERSPECTIVES

A  Listen to a survey about the future. Check (✓) the predictions you think will happen.

What will the future hold?

☐ Computers will recognize any voice command. You won't need a keyboard.

☐ Within 20 years, scientists will have discovered a cure for baldness.

☐ People will be living in cities under the ocean.

☐ By 2025, world leaders will have eliminated terrorism.

☐ Robots will be performing most factory jobs.

☐ By 2050, we will have set up human communities on Mars.

☐ Medical scientists will find a cure for Alzheimer's disease.

B Which of the predictions do you think will affect you?

10 GRAMMAR FOCUS

> ### Predicting the future with will ▶
>
> ***Use will to predict future events or situations.***
> Computers **will recognize** any voice command. You **won't need** a keyboard.
>
> ***Use future continuous to predict ongoing actions.***
> People **will be living** in cities under the ocean.
>
> ***Use future perfect to predict actions that will be completed by a certain time.***
> Within 20 years, scientists **will have discovered** a cure for baldness.
> By 2050, we **will have set up** human communities on Mars.

A Complete these predictions with the correct verb forms. (More than one answer is possible.) Then compare with a partner.

1. In ten years, flights from New York to Tokyo .... (take) less than two hours.
2. Soon, they .... (sell) computers that can translate perfectly from one language to another.
3. By the middle of the twenty-first century, scientists .... (discover) a way to prevent aging.
4. Sometime in the future, scientists .... (invent) a machine that transmits our thoughts.
5. In the future, people .... (live) on the moon.
6. In less than a decade, the polar ice caps .... (melt), and many islands .... (disappear).

B GROUP WORK Discuss each prediction in part A. Do you agree or disagree?

A: In ten years, flights from New York to Tokyo will take less than two hours. What do you think?
B: Oh, I totally agree. I think they'll use space-shuttle technology to build faster airplanes.
C: I'm not so sure. Those flights normally take about 14 hours. How are they going to come up with an invention that shortens the trip by 12 hours?

C CLASS ACTIVITY Discuss these questions.

1. What three recently developed technologies will have the greatest impact on our lives in the next 20 years?
2. What are the three most important changes that will have occurred on earth by 2050?
3. Which three jobs will people *not* be doing in 50 years? Why?

11 LISTENING *A perfect future?*

A ▶ Listen to people discuss changes that will affect these topics of interest in the future. Write down two changes for each topic.

Future changes		
1. work	....	....
2. transportation	....	....
3. education	....	....
4. health	....	....

B GROUP WORK Can you suggest one more possible change for each topic?

12 DISCUSSION *Things will be different!*

GROUP WORK Talk about these questions.

What do you think you'll be doing a year from now? five years from now?
Do you think you'll still be living in the same place?
What are three things you think you'll have accomplished within the next five years?
What are three things you won't have done within the next five years?
In what ways do you think you'll have changed by the time you retire?

B Group work

- Explain the task. Ask three Ss to model the conversation. Point out that if Ss don't agree, they can say what they think will happen instead. Elicit expressions for agreeing/disagreeing.
- Ss discuss the predictions in small groups. Set a time limit of about five minutes. Go around the class and note any problems with future tenses.
- When time is up, write general problems on the board. Elicit Ss' corrections.

C Class activity

- Explain the task. Read the questions.

11 LISTENING

Learning Objectives: *develop skills in listening for details; practice note-taking skills*

A ▶ [CD 2, Track 32]

- Point out the question mark on "A perfect future?" Elicit Ss' ideas about what this means.
- Write the following on the board. Brainstorm future changes. Ask Ss to add their ideas.

<u>Changes in the future</u>

work   transportation

education   health

- Explain the task. Ss listen as people discuss future changes. Remind Ss to write only key words and phrases for two future changes for each topic.

> **TIP** Discuss difficulties that Ss encounter while listening, and strategies for overcoming them. Ask Ss to write their strategies on the board. Offer suggestions (e.g., *key words are usually stressed; try to predict what you will hear*).

- Play the audio program two or three times. First Ss listen. Then they listen and make notes. Pause after each topic to give Ss time to write their notes.
- Finally, Ss write their notes in the chart.

12 DISCUSSION

Learning Objective: *discuss one's own future*

Group work

- Focus Ss' attention on the picture. Ask Ss to discuss the man's present and future.
- Ask different Ss to read the questions. Elicit or explain any new vocabulary.
- **Option:** Read each question. For pronunciation and intonation practice, Ss repeat chorally.

- Ss discuss the questions as a class. Remind Ss to use the same tense as the one in each question.
- **Option:** With the class, brainstorm some examples (e.g., *computing, cloning, robots, genetically modified crops, space exploration, wind farms, fuel cells*).
- **Option:** Adapt the discussion into an *aquarium.* Divide the class into A and B groups. Group A sits in a circle, the aquarium, while Group B stands around the seated Group A. Group A begins the discussion. At any point, a Student B who wants to join the discussion can tap a Student A on the shoulder and the two exchange places.

For more speaking practice using future tenses, try *Just One Minute* – download it from the website.

AudioScript

See page T-172.

Possible answers

1. Unemployment is going to keep getting worse. More people will be working at home instead of going into an office.
2. They'll have laws about what kind of car you can own and when you can use it. There will be fewer airports and more efficient train systems between cities, including trains under the oceans to connect continents.
3. Kids are going to stay in school longer. There will be a way to learn without teachers.
4. Drugs will have been discovered that will enable people to lose weight without dieting. They will have found cures for many diseases, so people will live to be over 100.

B Group work

- Explain the task.
- Ss work in small groups. They suggest another possible change for each topic in part A. Set a time limit of about five minutes. Then ask groups to share their suggestions with the rest of the class.

- Ss work in small groups. Ss take turns asking and answering the questions. Encourage Ss to ask questions of their own.

For another way to carry out the discussion, try the *Moving Dialog* – download it from the website.

Learning Objective: *develop skills in scanning, reading for main ideas and specific information, and summarizing*

- Books closed. Ask Ss if they have ever bought something because of social networking or online advertising. Elicit examples of businesses that use Twitter or other social networks to advertise. Use this discussion to open the topic of innovative business models.

- Books open. Read the pre-reading question. Give Ss a few minutes to scan the article. Elicit the answer to the pre-reading question. (Answer: Kogi BBQ uses social networking sites to do business instead of traditional advertising.)

- Ss read individually. Ask Ss to mark words that they can't guess from context, and to keep reading!

! For a new way to teach vocabulary, try *Vocabulary Mingle* – download it from the website. If you wish, you can join the activity. After you teach a S the meaning of a word, that S becomes a resource for other Ss to use.

- Elicit or explain any remaining new vocabulary.

Vocabulary

BBQ: a common abbreviation for barbecue; a style of cooking in which food is slowly cooked over a fire outdoors

evolve: grow, develop

emerge: become known; appear from somewhere

make the most of: use in a beneficial way

fusion: mix or blend of two or more things

concocted: created, invented

gourmet: relating to good food and drink

viral: infectious, spreading (including online)

be a sensation: become very popular

the wave of the future: an indication of how things will be in the future; a trend that will last

capitalize on something: use a situation to achieve something good for yourself

A

- Explain the task. Elicit or explain that a summary includes the most important points from an article.

- Ss complete the task individually. Point out that some answers can be phrased more than one way. Ss can write their answers on a separate sheet of paper.

- Ss compare answers in pairs. Ss may make changes if they wish.

- Check answers by asking Ss to read sentences or write them on the board.

Possible answers

Technology impacts they way people do **business.** Kogi BBQ, a trendy restaurant in Los Angeles, has developed a successful business **model** based on new technology. Kogi BBQ delivers gourmet fast food from five **food-service trucks**. To inform customers of their whereabouts, Kogi BBQ uses **social networking** sites, like Twitter. In so doing, Kogi BBQ has built an online **community** of enthusiastic customers who love and seek out its food.

B

- Explain the task. First Ss quickly look through the article to find key words or terms from the questions and re-read the related information. Remind Ss that a colon (:) sometimes comes before a definition or an example.

- Then tell Ss to cover the article and answer the questions in their own words.

- Ask six Ss to write their answers on the board.

Possible answers

1. Kogi BBQ does business in Los Angeles. Its trucks deliver food from various locations throughout the city.
2. It is a combination of Korean and Mexican food.
3. It goes to customers.
4. A "tweet" is a message sent through the social networking site, Twitter.
5. "Kogi Kulture" describes the interactive online community of Kogi BBQ fans.
6. To *capitalize* on something means to take advantage of it, often in terms of money.

C Group work

- Read the questions.

- Ss work in groups of three to five to discuss the questions. Ask one S in each group to write down the group's ideas.

- Ask one S from each group to share the group's ideas with the class.

- **Option:** Have Ss work in groups to develop an online marketing strategy for a company. It can be a real company or one that they make up. Have Ss explain to the class how social networking can help this business spread the word about its product or service.

End of Cycle 2

See the Supplementary Resources chart at the beginning of this unit for additional teaching materials and student activities related to this Cycle and for assessment tools.

Food Trends National.com

HOME | **FOOD TRUCKS** | RESTAURANTS | FAST FOOD | CATERERS

Tweet to eat

Skim the article. What's innovative about Kogi BBQ's business model?

As technology evolves, new business models emerge. For many years, businesses have sold their products and services online, but now social networking is changing the way people do business. Kogi BBQ in Los Angeles has found profitable ways to make the most of today's technology.

Kogi BBQ is a restaurant that serves a fusion of Korean and Mexican food concocted by Chef Roy Choi. The kimchi quesadilla and short rib taco are two favorites. Besides its menu, Kogi BBQ is different from other restaurants because people don't come to it; it goes to the people. Kogi BBQ uses five food-service trucks called Azul, Verde, Roja, Naranja, and Rosita to deliver cheap, gourmet fast food to long lines of hungry – and mostly young – customers throughout the city.

**Chef Roy Choi
of Kogi BBQ**

But how do people know where to find a Kogi BBQ truck? Technology is at the center of its business. Kogi BBQ uses the social networking site Twitter to inform customers where each of its trucks will be and when. The tweets (Twitter messages) look like this one:

> **Dinner time: Azul 6 PM - 9 PM @ Northridge (Devonshire and Reseda);
> 10:30 PM - 11:30 PM @ City of Industry (18558 Gale Ave.)**

Customers can even post requests, like this one:

> **Can you come to Colima in Rowland Heights earlier? Maybe around 6-9? Thanks.**

Kogi BBQ has been a viral sensation in Los Angeles. In addition to Twitter, Kogi BBQ uses YouTube, Facebook, blogs, and other electronic tools, like text messaging, to stay connected with its customers. By avoiding traditional advertising and building its business around an online community, Kogi BBQ has created a "Kogi Kulture," fueled by dedicated fans eager to spread the word.

Time will tell if this is a passing fad or the wave of the future. Either way, this much is true: As technology changes, businesses will figure out how to capitalize on it.

A Read the article. Then complete the summary with information from the article.

.... impacts the way people do .... Kogi BBQ, a trendy restaurant in Los Angeles, has developed a successful business .... based on new technology. Kogi BBQ delivers gourmet fast food from five .... To inform customers of their whereabouts, Kogi BBQ uses .... sites, like Twitter. In so doing, Kogi BBQ has built an online .... of enthusiastic customers who love and seek out its food.

B Use information in the article to answer the following questions in your own words.

1. Where does Kogi BBQ do business?
2. Why is Kogi BBQ considered fusion cuisine?
3. What is unique about Kogi BBQ?

4. What is a tweet?
5. What is "Kogi Kulture"?
6. What does it mean to *capitalize on* something?

C **GROUP WORK** What other companies use social networking to enhance their business? How might technology change the way people do business in the future?

Units 9–10 Progress check

SELF-ASSESSMENT

How well can you do these things? Check (✓) the boxes.

I can	Very well	OK	A little
Describe experiences of getting/having things done (Ex. 1)	☐	☐	☐
Ask for and give advice about problems (Ex. 2)	☐	☐	☐
Understand and give descriptions of historical events (Ex. 3)	☐	☐	☐
Make predictions about the future (Ex. 4)	☐	☐	☐

 1 **DISCUSSION** *Once in a while*

GROUP WORK Take turns asking questions about these services. When someone answers "yes," find out why and when the service was performed, and who performed it.

have your photo taken professionally
get your apartment painted
get your eyes checked
have your home redecorated or remodeled
get something translated

A: Have any of you ever had your photo taken professionally?
B: Yes, I have. I had one taken a few months ago.
C: Really? Why did you have it taken? . . .

have a photo taken

2 **ROLE PLAY** *A friend in need*

Student A: Choose one of these problems. Decide on the details of the
problem. Then tell your partner about it and get some advice.

I'm looking forward to my vacation, but I haven't saved enough money.
I don't get along with my . . . . We're always fighting.
I can't take care of my pet anymore. I don't know what to do.

Student B: Your partner tells you about a problem. Ask
questions about it. Then consider the situation
and offer two pieces of advice.

Change roles and choose another situation.

useful expressions
Have you thought about . . .?
It might be a good idea to . . .
Maybe you could . . .
Why don't you . . . ?

Units 9–10 Progress check

SELF-ASSESSMENT

Learning Objectives: *reflect on one's learning; identify areas that need improvement*

- Ask: "What did you learn in Units 9 and 10?" Elicit Ss' answers.
- Ss complete the Self-assessment. Encourage them to be honest, and point out they will not get a bad grade if they check (✓) "a little."

- Ss move on to the Progress check exercises. You can have Ss complete them in class or for homework, using one of these techniques:
  1. Ask Ss to complete all the exercises.
  2. Ask Ss: "What do you need to practice?" Then assign exercises based on their answers.
  3. Ask Ss to choose and complete exercises based on their Self-assessment.

 ## DISCUSSION

Learning Objective: *assess one's ability to talk about things people have or get done using the active and passive*

Group work

- Explain the task. Ask three Ss to model the conversation. Then ask different Ss to model the complete questions.

- Ss work in small groups. Ss take turns asking the questions. Remind Ss to ask follow-up questions with *why*, *when*, and *who*. Encourage Ss to ask other follow-up questions.
- Go around the class and give help as needed.
- Ask a S from each group to share a group member's experience.

 ## ROLE PLAY

Learning Objective: *assess one's ability to make suggestions with gerunds, infinitives, modals, and negative questions*

- Explain the task. Read the useful expressions.
- Divide the class into pairs, and assign A/B roles. Student As have a problem. Student Bs give advice.

- Ss role-play in pairs. Tell Student As to say whether or not they think the advice will work and why.
- Ss change roles and repeat the role play with another situation.
- Ask Ss to tell the class some of the best advice they got.

3 LISTENING

Learning Objective: *assess one's ability to listen to, understand, and refer to time in the past*

- **Option:** Bring a map of North America to class to show the position of Alaska and discuss its icy climate.

A [CD 2, Track 33]

- Explain the task. Ask Ss to read the questions. Use the photo to explain that the Iditarod is a sled-dog race in Alaska.
- Ss work in pairs. Ask Ss to discuss what kinds of words and information Ss might hear in the answers (e.g., *a year, a length of time, for/since*). For answers with dates, tell Ss to guess the approximate date.
- Play the audio program. Pause after each item for Ss to write. Play the audio program as many times as needed.

AudioScript

See page T-172.

- Go over answers with the class. If needed, play the audio program again. Ask Ss to focus on the correct answers.

Answers

1. in 1973
2. from 1948 to 1991
3. in 1997
4. for almost 30 years
5. since 1896

B Group work

- Explain the task.
- Give Ss time to write questions about historical events (achievements, disasters, or discoveries).
- Ss work in small groups. They take turns asking and answering their questions. Remind Ss to use prepositions of time.
- Find out how many correct answers Ss came up with.

4 SURVEY

Learning Objective: *assess one's ability to predict the future with* will, future continuous, *and* future perfect

A Class activity

- Explain the task. Ask two Ss to model the conversation.
- Ask different Ss to read the survey items as questions. If Ss are having trouble, ask Ss to write the questions on the board. Leave the questions on the board during the activity.
- Ss work in small groups. Ss take turns asking the questions. Remind Ss to ask follow-up questions.

- Tell Ss to write down the number of "yes" and "no" answers in the group.

B Group work

- Explain the task. Ask a S to read the example sentences.
- Give groups some time to make sentences about the results of their surveys.
- Ask each S in the group to report the results of at least one survey item to the class.

WHAT'S NEXT?

Learning Objective: *become more involved in one's learning*

- Focus Ss' attention on the Self-assessment again. Ask: "How well can you do these things now?"

- Ask Ss to underline one thing they need to review. Ask: "What did you underline? How can you review it?"
- If needed, plan additional activities or reviews based on Ss' answers.

3 **LISTENING** *How good is your history?*

A ▶ Listen to people discuss the questions. Write the correct answers.

1. When was the first Iditarod? ....
2. How long did apartheid exist in South Africa? ....
3. When did a spacecraft first land on Mars? ....
4. How long was the Berlin Wall up? ....
5. How long have the modern Olympics existed? ....

B **GROUP WORK** Write three more questions about historic events. (Make sure you know the answers.) Then take turns asking your questions. Who has the most correct answers?

4 **SURVEY** *Five years from now, . . .*

A **CLASS ACTIVITY** How many of your classmates will have done these things in the next five years? Write down the number of "yes" and "no" answers. When someone answers "yes," ask follow-up questions.

	"Yes" answers	"No" answers
1. move to a new city	....	....
2. get a (new) job	....	....
3. have a(nother) child	....	....
4. travel abroad	....	....
5. learn another language	....	....
6. get a college or master's degree	....	....

A: Five years from now, will you have moved to a new city?
B: Yes, I think I will have moved away from here.
A: Where do you think you'll move to?
B: I'd like to live in Shanghai.
A: Really? What will you be doing there?

B **GROUP WORK** Tally the results of the survey as a group. Then take turns telling the class any additional information you found out.

"Very few people think they will have moved to a new city in five years. Only two people think that they will move. One person thinks he'll move to Shanghai, and one person thinks she'll move to Boston."

Shanghai

WHAT'S NEXT

Look at your Self-assessment again. Do you need to review anything?

 Units 9–10 Progress check ▪ **71**

Unit 11 Supplementary Resources Overview

	After the following SB exercises	You can use these materials in class	Your students can use these materials outside the classroom
CYCLE 1	1 Snapshot		
	2 Conversation		**SSD** Unit 11 Speaking 1–2
	3 Grammar Focus		**SB** Unit 11 Grammar Plus focus 1 **SSD** Unit 11 Grammar 1 **ARC** Time clauses
	4 Listening		
	5 Speaking	**TSS** Unit 11 Extra Worksheet	
CYCLE 2	6 Word Power	**TSS** Unit 11 Vocabulary Worksheet **TSS** Unit 11 Listening Worksheet	**SSD** Unit 11 Vocabulary 1–2 **ARC** Behavior and personality
	7 Perspectives		
	8 Grammar Focus	**TSS** Unit 11 Grammar Worksheet	**SB** Unit 11 Grammar Plus focus 2 **SSD** Unit 11 Grammar 2 **ARC** Expressing regret 1–2 **ARC** Describing hypothetical situations
	9 Interchange 11		
	10 Pronunciation		
	11 Listening		
	12 Writing	**TSS** Unit 11 Writing Worksheet	
	13 Reading	**TSS** Unit 11 Project Worksheet **VID** Unit 11 **VRB** Unit 11	**SSD** Unit 11 Reading 1–2 **SSD** Unit 11 Listening 1–3 **SSD** Unit 11 Video 1–3 **WB** Unit 11 exercises 1–7

Key   **ARC:** Arcade   **SB:** Student's Book   **SSD:** Self-study DVD-ROM   **TSS:** Teacher Support Site
       VID: Video DVD   **VRB:** Video Resource Book   **WB:** Workbook

My Plan for Unit 11

Use the space below to customize a plan that fits your needs.

With the following SB exercises	I am using these materials in class	My students are using these materials outside the classroom

With or instead of the following SB section	I am using these materials for assessment

11 Life's little lessons

1 SNAPSHOT

Rites of Passage
Some important life events

- First birthday (or first 100 days, as in South Korea)
- First haircut
- Losing your first tooth
- First day of school
- Sweet 16 (or Sweet 15, as in Latin America)
- First job

- High school graduation
- 20th birthday (or 21st birthday, as in the United States and Canada)
- College graduation
- Marriage
- Becoming a parent
- Retirement

Source: *Peace Corps Handbook for RPCV Speakers*

Which rites of passage, or life events, are important in your country?
    Check (✓) the events.
What are other rites of passage for people in your country?
Have any of these things recently happened to you or someone you know?

2 CONVERSATION *I was really immature.*

A ◉ Listen and practice.

Alan: So what were you like when you were younger?
Carol: When I was a kid, I was kind of irresponsible.
Alan: You? Really? What made you change?
Carol: Graduating from high school.
Alan: What do you mean?
Carol: Well, until I graduated, I'd never had any important responsibilities. But then, I went off to college. . . .
Alan: I know what you mean. I was really immature when I was a teenager.
Carol: So what made *you* change?
Alan: I think I became more mature after I got my first job and moved away from home. Once I had a job, I became totally independent.
Carol: Where did you work?
Alan: I worked for my dad at the bank.

B ◉ Listen to the rest of the conversation.
What was another turning point for Carol? for Alan?

72

Life's little lessons

> In this unit, students discuss major life events, personal situations, and types of behavior. In Cycle 1, students talk about milestones in their lives using a variety of time clauses. In Cycle 2, students use should have + past participle and if clauses in the past perfect to describe regrets.

1 SNAPSHOT

Learning Objective: *talk about important life events*

 To introduce the topic, play **Line Up!** – download it from the website. Ss line up according to a major life event (e.g., their birthday, when they got married, etc.).

- Books closed. Ask: "What are some important events in a person's life?" Then ask Ss to open their books and compare their ideas with the Snapshot. Point out that *rite of passage* means important life event. Another word for this is *milestone*.

- **Option:** Books closed. With Ss, brainstorm some major events or milestones. Then tell Ss to open their books and quickly scan pages 72 to 74. Which of their guesses were correct?

- Elicit or explain any new vocabulary.

Vocabulary

Sweet 16: a girl's 16th birthday
retirement: when you leave your job and stop working, usually because you have worked for many years or are a certain age

- Read the first question. Ss work individually to check the life events that are important in their country.

- Then Ss compare their answers in pairs, if possible, pairs who are from different countries.

- Read the next two questions. Have Ss discuss them in pairs. If possible, pair Ss who are from different countries.

- Have Ss tell the class two things they learned from their partner.

2 CONVERSATION

Learning Objectives: *practice a conversation about becoming an adult; see time clauses in context*

A ▶ [CD 2, Track 34]

- Tell Ss to cover the text and look only at the picture. Ask: "What was Alan like when he was younger? What is he like now?" Ss discuss the picture in pairs.

> **TIP** To prepare Ss for the listening task, use the picture and title to elicit ideas before playing the audio program.

- Set the scene. Alan and Carol are on their first date, riding in a car. They are talking about their childhood. Write this chart on the board:

	What were they like as kids?	What life event changed them?
Carol		
Alan		

- Ss listen for answers to the questions on the board. Play the audio program. Ask two Ss to write the answers on the board. (Answers: Carol – was irresponsible, but going to college changed her; Alan – was immature, and then he got a job.)

- Text uncovered. Play the audio program again. Ss listen and read.

- Elicit or explain any new vocabulary.

Vocabulary

irresponsible: not carrying out one's duties or responsibilities
immature: behaving as though one is younger or less experienced than one is
turning point: a time when an important change starts to happen

- To elicit the humor, ask: "How much has Alan really changed? Was he independent later? Why not?" (Answer: Alan was probably not as independent as he imagined because he was working for his father.)

B ▶ [CD 2, Track 35]

- Explain the task. Read the focus questions.

- Tell Ss to listen and to take notes. Play the second part of the audio program.

AudioScript

See page T-173.

- Ss compare notes in pairs. Then check answers around the class.

Answers

Another turning point for Carol was when she got a dog. Another turning point for Alan was when he got his first bicycle.

- **Option:** In pairs, Ss discuss what they were like as kids and how they have changed.

T-72

Learning Objectives: *practice time clauses; learn to use subordinating conjunctions*

⏵ **[CD 2, Track 36]**

Time clauses

- Write the first time clause on the board. Label the subject (S) and verb (V), like this:

  S   V
  Before I had my first job, . . .

- Remind Ss of some important facts about clauses:
  1. All clauses require a subject and a verb.
  2. A time clause is a dependent clause. It can't stand alone; it must be connected to a main clause.
  3. The time clause can come before or after the main clause.
  4. When the time clause comes before the main clause, a comma separates the two clauses.

- Ask Ss to read the sentences in the Grammar Focus box. Tell Ss to underline the clauses.

- Play the audio program. Ss listen and repeat, focusing on intonation.

Conjunctions

- Go over the subordinating conjunctions in the Grammar Focus box. Elicit or explain the meanings as needed. Provide examples on the board.

  once/as soon as: when one event happens, another event happens soon afterward

  Once Sarah learned a little Spanish, she was able to talk to her neighbors, the Delgados.

  As soon as you're hired for your first job, you feel more confident.

  the moment: a particular point of time when two events happen together

  The moment John got married, he felt like an adult.

  until: to that time and then no longer

  Until I met Donna, I hadn't known what friendship was.

  by the time: one event is completed before another event

  By the time I graduated, I had already found a good job

- Point out the past perfect in the main clause with *until* and *by the time*. This shows that two events occurred in the past, but *meeting Donna* (action #1) *happened before knowing what friendship was* (action #2).

- Elicit additional examples from Ss around the class.

❗ For another way to practice time clauses, try **Substitution Dialog** – download it from the website.

A

- Explain the task. Point out the time clauses in column A and the main clauses in column B. Model the task with the first sentence.

- Ss complete the task individually. Go around the class and give help as needed.

- Ss work in pairs. Ss take turns reading aloud the sentences to compare answers.

- Elicit Ss' responses around the class.

Possible answers

1. e   2. g   3. b   4. d   5. f   6. c   7. a   8. h

B

- Explain the task. Have a S read the example sentence. Model sentences about yourself:

  T: I can make a sentence with number 1: "*By the time I was 15*, I had taken two years of German." Can you relate that to your life, Sandra?

  S: OK, let me see. Yes, I can relate that one to my life: "*By the time I was 15*, I had traveled to many places."

- Ss write sentences. Go around the class and spot-check verb tenses.

- Then Ss compare sentences with a partner.

C Group work

- Explain the task. Ask Ss to read the events. Read the example sentence.

- Ask: "What else happens after you get your driver's license?" Elicit suggestions.

- First, Ss work individually to write sentences. Remind Ss to use time clauses in the present *with you*. Point out that *you* here means "people in general;" it doesn't refer to any specific person.

- Then write a model conversation on the board:

  S1: After you get your driver's license, you find out that all your friends want rides.

  S2: Do you think so? I don't agree. After I got my driver's license, no one asked me for rides!

  S3: So, how did your life change after you got it?

  S2: Well, first I felt much freer. Also, I . . .

- Ss work in small groups. Ss take turns reading their sentences and discussing their ideas. Remind Ss to refer to the model on the board.

TIP Encourage Ss to use natural discourse markers when speaking, e.g., *well, so, you know, you see, actually,* etc. Ask Ss to look at previous Conversations and dialogs for examples.

Time clauses ▶

Before I had my first job, I was really immature.
After I got my first job, I became more mature.
Once I had a job, I became totally independent.
The moment I moved away from home, I felt like a different person.
As soon as I got my own bank account, I started to be more responsible.
Until I graduated, I'd never had any important responsibilities.
By the time I graduated from high school, I had already started working.

A Match the clauses in column A with appropriate information in column B.
Then compare with a partner.

A

1. By the time I was 15, ...
2. Until I started working part-time, ...
3. The moment I got my first paycheck, ...
4. As soon as I left home, ...
5. Once I started sharing an apartment, ...
6. After I began a relationship, ...
7. Before I traveled abroad, ...
8. Until I got really sick, ...

B

a. I didn't appreciate my own country.
b. I began to understand the value of money.
c. I learned that love can hurt!
d. I realized that I wasn't a child anymore.
e. I had learned how to take care of myself.
f. I learned how to get along better with people.
g. I had never saved any money.
h. I hadn't understood the importance of
   good health.

B Which of the clauses in column A can you relate to your life?
Add your own information to those clauses. Then compare with a partner.

"The moment I got my first paycheck, I became more independent."

C GROUP WORK What do you think people learn from these events? Write sentences
using time clauses in the present. Then take turns reading and talking about them.

1. getting a credit card
2. going out on your first date
3. getting your first job
4. getting your driver's license
5. buying your first bike, moped, or car
6. opening your own bank account
7. getting married
8. becoming a parent

> 1. Once you get a credit card, you learn
> it's important not to overspend.

4 LISTENING Important events

A ▶ Listen to three people describe important events in their lives. Complete the chart.

	Event	How it affected him or her
1. Sally	....	....
2. Henry	....	....
3. Debbie	....	....

B ▶ Listen again. What do these three people have in common?

5 SPEAKING Milestones

A PAIR WORK In your country, how old are people when these things happen?

get a driver's license
begin to date
move out of their parents' home

graduate from college
get married
retire

B GROUP WORK Choose three milestones. What do you think life is like before and after each one? Join another pair and discuss.

"Before people get a driver's license, they are very dependent on their parents. Once they get a license, they . . . "

6 WORD POWER Behavior and personality

A PAIR WORK At what age do you think people possess these traits? Check (✓) one or more ages for each trait.

	In their teens	In their 20s	In their 30s	In their 40s	In their 60s
ambitious	☐	☐	☐	☐	☐
argumentative	☐	☐	☐	☐	☐
carefree	☐	☐	☐	☐	☐
conscientious	☐	☐	☐	☐	☐
naive	☐	☐	☐	☐	☐
pragmatic	☐	☐	☐	☐	☐
rebellious	☐	☐	☐	☐	☐
sensible	☐	☐	☐	☐	☐
sophisticated	☐	☐	☐	☐	☐

B GROUP WORK Use the words in part A to describe people you know.

"My older brother is argumentative. He disagrees with me about everything!"

4 LISTENING

Learning Objective: *develop skills in listening for main ideas and note taking*

A ▶ *[CD 2, Track 37]*

- Books closed. Write these questions on the board. Ask Ss to discuss them in small groups:

  What event has been very important in your life? Why? How did it affect you or change you?

- Books open. Ss listen for each event and how it affected each person. Play the audio program. Pause after each speaker for Ss to write in the chart.

AudioScript

See page T-173.

B ▶ *[CD 2, Track 38]*

- Play the audio program again. Ss listen to find out what the three people have in common.

Answers

(for parts A and B)
1. She learned Spanish. She felt proud of herself.
2. He and his twin brother went to different colleges. He became more confident and independent.
3. She was the top student in her class. She became a lot more outgoing.

They discovered that they were good at doing things.

5 SPEAKING

Learning Objective: *talk about important events using time clauses*

A Pair work

- Explain the task. Read the question. Point out the expression "in their (teens)" in the Word Power.
- Focus Ss' attention on the picture and the first event. Model a discussion with two Ss.
- Ss discuss the events in pairs.

B Group work

- Explain the task. Read the example sentence.

Cycle 2, Exercises 6–13

- In pairs, discuss the events in part A and why they are important.
- Each pair joins another pair. Set a time limit of about ten minutes. Go around the class and listen in.
- When time is up, discuss any problems with the class.

End of Cycle 1

See the Supplementary Resources chart at the beginning of this unit for additional teaching materials and student activities related to this Cycle.

6 WORD POWER

Learning Objective: *learn adjectives for discussing behavior and personality*

A Pair work

- Explain the task. Give Ss some time to read the list of adjectives. Model with *ambitious*.
- Elicit or explain any new vocabulary. Also model stress or pronunciation if needed.

Vocabulary

ambitious: having a strong desire to be successful
argumentative: liking to argue or disagree with people
carefree: without any problems or worries
conscientious: hard-working
naive: lacking experience or knowledge
pragmatic: practical; making decisions based on facts rather than ideas

rebellious: reacting against rules or traditions
sensible: showing good judgment
sophisticated: confident, socially mature, and having knowledge about subjects like art, literature, and music

- Ss complete the task in pairs.

B Group work

- Model the task.
- Ss complete the task in pairs. As a final check, elicit Ss' responses around the class.

 For more practice, play ***Bingo*** – download it from the website. Recycle vocabulary from pages 3 and 30 to describe people and people's feelings.

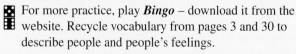

7 PERSPECTIVES

Learning Objectives: *listen to someone describing regrets; see* should have *and* if I'd *in context*

A ▶ [CD 2, Track 39]

- Ss cover the text and look only at the picture. Set the scene. Maya Misery is complaining about all the things she should or shouldn't have done. Elicit that *misery* means "unhappiness."
- Tell Ss to listen to find out how many regrets Maya has about school or college. Play the audio program. Elicit the answer. (Answer: four)

- Play the audio program again. Ss listen and read. Pause after each regret. Ask different Ss to summarize each one in their own words (e.g., *I didn't listen to my mother. Now I can't play a musical instrument.*).

B

- Explain the task. Read the questions.
- Ss discuss the questions in pairs.
- **Option:** Ss role-play Maya's session with her counselor. The counselor's goal is to ask Maya about her past and make her feel better.

8 GRAMMAR FOCUS

Learning Objectives: *practice expressing regrets and hypothetical situations with* should have + *past participle and* if *clauses*

▶ [CD 2, Track 40]

Should have + past participle

- Focus Ss' attention on the Perspectives. Ask Ss to find two sentences with *should have*. Write them on the board:

1	2	3	4	5
I	should	've	studied	something more . . .
I	shouldn't	have	waited	so long to choose . . .

- Elicit the rule:
  subject + *should have/'ve* + past participle
- Explain that we use *should have* to speculate about or imagine things that did or didn't happen (e.g., *Maya didn't study a practical subject, but now she realizes that she should have. She waited too long to choose a major, and now she regrets it.*).
- Encourage Ss to make up their own examples.
- **Option:** To practice *should have*, do part A now.

If + past perfect (or third conditional)

- Repeat the steps for *if I'd* . . . Elicit examples from the Perspectives. Write them on the board.
- Elicit the rule: *If* + subject + *had* + past participle, subject *could/would have* + past participle
- Explain that this structure describes hypothetical situations in the past. The *could/would have* clause shows what didn't happen.
- Encourage Ss to make up their own examples.
- Play the audio program. Ss listen and practice.

A

- Explain the task. Read the example.
- Ss complete the task individually. Go around the class and spot-check Ss' responses.

Possible answers

1. I should have been less rebellious when I was younger.
2. I should have paid attention to what I ate as a kid.
3. I should have made more friends when I was in high school.
4. I shouldn't have argued so much/should have argued less when I was a teenager.
5. I shouldn't have been so naive/should have been less naive when I started looking for my first job.

- Then Ss work in pairs. They talk about which statements are true about their own lives.

B

- Explain the task. Model how to do number 1. Then have Ss complete the task individually.
- Ss compare answers in pairs. Elicit answers around the class.

Answers

1. c   2. d   3. e   4. b   5. a

C

- Explain the task. Read number 1 in part B. Ask Ss to complete the clause.
- Ss work individually to complete the task. Go around the class and spot-check Ss' answers.
- Ss compare answers in small groups. Accept any answers that are both grammatical and logical.
- **Option:** Ss save their sentences for the Pronunciation on page 76.

7 PERSPECTIVES *I should have . . .*

A  Listen to Maya Misery talk about her regrets. Do you have any similar regrets?

"I should have studied something more practical while I was in college."

"If I'd listened to my mother, I would have learned to play a musical instrument."

"If I'd been more ambitious in college, I could have learned to speak another language."

"I shouldn't have waited so long to choose a major."

"If I hadn't wasted so much money last year, I would have moved into my own apartment by now."

"If I hadn't been so irresponsible, I could have gotten better grades."

B What do you suggest to help Maya feel better?

8 GRAMMAR FOCUS

Expressing regret and describing hypothetical situations ▸

Use **should have** + *the past participle to express regret.*
I should have studied something more practical when I was in college.
I shouldn't have waited so long to choose a major.

Use **would have** + *the past participle to express probable outcomes in hypothetical situations.*
Use **could have** + *the past participle to express possible outcomes.*
If I**'d listened** to my mother, I **would have learned** to play a musical instrument.
If I **hadn't been** so irresponsible, I **could have gotten** better grades.

A For each statement, write a sentence expressing regret. Then talk with a partner about which statements are true for you.

1. I was very rebellious when I was younger.
2. I didn't pay attention to what I ate as a kid.
3. I didn't make many friends in high school.
4. I was very argumentative as a teenager.
5. I was too naive when I started looking for my first job.

> 1. I should have been less rebellious when I was younger.

B Match the clauses in column A with appropriate information in column B.

A
1. If I'd listened to my parents, ...
2. If I'd been more active, ...
3. If I'd been more ambitious, ...
4. If I'd studied harder in school, ...
5. If I'd saved my money, ...

B
a. I wouldn't have had to borrow so much.
b. I could have learned a lot more.
c. I would have made more pragmatic decisions.
d. I wouldn't have gained all this weight.
e. I could have gotten a promotion.

C Add your own information to the clauses in column A. Then compare in groups.

9   INTERCHANGE 11   *When I was younger, . . .*

Imagine if things were different. Go to Interchange 11 on page 125.

10   PRONUNCIATION   *Reduction of* have *and* been

A ▶ Listen and practice. Notice how **have** and **been** are reduced in these sentences.

I should h̷a̷v̷e̷ b̷e̷e̷n̷ less selfish when I was younger.
If I'd b̷e̷e̷n̷ more ambitious, I could h̷a̷v̷e̷ gotten a promotion.

B   PAIR WORK   Complete these sentences and practice them. Pay attention to the reduced forms of **have** and **been**.

I should have been . . . when I was younger.   If I'd been more . . . , I could have . . .
I should have been . . . in high school.   If I'd been less . . . , I would have . . .

11   LISTENING   *Regrets*

A ▶ Listen to people describe their regrets. What does each person regret?

	What does he or she regret?	Why does he or she regret it?
1. Alex	....	....
2. Yi-yun	....	....
3. Jacob	....	....

B ▶ Listen again. Why does he or she regret it?

12   WRITING   *A letter of apology*

A Think about something you regret doing that you want to apologize for. Consider the questions below. Then write a letter of apology.

What did you do? What were the consequences?
Is there any way you can undo those consequences?

> Dear Jonathan,
>   I'm really sorry I forgot to tell you that my party was canceled. You worked so hard making all those cookies! I should've called or sent you a text before you started baking them, but I got really busy at work and didn't get around to it. If I'd been more conscientious, . . .

B   PAIR WORK   Read your partner's letter. Talk about what you would have done if you'd had a similar regret.

INTERCHANGE 11

See page T-126 for teaching notes.

 PRONUNCIATION

Learning Objective: *notice and use reductions of* have *and* been

A ▶ *[CD 2, Track 41]*

- Remind Ss that we stress key words. Words such as pronouns and auxiliary verbs are reduced. When *have* follows a modal (e.g., *should, could, would*), it is reduced to /əv/ (it sounds like the word *of*). The word *been* is reduced to /bɪn/.
- Ask Ss to listen for the reductions. Play the audio program. Ss listen and read.
- Play the audio program again. Ss listen and repeat.

B *Pair work*

- Explain the task. Model a few sentences with words from the Word Power on page 74 and others of your own.
- Ss complete the sentences in pairs. Then Ss practice the reductions.
- For more practice with reductions, have Ss work in groups and play the **Chain Game** – download it from the website.

11 LISTENING

Learning Objective: *develop skills in listening to main ideas and summarizing*

A ▶ *[CD 2, Track 42]*

- Explain the task. Draw the chart on the board.
- Tell Ss to listen the first time for the regret. Play the audio program. Pause after each speaker for Ss to complete the chart.

Answers

1. Alex regrets that he ever stopped exercising.
2. Yi-shun regrets that she didn't learn to play the guitar when she was a kid.
3. Jacob regrets not going to Europe with his friends the summer after they graduated college.

- For another way to set the scene, try **Cloud Prediction** – download it from the website.

B ▶ *[CD 2, Track 43]*

- Explain the task. This time Ss listen to find out what effect these regrets had.

- Play the audio program once or twice. Pause after each speaker to give Ss time to fill in the chart.
- Elicit Ss' responses.

TIP To check answers, draw the chart on the board and ask Ss to complete it. This way, those who are weak at listening will be able to see the answers.

AudioScript

See page T-173.

Answers

1. Alex has been trying to lose weight, and it's difficult. He wants to get healthy.
2. Yi-shun wishes she could bring a guitar to a party and play songs and have everyone sing along.
3. Jacob had the time to go, and he missed an amazing, unforgettable experience with his friends.

- For more practice with recognizing the grammar structures, play **Stand Up, Sit Down** – download it from the website. Use Variation 1.

 WRITING

Learning Objectives: *write a letter of apology; practice the new grammar structures*

A

- Focus Ss' attention on the picture. Ask what is happening. Then ask Ss to read the letter of apology.
- Explain the task. Read the questions.
- Give Ss time to make some notes.

- Ss use their notes to write a first draft.
- For a new way for Ss to think of and plan their content, try **Pass the Paper** – download it from the website.

B *Pair work*

- Explain the task. Ss work in pairs. They exchange letters and discuss what they would have done in a similar situation.

Learning Objectives: *develop skills in scanning and reading for main ideas; read about milestones around the world*

- Read the pre-reading question. Give Ss several minutes to scan the article. Elicit the answers. (Answers: El Sebou': Egypt, seven-day-old babies; La quinceañera: Mexico and other Latin American countries, 15 year-old girls; Land divers: Vanuatu, young men)

- *Option:* Elicit or have Ss write questions about the milestones using *who, what, when, where, why*, and *how*. When they read the article again, they can see if the article answers any of their questions.

! For another way to teach this Reading, try *Jigsaw Learning* – download it from the website. Have Ss read one paragraph each.

> **TIP** Remind Ss that an effective reader does not need to know the meaning of every word to understand the main ideas of a text. Encourage Ss to guess the meaning of words from context. Tell Ss to mark new words as they read and check the definitions only after they have finished reading.

- Ss read the article quickly and silently. Ask Ss to summarize each milestone in one or two sentences.

- Elicit or explain any new vocabulary.

Vocabulary

ancient: from a very long time ago
cradle: a bed for a baby
rocked: moved gently back and forth
gold-and silver-like: looking like gold and silver, but not actually made of those substances
attendees: people who attend or go to an event
passage: transition, change from one stage of life to another
spectacular: amazing, very beautiful
bouquet of flowers: a bunch of flowers arranged in a pleasing way
multilayered: having several layers or levels
hurl themselves: throw themselves; jump forcefully
vines: long rope-like plants attached to trees
break their fall: stop their fall
bungee: a long elastic cord
exact: precise

- *Option:* Assign the article for homework. Ask Ss to read the article once or twice and mark unfamiliar vocabulary. Also tell Ss to make a list of the words, check definitions in a dictionary, and write the definitions. During the next class, Ss work in groups to discuss and compare their lists.

A

- Explain the task. Read the list of words on the left.

- Ss re-read the article individually and look for the words. Then they match the words to their definitions.

- Ss compare answers in pairs. Encourage Ss to say where they found the information in the article.

- Check Ss' answers around the class.

Answers

1. d   2. a   3. e   4. f   5. c   6. b

B

- Explain the task. Point out the descriptions in the chart. Do the first item together as a class.

- Ss work individually to check the correct milestones for each description.

- Ss compare their charts in pairs. Then elicit answers from the class.

Answers

1. El Sebou', La quinceañera, Land divers
2. La quinceañera
3. El Sebou'
4. Land divers
5. La quinceañera

- *Option:* Have Ss work in pairs to write a similar chart with two or three more descriptions for each event. Then have pairs give their charts to another pair to complete.

C *Group work*

- Explain the task. Read the focus questions.

- Ss discuss the questions in small groups.

- *Option:* Each pair joins another pair. Ss take turns telling the others what their partner said. The partner makes corrections if needed.

- *Option:* Each S writes a paragraph about a milestone in his or her country, using the texts as a model.

End of Cycle 2

See the Supplementary Resources chart at the beginning of this unit for additional teaching materials and student activities related to this Cycle.

Milestones Around the World

Scan the article. Where does each milestone take place? Who is each milestone for?

EGYPT

In Egypt, many families with new babies celebrate *El Sebou'*, which means *the seventh*. Some say the ancient pharaohs believed that children who lived to be seven days old were ready for a long and healthy life. Family and friends meet at the parents' house, and the baby is put in a round wooden cradle called a *ghorbal*. Songs are sung, and the baby is rocked gently to awaken its senses. Salt is scattered to keep evil away, and the mother carries the baby around the house. Children follow with lit candles. Finally, bags full of candies, sweets, and gold- and silver-like coins are distributed to all attendees.

MEXICO

Families in Mexico and several other Latin American countries have a special celebration for *La quinceañera*, the birthday girl who turns 15 years old. It marks a girl's passage from girlhood to womanhood. Wearing a spectacular dress and carrying a bouquet of flowers, the girl arrives at a church for a thanksgiving service. Then there is a party with live music, dancing, and plenty of delicious food. An important moment is when the girl cuts a multilayered birthday cake.

VANUATU

On a single island in the South Pacific nation of Vanuatu, young men hurl themselves from a 30-meter wooden tower, with only vines tied around their ankles to break their fall. The original bungee jumpers, these "land divers" jump to prove their manhood. The goal is for the young man's shoulder to just touch the ground. The vines' measurement must be exact as there is no safety net. When a young man jumps, his mother holds a favorite childhood item. After the jump, she throws the item away, demonstrating that he is now a man.

A Read the article. Find the words in *italics* in the article. Then match each word with its meaning.

.... 1. *senses*   a. thrown in different directions
.... 2. *scattered*   b. demonstrate
.... 3. *spectacular*   c. throw
.... 4. *plenty*   d. sight, hearing, taste, touch, and smell
.... 5. *hurl*   e. very exciting to look at
.... 6. *prove*   f. more than enough

B Check (✓) the correct milestone(s) for each description.

	El Sebou'	La quinceañera	Land diving
1. The person's family participates.	☐	☐	☐
2. There is a religious ceremony.	☐	☐	☐
3. Children carry candles.	☐	☐	☐
4. The event is dangerous.	☐	☐	☐
5. The event requires special clothing.	☐	☐	☐

C **GROUP WORK** Which of the milestones do you think is the most serious? Which is the most fun? Why do you think people celebrate milestones like these?

Unit 12 Supplementary Resources Overview

	After the following SB exercises	You can use these materials in class	Your students can use these materials outside the classroom
CYCLE 1	1 Snapshot		
	2 Perspectives		
	3 Pronunciation		
	4 Grammar Focus		**SB** Unit 12 Grammar Plus focus 1 **SSD** Unit 12 Grammar 1 **ARC** Describing purpose
	5 Word Power	**TSS** Unit 12 Extra Worksheet	**SSD** Unit 12 Vocabulary 1–2 **ARC** Qualities for success
	6 Role Play		**WB** Unit 12 exercises 1–4
CYCLE 2	7 Conversation		**SSD** Unit 12 Speaking 1
	8 Grammar Focus	**TSS** Unit 12 Vocabulary Worksheet **TSS** Unit 12 Grammar Worksheet	**SB** Unit 12 Grammar Plus focus 2 **SSD** Unit 12 Grammar 2 **ARC** Describing purpose and Giving reasons **ARC** Giving reasons
	9 Listening	**TSS** Unit 12 Listening Worksheet	
	10 Interchange 12		
	11 Discussion		
	12 Writing	**TSS** Unit 12 Writing Worksheet	
	13 Reading	**TSS** Unit 12 Project Worksheet **VID** Unit 12 **VRB** Unit 12	**SSD** Unit 12 Reading 1–2 **SSD** Unit 12 Listening 1–3 **SSD** Unit 12 Video 1–3 **WB** Unit 12 exercises 5–8

With or instead of the following SB section	You can also use these materials for assessment
Units 11–12 Progress Check	**ASSESSMENT CD** Units 11–12 Oral Quiz **ASSESSMENT CD** Units 11–12 Written Quiz

Key   **ARC:** Arcade   **SB:** Student's Book   **SSD:** Self-study DVD-ROM   **TSS:** Teacher Support Site
         VID: Video DVD   **VRB:** Video Resource Book   **WB:** Workbook

My Plan for Unit 12

Use the space below to customize a plan that fits your needs.

With the following SB exercises	I am using these materials in class	My students are using these materials outside the classroom

With or instead of the following SB section	I am using these materials for assessment

12 The right stuff

1 SNAPSHOT

	COMPANY	MAIN PRODUCTS	FACT
SUCCESS STORIES	Coca-Cola	soft drinks, juice, and bottled water	Coca-Cola is the best-known English word in the world after *OK*.
	Sony	electronics equipment, movies, and TVs	Some early products included tape recorders and rice cookers.
	Levi Strauss	jeans and casual clothing	The first jeans were made for men looking for gold in California.
Five of the world's most successful businesses	Google	Internet-based products and services	Google comes from *googol*, which is the math term for the number 1 followed by 100 zeros.
	Nestlé	chocolate, instant coffee, and bottled water	Nestlé means *little nest*, which symbolizes security and family.

Sources: *Hoover's Handbook of American Business 2003*; www.sony.net; www.google.com; www.nestle.com

Which of these products exist in your country? Are they successful?
Can you think of three successful companies in your country? What do they produce?

2 PERSPECTIVES

A ⊙ Listen to the survey. What makes a business successful?
Number the choices from 1 (most important) to 3 (least important).

What makes a business successful?

1. In order for a language school to succeed, it has to have
   ☐ a variety of classes ☐ a convenient location ☐ inexpensive courses

2. To run a popular Internet café, it's a good idea to have
   ☐ plenty of computers ☐ good snacks and drinks ☐ a fast connection

3. In order to operate a successful movie theater, it has to have
   ☐ the latest movies ☐ good snacks and drinks ☐ big screens

4. To establish a trendy restaurant, it's important to have
   ☐ fashionable servers ☐ delicious food ☐ good music

5. For an athletic center to be profitable, it needs to have
   ☐ good trainers ☐ modern exercise equipment ☐ a variety of classes

6. For a concert hall to be successful, it should have
   ☐ excellent acoustics ☐ comfortable seats ☐ affordable tickets

① Most important
② Somewhat important
③ Least important

B GROUP WORK Compare your answers. Do you agree on the most important success factors?

The right stuff

In this unit, students talk about successful people, businesses, and products, as well as advertising. In Cycle 1, students use infinitive clauses and phrases to express purpose and describe qualities for success. In Cycle 2, students practice describing features and giving reasons.

1 SNAPSHOT

Learning Objective: *talk about successful businesses*

- Books closed. Give Ss or elicit a list of international companies. Elicit products that the companies make. For example:

International company	Product
Coca-Cola/Pepsi Cola	Soft drinks
Sony/Panasonic	Televisions/stereos
Levi Strauss	Jeans
Google	Internet-based products/ services
Nestlé	Chocolate

- Books open. Ask Ss to read the Snapshot. Ss may use their dictionaries.
- Ask Ss if any of the facts surprise them. Why?
- Elicit or explain any remaining new vocabulary.

Vocabulary

rice cooker: an electric pot used to cook rice
casual: not formal
symbolize: represent
nest: the place where birds lay their eggs

- **Option:** Read aloud the main products and facts (omitting the name of each). Ss listen and guess the company.
- Read the questions.
- Ss discuss the questions in pairs, small groups, or as a class.
- **Option:** If your class is made up of business Ss, have several Ss give a brief presentation (or "snapshot") of their company.

2 PERSPECTIVES

Learning Objective: *see ways to describe purpose in context*

> **TIP** To show Ss the purpose of activities, write the objectives on the board. As you finish each activity, check off the objective so that Ss know where they are. Then at the end of the class, tell Ss what they have achieved.

A [CD 3, Track 1]

- Books closed. With Ss, brainstorm some factors that make a language school successful. Ask Ss to write their suggestions on the board, like this:

What makes a language school successful?

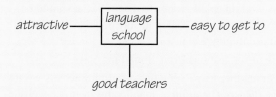

- Books open. Tell Ss to look at the first sentence. How similar were the Ss' opinions to the ones listed on the board?

- **Option:** Find out what Ss know about surveys. Ask: "What is a survey? Has anyone answered a real survey before? Why do businesses conduct surveys?"
- Explain the task. Point out the three options and explain the numbering system.
- Then ask the class to complete the first three boxes. To make sure that Ss understand the task, take a class vote. Which of the three options do Ss think is the most important?
- Ss complete the task individually. Go around the class and give help as needed. Write new words or expressions on the board, in your vocabulary column.
- Play the audio program. Ss listen and read. Ask Ss to raise their hands when they hear a category they rated *most important*.

B Group work

- Explain the task.
- Ss work in small groups. Ss discuss the most important factor in each case. Ask Ss to find out who is most similar to them.
- Then elicit Ss' ideas. How well do they agree?
- **Option:** Ss add one more success factor to each sentence.

3 PRONUNCIATION

Learning Objective: *notice and use reduced forms*

A [CD 3, Track 2]

- Point out that structure words such as *a, an, and, for,* and *to* are rarely stressed. The vowel in these words is usually reduced to /ə/. Explain that /ə/ is the most common sound in English.
- Play the audio program to present the reduced forms. Ss listen and read.
- Play the audio program again. Ss listen and repeat.

4 GRAMMAR FOCUS

Learning Objective: *practice using infinitive clauses to describe purpose*

[CD 3, Track 3]

- Write these sentences on the board. Ask Ss to fill in the blanks (answers in parentheses):

  Describing purpose with infinitive clauses

  1. _____ run a popular Internet café, it's a good idea to have plenty of computers. (To)

  2. _____ _____ _____ operate a successful movie theater, you need to make sure it shows the latest movies. (In order to)

  3. _____ a concert hall _____ _____ successful, it should have excellent acoustics. (For, to be)

  4. ___ ___ ___ a shopping mall _____ succeed, it has to have a variety of stores. (In order for, to)

- Explain the different types of infinitive clauses. Elicit or explain how sentences 1 and 2 are similar: (*In order*) + infinitive
  In order to succeed in business, you have to . . .
  To succeed in business, you have to . . .
- Point out that sentences 3 and 4 both use *for.*
  (*In order*) + *for* + noun + infinitive
  In order for a business to succeed, it . . .
  For a business to succeed, it . . .
- Elicit additional examples. Write some of the Ss' suggestions on the board.
- For more practice, play the **Chain Game** – download it from the website. Start with: "For a coffee bar to succeed, . . ."
- Play the audio program. Ss listen and read or repeat.

A

- Explain the task.
- Ss work individually and match goals with suggestions. Go around the class and give help as needed.

B Pair work

- Explain the task. Ss practice reading the sentences in Exercise 2 on page 78.
- **Option:** Play the audio program for Exercise 2 again. Ss listen and repeat.
- Ss work in pairs and take turns reading their first choices aloud. Go around the class and listen discreetly. Note: Ss will have additional practice using reduced forms in part A of Exercise 4.

- Go over answers with the class. If Ss have different answers, ask them to explain their choices. Accept any answers that are logical and grammatically correct.
- Then Ss work in pairs. They take turns reading their sentences. Remind Ss to use the reduced forms they practiced in Exercise 3.

Answers

1. e   2. a   3. d   4. b   5. c

B Pair work

- Explain the task.
- Ss work in pairs. They add one more suggestion for each goal in part A. Go around the class and give help as needed.
- Ask different Ss to come up and write their suggestions on the board. Accept any answers that are logical and grammatically correct.

C Group work

- Focus Ss' attention on the picture. Ask: "What is wrong with this coffee shop?" Elicit Ss' ideas.
- Explain the task. Ask two Ss to model the conversation.
- Ss work in small groups to discuss what should be done for the coffee shop to stay popular. Remind Ss to use infinitive clauses.
- Elicit suggestions from around the class.
- For another way to practice describing what's wrong, try **Picture Dictation** – download it from the website.
- For more practice, try **Vocabulary Tennis** – download it from the website. Choose a business (e.g., a cinema) and have teams take turns calling out success factors. Instead of words, Ss use sentences with infinitive clauses.

3 PRONUNCIATION *Reduced words*

A Listen and practice. Notice how certain words are reduced in conversation.

In order **før ä** café **tø** succeed, it needs **tø** have good food **ånd** service.
Før än airline **tø** be successful, it has **tø** maintain **ä** good safety record.

B PAIR WORK Take turns reading the sentences in Exercise 2 aloud. Use your
first choice to complete each sentence. Pay attention to reduced words.

4 GRAMMAR FOCUS

Describing purpose ▷

Infinitive clauses

To run a popular Internet café,	it's a good idea to have plenty of computers.
(In order) to establish a trendy restaurant,	it's important to have fashionable servers.

Infinitive clauses with for

For an athletic center **to be** profitable,	it needs to have modern exercise equipment.
(In order) for a language school **to succeed**,	it has to have a convenient location.

A Match each goal with a suggestion. Then practice the sentences with a partner.

Goals

1. For a health club to attract new people, ...
2. In order to run a profitable restaurant, ...
3. To establish a successful dance club, ...
4. For a coffee bar to succeed, ...
5. To run a successful clothing boutique, ...

Suggestions

a. you need to hire a talented chef.
b. it's a good idea to offer desserts, too.
c. you need to keep up with the latest styles.
d. it needs to have great music and lighting.
e. it has to offer the latest equipment.

B PAIR WORK Give another suggestion
for each goal in part A.

C GROUP WORK Look at the picture of
a coffee shop. For it to stay in business,
what should be done?

"For this coffee shop to stay in business, it needs . . ."

5 WORD POWER *Qualities for success*

A **PAIR WORK** What qualities are important for success?
Rank them from 1 to 5.

A model	A salesperson	A magazine
☐ fashionable	☐ clever	☐ affordable
☐ gorgeous	☐ charming	☐ attractive
☐ industrious	☐ knowledgeable	☐ entertaining
☐ muscular	☐ persuasive	☐ informative
☐ slender	☐ tough	☐ well written

B **GROUP WORK** Add one more adjective to each list.

"For a model to be successful, he or she needs to be . . ."

6 ROLE PLAY *You're hired!*

Student A: Interview two people for one of these jobs. What qualities do they need for success? Decide who is more qualified for the job.

Students B and C: You are applying for the same job. What are your best qualities? Convince the interviewer that you are more qualified for the job.

host for a political talk show   server at a trendy café   exercise equipment salesperson

A: To be a good host for a political talk show, you need to be knowledgeable. Are you?
B: Yes. I follow politics closely, and I'm also tough. I'm not afraid to ask hard questions.
C: I'm fascinated by politics, and I'm industrious, so I would do thorough research.

7 CONVERSATION *I thought you'd never ask!*

A ⏵ Listen and practice.

Mayumi: What's your favorite club, Ben?
   Ben: The Soul Club. They have fabulous music, and it's never crowded, so it's easy to get in.
Mayumi: That's funny. There's always a long wait outside my favorite club. I like it because it's always packed.
   Ben: Why do you think it's so popular?
Mayumi: Well, it just opened a few months ago, everything is brand-new and modern, and lots of fashionable people go there. It's called the Casablanca.
   Ben: Oh, right! I hear the reason people go there is just to be seen.
Mayumi: Exactly! Do you want to go some night?
   Ben: I thought you'd never ask!

B **CLASS ACTIVITY** What are some popular places in your city?
Do you ever go to any of these places? Why or why not?

5 WORD POWER

Learning Objective: *learn adjectives to describe successful businesses and businesspeople*

A *Pair work*

- Focus Ss' attention on the picture. With Ss, brainstorm some qualities that are important for a model to be successful. Write Ss' ideas on the board.
- Ask Ss to read the adjectives in each list. Elicit or explain any new vocabulary.

Vocabulary

industrious: hardworking
slender: thin
persuasive: able to influence other people
tough: strong; able to deal with difficult conditions
affordable: having a reasonable price
entertaining: amusing and interesting
informative: providing useful knowledge or ideas

- Ss work in pairs and rank the adjectives from 1 to 6. Remind Ss that 1 is most important. Encourage Ss to give reasons for their rankings and to try to come to agreement.
- Go around the room and offer help as needed.
- Elicit examples of the most important quality (ranked number 1) for success for each item.

B *Group work*

- Explain the task.
- Ss work in small groups to add one more adjective to each list.
- Elicit the new adjectives from each group. Encourage groups to explain their reason for adding that to the list.

6 ROLE PLAY

Learning Objective: *role-play a conversation between an interviewer and two job applicants*

- Explain the task. Ask three Ss to model the conversation.
- Students work in groups of three. Student A is the interviewer. He or she chooses a job from the list. Students B and C are applicants. Each tries to convince the interviewer that he or she is best for the job. Remind Ss to use vocabulary in the Word Power, as well as to recycle vocabulary from pages 3, 30, and 74.

- Set a time limit of about seven minutes. Go around the class and give help as needed.
- Ss change roles and do the role play again.

End of Cycle 1

See the Supplementary Resources chart at the beginning of this unit for additional teaching materials and student activities related to this Cycle.

Cycle 2, Exercises 7–13

7 CONVERSATION

Learning Objectives: *practice a conversation about fashionable places; see ways of giving reasons in context*

A *[CD 3, Track 4]*

- Tell Ss to cover the text and look only at the picture. Elicit details about the picture.
- Set the scene. Two friends, Mayumi and Ben, are talking about their favorite nightclubs. Tell Ss to listen to find out how the clubs are different.
- Play the audio program. Ss listen and take notes.

- Text uncovered. Tell Ss to read the conversation. Ask them to check the accuracy of their notes.
- Ask: "Which club would you rather go to? Why?"
- Ss practice the conversation in pairs.

❗ For another way to practice this Conversation, try the *Musical Dialog* – download it from the website.

B *Class activity*

- Explain the task. Read the questions. Hold a class discussion about "in" places. Ss compare and evaluate clubs they know.

Learning Objective: *practice giving reasons*

⏵ **[CD 3, Track 5]**

- Focus Ss' attention on the Grammar Focus box. Explain that the phrases in boldface are used for giving reasons. Present the following information and examples:

1. because *and* since
- They mean the same, although *since* is more formal.
- *Because* and *since* are followed by a subject and verb:
  subject + verb
  I love the Soul Club **because** the music is great.

- Ask Ss to underline the subject + verb phrases with *because* and *since* in the Grammar Focus box.

  - *Because* or *since* can begin or end a sentence. When the clause is at the beginning, it is followed by a comma.
    Since it's packed, there's a long wait. OR
    There's a long wait **since** it's packed.
  - The clause with *because* or *since* is a subordinate clause, not a main clause.

2. because of *and* due to
- They mean the same, although *due to* often has a negative connotation.
- *Because of* and *due to* are followed by a noun or noun phrase.

  This is my favorite club **because of** the great music.

- Ask Ss to underline the noun/noun phrases used with *because of* and *due to* in the Grammar Focus box.

  - *Because of* or *due to* can begin a sentence. When the clause is at the beginning, it is followed by a comma.
    Due to the crowds, it's difficult to get in. OR
    It's difficult to get in due to the crowds.
  - The clause with *because of* or *due* to is a subordinate clause, not a main clause.

3. for
  for + noun (or noun phrase)
  It's famous/well known/popular **for** its music.

4. the reason (that/why) ... is ...
  The reason (that/why) Julie goes there **is** to have fun.

- Play the audio program. Ss listen and read or repeat.

- **Option:** Ss choose a popular restaurant or club in their city and write sentences using the six patterns in the Grammar Focus box. Tell Ss to give reasons for the place's success. Go around the class and give help as needed.

A
- Books closed. Draw a circle on the board. Write *MTV* inside it. Ask: "What do you know about MTV? Do you ever watch it? Why is it so popular?" Ss come to the board to add their ideas to the mind map.
- Books open. Explain the task. Point out that more than one answer is possible.
- Ss complete the paragraph individually.
- Ss compare answers in pairs. Check Ss' responses around the class.

Answers

MTV is one of the most popular television networks in the world. People love MTV not only **because of** its music videos, but also **because of/due to** its clever and diverse programming. **Since/Because** it keeps its shows up-to-the-minute, young people watch MTV for the latest fads in music and fashion. MTV is also well known **for** its music awards show. **The reason (why/that)** so many people watch it is to see all the fashionable guests. MTV even has reality shows. These shows are popular **because** they appeal to young people. **Because of/Due to** MTV's widespread popularity, many teenagers have become less industrious with their homework!

B
- Explain the task. Model the first sentence with the class.
- Ss complete the task individually or in pairs. Then check Ss' responses.

TIP If a S finishes the task early, check his or her work, and send the S to work with another person. Alternatively, ask the S to start writing the answers on the board.

Answers

1. b   2. c   3. e/g   4. a/f   5. g   6. d   7. h   8. f

C *Pair work*
- Explain the task. Ask a S to read the example sentence. Ss suggest two more reasons for each success in part B.
- Ss work in pairs. Elicit responses from the class.
- **Option:** Ask Ss to write one idea each on the board. Use those suggestions to go over any problems Ss may still have with these structures.

⚁ For more practice with giving reasons, try ***Just One Minute*** – download it from the website. Ss describe a business, TV show, or product, and the reasons for its success.

Giving reasons ▶

I like the Casablanca **because** it's always packed.
Since it's always so packed, there's a long wait outside the club.
It's popular **because of** the fashionable people.
The Soul Club is famous **for** its fantastic music.
Due to the crowds, the Casablanca is difficult to get in to.
The reason (that/why) people go there **is** just to be seen.

A Complete the paragraph with *because, since, because of, for, due to*, and *the reason*. Then compare with a partner. (More than one answer is possible.)

MTV is one of the most popular television networks in the world. People love MTV not only .... its music videos, but also .... its clever and diverse programming. .... it keeps its shows up-to-the-minute, young people watch MTV for the latest fads in music and fashion. MTV is also well known .... its music awards show. .... so many people watch it is to see all the fashionable guests. MTV even has reality shows. These shows are popular .... they appeal to young people. .... MTV's widespread popularity, many teenagers have become less industrious with their homework!

B What reason explains the success of each situation? (More than one answer is possible.) Compare ideas with a partner.

Situation

1. Nokia is a successful company ....
2. People love Levi's jeans ....
3. The BBC is well known ....
4. Huge supermarket chains are popular ....
5. People everywhere drink Coca-Cola ....
6. Apple products are famous ....
7. Nike is a popular brand of clothing ....
8. Many people like megastores ....

Reason

a. since prices are generally more affordable.
b. due to its ever-changing product line.
c. because they have always been fashionable.
d. for their innovative designs.
e. because of its informative programming.
f. for their big choice of products.
g. since it advertises worldwide.
h. because the advertising is clever and entertaining.

C **PAIR WORK** Suggest two more reasons for each success in part B.

A: Nokia is a successful company because its commercials are very clever.
B: I think another reason why they are successful is . . .

9 LISTENING *Radio commercials*

A ▶ Listen to radio commercials for three different businesses.
What are two special features of each place?

	Maggie's	Sports Pro	Mexi-Grill
1.	....	....	....
2.	....	....	....

B ▶ Listen again. Complete each slogan.

1. "If you don't .... what you want in your .... , come .... ours!"
2. "We're here to .... you have .... !"
3. "You won't find a .... , ... meal – anywhere!"

10 INTERCHANGE 12 *Catchy slogans*

How well do you know the slogans companies use for their products?
Go to Interchange 12 on page 127.

11 DISCUSSION *TV commericials*

GROUP WORK Discuss these questions.

When you watch TV, do you pay attention to the commercials? Why or why not?
What commercials do you remember from the last time you watched TV?
What are some effective commercials you remember? What made them effective?
What is the funniest commercial you've ever seen? the dumbest? the most shocking?
Which celebrities have been in commercials? Has this affected your opinion of the product?
    Has it affected your opinion of the celebrity?
What differences are there between commercials today and commercials from the past?

12 WRITING *A commercial*

A Choose one of your favorite products. Read the questions and make notes
about the best way to sell it. Then write a one-minute radio or TV commercial.

What's good or unique about the product?
Why would someone want to buy or use it?
Can you think of a clever name or slogan?

B **GROUP WORK** Take turns presenting your
commercials. What is good about each one?
Can you give any suggestions to improve them?

> Are you looking for a high-quality
> TV that is also attractively designed?
> Buy a Star TV. Star is the most popular
> name in electronics because of its
> commitment to excellence and . . .

9 LISTENING

Learning Objectives: *listen to three radio commercials; practice listening for specific information and taking notes*

A *[CD 3, Track 6]*

- Explain the task. Then ask Ss to read the names of the businesses and predict what kind of business each is.
- Tell Ss to listen to the commercials for the special features. Remind Ss to write down only key words.
- Play the audio program. Ss listen and complete the features columns. Were Ss' predictions correct?
- Elicit the answers.

> **AudioScript**
>
> See page T-174.

> **Answers**
>
> Maggie's: 1. designer fashions at the lowest prices;
>   2. accepts all major credit cards
> Sports Pro: 1. knowledgeable salespeople;
>   2. open every day
> Mexi-Grill: 1. any combination of fillings available;
>   2. fast service at low prices

B *[CD 3, Track 7]*

- Play the audio program again. Ss listen and complete the slogan for each place. Then check Ss' answers.

> **Answers**
>
> 1. If you don't **see** what you want in your **closet**, come **check out** ours! **Maggie's**
> 2. We're here to **help** you have **fun! Sports Pro**
> 3. You won't find a **cheaper, tastier** meal—anywhere! **Mexi-Grill**

❗ For another way to teach this exercise, try ***Jigsaw Learning*** – download it from the website. Student A listens for the feature, Student B listens for the slogan.

10 INTERCHANGE 12

See page T-127 for teaching notes.

11 DISCUSSION

Learning Objective: *talk about TV commercials*

Note: If possible, show some recordings of TV commercials in class.

Group work

- Read the discussion questions. Explain the task. Encourage Ss to ask follow-up questions.
- Ss work in small groups to discuss the questions. Go around the room and offer help as needed.

- ***Option:*** Write each question on a card. Divide the class into seven groups, if possible. Give each group a card with a question. Set a time limit of three minutes for groups to discuss the question. Then have groups pass their question on to another group, and repeat the process until groups have discussed all seven questions.

12 WRITING

Learning Objective: *write a radio or TV commercial*

A

- Explain the task. Read the questions. Explain that Ss can use them to help organize their ideas. Ask a S to read the example commercial.
- Ss work individually. Tell Ss to choose one product and make notes on how it could be advertised. Ss use their notes to write a first draft.
- ***Option:*** The first draft can be assigned for homework.

B Group work

- Explain the task. Ss present their one-minute commercials to their group. The rest of the group offers feedback on the presentation.
- ***Option:*** Encourage Ss to include props and music.
- ***Option:*** Ss create a storyboard for their commercial and present it to the group or the class. The storyboard could show, using a comic-book style, the main scenes in the TV commercial.

13 READING

Learning Objective: *develop skills in predicting and making inferences*

- Focus Ss' attention on the cartoon. Ask if anyone understands why this is humorous. Tell Ss they will get the joke after they read the article.

- Read the pre-reading task. Elicit or explain that *market research* studies ways to advertise a product, what price to charge for it, and who might want to buy it.

- Elicit Ss' ideas about the title and the pre-reading question. Ask: "Do you know any products that sell well in one country but not in another? Why?"

A

- Explain the task. Then go over statements 1-6. Point out that sometimes the answer is not given.

- Ss read the article individually. Tell Ss to guess the meanings of unfamiliar words while quickly reading for main ideas. Remind Ss to mark any words they don't understand.

- Elicit the problem with "Nova."

- For another way to teach this reading, try ***Reading Race*** – download it from the website.

- Then Ss work in pairs or small groups to discuss vocabulary. Tell Ss to ask each other about words they still don't understand. Ss may use their dictionaries for a final check.

- Elicit or explain any remaining new vocabulary.

Vocabulary

learned the hard way: made a lot of mistakes or had a lot of difficulty before learning something

overlooked: didn't notice something or didn't realize how important it was

Sure enough: expression used to say that something happened exactly the way someone thought it would

translated . . . literally: translated from one language to another, word by word, according to its most basic meaning rather than the general meaning

As it turned out: the way something actually happened

pleading: asking for something in an urgent and anxious way

ancestors: family members who lived long ago

packaging: the container a product is sold in

countless: too many to be counted

pure coincidence: two things happening together completely by chance, in a surprising way

signature: a person's handwritten name

Arabic script: the written form of the Arabic language

- Ss work individually or in pairs to choose the correct answers.

- Go over answers with the class.

Answers

1. false   3. not given   5. false
2. true   4. not given   6. false

B

- Explain the task. Read the two problems.

- ***Option:*** Ask a S to point out something made of leather. "Fly in leather" translates into Spanish as *Volar en cuero.*

- Ss work individually.

- Go over answers with the class.

Answers

1. N   2. T

C Group work

- Explain the task. Brainstorm products from Ss' countries.

- Ss complete the task in groups. Ask Ss from the same country to work together if possible. Go around the class and give help as needed.

- For more practice, try ***Twenty Questions*** – download it from the website. Ss think of an advertisement.

End of Cycle 2

See the Supplementary Resources chart at the beginning of this unit for additional teaching materials and student activities related to this Cycle and for assessment tools.

The Wrong Stuff

Look at the picture and the first sentence of the article. Why is market research important to companies that want to sell their products internationally?

If a business wants to sell its product internationally, it had better do some market research first. This is a lesson that some large American corporations have learned the hard way.

What's in a name?

Sometimes the problem is the name. When General Motors introduced its Chevy Nova into Latin America, it overlooked the fact that *No va* in Spanish means "It doesn't go." Sure enough, the Chevy Nova never went anywhere in Latin America.

Translation problems

Sometimes it's the slogan that doesn't work. No company knows this better than Pepsi-Cola, with its "Come alive with Pepsi!" campaign. The campaign was so successful in the United States that Pepsi translated its slogan literally for its international campaign. As it turned out,

the translations weren't quite right. Pepsi was pleading with Germans to "Come out of the grave" and telling the Chinese that "Pepsi brings your ancestors back from the grave."

A picture's worth a thousand words

Other times, the problem involves packaging. A picture of a smiling, round-cheeked baby has helped sell countless jars of Gerber baby food. So when Gerber marketed its products in Africa, it kept the picture on the jar. What Gerber didn't realize was that in many African countries, the picture on the jar shows what the jar has in it.

Twist of fate

Even cultural factors can be involved. The cosmetics company Revlon

made a costly mistake when they launched a new perfume in Brazil. The perfume smelled like Camellia flowers. It overlooked the fact that Camellia flowers are associated with funerals in Brazil. Unsurprisingly, the perfume failed. The entire Revlon brand suffered as many felt the company disrespected the culture.

Here's a great new car. The Nova!

It doesn't run?

A Read the article. Then for each statement, check (✓) True, False, or Not given.

	True	False	Not given
1. General Motors did a lot of research before naming the Chevy Nova.	☐	☐	☐
2. The "Come alive with Pepsi!" campaign worked well in the U.S.	☐	☐	☐
3. Pepsi still sold well in Germany and China.	☐	☐	☐
4. Gerber changed its packaging after the problem in Africa.	☐	☐	☐
5. The problem for Revlon was the name "Camellia."	☐	☐	☐
6. Revlon no longer sells cosmetics in Brazil.	☐	☐	☐

B Look at the marketing problems below. In each situation, was the problem related to the product's name (**N**) or slogan (**S**)?

.... 1. The Ford Fiera didn't sell well in Spain, where *fiera* means "ugly old woman."

.... 2. Braniff Airline's "Fly in leather" campaign was meant to promote its comfortable new seats. In Spanish, the company was telling passengers to "Fly with no clothes on."

C **GROUP WORK** Think of two products sold in your country: one that has sold well, and one that hasn't. Why did one sell well, but not the other? What changes could help the second product sell better?

Units 11–12 Progress check

SELF-ASSESSMENT

How well can you do these things? Check (✓) the boxes.

I can	Very well	OK	A little
Describe important life events and their consequences (Ex. 1)	☐	☐	☐
Describe and explain regrets about the past (Ex. 2)	☐	☐	☐
Describe hypothetical situations in the past (Ex. 2)	☐	☐	☐
Understand and give reasons for success (Ex. 3, 4)	☐	☐	☐
Describe the purpose of actions (Ex. 4)	☐	☐	☐

 SPEAKING *Lessons to live by*

A What are two important events for each of these age groups? Complete the chart.

Children	Teenagers	People in their 20s	People in their 40s
....	....	....	....
....	....	....	....

B GROUP WORK Talk about the events. Why is each event important? What do people learn from each event?

A: Starting school is an important event for children.
B: Why is starting school an important milestone?
A: Once they start school, . . .

useful expressions	
after	once
as soon as	before
the moment	until
by the time	

2 *GAME* A chain of events

A Write three regrets you have about the past.

B GROUP WORK What if the situations were different? Take turns. One student expresses a regret. The next student adds a hypothetical result, and so on, for as long as you can.

A: I should have been more ambitious during college.
B: If you'd been more ambitious, you would have gone abroad.
C: If you'd gone abroad, you could have . . .

Units 11-12 Progress check

SELF-ASSESSMENT

Learning Objectives: *reflect on one's learning; identify areas that need improvement*

- Ask: "What did you learn in Units 11 and 12?" Elicit Ss' answers.
- Ss complete the Self-assessment. Encourage them to be honest, and point out they will not get a bad grade if they check (✓) "a little."

- Ss move on to the Progress check exercises. You can have Ss complete them in class or for homework, using one of these techniques:
  1. Ask Ss to complete all the exercises.
  2. Ask Ss: "What do you need to practice?" Then assign exercises based on their answers.
  3. Ask Ss to choose and complete exercises based on their Self-assessment.

 ## SPEAKING

Learning Objective: *assess one's ability to describe important events with time clauses*

A
- Explain the task. Ss come up with important events at several points in people's lives.
- Ss work individually to complete the chart. Go around the class and give help with vocabulary.

B *Group work*
- Explain the task. Read the focus questions. Ask Ss to read the useful expressions. Ask three Ss to model the conversation.

- Ss work in small groups to discuss the events. Go around the class and note errors you hear. Also note time clauses you hear used correctly.
- After the discussion, write errors you heard on the board. Ask the class to correct them. Point out examples of time clauses you heard used correctly.
- Ask each group to share one or two of the important events they discussed.

 ## GAME

Learning Objectives: *assess one's ability to talk about behavior and personality; assess one's ability to express regrets about the past using past modals; assess one's ability to describe hypothetical situations using if clauses*

A
- Explain the task.
- Ss work individually to write three regrets. Remind Ss that they will be sharing these regrets, so they should avoid anything too personal to share.
- Go around the class to check grammar and give help as needed.

B *Group work*
- Explain the task. Ask three Ss to model the conversation.
- Ss work in small groups. Ss take turns talking about regrets. Group members add hypothetical results. Challenge Ss to think of several hypothetical results for each situation.
- **Option:** Ask Ss to write their sentences. Ss can read them aloud or turn them in to you to check.

3 LISTENING

Learning Objective: *assess one's ability to listen to, understand, and give reasons for success*

A [CD 3, Track 8]

- Explain the task. Ask Ss to read the factors. Elicit or explain any new vocabulary.
- Tell Ss to listen and check (✓) the factors they hear. Play the audio program once or twice.

> **AudioScript**
>
> See page T-174.

- Go over answers with the class.

> **Answers**
>
> concept, location, advertising

B ⏵ [CD 3, Track 9]

- Explain the task.

- Tell Ss to listen for the reason each factor is important. Play the audio program again. Pause after each section for Ss to write. Remind Ss to answer in their own words. Play the audio program as many times as needed.
- Ss compare answers with a partner. If they have any disagreements, play the audio program again.
- Go over answers with the class.

> **Possible answers**
>
> 1. concept: A restaurant needs to be unique and special to compete with other restaurants.
> 2. location: A restaurant needs to be seen by many people so it will attract customers.
> 3. advertising: If you have a new restaurant, you need to have a way to let people know about it.

- ***Option:*** Ss work in groups. They discuss the factors not mentioned in the audio program. Ask groups to share their ideas with the class.

4 DISCUSSION

Learning Objectives: *assess one's ability to give reasons for success; assess one's ability to describe purpose with infinitive clauses and clauses with* for

A *Pair work*

- Explain the task. Ask Ss to read the list of businesses. Elicit or explain any new vocabulary.
- Ss work in pairs. First, Ss discuss the factors affecting success. Remind Ss to choose two businesses.
- Then Ss write three sentences describing the most important factors. Go around the class and give help as needed.

B *Group work*

- Explain the task. Ask two Ss to model the conversation.

- Each pair joins another pair. Ss take turns sharing their ideas.
- Ask groups which ideas they agreed and disagreed about.

C *Group work*

- Explain the task. Read the example sentence. Ask Ss to read the useful expressions.
- Ss work in the same groups or in different groups. Ss choose a successful business to discuss. Encourage Ss to name factors like the ones in Exercise 3.
- Ask groups to share ideas with the class.

WHAT'S NEXT?

Learning Objective: *become more involved in one's learning*

- Focus Ss' attention on the Self-assessment again. Ask: "How well can you do these things now?"

- Ask Ss to underline one thing they need to review. Ask: "What did you underline? How can you review it?"
- If needed, plan additional activities or reviews based on Ss' answers.

3 LISTENING *Success story*

A ▶ Listen to a business consultant discuss the factors necessary for a restaurant to be successful. Check (✓) the ones she says are important.

☐ advertising   ☐ concept   ☐ decor   ☐ food   ☐ location   ☐ name

B ▶ Listen again. In your own words, write the reason why each factor is important.

Factor	Why is it important?
1.	....
2.	....
3.	....

4 DISCUSSION *The secrets of success*

A **PAIR WORK** Choose two businesses and discuss what they need to be successful. Then write three sentences describing the most important factors.

☐ a car wash   ☐ a gourmet supermarket   ☐ a juice bar
☐ a dance club   ☐ a high-rise hotel   ☐ a used clothing store

> 1. In order for a hotel to be successful, it has to be affordable.

B **GROUP WORK** Join another pair. Share your ideas. Do they agree?

A: We think in order for a hotel to be successful, it has to be affordable.
B: Really? But some of the most successful hotels are very expensive.

C **GROUP WORK** Now choose a popular business that you know about. What are the reasons for its success?

W Santiago

"I think W hotels are successful because the decor is so beautiful."

useful expressions
It's successful because (of) . . .   It's become popular since . . .
It's popular due to . . .   It's famous for. . .
The reason it's successful is . . .

WHAT'S NEXT?

Look at your Self-assessment again. Do you need to review anything?

Unit 13 Supplementary Resources Overview

	After the following SB exercises	You can use these materials in class	Your students can use these materials outside the classroom
CYCLE 1	1 Snapshot		
	2 Conversation		**SSD** Unit 13 Speaking 1–2
	3 Pronunciation		
	4 Grammar Focus		**SB** Unit 13 Grammar Plus focus 1 **SSD** Unit 13 Grammar 1 **ARC** Past modals for degrees of certainty 1–2
	5 Listening		
	6 Speaking	**TSS** Unit 13 Extra Worksheet	
	7 Interchange 13		**WB** Unit 13 exercises 1–4
CYCLE 2	8 Perspectives		
	9 Grammar Focus	**TSS** Unit 13 Grammar Worksheet **TSS** Unit 13 Listening Worksheet	**SB** Unit 13 Grammar Plus focus 1 **SSD** Unit 13 Grammar 2 **ARC** Past modals for judgments and suggestions
	10 Word Power	**TSS** Unit 13 Vocabulary Worksheet	**SSD** Unit 13 Vocabulary 1–2 **ARC** Reactions 1–2
	11 Listening		
	12 Discussion	**TSS** Unit 13 Writing Worksheet	
	13 Writing		
	14 Reading	**TSS** Unit 13 Project Worksheet **VID** Unit 13 **VRB** Unit 13	**SSD** Unit 13 Reading 1–2 **SSD** Unit 13 Listening 1–3 **SSD** Unit 13 Video 1–3 **WB** Unit 13 exercises 5–7

Key **ARC:** Arcade   **SB:** Student's Book   **SSD:** Self-study DVD-ROM   **TSS:** Teacher Support Site
VID: Video DVD   **VRB:** Video Resource Book   **WB:** Workbook

My Plan for Unit 13

Use the space below to customize a plan that fits your needs.

With the following SB exercises	I am using these materials in class	My students are using these materials outside the classroom

With or instead of the following SB section	I am using these materials for assessment

13 That's a possibility.

Pet Peeves

Why is it that some people...?

- ◆ are noisy eaters
- ◆ always ask for favors
- ◆ constantly interrupt
- ◆ are late all the time
- ◆ read over my shoulder on the subway
- ◆ chat online while talking on the phone
- ◆ always want to get in the last word
- ◆ throw their garbage in the recycling bin
- ◆ don't cover their mouths when they cough
- ◆ make popping sounds when they chew gum

Source: Interviews with people between the ages of 16 and 45

Which of the pet peeves do you have about people you know? Which one is the worst?
Underline a pet peeve you could be accused of. When and why are you guilty of it?
Are there any pet peeves in the list that don't annoy you?

2 CONVERSATION *What happened?*

A ⊙ Listen and practice.

Jackie: You asked Beth to be here around 7:00, didn't you?
Bill: Yes. What time is it now?
Jackie: It's almost 8:00. I wonder what happened.
Bill: Hmm. She might have forgotten the time. Why don't I call and see if she's on her way?

A few minutes later

Bill: I got her voice mail, so she must not have turned on her cell phone.
Jackie: I hope she didn't have a problem on the road. Her car could have broken down or something.
Bill: Of course she may have simply forgotten and done something else today.
Jackie: No, she couldn't have forgotten – I just talked to her about it yesterday. I guess we should start without her.

B ⊙ Listen to the rest of the conversation. What happened?

That's a possibility.

> In this unit, students discuss social habits, predicaments, and mysteries. In Cycle 1, students give explanations, reasons, and suggestions using past modals *must have, may have, and* could have. *In Cycle 2, students give opinions and advice with past modals* should have, could have, *and* would have.

1 SNAPSHOT

Learning Objective: *talk about annoying social habits*

- Books closed. Write the subtitle "Pet Peeves" on the board. List one or two pet peeves not shown in the Snapshot:

  Why is it that some people :

  - always talk about how much things cost?

  - never help clean up after a party?

  Note: Ss discuss their own pet peeves later.

- Elicit that *pet peeves* are things that always annoy you.
- Books open. Ask Ss to look at the Snapshot in pairs.
- Elicit or explain any new vocabulary.

Vocabulary

get in the last word: say something else, even when a conversation seems to be over

- Read the questions. Make sure Ss understand that *you could be accused of* and *are you guilty of it?* mean "Do you ever do unacceptable things like these?"
- Ss discuss the questions in small groups. Remind Ss to use "I hate it when/It bothers me when," etc. from Unit 1.
- ***Option:*** Ss work in small groups. Each group writes ten rules for good manners (e.g., *People should always:.*

  - hold the door open for the next person

  - call if they're going to be late).

- For more practice with the vocabulary, play ***True or False?*** – download it from the website. Ss cover the text and look at the picture for one minute. Then ask Ss to close their books and test their memory (e.g., *The man's shirt is blue [false]*).

2 CONVERSATION

Learning Objectives: *practice a conversation about offering explanations; see past modals in context*

A ▶ [CD 3, Track 10]

- Books closed. Set the scene. Two people are talking about a guest who is late for their barbecue.
- Write these questions on the board:

  What time was Beth asked to come? (7:00)

  What time is it now? (almost eight o'clock)

  What does Bill decide to do? (call Beth)

  Why can't Bill contact Beth? (her cell phone is off)

  What do they decide to do? (start without Beth)

- Tell Ss to listen for the answers. Play the audio program. Then elicit the answers. Ask: "What would you do in a similar situation? In your opinion, did they do the right thing?"
- Write these sentence starters on the board (answers in parentheses):

  What has happened to Beth?

  Bill: She might have ___ ___ ___ (forgotten the time)

  Jackie: Her car could have ___ ___ . (broken down)

  Bill: She may have simply forgotten and ___ ___ ___ ___ . (done something else today)

- Tell Ss to listen for the answers. Play the audio program again.
- Ask Ss to come to the board to fill in the answers. Ask the class to correct answers if needed.
- Books open. Play the audio program. Ss listen and read or repeat.

B ▶ [CD 3, Track 11]

- Explain the task. Tell Ss to listen to what really happened to Beth. Play the second part of the audio program. Elicit Ss' responses.

AudioScript

See page T-174.

Answers

Beth's dog was sick, and she had to take her to the vet.

T-86

3 PRONUNCIATION

Learning Objective: *notice and use reduced forms of past modals*

A ▶ *[CD 3, Track 12]*

- Play the audio program. Ss listen. Point out that in past modals, *have* is reduced to /əv/. The reduced *have* sounds like *of*.
- Play the audio program again. Ss listen and repeat.

B ▶ *[CD 3, Track 13]*

- Play the audio program. Ss listen and focus on the full form of *not*.
- Play the audio program again. Ss listen and repeat.

❗ For a different way to practice reductions, try **Walking Stress** – download it from the website. Ss identify key words first.

4 GRAMMAR FOCUS

Learning Objective: *practice using past modal verbs for degrees of certainty*

▶ *[CD 3, Track 14]*

Past modals of possibility (**may/might/could have**)

- Point out that we use *may, might,* and *could* when something is possible, but we don't know for sure. Write the rule on the board. Elicit other possible reasons for Beth's lateness, using *may/might/ could have.*

  subject + *may/might/could* + *have* + past participle
  She   may   have   gotten lost.

Past modals of certainty (**must/couldn't have**)

- Ask Ss to find an example of *must (not) have* in the Conversation on page 86. Write it on the board.
- Tell Ss that we use *must not have* when we are almost certain. Remind Ss: Bill gets Beth's voice mail, so he is pretty sure *she must not have turned on her phone.*
- Explain that when we are more certain, we use *couldn't have.* Ask Ss to find the example of *couldn't have* in the Conversation. Write it on the board.

- Play the audio program. Ss listen and read or repeat.

❗ For another way to practice past modals, try **Disappearing Dialog** – download it from the website, using the Conversation on page 86. Erase the past modals first.

A

- Explain the task. Read the situations and explanations. Elicit or explain any unfamiliar words.
- Ss complete the task individually. Go over answers with the class.
- Then Ss practice reading their answers in pairs. Remind Ss to use reduced forms.

Answers

1. b   2. f   3. a   4. d   5. c   6. e

B *Pair work*

- Explain the task.
- Ss work in pairs and take turns suggesting explanations for each situation.

5 LISTENING

Learning Objective: *develop skills in giving explanations*

A *Group work*

- Focus Ss' attention on the subtitle, "Jumping to conclusions." Elicit or explain that this means "forming an opinion before you have all the facts."
- Explain the task. Ask Ss to form small groups.
- Invite Ss to give explanations for the events pictured. Remind Ss to use past modals.

B ▶ *[CD 3, Track 15]*

- Explain the task. Remind Ss to take notes.
- Play the audio program. Then ask: "What *did* happen?" Elicit Ss' responses. Discuss how similar their part A explanations were to what really happened.

AudioScript

See page T-175.

Answers

1. There were dolphins following the cruise ship, and the people were looking at them.
2. She got locked out of her own house. The wind blew the door shut when she went outside to get the newspaper, so she tried to enter through her bedroom window.

3 PRONUNCIATION *Reduction in past modals*

A ▶ Listen and practice. Notice how **have** is reduced in these sentences.

He must **have** forgotten the date.   She might **have** had a problem on the road.

B ▶ Listen and practice. Notice that **not** is not contracted or reduced in these sentences.

He may **not** have remembered it.   She must **not** have caught her bus.

4 GRAMMAR FOCUS

> ### Past modals for degrees of certainty ▶
>
> **It's almost certain.**
> She **must have left** already.
> She **must not have turned on** her phone.
>
> **It's not possible.**
> She **couldn't have been** at home.
>
> **It's possible.**
> She **may/might have forgotten** the time.
> She **may/might not have remembered** the time.
> Her car **could have broken down**.

A Read each situation and choose the best explanation. Then practice with a partner.
(Pay attention to the reduced forms in past modals.)

Situation

1. Maura couldn't keep her eyes open. ....
2. Brian got a call and looked worried. ....
3. The teacher looks very happy today. ....
4. Jane is in a terrible mood today. ....
5. Jeff was fired from his job. ....
6. My cousin is broke again. ....

Explanation

a. He may have gotten a raise.
b. She must not have gotten enough sleep.
c. He might not have done his work on time.
d. She could have had a fight with her boyfriend.
e. She must have spent too much last month.
f. He couldn't have heard good news.

B PAIR WORK Suggest different explanations for each situation in part A.

5 LISTENING *Jumping to conclusions*

A GROUP WORK What do you think happened? Offer an explanation for each event.

B ▶ Listen to the explanations for the two events in part A and take notes.
What *did* happen? How similar were your explanations?

6 SPEAKING *What's your explanation?*

A PAIR WORK What do you think were the reasons for these events? Suggest two different explanations for each.

1. Two people were having dinner in a restaurant. One suddenly got up and ran out of the restaurant.
2. A woman living alone returned home and found the TV and radio turned on. They weren't on when she went out.
3. Two friends met again after not seeing each other for many years. One looked at the other and burst out laughing.

B GROUP WORK Each student thinks of two situations like the ones in part A. Others suggest explanations.

A: Last night, a wife handed her husband a large bag of money.
B: Well, she might have returned some money she'd taken from him.

7 INTERCHANGE 13 *Photo plays*

What's your best explanation for some unusual events? Go to Interchange 13 on page 128.

8 PERSPECTIVES *She's driving me crazy!*

A Listen to three friends talking to one another on the phone. Check (✓) the response you think is best for each person's problem.

Michi / **Molly**

Hi Molly. Ramona's mad because she thinks I didn't ask her to go hiking with us. I sent her four emails, but she never responded!

☐ Well, you know Ramona never answers emails. You should have called her on the phone.

☐ Oh, forget it! I wouldn't have sent so many messages. If Ramona can't bother to check her email, she'll just miss out on things.

Molly / **Ramona**

Ramona, hi! I just got off the phone with Michi. She asked me for advice, but she never stops talking long enough to listen!

☐ You could have been more understanding. Michi must have been upset and just needed to talk.

☐ I would have asked Michi to be quiet for a minute. How can you give her advice if she doesn't give you a chance to talk?

Ramona / **Michi**

Michi, I can't believe that Molly still has my notes! I needed them for a test today. She never returns things!

☐ Molly shouldn't have kept your notes this long! But I wouldn't have lent them to her the week before a test.

☐ Oh, Molly may have just forgotten about them. I would have just borrowed someone else's notes.

B Do you talk about pet peeves with your friends? Do they give you advice?

6 SPEAKING

Learning Objective: *talk about reasons for events using past modals*

A *Pair work*

- Explain the task. Focus Ss' attention on the picture.
- Read the first situation. Model the task with a S:

  T1: I have an explanation. The woman could have remembered that she left the water running in her bathroom, so she had to rush home to turn it off. What do you think?

  S1: Well, she might have just heard her car alarm go off. She was running out to see if someone was stealing her car.

- Read the other two situations. Elicit or explain that *burst out* means "suddenly started."
- Ss work in pairs. They take turns suggesting explanations. Tell Ss to be creative and to use past modals. Go around the class and give help as needed.

Possible answers

1. One of them might have noticed someone trying to break into his car./The couple could have had a fight, and one of them was too upset to stay and finish his dinner.

2. The woman might have forgotten that her brother had asked to stay overnight. He must have been asleep when she came home./The woman's cat could have played with the remote control for the radio and TV, accidentally turning them both on.

3. Both men must have gone bald since the last time they saw each other./The one who laughed might have been surprised at how fit the other was, so he laughed at the great change in his old "couch potato" friend.

B *Group work*

- Explain the task. Ask two Ss to model the conversation. Elicit additional explanations.
- Ss work individually to think of situations like the ones in part A. Go around and give help as needed.
- Then Ss work in small groups. Ss read their situations. Group members offer explanations. Set a time limit of about ten minutes.

> **TIP** Ss like to receive feedback after Speaking activities. Include positive reinforcement on issues like creativity, accuracy, fluency, use of new language, and participation.

7 INTERCHANGE 13

See page T-128 for teaching notes.

End of Cycle 1

Cycle 2, Exercises 8–14

See the Supplementary Resources chart at the beginning of this unit for additional teaching materials and student activities related to this Cycle.

8 PERSPECTIVES

Learning Objectives: *listen to friends discussing problems on the phone; see could have and would have in context*

A ▶ *[CD 3, Track 16]*

- Write these questions on the board. Ss discuss them in pairs.

  Do you know someone who drives you crazy? What does he or she do? How do you react?

- Set the scene. Three friends are talking on the phone. Each friend is mad at another.
- Ask Ss to read the three boxes on the left. Then ask: "Who is calling who(m)? Who(m) is she complaining about? What's the problem?"

- Books closed. Explain the task.
- Play the audio program. Ss listen to three calls. In each case, they will hear two possible responses. Pause after the responses. Ss decide which response is best.
- Books open. Ss check their responses. Ask Ss which response they prefer, and why.

B

- Explain the task. Read the questions.
- Ss discuss the questions in pairs or small groups.
- **Option:** Ask Ss how many of them share problems with their friends. Who shares more, men or women? Discuss possible reasons.

9 GRAMMAR FOCUS

Learning Objective: *practice past modals for giving opinions and suggestions on real and hypothetical past events*

⏵ *[CD 3, Track 17]*

Giving opinions (should have)

- Explain that we use *should/shouldn't have* to give opinions. Focus Ss' attention on the Perspectives on page 88. Ask Ss to find two examples with *should(n't) have*. Write them on the board in columns:

1	2	3	4	5
You	should	have	called	her . . .
Molly	shouldn't	have	kept	your notes . . .

- Elicit or explain the examples:

  You should have called her . . . (Molly is giving an opinion. She thinks Michi was wrong to send emails.)

  Molly shouldn't have kept your notes . . . (Michi is giving an opinion. She thinks Molly was wrong to keep the notes.)

- Elicit the rule. Write it on the board:

  subject + should (not) + have + past participle

- Encourage Ss to think of more examples.

Giving advice (would have/could have)

- Repeat the above steps. Note: There are four examples of *would(n't) have* in the Perspectives.

- Explain the meaning *of would have* like this:

  I wouldn't have sent so many messages. (Molly is imagining this [hypothetical] situation happening to her and saying she would have done things differently.)

Ask Ss to listen for the reduced form of *have* in past modals. Play the audio program. Ss listen and read or repeat.

A

- Explain the task. Tell Ss to look at the picture as you model the first conversation.

- Ss complete the task individually. Ss use past modals to complete the conversations. Go around the class and give help as needed.

- Elicit or explain any new vocabulary.

> **Vocabulary**
>
> **dented:** hit something so that its surface was bent and marked
> **exhausted:** very tired
> **yawning:** opening the mouth wide, showing lack of sleep
> **gotten the hint:** understood an indirect message
> **ended up:** did something no matter what

- Go over answers with the class.

> **Possible answers**
>
> 1. could have dressed; would have asked
> 2. should have told; wouldn't have lent
> 3. shouldn't have stayed; could have started
> 4. wouldn't have paid; shouldn't have invited

- Ss practice the conversations in pairs.

B Pair work

- Ss work in pairs to think of another suggestion or comment for each situation in part A.

10 WORD POWER

Learning Objective: *learn nouns for discussing reactions*

A

- Explain the task. Set the scene: Megan's boyfriend forgot her birthday.

- Give Ss time to read the reactions and examples. Elicit or explain any vocabulary Ss ask about (without giving away the answers).

- Model the task with the first word. Elicit that *assumption* means "jumping to conclusions." Then ask Ss to find the example. (Answer: f)

- Ss complete the task individually. Ss may use a dictionary.

- Then Ss compare answers in pairs or small groups. Elicit Ss' responses to check answers.

> **Answers**
>
> 1. f   2. c   3. e   4. h   5. d   6. g   7. b   8. a

B Group work

- Explain the task. Model the task making an assumption:

  T: Rob isn't in class today. He must have had a doctor's appointment.

- Ss work in small groups. Each group chooses a situation. Then Ss take turns giving examples of each reaction (1–8). Remind Ss to use past modals for opinions and advice.

 For more practice with the vocabulary, play *Tic-Tac-Toe* – download it from the website. Add one more reaction (e.g., a reason).

9 GRAMMAR FOCUS

Past modals for judgments and suggestions ▶

Judging past actions	Suggesting alternative past actions
You **should have called** her on the phone.	You **could have been** more understanding.
She **shouldn't have kept** your notes this long.	I **wouldn't have lent** them to her.

A Complete the conversations using past modals with the verbs given. Then practice with a partner.

1. A: I invited my boyfriend over to meet my parents, but he arrived wearing torn jeans. He looked so messy!
   B: Well, he .... (dress) neatly.
   I .... (ask) him to wear something nicer.

2. A: John borrowed my car and dented it. When he returned it, he didn't even say anything about it!
   B: He .... (tell) you! Well, I
   .... (not lend) it to him in the first place.
   He's a terrible driver.

3. A: I'm exhausted. Mary came over and stayed until 2:00 A.M.!
   B: She .... (not stay) so late. You
   .... (start) yawning. Maybe she would have gotten the hint!

4. A: Tom invited me to a play, but I ended up paying for us both!
   B: I .... (not pay) for him. He
   .... (not invite) you if he didn't have enough money.

B PAIR WORK Think of another suggestion or comment for each situation above.

10 WORD POWER Reactions

A Megan's boyfriend forgot her birthday. How does she react?
Match each reaction with the best example.

Reaction	Example
1. an assumption	a. "If you do it again, you'll have to find a new girlfriend."
2. a criticism	b. "I bet you were out with another woman!"
3. a demand	c. "You can be so inconsiderate."
4. an excuse	d. "You'll probably forget our anniversary, too!"
5. a prediction	e. "Now you have to take me out to dinner . . . twice."
6. a suggestion	f. "You must have wanted to break up with me."
7. a suspicion	g. "You know, you ought to buy me flowers."
8. a warning	h. "I know you've been busy lately. It just slipped your mind."

B GROUP WORK Imagine that someone was late for class, or choose another situation. Give an example of each reaction in the list above.

11 LISTENING What should they have done?

A ▶ Listen to descriptions of three situations. What would have been the best thing to do in each situation? Check (✓) the best suggestion.

1. ☐ Dennis should have called a locksmith.
   ☐ He should have broken a window.
   ☐ He did the right thing.

2. ☐ Diana should have turned up her radio to keep out the noise.
   ☐ She should have called the neighbors to see what was happening.
   ☐ She did the right thing.

3. ☐ Simon should have kept the ring for himself.
   ☐ He should have taken the ring and called the police.
   ☐ He did the right thing.

B PAIR WORK What would you have done in each situation in part A?

12 DISCUSSION You could have . . .

GROUP WORK Read each situation. Say what you could have or should have done.

"I went to my neighbor's house for dinner last night. He had cooked all day, but the food was awful! I didn't want to hurt his feelings, so I ate it."

"My friend forgot to do her homework, so she asked if she could look at mine. I did mine, but I told her I hadn't."

"I didn't have any money to buy my cousin a birthday present, so I gave her something I had received previously as a gift. My brother told my cousin and now she's mad at me."

"My friend started dating this guy I don't really like. She asked what I thought of him, and I told her the truth."

A: You should have told him you weren't feeling well.
B: Or you could have eaten it really slowly.
C: I think I would have . . .

13 WRITING A complicated situation

A Think of a complicated situation from your own experience. Write a paragraph describing the situation, but don't explain how you resolved it.

One friend of mine is very demanding of my time. He wants to do everything with me, and I have a hard time saying no. I have other friends I want to spend time with as well. Last night, he asked me to spend all day Saturday with him. I didn't want to hurt his feelings. . . .

B PAIR WORK Exchange papers. Write a short paragraph about how you would have resolved your partner's situation.

C PAIR WORK Read your partner's resolution to your situation. Tell your partner how you resolved it. Whose resolution was better?

11 LISTENING

Learning Objective: *develop skills in listening for information*

A *[CD 3, Track 18]*

- Explain the task. Ss will listen to descriptions of three situations. Ask Ss to read the three suggestions for each situation.
- Elicit or explain any new vocabulary.

Vocabulary

locksmith: someone who makes and repairs locks and who can open a locked door

- Tell Ss to listen and decide what would have been the best thing to do.
- Play the audio program. Pause after each situation. Ss check (✓) what they think is the best suggestion. Make sure Ss understand there are no "correct" answers.

AudioScript

See page T-175.

- Elicit Ss' responses around the class.

> **TIP** To increase talking time, have Ss try the activity again. Be sure to give Ss a new challenge (e.g., *work with a new partner, focus on intonation, give longer answers*).

B *Pair work*

- Explain the task. Model the task by encouraging Ss to explain their choices in part A. For example:

  T: Kenita, what would you have done if you had been Dennis (in number 1)?

  S1: I would have taken a bus home and gotten my spare key.

  S2: Really? I think that would have taken too long. I would have . . .

- Ss discuss their ideas in pairs. Go around the class and give help as needed.

12 DISCUSSION

Learning Objective: *discuss opinions and advice using past modals*

Group work

- Explain the task. Read the first situation. Ask three Ss to read the example responses. Ask Student C to complete the third sentence in the example.
- Have Ss work in groups of four, if possible. Ss take turns reading a situation from the box. The group members discuss opinions and advice for each complicated situation.
- Set a time limit of about ten minutes. Go around the class and listen in. Make note of common errors to

go over after the activity. Remember to give positive feedback, too!

- **Option:** Ss work in groups. They think of three more problem situations. Suggest that pairs jot down each situation in note form. Set a time limit of five to eight minutes. Go around the class and give help as needed. Then Ss give their situations to another group to discuss.

> **TIP** Tell Ss to make a "time out" signal (forming a T-shape with their hands) if they want to use their first language. Give Ss a limit for the number of time outs.

13 WRITING

Learning Objective: *write a paragraph about a complicated situation in the past*

A

- Explain the task.
- Ss write about a situation they personally experienced. Remind Ss not to write about how they resolved the problem.
- Encourage Ss to brainstorm or note ideas before starting their drafts. Go around the class and give help as needed.
- **Option:** The first draft can be assigned for homework.

B *Pair work*

- Explain the task.
- Ss exchange papers in pairs. Then Ss work individually to write a response. Remind Ss to use past modals in their advice.

C *Pair work*

- Explain the task. Ss return papers and read the advice.
- Then Ss tell each other how they actually resolved the problem. Finally, Ss discuss whose solution was better.

14 READING

Learning Objective: *develop skills in reading for main ideas and specific information and distinguishing between fact and opinion*

- Read the pre-reading question. Elicit Ss' ideas about the picture.
- Tell Ss to read the article. Remind Ss to mark any vocabulary they can't guess from context or with the help of the picture.
- Ss work in pairs or groups to go over marked vocabulary. If no one knows the meaning of a certain word, then Ss may use their dictionaries.
- Elicit or explain any remaining new vocabulary.

Vocabulary

prosperous: wealthy and successful

mining town: a place where people took precious metals like gold or silver out of the earth

making their fortune: becoming rich

graveyard: a place where dead people are buried (put underground)

flamelike: like the flames of a fire

ethereally: very delicately and lightly, in way that doesn't seem real

vanished: disappeared suddenly, especially in a way that can't be easily explained

eerie: frightening; often used for something not natural or not understood

tombstone: a stone that marks a grave; it usually gives the name and birth and death dates for the person buried there

radioactive ore/radioactivity: a substance or a quality in a substance that sends out a form of energy that is harmful to living things

rotting matter: naturally dead substance like plants

helmets: protective hats; miners' helmets have lights on them to help the miners see while working underground

TIP If you are short of time, limit the number of words you explain. Ss choose the key words to ask you about, and look up the rest in a dictionary for homework.

A

- Explain the task. Read the four questions.
- Ss complete the task individually, in pairs, in small groups, or as a class. Ss can write their answers or give them orally. Encourage Ss to use their own words in their answers.

- If the activity is done individually, in pairs, or in groups, elicit Ss' answers around the class.

Possible answers

1. Silver Cliff was a prosperous mining town with thousands of people in the 1880s, but now it has a population of only 100.
2. The blue lights were first seen in a graveyard on a hill outside Silver Cliff.
3. A group of miners saw the lights first.
4. The blue lights are eerie. They look like flickering candle flames or dim, round spots of blue-white light.

❗ For a different way to do this exercise, try *Jigsaw Learning* – download it from the website.

B

- Explain the task. Make sure Ss know the difference between a fact (something that can be proved to be true) and an opinion (someone's belief).
- Ss work individually to complete the chart.
- Then Ss compare answers in pairs. Ask Ss to discuss any disagreements.
- Go over answers with the class.

Answers

1. Fact   2. Fact   3. Fact   4. Opinion   5. Fact   6. Opinion

- **Option:** Ss role-play an interview between the miners and a journalist.

C *Group work*

- Explain the task. Read the questions.
- Ss discuss the questions in small groups. Set a time limit of five to ten minutes. Go around the class and give help as needed.
- Ask groups to share their ideas around the class. Take a class vote to find out which group's explanation is the most reasonable.

End of Cycle 2

See the Supplementary Resources chart at the beginning of this unit for additional teaching materials and student activities related to this Cycle.

The Blue Lights of Silver Cliff

Look at the picture. What do you think the "blue lights" are?

Today, the town of Silver Cliff, Colorado, has a population of only 100 people. Once, however, it was a prosperous mining town where thousands came with dreams of finding silver and making their fortune.

Late one night in 1880, a group of miners were headed back to their camp after a good time in town. They were still laughing and joking as they approached the graveyard on a hill outside Silver Cliff. Then one of the men yelled and pointed toward the graveyard. The others fell silent. On top of each grave, they saw flamelike blue lights. These eerie lights seemed to be dancing on the graves, disappearing and then appearing again.

This was the first sighting of the blue lights of Silver Cliff. There have been many other sightings over the years. In 1969, Edward Lineham from National Geographic magazine visited the graveyard. Lineham's article tells of his experience: "I saw them. . . . Dim, round spots of blue-white light glowed ethereally among the graves. I . . . stepped forward for a better look. They vanished. I aimed my flashlight at one eerie glow and switched it on. It revealed only a tombstone."

Lineham and others have suggested various explanations for the lights. The lights might have been reflections of lights from the town, but Silver Cliff's lights seemed too dim to have this effect. They could have been caused by radioactive ore, though there's no evidence of radioactivity. They may also have been caused by gases from rotting matter. This usually happens in swamps, however, and the area around Silver Cliff is dry. Or, perhaps, the lights are from the helmets of dead miners wandering the hills in search of their fortune.

A Read the article. Then answer these questions.

1. How has Silver Cliff changed over the years?
2. Where were the blue lights first seen?
3. Who saw the blue lights first?
4. What do the blue lights look like?

B Which of these statements are facts? Which are opinions? Check (✓) Fact or Opinion.

	Fact	Opinion
1. Today, the town of Silver Cliff has a population of 100 people.	☐	☐
2. The miners saw flamelike blue lights on top of each grave.	☐	☐
3. Edward Lineham suggested various explanations for the lights.	☐	☐
4. The lights were actually reflections of lights from the town.	☐	☐
5. There was no evidence of radioactivity.	☐	☐
6. The lights were from the helmets of dead miners.	☐	☐

C GROUP WORK Which of the explanations for the blue lights do you think is the most satisfactory? Why? Can you think of any other possible explanations?

Unit 14 Supplementary Resources Overview

After the following SB exercises	You can use these materials in class	Your students can use these materials outside the classroom
CYCLE 1 1 Snapshot		
2 Conversation		**SSD** Unit 14 Speaking 1–2
3 Grammar Focus		**SB** Unit 14 Grammar Plus focus 1 **SSD** Unit 14 Grammar 1 **ARC** The passive to describe process 1–3
4 Listening	**TSS** Unit 14 Extra Worksheet	
5 Speaking		
6 Writing		**WB** Unit 14 exercises 1–4
CYCLE 2 7 Word Power	**TSS** Unit 14 Vocabulary Worksheet **TSS** Unit 14 Listening Worksheet	**SSD** Unit 14 Vocabulary 1–2 **ARC** Media professions
8 Perspectives		
9 Pronunciation		
10 Grammar Focus	**TSS** Unit 14 Grammar Worksheet **TSS** Unit 14 Writing Worksheet	**SB** Unit 14 Grammar Plus focus 2 **SSD** Unit 14 Grammar 2 **ARC** Relative clauses
11 Interchange 14		
12 Reading	**TSS** Unit 14 Project Worksheet **VID** Unit 14 **VRB** Unit 14	**SSD** Unit 14 Reading 1–2 **SSD** Unit 14 Listening 1–3 **SSD** Unit 14 Video 1–3 **WB** Unit 14 exercises 5–8

With or instead of the following SB section	You can also use these materials for assessment
Units 13–14 Progress Check	**ASSESSMENT CD** Units 13–14 Oral Quiz **ASSESSMENT CD** Units 13–14 Written Quiz

Key

ARC: Arcade	**SB:** Student's Book	**SSD:** Self-study DVD-ROM	**TSS:** Teacher Support Site
VID: Video DVD	**VRB:** Video Resource Book	**WB:** Workbook	

My Plan for Unit 14

Use the space below to customize a plan that fits your needs.

With the following SB exercises	I am using these materials in class	My students are using these materials outside the classroom

With or instead of the following SB section	I am using these materials for assessment

14 Behind the scenes

1 SNAPSHOT

Movie Firsts

The first...
- Movie-length music video – *Pink Floyd: The Wall* (1982)
- Advanced computer technology – *Terminator 2* (1991)
- Movie with Dolby Digital sound – *Batman Returns* (1992)
- Computer-animated feature film – *Toy Story* (1995)
- Movie to be released on DVD – *Twister* (1996)
- Movie to gross over $1 billion – *Titanic* (1998)
- 3-D movie to gross over $2 billion worldwide – *Avatar* (2009)
- Movie to make over $92 million in one day – *Harry Potter and the Deathly Hallows – Part 2* (2011)

Sources: www.imdb.com; www.listology.com

Have you seen any of these movies? Did you enjoy them?
What's the most popular movie playing right now? Have you seen it? Do you plan to?
Are there many movies made in your country? Name a few of your favorites.

2 CONVERSATION *Movies are hard work!*

A ▶ Listen and practice.

Ryan: Working on movies must be really exciting.
Nina: Oh, yeah, but it's also very hard work. A one-minute scene in a film can take days to shoot.
Ryan: Really? Why is that?
Nina: Well, a scene isn't filmed just once. Lots of different shots have to be taken. Only the best ones are used in the final film.
Ryan: So, how many times does a typical scene need to be shot?
Nina: It depends, but sometimes as many as 20 times. One scene may be shot from five or six different angles.
Ryan: Wow! I didn't realize that.
Nina: Why don't you come visit the studio? I can show you how things are done.
Ryan: Great, I'd love to!

B ▶ Listen to the rest of the conversation. What else makes working on movies difficult?

Behind the scenes

Cycle 1, Exercises 1–6

In this unit, students discuss the production of movies, TV programs, theater performances, and newspapers. In Cycle 1, students describe processes using the passive. In Cycle 2, students discuss jobs using defining and non-defining relative clauses.

1 SNAPSHOT

Learning Objective: *talk about the movie industry*

- ***Option:*** Show a popular English-language movie during this unit. Use it to explain useful vocabulary and concepts.

 As a warm-up, Ss play ***Line Up!*** – download it from the website. Ss line up according to when they last saw a movie (on TV, DVD, video, or at a movie theater).

- Books closed. Explain that Ss are going to discuss some movie "firsts." Write this information on the board. Ask Ss to match the "first" with the date:

The first movie-length music video	1998
The first computer-animated feature film	1982
The first movie to make over $ 1 billion	2009
The first 3-D movie to make over $ 2 billion worldwide	1995

- Books open. Ss read the Snapshot individually. Tell Ss to check their "firsts" in the Snapshot.

- Elicit or explain any new vocabulary.

Vocabulary

Dolby: a sound engineering company
digital sound: an electronic sound system
animated: using cartoons rather than live actors
feature film: a full-length movie
gross: bring a total income

- Read the questions. Ss discuss the questions in small groups.

2 CONVERSATION

Learning Objectives: *practice a conversation about working in the movies; see the passive in context*

A [CD 3, Track 19]

- Ask Ss to cover the text and describe the picture.

- ***Option:*** Ask: "Have you ever seen a movie being shot? Have you ever taken part in a movie?" If so, the class asks the S questions.

- Set the scene. Nina works on movies. Ryan is asking her how movies are made.

- Ask: "What do Ryan and Nina think about working on movies?" Play the first two lines of the audio program. Elicit answers. (Answer: He thinks it must be really exciting; she thinks it's hard work.)

- Ask: "Why is making movies 'hard work'?" Elicit suggestions. Play the audio program. Ss listen and take notes.

- Ss compare notes in pairs.

- Tell Ss to read the conversation to check their notes.

- Elicit or explain any new vocabulary.

Vocabulary

shoot: film
shot: filmed parts of a scene
angles: different views of the same scene
studio: the place where movies are filmed

- Play the audio program again. Ss listen and read or repeat.

- Ss practice the conversation in pairs.

> **TIP** To encourage Ss to look at each other while practicing Conversations, ask them to stand up and face each other. This also makes the conversation more active and natural.

- For another way to practice the conversation, try the ***Onion Ring*** technique – download it from the website.

- ***Option:*** Ask questions like these: "Did you just learn anything new about how movies are made? Would you like to visit a film studio? Would you like to work on movies? Why or why not?"

B [CD 3, Track 20]

- Explain the task. Read the question.

- Tell Ss to listen for the answer. Play the second part of the audio program. Elicit answers.

AudioScript

See page T-175.

Answers

The hours are dreadful.

3 GRAMMAR FOCUS

Learning Objective: *practice the passive to describe process*

▶ **[CD 3, Track 21]**

- Elicit that the basic passive is *be* + past participle. Review the reasons for using the passive:

  a. we don't know who does the action
  b. it's not important who does the action

Passive with modals

- Write these sentences on the board. Ask Ss to find them in the Conversation on page 92 and complete them:

  Lots of different shots _____ . *(have to be taken)*

  One scene _____ from five or six angles. *(may be shot)*

- Explain or elicit the rule. Write it on the board: modal + *be* + past participle

- Play the audio program. Ss listen and read or repeat.

A

- Explain the task. Model the first sentence.

- Ss complete the task individually or in pairs. Remind Ss to use *be* + past participle. Go around the class and give help as needed.

- Elicit or explain any new vocabulary.

Answers

Before filming
To complete the script, it has to **be divided** into scenes, and the filming details need to **be written out**. First, an outline of the script has to **be prepared**.
Next, actors **are chosen**, locations **are picked**, and costumes **are designed**. Filming can then begin.
Then the outline **is expanded** into a script.
After the script **is completed**, a director must **be hired**.
During and after filming
The final film you see on the screen **is created** by the director and editor out of thousands of different shots.
Soon after the film has been edited, music **is composed** and sound effects may **be added**.
After the filming **is finished**, the different shots can then **be put together** by the editor and director.
Once shooting begins, different shots **are filmed** separately. Scenes may **not be shot** in sequence.

B *Pair work*

- Explain the task. Model how to do the sequencing. Ask Ss to read the first sentence. Then Ss scan each sentence to find which event comes next.

- Suggest that Ss look for the same key words (e.g., *outline* and *script*, which appear in number 1, are also in number 2).

- Ss complete the task in pairs. Elicit responses.

Answers

(from top to bottom)
Before filming: 3, 1, 5, 2, 4
During and after filming: 9, 8, 7, 6

 For more practice, have Ss act out the sentences using *Mime* – download it from the website.

4 LISTENING

Learning Objective: *develop skills in listening for specific information*

A ▶ **[CD 3, Track 22]**

- Books open. Explain the task. Ss listen for what a producer does. Play the audio program.

AudioScript

See page T-175.

Possible answers

Things a producer does: A producer makes sure everything is done correctly, on time, and within the budget. A producer also does research, thinks up ideas for shows, and works with directors and performers.
Personality traits: A producer has to have a strong personality (to be in charge), be decisive, and work well under pressure.

B ▶ **[CD 3, Track 23]**

- Explain the task. Ss listen for the personality traits. Play the audio program again. Check responses.

GRAMMAR FOCUS

> ### The passive to describe process ⊙
>
> **is/are + past participle**
> A scene **isn't filmed** just once.
> Only the best shots **are used**.
>
> **Modal + be + past participle**
> One scene **may be shot** from five or six different angles.
> Lots of different shots **have to be taken**.

A The sentences below describe how a movie is made. First, complete the sentences using the passive. Then compare with a partner.

Before filming

☐ To complete the script, it has to .... (divide) into scenes, and the filming details need to .... (write out).

1 First, an outline of the script has to .... (prepare).

☐ Next, actors .... (choose), locations .... (pick), and costumes .... (design). Filming can then begin.

☐ Then the outline .... (expand) into a script.

☐ After the script .... (complete), a director must .... (hire).

During and after filming

☐ The final film you see on the screen .... (create) by the director and editor out of thousands of different shots.

☐ Soon after the film has been edited, music .... (compose) and sound effects may .... (add).

☐ After the filming .... (finish), the different shots can then .... (put together) by the editor and director.

6 Once shooting begins, different shots .... (film) separately. Scenes may .... (not shoot) in sequence.

B **PAIR WORK** Number the sentences in part A (before filming: from 1 to 5; during and after filming: from 6 to 9).

 4

LISTENING *I love my job!*

A ⊙ Listen to an interview with a TV producer. Write down three things a producer does.

Things a producer does	Personality traits
1.	....
2.	....
3.	....

B ⊙ Listen again. What are three personality traits a producer should have? Complete the chart.

5 SPEAKING Step by step

A PAIR WORK What do you think is required to prepare for a theater performance? Put the pictures in order and describe the steps. Use the vocabulary to help you.

make the costumes

rehearse the lines

build the sets

choose the actors

find a venue

write the script

A: Preparing for a theater performance requires many steps.
   First, the script must be written.
B: Right! And after that, the actors are chosen.
A: I agree. Then . . .

B PAIR WORK Choose one of these topics. Come up with as many steps as you can.

creating a student newspaper   planning a wedding   preparing for a rock concert
making a short video   preparing for a fashion show   putting on a school musical

C GROUP WORK Share your information from part B with another pair.

6 WRITING Describing a process

A Write about one of the topics from Exercise 5 or use your own idea. Describe the different steps in the process.

> Putting on a school musical requires a lot of planning. First, the director and production team must be chosen. Then the dates for the musical should be decided. After that, the actual musical can be chosen. Then auditions for the various roles can be held and . . .

B PAIR WORK Read your partner's paper. Can you think of any more steps?

5 SPEAKING

Learning Objective: *talk about steps in a process*

A *Pair work*

- Focus Ss' attention on the pictures and ask Ss to explain what happens at each stage, using the passive and the vocabulary given.

Vocabulary

performance: presentation of a play
rehearse: practice
sets: things built for a performance
venue: place for a performance or event

- Explain the task. Ask two Ss to help put the pictures in order. Remind Ss to use the passive to describe the process:

    T: Look at the first four pictures. Which one probably comes first when putting on a play?

    S1: I think it's the second picture. The script is rehearsed by the actors.

    S2: Yes, I agree. After that, the sets are built. That's the first picture.

    S1: Right. Then the next step is . . .

- Ss order the pictures in pairs. Allow Ss to add more steps in the process.

- Set a time limit of about five minutes. Go around the class and give help as needed. Note problems Ss are having, especially with passives.

- When time is up, write the more common problems on the board. Ask Ss to suggest corrections.

- Check the order. Then ask three Ss to model the conversation.

Possible answers

(as pictured from left to right)
A theater performance
6 The costumes are made.
3 The lines are rehearsed.
5 The sets are built.
2 The actors are chosen.
4 A venue is found.
1 The script is written.

B *Pair work*

- Explain the task.

- Ss choose another event to discuss. Ss work in groups to come up with as many steps as possible.

- For another way to practice this activity, try *Just One Minute* – download it from the website. Ss take turns coming up with as many steps as possible.

C *Group work*

- Each pair joins another pair. Ss take turns presenting their work. Ss discuss any missing steps.

- *Option:* Ask Ss to look at the pictures again. Then, without looking, Ss describe the steps from memory. Tell Ss to include any new steps.

6 WRITING

Learning Objective: *write about the steps in a process*

A

- Explain the task.

- Model the task. Ask Ss to look at the pictures in Exercise 5 as you read the example.

- Point out the passives in the example. Also point out the sequence markers. Remind Ss to use these, as well as time clauses (see Exercise 3 on page 73). Write suggestions on the board:

    <u>Sequence markers</u>

    first, second, next, then, after that, afterward, finally

    <u>Time-clause markers</u>

    before, once, after, as soon as

- Ss work individually to choose a topic. Remind Ss to brainstorm key words involved in the steps or process.

> **TIP** To prevent Ss from copying the model paragraph too closely, ask Ss to close their books after reading it.

- Next, Ss write their first draft.

- *Option:* The brainstorming and draft can be done as homework.

B *Pair work*

- Explain the task.

- Ss work in pairs. They give each other feedback. Ss exchange papers and point out any missing steps.

- Ss write a final draft. Remind Ss to use their partner's suggestions if they wish and their own ideas.

End of Cycle 1

See the Supplementary Resources chart at the beginning of this unit for additional teaching materials and student activities related to this Cycle.

7 WORD POWER

Learning Objective: *learn vocabulary for professions in the media*

A

- Elicit or explain that media are all the ways to communicate and exchange information (e.g., *radio, TV, newspapers, magazines*).
- Explain the task. Elicit that *compound nouns* are made up of two nouns (e.g., *film + editor*) or an adjective and a noun (e.g., *foreign + correspondent*).
- Ss work individually to complete the chart. Point out that more than one answer is possible.
- Go over answers with the class.

> **Possible answers**
>
> Film jobs: film composer, movie extra, stunt person
> Publishing jobs: editorial director, page designer, photo editor
> TV jobs: newscaster, sitcom writer, talk show host
> Computer jobs: computer programmer, network installer, software designer

B *Group work*

- Explain the task. Read the question and example.
- Ss complete the task in groups. They describe the occupations in part A.
- **Option:** Have Ss choose one of the jobs from the chart and do research online to find out more about it. Have Ss report back to their group or the class with three additional details about that job.
- For more practice with the vocabulary, play ***Twenty Questions*** – download it from the website. Ss think of a media profession.

 8 PERSPECTIVES

Learning Objective: *see defining and non-defining relative clauses in context*

A ▶ *[CD 3, Track 24]*

- Books closed. Write the occupations on the board. Ss work in pairs to guess what each person does.
- Set the scene. Ss will hear a quiz show. As Ss hear each job description, they call out the occupation.
- Play the audio program. Ss call out the answers.
- Books open. Play the audio program again. Ss write the answers. Go over answers with the class.

> **Answers**
>
> 1. location scout   3. prop designer   5. dialect coach
> 2. casting director   4. screenwriter   6. script doctor

B

- Explain the task. Ss choose the occupations they think would be interesting. Encourage Ss to say *why* the jobs would be interesting.
- For more practice with vocabulary for jobs, try ***Vocabulary Steps*** – download it from the website.

9 PRONUNCIATION

Learning Objective: *notice and review stress in compound nouns*

A ▶ *[CD 3, Track 25]*

- Explain the task. Remind Ss that the first word in a compound noun usually has stronger stress, but that there are some exceptions to this rule.
- Play the audio program. Have Ss mark the stress that they hear on each word.

- Elicit answers. Then play the audio program again. Ss listen and repeat.

B

- Explain the task. Ss identify the compound nouns in the sentences in Exercise 8.
- Ss read the sentences to a partner.
- Go around the class and have different Ss read the sentences aloud. Correct any pronunciation problems.

WORD POWER *Media professions*

A What kind of jobs are these? Complete the chart with the compound nouns.

computer programmer   network installer   photo editor   software designer
editorial director   newscaster   movie extra   stunt person
film composer   page designer   sitcom writer   talk show host

Film jobs	Publishing jobs	TV jobs	Computer jobs
....	....	....	....
....	....	....	....
....	....	....	....

B GROUP WORK Choose four jobs from part A and describe what they do.

"A computer programmer writes the instructions that direct computers to process information."

 PERSPECTIVES *Quiz show*

A ⊙ Listen to a quiz show. Can you guess the occupations?

casting director	**1.** A _____, who finds appropriate places to shoot scenes, gets to travel all over the world.
location scout	**2.** A _____ is someone who chooses an actor for each part in a movie.
screenwriter	**3.** A _____, who makes sure that everything on a movie set looks realistic, creates the objects that the characters use.
dialect coach	**4.** A _____ is someone who develops and expands a story idea into a full movie script.
prop designer	**5.** A _____ is a language specialist who works with actors on their accents.
script doctor	**6.** A _____, who is used when an original screenplay needs more work, makes jokes funnier and dialogs more realistic.

B Which of the jobs in part A do you think would be the most interesting? Why? Tell the class.

 PRONUNCIATION *Review of stress in compound nouns*

A ⊙ Listen and practice. Notice how the first word in a compound noun usually receives greater stress.

newscaster   photo editor   movie extra   sitcom writer   stunt person

B Practice the sentences in Exercise 8. Pay attention to the word stress in the compound nouns.

> **Defining and non-defining relative clauses** ▶
>
> *Defining relative clauses are used to identify people.*
>
> A dialect coach is a language specialist. ⟶ A dialect coach is a language specialist **who/that**
> She works with actors on their accents. **works with actors on their accents**.
>
> *Non-defining relative clauses give further information about people.*
>
> A location scout finds places to shoot ⟶ A location scout, **who finds places to**
> scenes. He travels all over the world. **shoot scenes**, travels all over the world.

A Do these sentences contain defining (**D**) or non-defining (**ND**) clauses? Add commas to the non-defining clauses. Then compare with a partner.

a stunt person

1. A stunt person is someone who "stands in" for an actor during dangerous scenes. ....
2. A computer-graphics supervisor who needs advanced technical knowledge often spends millions of dollars on computer graphics. ....
3. A stagehand is the person who moves the sets on stage in a theater production. ....
4. A movie producer who controls the budget decides how money will be spent. ....

B Add the non-defining relative clauses in parentheses to the sentences.

1. A movie extra appears in the background scenes. (who never has any lines)

   ....
   ....

2. A newscaster presents the news and introduces videos from reporters. (who should be trustworthy)

   ....
   ....

3. A photo editor selects the photos that go into magazines. (who is responsible for the quality and content of images)

   ....
   ....

4. A film composer must know music theory and interpretation. (who writes the background music for movies)

   ....
   ....

C Write three sentences with relative clauses about jobs you know. Compare with a partner.

11 INTERCHANGE 14 *Who makes it happen?*

What kinds of people does it take to make a movie? Go to Interchange 14 on page 129.

10 GRAMMAR FOCUS

Learning Objective: *practice defining and non-defining relative clauses*

 [CD 3, Track 26]

Defining and non-defining relative clauses

- Focus Ss' attention on the Perspectives on page 95. Ask Ss to underline the relative clause (i.e., the part beginning with *who* or *that*) in each sentence.

- Explain that there are two types of relative clauses: defining and non-defining relative clauses. Point out the differences between them:

  1. **Defining relative clause:** The information in the clause is necessary. It shows us which person is being described or talked about.

     The actor <u>who starred in that movie</u> is very talented.

  2. **Non-defining relative clause:** The information isn't necessary. It is extra information that is added to the sentence.

     Tom Cruise, <u>who starred in that movie</u>, is very talented.

> **TIP** To help Ss remember the difference between two structures, write the two examples using different colored chalk or markers.

- Again focus Ss' attention on the Perspectives. Ss decide whether the clauses are necessary to the sentences (defining) or extra information (non-defining).

- Ask Ss to label each sentence Defining (**D**) or Non-defining (**ND**). (Answers: D – 2, 4, 5; ND – 1, 3, 6)

- Point out that commas are used before and after a non-defining relative clause.

- **Option:** To check Ss' comprehension, ask Ss to give a quick summary of the rules.

- Play the audio program. Ss listen and read or repeat.

- For more practice with relative clauses, play **Run For It!** – download it from the website. Read out sentences that contain defining and non-defining relative clauses.

A

- Explain the task. Model the first sentence.

- Ss complete the task individually. They decide if clauses are defining or non-defining. Remind Ss to add commas to non-defining clauses. Go around the class and give help as needed.

- Go over answers with the class.

> **Answers**
>
> 1. D
> 2. ND: A computer-graphics supervisor, who needs advanced technical knowledge, often spends millions of dollars on computer graphics.
> 3. D
> 4. ND: A movie producer, who controls the budget, decides how money will be spent.

B

- Explain the task. Model the first sentence.

- Ss complete the task individually. They add non-defining relative clauses. Remind Ss to add commas in the correct places. Go around the class and give help as needed.

- Ask an early finisher to write the answers on the board. Go over answers with the class.

> **Answers**
>
> 1. A movie extra, who never has any lines, appears in the background scenes.
> 2. A newscaster, who should be trustworthy, presents the news and introduces videos from reporters.
> 3. A photo editor, who is responsible for the quality and content of images, selects the photos that go into magazines.
> 4. A film composer, who writes the background music for movies, must know music theory and interpretation.

C

- Explain the task.

- Ss work individually. Ss write three sentences with relative clauses about jobs they know. Point out that they do not have to be media jobs.

- Ss compare their sentences in pairs.

11 INTERCHANGE 14

See page T-129 for teaching notes.

Learning Objectives: *develop skills in scanning; distinguish between main ideas and supporting ideas*

- Books closed. Ask if anyone knows what "Bollywood" is. If anyone answers "yes," let the rest of the class ask questions.
- Books open. Ask Ss to look at the picture. Read the pre-reading task. Tell Ss to scan the article to answer the question. Elicit answers from the class. (Answer: It was written for the general public.)
- Ss read individually. Remind them to mark any words or expressions they want clarified.

! For another way to teach vocabulary, try the *Vocabulary Mingle* – download it from the website.

- Elicit or explain any new vocabulary.

Vocabulary

deserted: having no people
shelter: housing; protection from the weather
spooky: frightening; eerie
defenseless: helpless; with no power
elaborate song-and-dance number: long, fancy entertainment routine
pack into: enter a crowded place
runs: lasts
melodramatic: exaggerated; with strong feelings
flashy: expensive and showy
twirl around: spin; dance in circles
triumphs: beats; wins over
villain: bad guy
beloved: appreciated with strong affection

A

- Explain the task. Model the task with the first question.
- Ss complete the task individually, then they compare answers in pairs.
- Go over answers with the class.

Answers

1. While Bollywood is as old as Hollywood, Bollywood is much bigger.
2. Bollywood produces more than 1,100 films every year.
3. A typical Bollywood movie is about three hours long.
4. The stars of Bollywood movies are beloved by audiences throughout Asia, Africa, and the Middle East.

B

- Explain the task. Model how to find the first sentence in the article. Elicit that the paragraph number is in parentheses.
- Contrast *main idea* (a general idea that covers the topic of a paragraph) and *supporting idea* (a specific point that adds information to or an explanation of the main idea).
- Ss complete the task individually. Point out that ellipses (. . .) indicate omitted text.
- Then Ss compare answers in pairs.
- Go over answers with the class.

Answers

1. Main idea
2. Supporting idea
3. Main idea
4. Supporting idea
5. Main idea

- **Option:** Assign each S a paragraph. Ss change two facts in their paragraph. Then they read their "changed" text to the class. Ss try to spot the incorrect facts.

C Group work

- Explain the task. Read the questions.
- Ask: "Who has seen a Bollywood movie?" Include one person who has seen a Bollywood movie in each pair. It may be necessary for Ss to work in small groups instead of pairs.
- **Option:** If no one has seen a Bollywood movie, offer alternative discussion questions about movie types (e.g., *Do you like animated movies / science fiction movies / documentaries / musicals? Why or why not?*).
- Ss discuss the question in pairs or small groups. Remind Ss to ask follow-up questions and to add information.

End of Cycle 2

See the Supplementary Resources chart at the beginning of this unit for additional teaching materials and student activities related to this Cycle and for assessment tools.

Hooray for Bollywood!

Scan the article. Who do you think it was written for?
☐ people in the film industry ☐ the general public ☐ fans of Bollywood movies

1 A storm forces a plane to make an emergency landing on a deserted island. The only shelter is a spooky house, where a murderer begins killing passengers. So what do these defenseless people do? They have a beach party and perform an elaborate song-and-dance number.

2 This is the world of Bollywood. The scene described above is from the classic Indian film *Gumnaam*, which was made in the 1960s. It is typical of the kind of movies that are still made in India today.

3 For as long as Hollywood has existed, there has also been an Indian film industry. Because it is based in Mumbai (formerly Bombay), it is popularly called Bollywood – from the words Bombay and Hollywood. While it is as old as Hollywood, it is much bigger. Bollywood currently has the largest movie industry in the world. It produces more than 1,100 films a year – and as many as 20 million people a day pack into movie theaters to see Bollywood films.

4 While there are many types of films made in India, the most popular are the movies made in Bollywood. The films, which are made in the

Hindi language, generally deal with Indian history and social issues. The average Bollywood film runs about three hours but audiences don't seem to mind the length. The stories are melodramatic: Heroes drive around in flashy cars, actresses twirl around in beautiful costumes, and the poor boy always triumphs against the rich villain. They also feature many musical numbers, usually love songs.

5 Although the films may seem exaggerated to some, that's not how most filmgoers feel. These movies and their stars are beloved by audiences throughout Asia, Africa, and the Middle East. "Every South Asian grows up with some kind of connection to Bollywood," notes Indian writer Suketu Mehta. "In certain ways, it's what unites us."

A Read the article. Find and underline a sentence in the article that answers each question below.

1. How does Bollywood compare to Hollywood?
2. How many Bollywood films are made every year?
3. How long is a typical Bollywood movie?
4. How do audiences feel about the stars of Bollywood movies?

B Find these sentences in the article. Decide whether each sentence is the main idea or a supporting idea in that paragraph. Check (✓) the correct boxes.

	Main idea	Supporting idea
1. This is the world of Bollywood. (par. 2)	☐	☐
2. It produces more than . . . to see Bollywood films. (par. 3)	☐	☐
3. While there are many . . . made in Bollywood. (par. 4)	☐	☐
4. The average Bollywood film . . . mind the length. (par. 4)	☐	☐
5. Although the films may seem . . . filmgoers feel. (par. 5)	☐	☐

C **GROUP WORK** Have you ever seen a Bollywood movie? If so, how did you like it?

Units 13–14 Progress check

SELF-ASSESSMENT

How well can you do these things? Check (✓) the boxes.

I can	Very well	OK	A little
Understand and speculate about past events (Ex. 1)	☐	☐	☐
Make judgments and suggestions about past events (Ex. 2)	☐	☐	☐
Describe processes (Ex. 3)	☐	☐	☐
Describe people's appearance, personality, and typical behavior (Ex. 4)	☐	☐	☐

1 LISTENING *Where did it take place?*

A Listen to three conversations. Where do you think each conversation takes place? What do you think might have happened? Take notes.

Where the conversation takes place	What might have happened
1.	....
2.	....
3.	....

B PAIR WORK Compare your notes. Decide on what happened.

2 DISCUSSION *Tricky situations*

A PAIR WORK React to these situations. First, make a judgment or suggestion using a past modal. Then add another statement using the reaction in parentheses.

1. John was driving too fast, and the police stopped him. (a warning)
2. Lisa got an F on her English test. (a criticism)
3. Bill went shopping and spent too much money. (an excuse)
4. Crystal is late to class every morning. (a suggestion)
5. Oscar studied all night for his final exam and didn't sleep at all. (a prediction)

"John shouldn't have driven so fast. He'd better be careful, or . . ."

B GROUP WORK Join another pair and compare your comments. Who has the most interesting reaction to each situation?

Units 13–14 Progress check

SELF-ASSESSMENT

Learning Objectives: *reflect on one's learning; identify areas that need improvement*

- Ask: "What did you learn in Units 13 and 14?" Elicit Ss' answers.
- Ss complete the Self-assessment. Encourage them to be honest, and point out they will not get a bad grade if they check (✓) "a little."

- Ss move on to the Progress check exercises. You can have Ss complete them in class or for homework, using one of these techniques:
  1. Ask Ss to complete all the exercises.
  2. Ask Ss: "What do you need to practice?" Then assign exercises based on their answers.
  3. Ask Ss to choose and complete exercises based on their Self-assessment.

LISTENING

Learning Objective: *assess one's ability to listen to, understand, and express degrees of certainty using past modals*

A ▶ [CD 3, Track 27]
- Explain the task.
- Ss work individually to complete the chart. Play the audio program two or three times. Pause between conversations for Ss to write. Remind Ss to write notes, not complete sentences.
- Don't check answers before completing part B.

> **AudioScript**
>
> See page T-176.

- **Option**: For lower-level classes, ask Ss to listen first for "where" and then for "what."

B *Pair work*
- Explain the task.
- Ss work in pairs to compare notes from part A. Remind Ss to use modal expressions (e.g., *It could have taken place . . . They might have . . . She must have . . . He may have . . .*).
- Ask Ss to share ideas with the class.

> **Possible answers**
>
> (for parts A and B)
> 1. at a restaurant/café: The waiter might have given bad service. The chef may have been new, and the food might have tasted terrible.
> 2. in an elevator: The man must have gotten stuck in the elevator. The elevator might have malfunctioned.
> 3. in a car: The car may not have been fixed properly. The car might be having engine trouble.

DISCUSSION

Learning Objectives: *assess one's ability to give opinions and advice using past modals; assess one's ability to react to different situations*

A *Pair work*
- Explain the task.
- Read the example warning. Point out the past modal in the example. Elicit additional warnings from the class.
- Ss work in pairs to react to each situation. Go around the class to check use of past modals and give help as needed.

B *Group work*
- Explain the task.
- Each pair joins another pair. Ss take turns reading their sentences. The other Ss comment on the opinions or advice.
- Ask groups to share comments with the class.

3 GAME

Learning Objective: *assess one's ability to use the passive to describe process with* be *and modals*

A Group work

- Explain the task. Ask Ss to read the opening and closing sentences of each topic.
- Ss work in small groups. Ask each group to choose one process. Tell Ss to describe the entire process orally before they write.
- Ss write the steps in the process. Remind Ss to use passives and modals. Ss can use a separate sheet of paper if needed.
- Go around the class to check sentences and to give help as needed.

B Class activity

- Explain the task. Ask: "Who has more than five steps? More than six steps?" until you find the group with the most steps. Ask that group to read the steps to the class.
- **Option:** Ask each group to read their steps. Award one point for each step that correctly uses the passive. The group with the most points "wins."
- **Option:** Each pair joins another pair. Ss in one pair take turns reading the steps in the process. Ss in the other pair mime the actions. Then the pairs switch roles.

4 SPEAKING

Learning Objective: *assess one's ability to describe people with defining and non-defining relative clauses*

A

- Explain the task. Model the task by completing two or three sentences about someone in your life.
- Ss work individually to write their statements. Go around the class and give help as needed.

B Pair work

- Explain the task. Ask two Ss to model the conversation. Point out the follow-up question.

- Ss compare their answers in pairs.
- Ask Ss to share interesting things they learned about people in their partner's life.
- **Option:** Ss write a paragraph about one of the people in part A. Ss can exchange paragraphs, post them around the room, or hand them in for you to check.

WHAT'S NEXT?

Learning Objective: *become more involved in one's learning*

- Focus Ss' attention on the Self-assessment again. Ask: "How well can you do these things now?"

- Ask Ss to underline one thing they need to review. Ask: "What did you underline? How can you review it?"
- If needed, plan additional activities or reviews based on Ss' answers.

3 GAME *From first to last*

A **GROUP WORK** Look at these topics. Set a time limit. Talk with your group and write as many steps as you can between the first and last parts of each process.

sending an email

making a cup of tea

First, the computer has to be turned on.

....
....
....
....

Finally, the email is delivered to the person's in-box.

First, some water must be boiled.

....
....
....
....

Finally, the tea has to be poured from the teapot into the cup.

B **CLASS ACTIVITY** Compare your answers. Which group has the most steps?

4 SPEAKING *People in your life*

A Complete these statements about people in your life.

My mother is a person who ....
My neighbor, who .... , always ....
My father is a .... who ....
My teacher, who .... , is ....
My best friend is someone that ....

B **PAIR WORK** Compare your answers. Ask two follow-up questions about each of your partner's statements.

A: My mother is a person who takes care of everyone's needs before her own.
B: Does she ever get tired of helping everyone but herself?

WHAT'S NEXT?

Look at your Self-assessment again. Do you need to review anything?

Unit 15 Supplementary Resources Overview

	After the following SB exercises	You can use these materials in class	Your students can use these materials outside the classroom
CYCLE 1	1 Snapshot		
	2 Perspectives		
	3 Grammar Focus		**SB** Unit 15 Grammar Plus focus 1 **SSD** Unit 15 Grammar 1 **ARC** Giving recommendations and opinions 1–2
	4 Discussion		
	5 Listening	**TSS** Unit 15 Listening Worksheet	
	6 Interchange 15	**TSS** Unit 15 Writing Worksheet	**WB** Unit 15 exercises 1–5
CYCLE 2	7 Word Power	**TSS** Unit 15 Vocabulary Worksheet	**SSD** Unit 15 Vocabulary 1–2 **ARC** Local concerns
	8 Conversation		**SSD** Unit 15 Speaking 1–2
	9 Grammar Focus	**TSS** Unit 15 Grammar Worksheet	**SB** Unit 15 Grammar Plus focus 2 **SSD** Unit 15 Grammar 2 **ARC** Tag questions for opinions 1–2
	10 Pronunciation	**TSS** Unit 15 Extra Worksheet	
	11 Listening		
	12 Writing		
	13 Reading	**TSS** Unit 15 Project Worksheet **VID** Unit 15 **VRB** Unit 15	**SSD** Unit 15 Reading 1–2 **SSD** Unit 15 Listening 1–3 **SSD** Unit 15 Video 1–3 **WB** Unit 15 exercises 6–9

Key

ARC: Arcade	**SB:** Student's Book	**SSD:** Self-study DVD-ROM	**TSS:** Teacher Support Site
VID: Video DVD	**VRB:** Video Resource Book	**WB:** Workbook	

My Plan for Unit 15

Use the space below to customize a plan that fits your needs.

With the following SB exercises	I am using these materials in class	My students are using these materials outside the classroom

With or instead of the following SB section	I am using these materials for assessment

There should be a law!

1 SNAPSHOT

It's Against the Law!

In the United States and Canada	In other countries

- In Arizona, you may go to prison for 25 years if you cut down a saguaro cactus.
- In New Britain, Connecticut, fire trucks must travel at 25 miles per hour even when going to a fire.
- In the state of Washington, it is illegal to pretend your parents are rich.
- In Canada, 35% of radio broadcasting time must have Canadian content.

- In Switzerland, it's an offense to hang clothes out to dry on a Sunday.
- In Australia, it is illegal to walk on the right side of footpaths.
- It is against the law not to flush a public toilet in Singapore.
- In Finland, taxi drivers must pay royalties if they play music for customers.

Sources: www.dumblaws.com

Which of these laws would you like to have in your city or country? Why?
Can you think of reasons for these laws?
Do you know of any other unusual laws?

2 PERSPECTIVES

A ▶ Listen to people make recommendations at a community meeting. Would you agree with these proposals if they were made in your community? Check (✓) your opinion.

Community Meeting Notes

	strongly agree	somewhat agree	disagree
1. Cyclists should be required to wear helmets.	☐	☐	☐
2. Pet owners shouldn't be allowed to walk dogs without a leash.	☐	☐	☐
3. People ought to be required to end parties at midnight.	☐	☐	☐
4. Something has got to be done to stop littering.	☐	☐	☐
5. People mustn't be permitted to park motorcycles on the sidewalks.	☐	☐	☐
6. Laws must be passed to control the noise from car alarms.	☐	☐	☐
7. Drivers should only be permitted to honk their horns in case of an emergency.	☐	☐	☐

B GROUP WORK Compare your opinions. If you have different opinions, give reasons for your opinions to try to get your classmates to agree with you.

There should be a law!

> *In this unit, students practice giving opinions about laws and social issues. In Cycle 1, students make recommendations using passive modals. In Cycle 2, students express opinions with tag questions.*

1 SNAPSHOT

Learning Objective: *talk about unusual laws*

Note: If possible, bring in a world map to help Ss find the places mentioned in the Snapshot.

- Introduce the topic of laws by asking Ss some questions about laws on marriage, driving, ID cards, etc., in their country (e.g., *How old do you have to be in order to get married?*). Check Ss' use of *must* and *have to*.
- Explain that this Snapshot is about unusual laws.
- Ss read individually. Encourage Ss to use context to guess the meaning of new words. Ss may check their dictionaries if they wish.
- Elicit or explain any remaining new vocabulary.

Vocabulary

cactus: a prickly plant that grows in the desert
illegal: not legal, against the law
pretend: act as if something is true when it is false
offense: a crime

flush: pull a lever or cord to make water go through a toilet
royalties: money that is paid to a musician (or writer, actor, or other performer) each time their work is sold, played, or performed

- Elicit some useful expressions from the Snapshot (e.g., *It's an offense to, It's against the law to, The law requires people to, It's illegal to,* etc.).
- Read the questions. Ss discuss the questions in groups. Model some imaginative answers:

T: Paul, why do you think it's an offense to hang clothes out to dry on a Sunday?

S1: Well, people who are going to religious services might not like to see that. For some people, Sunday is a day of rest.

S2: Yeah, or maybe the laundry hanging out to dry distracts drivers.

2 PERSPECTIVES

Learning Objective: *see recommendations and opinions in context*

A ▶ [CD 3, Track 28]

- Books closed. Write these categories on the board. With Ss, brainstorm some problems associated with these people:

  - people who have parties   - cyclists   - pet owners
  - motorcyclists   - people who litter   - car owners

- Set the scene. Some people are discussing the problems on the board. They are making recommendations about what should be done.
- Ask Ss to copy the points on the board. Play the audio program. Ss listen and number the problems in the order they are discussed.
- Books open. Ss read the recommendations and check the order. Point out that sentences 6 and 7 are both about car owners.
- Elicit or explain any remaining new vocabulary.

Vocabulary

helmet: a hard, protective hat
leash: a chain or leather strap used to lead a dog
honk: make a noise with a horn

> **TIP** To avoid teaching words that Ss already know, let Ss *tell you* what they need to know. Also, make the most of your Ss' knowledge: elicit meanings from them whenever possible.

- Elicit the meaning of "strongly agree," "somewhat agree," and "disagree." Explain that Ss should check only one box for each recommendation.
- Ss work in pairs. Tell Ss to re-read the recommendations and check (✓) their own opinions. Set a time limit of about five minutes. Go around the class and give help as needed.
- Take a class poll. Play the sentences again and ask Ss to raise their hands. What do most Ss think about these issues?

B Group work

- Explain the task. Encourage Ss to give reasons and come to a consensus, or get everyone to agree.
- Ss compare their opinions in groups.
- Ask Ss how easy or difficult it was to get group members to agree with their opinions. Ask for examples of how they persuaded people to have the same opinion about a proposal.

3 GRAMMAR FOCUS

Learning Objective: *practice giving recommendations and opinions with* ought to, should, have (got) to, *and* must

▶ *[CD 3, Track 29]*

- Focus Ss' attention on the Perspectives on page 100. Explain that passive modals were used for recommendations. If needed, remind Ss that a passive modal is modal + *be* + past participle.
- Ask Ss to underline the passive modal in each sentence.
- Point out that some opinions are stronger than others. Explain the following. Then write the chart on the board:
  1. We use *should* and *ought to* when we think something is a good idea.
  2. We use *must* and *have (got) to* when we think something is absolutely necessary. Note: It may even be a law.

A good idea	Absolutely necessary
should	must
ought to	have to/have got to

- Ask Ss to look at the Perspectives. Ask: "Which were considered 'absolutely necessary'?" (Answers: 4, 5, 6)
- Write these two sentences on the board. Ask if Ss can understand the difference:

  Cyclists should be required to wear a helmet.

  Cyclists must be required to wear a helmet.

- Play the audio program. Ss listen and read or repeat.

A

- Explain the task. Ask Ss to describe what is happening in the picture.
- Tell Ss to look at the first sentence. Ask: "Who thinks people *shouldn't* be allowed to use cell phones while driving? Who thinks people *should* be allowed to use cell phones while driving? Does anyone think

it *mustn't* be allowed?" Elicit possible answers for number 1.
- Give Ss time to read the issues.
- Elicit or explain any new vocabulary.

Vocabulary

periodic: from time to time
high-rise: tall building; having many stories
ban: prohibit; forbid
fur: animal skins

- Ss complete the task individually. Check answers, accepting any that are logical and grammatically correct.

Possible answers

1. People **shouldn't be allowed** to use cell phones while driving. (or: **mustn't be allowed**)
2. Young people **mustn't be permitted** to get married before age 15. (or: **shouldn't be permitted**)
3. Companies **ought to be required** to give workers periodic breaks. (or: **must be required**)
4. People **should be allowed** to have pets in high-rise apartments. (or: **shouldn't**)
5. Scientists **mustn't be permitted** to use animals for research. (or: **have got to be permitted**)
6. Laws **have got to be passed** to ban the sale of handguns. (or: **must be passed**)
7. The sale of fur products **should be prohibited**. (or: **shouldn't be permitted**).
8. Something **has to be done** to stop clubs from staying open so late. (or: **must be done**)

B *Group work*

- Explain the task. Ask three Ss to model the conversation.
- Ss work in pairs. Ss take turns reading their statements. Remind Ss to say whether they agree or not and to give reasons for their opinions.

 For more practice with recommendations and opinions, play *Mime* – download it from the website.

4 DISCUSSION

Learning Objective: *develop the skill of giving opinions*

A *Group work*

- Explain the task. Read the topics. Model the conversation with a S.
- Ask Ss to read the phrases in the box. Explain that these are polite ways of disagreeing.
- Elicit or explain any new vocabulary.

- Ss work individually. Set a time limit of about five minutes.
- Ss discuss their ideas in groups. Remind Ss to use passive modals and phrases such as *due to, because of, because, since.*
- **Option:** Adapt the discussion into an *aquarium*. See page T-68, Exercise 10, part C.

B *Class activity*

- Explain the task. Ss share the group's ideas.

3 GRAMMAR FOCUS

Giving recommendations and opinions ▶

When you think something is a good idea
Cyclists **should be required** to wear a helmet.
Pet owners **shouldn't be allowed** to walk dogs without a leash.
People **ought (not) to be required** to end parties at midnight.

When you think something is absolutely necessary
Laws **must be passed** to control the noise from car alarms.
People **mustn't be permitted** to park motorcycles on the sidewalks.
A rule **has to be made** to require cycling lanes on city streets.
Something **has got to be done** to stop littering.

A Complete the sentences positively or negatively. Choose a modal that shows how strongly you feel about these issues.

1. People .... (allow) to use cell phones while driving.
2. Young people .... (permit) to get married before age 15.
3. Companies .... (require) to give workers periodic breaks.
4. People .... (allow) to have pets in high-rise apartments.
5. Scientists .... (permit) to use animals for research.
6. Laws .... (pass) to ban the sale of handguns.
7. The sale of fur products .... (prohibit).
8. Something .... (do) to stop clubs from staying open so late.

B GROUP WORK Compare your statements. Do you agree with one another? If not, why not?

A: People shouldn't be allowed to use cell phones while driving. It's dangerous.
B: You may have a point, but laws shouldn't be passed to prevent it. That's too strict.
C: Maybe, but in my opinion, . . .

4 DISCUSSION What's your opinion?

A GROUP WORK Think of three reasons for, and three reasons against, each idea below. Then discuss your views. As a group, form an opinion about each idea.

imposing strict dress codes for students
requiring people to do volunteer work
paying teachers less when their students fail

offering a different opinion
That sounds interesting, but I think . . .
That's not a bad idea. On the other hand, I feel . . .
You may have a point. However, I think . . .

A: What do you think about imposing strict dress codes for students?
B: I think it's a terrible idea! Students shouldn't be required . . .

B CLASS ACTIVITY Share your group's opinions and reasons. Who has the most persuasive reasons for and against each position?

5 LISTENING *What should be done?*

A ▶ Listen to people discuss problems. What solutions do they suggest?
Take notes in the chart.

1. people talking loudly on cell phones in restaurants

2. car alarms going off at night

3. telemarketing salespeople calling too often

Solutions
1. ....
2. ....
3. ....

B GROUP WORK Do you agree or disagree with the solutions?
What do you think should be done about each problem?

6 INTERCHANGE 15 *You be the judge!*

What if you could make the rules? Go to Interchange 15 on page 130.

7 WORD POWER *Local concerns*

A PAIR WORK Which of these issues are problems in your community?
Check (✓) the appropriate boxes.

- bullying
- company outsourcing
- graffiti
- homelessness
- inadequate health care
- lack of affordable child care
- noise pollution
- overcrowded classrooms
- stray animals
- street crime

noise pollution

B GROUP WORK Join another pair of students. Which three problems
concern your group the most? What should or can be done about them?

LISTENING

Learning Objective: *develop skills in listening for specific information*

A [CD 3, Track 30]

- Ask Ss to cover the text and look only at the pictures. Ask: "What problems are illustrated here? How do you feel about these things?"

> **TIP** Use pre-listening activities to prepare Ss for a Listening. Brainstorming or discussing the topic, exploiting the picture and subtitle, and prediction tasks get Ss thinking about what they are going to hear.

- Text uncovered. Explain the task. Ask Ss to read the captions. Elicit or explain that *telemarketing* is unsolicited phone calls by people selling goods or services.
- Play the audio program, pausing after each discussion. Ss listen and complete the chart. Ask Ss to write full sentences.

AudioScript

See page T-176.

Answers

1. People with cell phones should be asked to leave them at the door.
2. People who park regularly on the street ought to be required to let their neighbors know their license plate number and their telephone number.
3. The telephone companies should offer a service that automatically blocks telemarketing calls.

B *Group work*

- Explain the task. Read the questions.
- Ss discuss the problems and solutions in groups. Remind Ss to disagree politely, give reasons, and ask follow-up questions.

INTERCHANGE 15

See page T-130 for teaching notes.

> **End of Cycle 1**

See the Supplementary Resources chart at the beginning of this unit for additional teaching materials and student activities related to this Cycle.

> **Cycle 2, Exercises 7–13**

WORD POWER

Learning Objective: *learn vocabulary for discussing social and health issues*

A *Pair work*

- Explain the task. Ask Ss to read the issues. Point out that these are examples of *social issues*.
- Use the picture to model the task. Write *lack of affordable child care* on the board. Elicit that *lack of* means "not enough." Ask: "Is there not enough affordable child care in your community?" If so, Ss check (✓) that box.
- Ss work in pairs. Tell Ss that they can respond to issues in their country if they wish.
- Elicit or explain any new vocabulary.

Vocabulary

bullying: intentionally frightening someone who is smaller or weaker (often a problem in schools)
outsourcing: hiring people outside the company to perform certain jobs

graffiti: words or pictures written or drawn illegally on walls of buildings and public property
inadequate: not acceptable; not up to minimum or basic standards; not able to meet basic needs
stray animals: dogs and cats that don't belong to anyone

- **Option:** Write these stress patterns on the board. Ask Ss to find the words that fit the patterns:

  Ｏo   (ethnic, conflict)
  Ｏoo   (company, outsourcing, homelessness)
  oＯo   (pollution, graffiti)
  oＯoo   (inadequate, affordable)

For more practice with the vocabulary, play *Tic-Tac-Toe* – download it from the website.

B *Group work*

- Explain the task. Read the questions.
- Each pair joins another pair. Go around the class and give help as needed.

8 CONVERSATION

Learning Objectives: *practice a conversation about social issues; see tag questions for opinions in context*

A [CD 3, Track 31]

- Use the picture to set the scene. Sarah is mailing some bills and telling Todd her problems. Ask: "What kinds of problems do you think Sarah has?" Ss brainstorm in pairs.
- **Option:** Ask Ss to cover the text and look only at the picture. Ask pairs to tell a story about the people in the picture. Encourage Ss to be creative!
- Tell Ss to listen for what is making life difficult for Sarah. Play the audio program several times. Ss listen and take notes.
- Ss to open their books and read the conversation. Ss check their notes.
- Elicit or explain any new vocabulary.

- Play the audio program again. Ss listen and read.
- Ss practice the conversation in pairs.
- ! Ss practice the conversation in pairs, using **Say It With Feeling!** – download it from the website.

B ▶ [CD 3, Track 32]

- Explain the task. Read the focus question.
- Play the audio program. Then elicit Ss' answers.

> ### AudioScript
> See page T-176.

> ### Answers
> Todd is concerned about what he's going to do after he graduates.

9 GRAMMAR FOCUS

Learning Objective: *practice tag questions for opinions*

▶ [CD 3, Track 33]

- Focus Ss' attention on how Sarah used tag questions in the previous Conversation. Explain that tag questions are used when we expect someone to agree with us or when we are asking for confirmation.
- Next, focus Ss' attention on the Grammar Focus box. Point out the difference between the two columns. Explain that when a statement is affirmative, the tag question is negative, and vice versa. For example: + / - Health insurance **is** really expensive, **isn't** it? - / + Child care **isn't** cheap, **is** it?
- Explain that when *be* is the main verb, *be* is also used in the tag question. Similarly, we use the same modal in the main clause and the tag (e.g., *We should pay our taxes, shouldn't we?*).
- However, simple present and past verbs use the auxiliary verb in the tag. Write these examples on the board:
  Graffiti *makes* everything look ugly, *doesn't* it?
  You *found* affordable child care, *didn't* you?
- Play the audio program. Ss listen and read or repeat.

A

- Explain the task.
- Ss complete the task individually. They complete the sentences with tag questions. Go around the class and give help as needed.

- Then Ss compare answers in pairs. Go over answers with the class.

> ### Answers
> 1. You can't escape advertising nowadays, **can you**?
> 2. There aren't any noise pollutions laws, **are there**?
> 3. School bullying is a major problem here, **isn't it**?
> 4. Overcrowded classrooms can be hard to manage, **can't they**?
> 5. The sales tax should be lowered, **shouldn't it**?
> 6. It isn't easy to save money these days, **is it**?
> 7. The city doesn't do enough for stray animals, **does it**?
> 8. There are more homeless people on the streets, **aren't there**?

B

- Explain the task. Read the question.
- Ss work individually. Set a time limit of about ten minutes. Go around the class and give help as needed.

C Group work

- Explain the task. Ask three Ss to model the conversation.
- Ss work in small groups. Ss take turns reading their statements and giving opinions on others'. Set a time limit of ten minutes.

CONVERSATION *It isn't cheap, is it?*

A ▶ Listen and practice.

Sarah: Health insurance, child-care bills, rent! Now that I'm going to school and only working part-time, I have a hard time making ends meet.

Todd: Health insurance is really expensive, isn't it?

Sarah: Yeah! My company used to pay for it when I was working full-time.

Todd: And child care isn't cheap, is it?

Sarah: No, it's not. After I pay for rent and groceries, almost all my money goes to pay for my son's day care.

Todd: Colleges should provide free day care for students with children.

Sarah: I think so, too. But they don't have any services like that at my school.

B ▶ Listen to the rest of the conversation. What is Todd concerned about?

9 GRAMMAR FOCUS

Tag questions for opinions ▶

Affirmative statement + negative tag	**Negative statement + affirmative tag**
Health insurance is really expensive, **isn't it**?	Child care isn't cheap, **is it**?
There are lots of criminals in the city, **aren't there**?	There aren't enough police, **are there**?
Graffiti makes everything look ugly, **doesn't it**?	People don't care about our city, **do they**?
Colleges should provide day care, **shouldn't they**?	You can't find affordable child care, **can you**?

A Add tag questions to these statements. Then compare with a partner.

1. You can't escape advertising nowadays, . . . ?
2. There aren't any noise pollution laws, . . . ?
3. School bullying is a major problem here, . . . ?
4. Overcrowded classrooms can be hard to manage, . . . ?
5. The sales tax should be lowered, . . . ?
6. It isn't easy to save money these days, . . . ?
7. The city doesn't do enough for stray animals, . . . ?
8. There are more homeless people on the streets, . . . ?

B What are some things you feel strongly about in your school or city? Write six statements with tag questions.

C **GROUP WORK** Take turns reading your statements. Other students respond by giving their opinions.

A: The food in the cafeteria is terrible, isn't it?
B: Yes, it is. They should get a new cook.
C: On the other hand, I like the hamburgers because . . .

10 PRONUNCIATION Intonation in tag questions

A ▶ Listen and practice. Use falling intonation in tag questions when you are giving an opinion and expect the other person to agree.

Street crime is a terrible problem, isn't it?

People should have access to quality health care, shouldn't they?

B **PAIR WORK** Take turns reading the statements with tag questions from Exercise 9, part A. Give your own opinions when responding.

11 LISTENING You agree, don't you?

A ▶ Listen to people give their opinions about current issues in the news. What issues are they talking about?

Issue	Opinions for	Opinions against
1.	....	....
	....	....
2.	....	....
	....	....

B ▶ Listen again. What opinions do you hear? Complete the chart.

C **GROUP WORK** What do you think about the issues in part A?

12 WRITING A new law

A Think about a local problem that needs to be solved, and write a persuasive essay suggesting a new law to help solve it. Be creative! Use these questions to help you.

What is the problem, and how does it affect your community?
What can be done to help solve it?
Who might disagree with you, and how will you convince them that your law is a good idea?

> I think students in our town should be required to wear school uniforms. Students shouldn't be permitted to wear the latest fashions because this promotes jealousy and competition. Also, students would be able to concentrate on their studies better if . . .

B **GROUP WORK** Try to convince your classmates to pass your new law. Then vote on it.

PRONUNCIATION

Learning Objective: *notice and use intonation in tag questions*

A [CD 3, Track 34]

- Explain that we use falling intonation on tag questions. This shows that we are giving an opinion, not asking a real question. Also, we expect the listener to agree with us.

- Play the audio program. Ss practice. Check Ss' individual pronunciation.

B *Pair work*

- Ss work in pairs. They take turns reading the tag questions from part A of Exercise 9. Remind Ss to respond with their own opinions.

 # LISTENING

Learning Objective: *develop skills in listening to opinions about issues in the news*

❗ To set the scene for the Listening, try *Cloud Prediction* – download it from the website. Use these words: 1. ban, research, cruel, killed, chimpanzees; 2. download, music, protected, file sharing, copying, CDs.

A [CD 3, Track 35]

- Explain the task.
- Tell Ss to listen and fill in the issues in the chart. Play the audio program. Pause between issues for Ss to complete the chart.

AudioScript

See page T-176.

Answers

1. stopping all research that uses animal subjects
2. downloading music off the Internet

B [CD 3, Track 36]

- Explain the task. Remind Ss to listen for key words and take notes.

- Tell Ss to listen and fill in the "for" opinions in the chart first. Play the audio program. Pause between issues for Ss to complete the chart. Ss listen and write.

- Play the audio program again. This time Ss fill in the "against" opinions.

- Ask Ss to write the answers on the board.

Possible answers

1. banning research using animals: *For (1)* it's cruel and unnecessary (2) animals shouldn't be killed so that professors can publish; *Against (1)* advances in medical research on diseases depends on animals (2) research can't be done on humans
2. downloading music off the Internet: *For (1)* people have a right to share with their friends (2) CDs are too expensive; *Against (1)* people should have to pay for their music (2) musicians depend on people buying music to make money

C *Group work*

- Explain the task.
- Ss work in groups. They discuss the issues in part A. Go around the class and listen in. Note errors to go over after the activity.

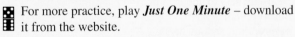 For more practice, play *Just One Minute* – download it from the website.

WRITING

Learning Objective: *write a persuasive essay suggesting a new law to help solve a local problem*

A

- Explain the task. Elicit or explain the meaning of *persuasive essay* (an essay that tries to get people to agree with your opinion or proposal).

- Focus Ss' attention on the picture. Ask Ss to predict what this essay is about. Then read the example essay. Point out the use of opinions and reasons.

- Read the focus questions. Give Ss a few minutes to choose a topic.

- Explain how to organize the essay. The first paragraph should include a brief description of the issue, the writer's opinions, and supporting reasons. The second paragraph should include a proposal for a new law, with recommendations on what needs to be done or reasons for why it will help solve the problem.

- After Ss generate ideas and organize their thoughts, have them write a first draft.

B *Group work*

- Explain the task. Encourage Ss to ask each other questions about the proposed laws or about their opinions. Have Ss vote by having them write "yes" or "no" on a slip of paper.

13 READING

Learning Objectives: *develop skills in scanning, sequencing, reading for main ideas, and critical thinking; read an article about plagiarism*

- Read the pre-reading question.
- Ss scan the article quickly. Ask Ss to raise their hands or look up when they are done.
- Elicit answers from the class. (Answer: *Plagiarism* is copying material without giving credit to the source or getting someone else to do your work.)
- Ask: "Where did you find the answer?" (Answer: The end of paragraph two poses the question, and it is answered directly in paragraph three.)
- Then ask: "What is the first paragraph about?" (Answer: a story about an incident of plagiarism) Point out that opening with a story to illustrate a broader issue is a common technique in magazine and newspaper articles.
- Ss read the article individually. Encourage Ss to guess the meaning of new words. Remind Ss to circle or underline words they can't guess from context.
- Ss work in pairs or groups to discuss marked words. Ss may look up definitions if needed.
- Elicit or explain any new vocabulary.

Vocabulary

school policy: rules of the school
school board: the government of the school system
resigned: quit her job
in protest: to show that she was unhappy with the decision
significant: important; large or well-known
giving credit to the source: saying where the material came from originally
a big deal: an important problem
clear-cut: easy to understand
deserve: earn or merit
severe: strict; serious; harsh

- *Option:* Assign the article for homework. Ask Ss to read it once or twice for comprehension. Then they should mark new vocabulary. Tell Ss to list the marked words, use a dictionary to check definitions, and write the definitions on the list. In class, Ss work in groups to discuss and compare their lists.

A

- Explain the task.
- Ss complete the task individually. They reread the article and number the events in sequence. Tell Ss to order the events as they happened in real time, not as described in the article.
- Go over answers with the class.

Answers

| a. 6 | b. 2 | c. 3 | d. 5 | e. 1 | f. 4 |

B

- Explain the task.
- Ss complete the task individually. They complete the chart with arguments from the reading. Then Ss compare charts with a partner. Ss may make changes if they wish.
- Go over answers with the class.

Possible answers

Arguments to justify plagiarism	Arguments against plagiarism
1. It's necessary to do well in school. 2. Everyone does it, so it's no big deal.	Students who plagiarize benefit unfairly. It is morally wrong because it is stealing.

- *Option:* Ss work with a partner and add their own ideas to the chart. Student A thinks of reasons to justify plagiarism; Student B thinks of arguments against.

C Group work

- Explain the task. Read the focus questions.
- Ss discuss the questions in small groups. Tell Ss they can discuss related issues if they wish.
- *Option:* Ss take notes as they talk. Then ask Ss to share ideas with the class.

End of Cycle 2

See the Supplementary Resources chart at the beginning of this unit for additional teaching materials and student activities related to this Cycle.

How Serious Is Plagiarism?

Read the title and first paragraph of the article. What do you think the word plagiarism *means?*

In 2002, a biology teacher in Kansas – a state in the American Midwest – made national, and even international, news. After Christine Pelton discovered that 28 of her 118 students had plagiarized parts of a major project, she gave them failing grades. Although this was the school policy, the students' parents complained. The school board directed Ms. Pelton to change the punishment: They told her that 600 points should be taken from the offenders, rather than the entire 1,800 points. Ms. Pelton resigned in protest.

Why did this become such a significant story? Perhaps it is because so many people feel strongly about what is right and wrong. The incident raised some important questions: What is plagiarism? How serious is it?

The simplest form of plagiarism occurs when someone copies material without giving credit to the source. However, there are also more serious forms, such as when a student pays someone else to write an essay.

Some people claim that copying is necessary to do well in school. They have realized that their own words are not as good as someone else's. Another common argument is that everyone does it, so it's not a big deal. In fact, it has been learned that even some highly respected figures, including Martin Luther King Jr., have plagiarized.

Although some people find reasons to justify plagiarism, others feel the issue is clear-cut: They feel it is morally wrong, and consider it stealing – a theft of ideas rather than money. These people believe that students who plagiarize benefit unfairly. They receive a better grade than they deserve.

So what about the incident in Kansas? Was the original punishment too severe? Do teachers have the right to tell students and parents what is right or wrong? Ms. Pelton would probably say that the job of a teacher is to do exactly that.

A Read the article. Then number these sentences from 1 (first event) to 6 (last event).

.... a. The teacher's story appeared in national news.
.... b. The teacher gave the students failing grades.
.... c. The students' parents were angry.
.... d. The teacher left her job.
.... e. The group of students cheated on an assignment.
.... f. The school board told the teacher to change the scores.

B Complete the chart with the arguments for and against plagiarism presented in the article.

Arguments to justify plagiarism	Arguments against plagiarism
1.	....
2.	....

C **GROUP WORK** Is it ever OK to copy other people's work? Why or why not?
Should teachers have the right to tell students and parents what is right or wrong?

Unit 16 Supplementary Resources Overview

	After the following SB exercises	You can use these materials in class	Your students can use these materials outside the classroom
CYCLE 1	1 Snapshot		
	2 Perspectives		
	3 Grammar Focus		**SB** Unit 16 Grammar Plus focus 1 **SSD** Unit 16 Grammar 1 **ARC** Complex noun phrases containing gerunds
	4 Pronunciation		**ARC** Stress and rhythm
	5 Interchange 16		
	6 Listening		
	7 Word Power	**TSS** Unit 16 Vocabulary Worksheet	**SSD** Unit 16 Vocabulary 1–2
	8 Discussion	**TSS** Unit 16 Writing Worksheet	**WB** Unit 16 exercises 1–5
CYCLE 2	9 Conversation		**SSD** Unit 16 Speaking 1
	10 Grammar Focus	**TSS** Unit 16 Grammar Worksheet	**SB** Unit 16 Grammar Plus focus 2 **SSD** Unit 16 Grammar 2 **ARC** Accomplishments and goals 1–2
	11 Listening	**TSS** Unit 16 Listening	
	12 Writing		
	13 Reading	**TSS** Unit 16 Extra Worksheet **TSS** Unit 16 Project Worksheet **VID** Unit 16 **VRB** Unit 16	**SSD** Unit 16 Reading 1–2 **SSD** Unit 16 Listening 1–3 **SSD** Unit 16 Video 1–3 **WB** Unit 16 exercises 6–8

With or instead of the following SB section	You can also use these materials for assessment
Units 15–16 Progress Check	**ASSESSMENT CD** Units 15–16 Oral Quiz **ASSESSMENT CD** Units 15–16 Written Quiz **ASSESSMENT CD** Units 9–16 Test

Key

ARC: Arcade	**SB:** Student's Book	**SSD:** Self-study DVD-ROM	**TSS:** Teacher Support Site
VID: Video DVD	**VRB:** Video Resource Book	**WB:** Workbook	

My Plan for Unit 16

Use the space below to customize a plan that fits your needs.

With the following SB exercises	I am using these materials in class	My students are using these materials outside the classroom

With or instead of the following SB section	I am using these materials for assessment

16 Challenges and accomplishments

1 SNAPSHOT

VOLUNTEER! What are you interested in? Consider these volunteering opportunities.

COSTA RICA

- helping at a wildlife center
- monitoring endangered birds
- assisting with reforestation
- teaching computer skills
- organizing environmental activities

THAILAND

- repairing rural roads
- building schools
- designing websites
- taking care of elephants
- working in rural health clinics

MOZAMBIQUE

- building houses
- working at an orphanage
- conducting health surveys
- teaching English
- working on a marine conservation project

Sources: www.volunteerabroad.com; www.kayavolunteer.com

Which project sounds the most interesting? the least interesting?
Can you think of any other interesting projects that volunteers could do?
Do you know anyone who has volunteered? What did they do?

2 PERSPECTIVES *Volunteers talk about their work.*

A ▶ Listen to people talk about their volunteer work. What kind of work do they do? Write the names in the sentences below.

> The most rewarding thing about helping them is learning from their years of experience.
> —*Paul*

> One of the most difficult aspects of working abroad is being away from my family.
> —*Sho-fang*

> One of the rewards of working with them is experiencing their youthful energy and playfulness.
> —*Mariela*

> The most challenging thing about doing this type of work is determining their strengths and weaknesses.
> —*Jack*

1. .... **teaches in a developing country.**
2. .... **tutors in an adult literacy program.**
3. .... **visits senior citizens in a nursing home.**
4. .... **plays games with children in an orphanage.**

B Which kind of volunteer work would you prefer to do? What do you think would be rewarding or challenging about it?

106

Challenges and accomplishments

> In this unit, Ss discuss the challenges and rewards in life. In Cycle 1, students discuss volunteer work using complex noun phrases with gerunds. In Cycle 2, students talk about things they have achieved and would like to achieve, using past and future tenses, including the future perfect.

 SNAPSHOT

Learning Objective: read about volunteering opportunities

- Books closed. Elicit the meaning of *volunteer* (someone who works for or helps an organization, but does not get paid). Elicit examples of the kind of work volunteers do and write Ss' suggestions on the board. (You can write a few ideas to get them started: teaching computer skills, repairing roads, building houses.)

- Books open. Ask Ss to cover up the text and look only at the pictures. Ask which volunteer work ideas listed on the board might be useful in these three places.

- Have Ss uncover the text and read the information. Have them check to see if any of the volunteer work opportunities they guessed from the board were listed in the Snapshot.

! For another way to present the Snapshot, try
● *Jigsaw Learning* – download it from the website. Each S reads about a volunteering opportunity and summarizes the information for the other two.

- Elicit or explain any new vocabulary.

Vocabulary

monitor: watch something carefully and record results
endangered: at the point of no longer existing as a species
assisting: helping
rural: country (not in the city)
orphanage: a home for children who do not have parents or whose parents cannot care for them
conduct: organize or do something (such as a study, survey, or experiment)
conservation: the protection of nature

- Read the questions. Ask Ss to think about their answers first.

- Ss work in pairs or small groups. They take turns sharing their responses.

 PERSPECTIVES

Learning Objectives: discuss volunteer work; see complex noun phrases containing gerunds in context

A ▶ [CD 3, Track 37]

- Books closed. Ask: "What are some things that might be difficult, or challenging, about volunteer work? What are some things that might be satisfying, or make you feel good?"

- Books open. Explain the task. Ask Ss to read Paul's experience and write his name in the correct sentence. Ask Ss which words were clues.

- Play the audio program, pausing after each speaker. Remind Ss to look for clues (e.g., *years of experience* tells us this sentence refers to older people).

- Go over answers with the class.

- Elicit or explain any new vocabulary.

Vocabulary

rewarding: satisfying; causing good feelings
aspects: points; areas
abroad: in a foreign country
youthful: young

playfulness: wanting to have fun or a good time
determining: finding
developing country: a country that has little money or industry but is growing economically
literacy program: a course to teach people how to read
senior citizen: a person over age 65
nursing home: a type of home for people who need long-term medical care

Answers

1. Shao-fang   2. Jack   3. Paul   4. Mariela

- Play the audio program again if needed. Ss listen and read or repeat.

B

- Explain the task. Read the questions.

- Ss work in pairs or small groups. Ss take turns sharing their responses.

3 GRAMMAR FOCUS

Learning Objective: *practice ways of forming sentence subjects that include complex noun phrases with gerunds*

▶ ***[CD 3, Track 38]***

- Books closed. Dictate these two sentence starters: "One of the most difficult aspects of working abroad . . . The most rewarding thing about helping them . . ."
- Explain that these are examples of complex noun phrases with gerunds. They are made up of three parts:

  a. a noun phrase (e.g., the nouns *aspects* and *thing*, and all the words that come before them). Ask Ss to underline the noun phrases (e.g., *one of the most difficult aspects, the most rewarding thing*).

  b. a preposition (e.g., *of, about*). Ask Ss to draw a box around the two prepositions.

  c. a gerund (e.g., *working, helping*). Ask Ss to circle the gerunds.

- ***Option:*** Use three cards of different colors. Write on the cards: (1) *one of the most difficult aspects* (2) *of* (3) *working abroad.* Use this to help Ss visualize the three parts of a complex noun phrase with a gerund.
- Books open. Focus Ss' attention on the Grammar Focus box. Read the first sentence. Point out that the whole **boldface** section is the <u>subject</u> of the sentence!
- Play the audio program. Ss listen and read or repeat.

A ***Pair work***

- Explain the task.
- Ss complete the first task individually. They match each question with the best response. Go around the class and give help as needed.

- Write answers on the board and ask Ss to check their own work.

Answers

1. g   2. f   3. d   4. a   5. c   6. b   7. e

- Explain the second task. Ask two Ss to model the conversation.
- Ss work in pairs. They take turns asking and answering the questions.

B ***Group work***

- Explain the task. Model the task by asking different Ss to respond to number 1 in part A:

  T: What's the most challenging thing about working from home?

  S1: I can work whenever I want, but sometimes I don't know when to stop. It's hard to leave work when you live with it!

- ***Option:*** Ss work individually to write their own responses. Go around the class and give help as needed.
- Ss work in small groups. Ss take turns asking questions and giving their own answers. Encourage Ss to agree and disagree, ask follow-up questions, and add information.
- Go around the class and listen in. Note any problems. After the activity, write some of the problems on the board. Elicit ideas for corrections from Ss.
- For more practice, play the ***Chain Game*** – download it from the website. Choose a starting sentence that your Ss can relate to (e.g., *the worst thing about being a teenager/student/office worker/homemaker is . . .*).

4 PRONUNCIATION

Learning Objective: *notice and use stress and rhythm*

A ▶ ***[CD 3, Track 39]***

- Remind Ss that usually only key words are stressed in a sentence. These stressed words occur with regular rhythm.
- Play the audio program. Ss listen and focus on sentence stress and rhythm.
- Play the audio program again. Ss listen and repeat. If needed, clap your hands in time to the stress. Ss clap with you.

❗ For another way to practice stress and rhythm, try ***Walking Stress*** – download it from the website. (Note: When practicing the first sentence, Ss should

place their foot on the floor on the syllables *ward, trav, learn,* and *cult*.)

B ***Pair work***

- Explain the task. Ss practice saying the sentences in the Grammar Focus box, using correct stress and rhythm.
- ***Option:*** For more practice, Ss can practice saying the sentences in the Perspectives on page 106.

> **TIP** To reduce anxiety, tell Ss to say the sentences faster and faster. This is fun and forces Ss to say non-stressed sounds with the schwa /ə/ sound.

3 GRAMMAR FOCUS

> ### Complex noun phrases containing gerunds
>
> **The most rewarding thing about helping them** is learning from their years of experience.
> **One of the most difficult aspects of working abroad** is being away from my family.
> **One of the rewards of working with them** is experiencing their youthful energy.

A **PAIR WORK** Match the questions and responses. Then ask and answer the questions. Respond using a complex noun phrase followed by a gerund.

Questions

1. What's the most challenging thing about working from home? ....
2. What's the best thing about being a police officer? ....
3. What's one of the rewards of being a teacher? ....
4. What's one of the most difficult things about being an emergency-room nurse? ....
5. What's one of the most interesting aspects of working abroad? ....
6. What's one of the most difficult aspects of doing volunteer work? ....
7. What's the hardest part about being overseas? ....

Responses

a. dealing with life-or-death situations every day
b. finding enough time to do it on a regular basis
c. learning how people in other cultures live and think
d. helping people learn things that they couldn't learn on their own
e. not talking with my family regularly
f. getting to know people from all parts of society
g. not being distracted by household chores or hobbies

A: What's the most challenging thing about working from home?
B: The most challenging thing about working from home is not being distracted by household chores or hobbies.

B **GROUP WORK** Ask the questions in part A again and answer with your own ideas.

4 PRONUNCIATION *Stress and rhythm*

A ⊙ Listen and practice. Notice how stressed words and syllables occur with a regular rhythm.

The most rewarding thing │ about traveling │ is learning │ about other cultures.

The most frustrating thing │ about working │ in a foreign country │ is missing │ friends and family.

B **PAIR WORK** Take turns reading the sentences in the grammar box in Exercise 3. Pay attention to stress and rhythm.

5 INTERCHANGE 16 *Viewpoints*

Take a survey about volunteering. Go to Interchange 16 on page 131.

6 LISTENING *Challenges and rewards*

▶ Listen to these people talk about their work. What is the biggest challenge of each person's job? What is the greatest reward? Complete the chart.

	Biggest challenge	Greatest reward
1. psychologist	....	....
2. camp counselor	....	....
3. firefighter	....	....

7 WORD POWER *Antonyms*

A Complete the pairs of opposites with the words in the box. Then compare with a partner.

compassionate	cynical	dependent	rigid	timid	unimaginative

1. adaptable   ≠ ....
2. courageous ≠ ....
3. insensitive ≠ ....
4. resourceful   ≠ ....
5. self-sufficient ≠ ....
6. upbeat   ≠ ....

B GROUP WORK How many words or things can you associate with each word in part A?

A: What words or things do you associate with *adaptable*?
B: Flexible.
C: Easy to get along with.

8 DISCUSSION *Rewarding work*

GROUP WORK What are the special challenges and rewards of working in these situations? Would you ever consider working in one of these areas? Why or why not?

working with animals
teaching gifted children
cooking food at a homeless shelter
working for a nonprofit organization
working in a home for the visually impaired

A: I suppose the most challenging thing about working with animals is . . .
B: But one of the rewards of working with animals must be . . .

INTERCHANGE 16

See page T-131 for teaching notes.

 LISTENING

Learning Objective: *develop skills in listening for main ideas and taking notes*

 [CD 3, Track 40]

- Books closed. Write the three jobs on the board:
  psychologist   camp counselor   firefighter
- Ask: "What do you think is the biggest challenge of each job? What is the greatest reward?" Ask Ss to predict what they will hear.
- For another way to predict, play **Prediction Bingo** – download it from the website.
- Tell Ss to listen for the answers to the questions. Play the audio program. Ss listen and take notes.

AudioScript

See page T-177.

- Give Ss time to fill in the chart.
- Elicit Ss' answers. Ask Ss to give full sentences.

Answers

1. listening to people talk about their problems all day; seeing patients making real progress
2. getting kids with problems to trust him and open up; seeing kids develop confidence and a sense of self-worth
3. going into a burning building; getting someone out safely

- Ask: "Which job would you prefer to do? Why?"
- Ss discuss the questions in pairs or as a class.

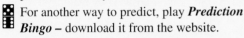 **WORD POWER**

Learning Objective: *learn antonyms and vocabulary for personality types*

A

- Elicit that the word *antonyms* means "opposites."
- Ask Ss to read the words. Elicit or explain that they are adjectives that describe people.
- Ss work individually or in pairs to fill in the blanks. Ss compare answers in pairs.

Answers

1. rigid
2. timid
3. compassionate
4. unimaginative
5. dependent
6. cynical

- **Option:** Ss decide if the adjectives are positive (**P**) or negative (**N**) (e.g., *cynical = N; upbeat = P*).

B Group work

- Explain the task. Ask three Ss to model the conversation.
- Ss work in groups. They associate words with the adjectives in part A. Tell Ss to make whatever associations come to mind.
- For more practice with antonyms, try **Vocabulary Tennis** – download it from the website.

 DISCUSSION

Learning Objective: *develop skills in giving opinions*

Group work

- Explain the task. Ask Ss to read the four jobs.

Vocabulary

gifted children: highly intelligent or talented children
homeless shelter: a place where people with no home can stay temporarily
nonprofit organization: an organization or company whose goal is not to make money for itself but instead to provide a charitable service

visually impaired: blind

- Ask two Ss to read the conversation.
- Ss discuss the jobs in small groups. Encourage Ss to think of at least three challenges and rewards for each job.

End of Cycle 1

See the Supplementary Resources chart at the beginning of this unit for additional teaching materials and student activities related to this Cycle.

9 CONVERSATION

Learning Objectives: *practice a conversation about accomplishments and goals; see verb tenses in context*

A ⏵ [CD 3, Track 41]

- Books closed. Elicit or explain that in some cultures, turning 21 marks a rite of passage into adulthood.
- Ask questions to stimulate discussion on goals and accomplishments:
  For Ss under 21 years old
  How do you think you'll feel when you're 21?
  What major plans do you want to achieve?
  For Ss over 21 years old
  How did you feel when you turned 21?
  What goals did you have at that time?
  Have you accomplished a lot since then? What?
- Set the scene. Alison is 21 today. She is talking to her uncle about what she's achieved and what her plans are.

- Tell Ss to listen to find out how Alison feels about her past, present, and future. Play the audio program. (Note: Ss will have to make inferences.) Elicit ideas.
- Write these questions on the board:
  What has Alison achieved in the last few years? What hasn't she achieved? What two things does she hope she'll have accomplished by the time she's 30?
- Play the audio program again. Ss listen and answer the questions.
- Books open. Ss check their answers by reading the conversation.

B *Class activity*

- Explain the task. Read the focus questions.
- Use the questions for a class discussion.

10 GRAMMAR FOCUS

Learning Objective: *practice the present perfect, simple past, future perfect, and* would like to have

⏵ [CD 3, Track 42]

- Play the audio program. Ss listen and read or repeat.
- Review how to form the various structures. Elicit rules and example sentences from Ss.

Talking about past accomplishments

1. the present perfect (*have* + past participle)
   What <u>have</u> you <u>accomplished</u> in the last few years?
   I've <u>managed</u> to buy a new car.
   <u>I've been able</u> to . . .

2. the simple past
   What <u>did</u> you <u>accomplish</u> in the last five years?
   I <u>managed</u> to get a good job two years ago
   <u>I learned/was able to</u> . . . last year/in 2011.

Talking about possible future accomplishments

3. the future perfect (*will have* + past participle)
   What do you hope you<u>'ll have achieved</u> in the next five years?
   I hope (that) I<u>'ll have taken</u> a trip to Europe.

4. *would like to have* + past participle
   What <u>would you like to have accomplished</u> in the next five years?
   <u>I'd like to have bought</u> my own home.
   <u>I'd like to have seen/made</u> . . .

A

- Explain the task. Read the statements.
- Model the task:
  T: (reading aloud number 1) "I've met the person who's right for me." Yes, that's true for me. I've accomplished that, and so I'll check it. (T checks the box.)
- Ss answer the questions individually.
- Ss write four statements about their past accomplishments. Go around the class and spot-check Ss' answers. Decide if they need more practice with the tenses.
- For more practice with past and future tenses, play *True or False?* – download it from the website. Ss talk about their accomplishments.

B

- Explain the task. Ss complete the sentences with goals.

C *Group work*

- Explain the task.
- Ss work in groups. Each group chooses a secretary. This person records how many Ss share the same accomplishments and how many have the same goals. Ss compare sentences from parts A and B.
- For another way to practice the tenses, try the *Substitution Dialog* – download it from the website. Ss use the Conversation on page 109.

9 CONVERSATION *I've managed to get good grades, but . . .*

A ▶ Listen and practice.

Uncle Ed: Happy birthday, Alison! So how does it feel to be 21?
Alison: Kind of strange. I suddenly feel a little anxious, like I'm not moving ahead fast enough.
Uncle Ed: But don't you think you've accomplished quite a bit in the last few years?
Alison: Oh, I've managed to get good grades, but I still haven't been able to decide on a career.
Uncle Ed: Well, what do you hope you'll have achieved by the time you're 30?
Alison: For one thing, I hope I'll have seen more of the world. But more important than that, I'd like to have made a good start on my career by then.

B CLASS ACTIVITY How similar are you to Alison? Are you satisfied with your accomplishments so far? What do you want to accomplish next?

10 GRAMMAR FOCUS

Accomplishments and goals ▶

Accomplishments with the present perfect or simple past	**Goals with the future perfect or would like to have + past participle**
I**'ve managed** to get good grades. (I **managed** to . . .) I**'ve been able** to accomplish a lot in college. (I **was able** to . . .)	What do you hope you**'ll have achieved**? I hope I**'ll have seen** more of the world. I**'d like to have made** a good start on my career.

A What are some of your accomplishments from the last five years? Check (✓) the statements that are true for you. Then think of four more statements about yourself.

☐ 1. I've met the person who's right for me.
☐ 2. I've learned some important life skills.
☐ 3. I was able to complete my degree.
☐ 4. I've made an important career move.

B What are some goals you would like to have accomplished in the future? Complete the sentences.

1. By this time next year, I hope I'll have . . .
2. Three years from now, I'd like to have . . .
3. In ten years, I'd like to have . . .
4. By the time I'm 60, I hope I'll have . . .

C GROUP WORK Compare your sentences in parts A and B. What accomplishments do you have in common? What goals?

11 LISTENING *Future plans*

A 🔘 Listen to three young people discuss their plans for the future. What do they hope they'll have achieved by the time they are 30?

1. Rick	2. Jasmine	3. Bianca
....	....	....
....	....	....
....	....	....

B PAIR WORK Who do you think has the most realistic expectations?

12 WRITING *A personal statement for an application*

A Imagine you are applying to a school or for a job that requires a personal statement. Use these questions to organize your ideas. Make notes and then write a draft.

1. What has your greatest accomplishment been? Has it changed you in any way? How?
2. What are some interesting or unusual facts about yourself that make you a good choice for the job or school?
3. What is something you hope to have achieved ten years from now? When, why, and how will you reach this goal? Will achieving it change you? Why or why not?

> I think my greatest accomplishment has been finally getting my diploma at age 30. I've been able to achieve many things in school with the support of my family, and . . .
> There are two things I'd really like to have achieved by the time I'm 40. First, I hope I'll have done some traveling. . . .

B GROUP WORK Share your statements and discuss each person's accomplishments and goals. Who has the most unusual accomplishment or goal? the most realistic? the most ambitious?

11 LISTENING

Learning Objective: *develop skills in listening for main ideas and note taking*

A [CD 3, Track 43]

- Read the situation and the question. Present each picture and the person's name in the chart.
- **Option:** Ask Ss to look at the photos and make predictions. Ask: "Which person will probably be a volunteer? Be a model? Have a successful career?" Tell Ss to discuss and justify their guesses. Take a poll and write the guesses on the board. Later compare Ss' answers to the chart.
- Tell Ss to listen for what each person hopes to achieve. Play the audio program. Ss listen and take notes.

AudioScript

See page T-177.

> **TIP** If Ss have problems understanding the audio program, try to establish where the problem lies. Then replay that segment only.

- Elicit Ss' answers around the class. Encourage Ss to give full-sentence answers with the future perfect.

Answers

1. Rick hopes he'll have opened his own restaurant.
2. Jasmine hopes she'll have finished medical school and will have started her career as a pediatrician.
3. Bianca hopes she'll have had a successful modeling career.

B Pair work

- Explain the task. Read the focus question. Elicit or explain that realistic expectations are hopes or dreams that may actually happen (as opposed to *unrealistic* expectations).
- Ss discuss the question in pairs. Encourage Ss to give reasons for their answers. Accept any answer that Ss can defend in a clear, logical way.
- **Option:** Take a quick class poll on which person has the most realistic expectations. Ask Ss to share reasons for their opinions.

12 WRITING

Learning Objective: *write a personal statement for an application*

A

- Explain the task. Ss write a personal statement. Ask Ss to read the questions and example.
- Tell Ss to use the questions to guide their writing. Ss first brainstorm accomplishments, then interesting or unusual facts, and finally future goals. Go around the class and give help as needed.
- Ss use their brainstorming notes to compose a first draft.
- **Option:** Step 3 can be done for homework.

B Group work

- Explain the task. Read the focus questions.
- Ss work in small groups. Give Ss the choice of reading the letters silently or of having the writers read their letters to the group. Set a time limit of about ten minutes.
- Ss discuss the questions. Remind Ss to keep the discussion friendly and lighthearted.

- **Option:** Ss role-play an interview for the school or job.
- **Option:** To find out if, and how, Ss want to celebrate the end of the course, try this game:

Hooray! It's the end of the course!

- Take a class vote (through a show of hands or by secret ballot) on whether Ss are interested in doing something special to celebrate the end of the course. If the majority decides they want to, have them make plans:
  1. Brainstorm with the class some ways or ideas on how to celebrate; write them on the board.
  2. Take a class vote on which idea they like the best.
  3. Let a volunteer take over the brainstorming on what kinds of plans the class needs to make and who will be in charge of each part (e.g., choosing the date/place/time; organization of transportation or entertainment; food/drinks; cost per student).
  4. In groups, Ss plan certain parts of the celebration.
  5. Ss celebrate!

Learning Objective: *develop skills in scanning, making inferences, and understanding vocabulary in context*

- Books closed. Ask: "Have you ever heard of (or known) a young person who was very talented in some way?" Elicit Ss' responses around the class.

- Books open. Present the title, picture, and pre-reading questions. Elicit or remind Ss that *gifted* means "extremely talented."

- Ask Ss to scan the article to answer the pre-reading questions. Tell Ss to raise their hands or look up when they are done. Elicit answers around the class. (Answers: Jessica Watson is happy to spend time alone; Ali Pirhani is multilingual; Samson Diamond has done community service.)

- Ss read the article individually. Remind Ss to mark new words they can't guess from context. Ask Ss not to check a dictionary until they complete Exercise A.

! For a new way to present the article, try the ***Reading Race*** **–** download it from the website.

A

- Explain the task.
- Ss work individually or in pairs to match words with meanings. Remind Ss to use context clues.
- Go over answers with the class.

Answers

1. c   2. d   3. a   4. b

- Ss work in pairs or groups to discuss any additional vocabulary they marked. Encourage Ss to use their dictionaries.

> **TIP** Encourage Ss to use cooperative learning to learn new vocabulary. For example, they can discuss the meaning of the new words in groups or try Vocabulary Mingle on page T-153.

- Elicit or explain any remaining new vocabulary.

Vocabulary

multilingual: able to speak more than two languages (bilingual = two languages)
fluent: able to use a language naturally without stopping or making mistakes
diverse: varied, different
polyglot: able to speak many languages
promote: encourage

claims: says that something is true or that you have done something
circumnavigation: going around the world (usually in a boat)
nautical: relating to boats or sailing
obtained: got something
underprivileged: poor and having fewer opportunities than most people
empower: give someone the confidence, skills, or freedom to do something
philosophy: belief; way of thinking

B

- Explain the task. Elicit or explain that *inferences* are logical conclusions made from information in the reading and *restatements* are the same information said another way.
- Ss complete the task individually or in pairs.
- Go over answers with the class.

Answers

1. I   2. R   3. R   4. NG   5. I   6. NG

C *Group work*

- Explain the task. Read the focus questions.
- Give Ss time to plan what they want to say.
- Ss discuss the questions in small groups. Remind Ss that they should be able to explain their opinions.
- Ask groups to share ideas with the whole class.
- ***Option:*** Ss role-play. Student A is one of the people in the article. Student B is a journalist. Student B interviews Student A about accomplishments and goals. Then Ss change roles and role-play again.

End of Cycle 2

See the Supplementary Resources chart at the beginning of this unit for additional teaching materials and student activities related to this Cycle and for assessment tools.

Young and Gifted

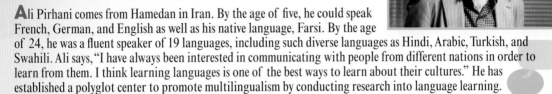

Ali Pirhani comes from Hamedan in Iran. By the age of five, he could speak French, German, and English as well as his native language, Farsi. By the age of 24, he was a fluent speaker of 19 languages, including such *diverse* languages as Hindi, Arabic, Turkish, and Swahili. Ali says, "I have always been interested in communicating with people from different nations in order to learn from them. I think learning languages is one of the best ways to learn about their cultures." He has established a *polyglot* center to promote multilingualism by conducting research into language learning.

A lot of people have sailed, nonstop and alone, around the world, but Jessica Watson claims to be the first 16-year-old to have done so. On May 15, 2010, she returned to Sydney, Australia, after 210 days at sea. However, her claim is not recognized by the World Sailing Speed Record Council. As its name suggests, the council only considers speed records, not factors such as age. Also, the council's minimum distance to qualify for *circumnavigation* is 26,000 nautical miles, but Jessica's route, via the southern oceans, was shorter than this. Her reaction to the council's decision? "It really doesn't bother me."

At age 10, Samson Diamond joined a music project in Soweto, South Africa, and picked up a violin. He soon became leader of the project's Buskaid Soweto String Ensemble, which plays classical music. Later, he obtained a master's degree in music performance. He has also used his talent to serve poor communities in England, Jamaica, and his home country by teaching *underprivileged* people how to empower themselves through music. He says, "My philosophy is 'the further you go, the further there is to go. Never stop searching.' "

A Read the article. Find the words in *italics* in the article.
Then match each word with its meaning.

- .... 1. *diverse*
- .... 2. *polyglot*
- .... 3. *circumnavigation*
- .... 4. *underprivileged*

- a. sailing (or flying) around something
- b. poor, not having the things most people have
- c. different
- d. speaking or using many different languages

B Which statements are inferences (**I**)? Which are restatements (**R**)?
Which are not given (**NG**)?

- .... 1. Ali Pirhani learned a lot of languages when he was a teenager.
- .... 2. He believes that culture and language are closely connected.
- .... 3. Jessica Watson circumnavigated the world via the southern oceans.
- .... 4. She plans to circumnavigate the world via a longer route.
- .... 5. Samson Diamond was a fast learner on the violin
- .... 6. He wants young people to play sports as well as music.

C **GROUP WORK** Which person do you think is making the biggest contribution to society? Why? What personal characteristics made it possible for him or her to achieve so much?

Units 15–16 Progress check

SELF-ASSESSMENT

How well can you do these things? Check (✓) the boxes.

I can	Very well	OK	A little
Give recommendations and opinions about rules (Ex. 1)	☐	☐	☐
Understand and express opinions, and seek agreement (Ex. 2)	☐	☐	☐
Describe qualities necessary to achieve particular goals (Ex. 3)	☐	☐	☐
Describe challenges connected with particular goals (Ex. 3)	☐	☐	☐
Ask about and describe personal achievements and ambitions (Ex. 4)	☐	☐	☐

 DISCUSSION *Setting the rules*

A **PAIR WORK** What kinds of rules do you think should be made for these places? Talk with your partner and make three rules for each. (Have fun! Don't make your rules too serious.)

a health club   an apartment building
a school   the school library

B **GROUP WORK** Join another pair. Share your ideas. Do they agree?

A: People should be required to use every machine in a health club.
B: That sounds interesting. Why?
A: Well, for one thing, people would be in better shape!

2 LISTENING *Social issues*

A ▶ Listen to people give opinions. Check (✓) the correct responses.

1. ☐ Yes, it is.
   ☐ Yes, they are.

2. ☐ Yes, they do.
   ☐ Yes, they should.

3. ☐ Yes, we do.
   ☐ Yes, it does.

4. ☐ Yes, it does.
   ☐ Yes, it should.

5. ☐ No, they can't.
   ☐ No, it isn't.

6. ☐ No, they don't.
   ☐ No, you can't.

B **PAIR WORK** Write a tag question for each response you did not check.

1. Stray animals are so sad, aren't they? Yes, they are.

Units 15–16 Progress check

SELF-ASSESSMENT

Learning Objectives: *reflect on one's learning; identify areas that need improvement*

- Ask: "What did you learn in Units 15 and 16?" Elicit Ss' answers.
- Ss complete the Self-assessment. Encourage them to be honest, and point out they will not get a bad grade if they check (✓) "a little."

- Ss move on to the Progress check exercises. You can have Ss complete them in class or for homework, using one of these techniques:
  1. Ask Ss to complete all the exercises.
  2. Ask Ss: "What do you need to practice?" Then assign exercises based on their answers.
  3. Ask Ss to choose and complete exercises based on their Self-assessment.

DISCUSSION

Learning Objective: *assess one's ability to give recommendations and opinions using passive modals*

A *Pair work*

- Explain the task. Ask Ss to read the list of places.
- Elicit one or two examples of fun rules (e.g., *People should be required to use every machine in a health club.*). Write the examples on the board.
- Ss work in pairs. Ss choose a place and talk about possible rules. Remind Ss to use passive modals.
- Ss choose three rules to tell a group. Ss can memorize their rules or write them down.

B *Group work*

- Explain the task. Ask two Ss to model the conversation.
- Focus Ss' attention on the picture. Ask Ss what would be the *bad* points of the example rule.
- Each pair joins another pair. Pairs take turns telling and discussing their rules.
- Ask each pair to share the most interesting rule the other pair described.

LISTENING

Learning Objective: *assess one's ability to listen to, understand, and use tag questions to ask for agreement*

A ⏵ *[CD 3, Track 44]*

- Explain the task.
- Ss work in pairs. They decide what tag question would fit each response (e.g., for number 1, the tag questions would be *isn't it?* or *aren't they?*).
- Play the audio program as many times as needed. Ss listen and check (✓) the correct response.

> **AudioScript**
>
> See page T-177.

- Go over answers with the class.

> **Answers**
>
> 1. Yes, it is.
> 2. Yes, they should.
> 3. Yes, we do.
> 4. Yes, it does.
> 5. No, it isn't.
> 6. No, you can't.

- ***Option:*** Play the audio program again. Pause after each question. Ask Ss to repeat the question (a paraphrase is OK).

B *Pair work*

- Explain the task. Read the example question and answer. Point out that the question can be anything that fits the answer.
- Ss work in pairs to write questions.
- Ask Ss to read their questions aloud. Elicit answers from the rest of the class.
- ***Option:*** Ss work in pairs to write tag questions to fit any six answers in part A. Then each pair joins another pair. Pairs take turns reading their questions. The other pair answers.

DISCUSSION

Learning Objectives: *assess one's ability to identify qualities necessary to achieve certain goals; assess one's ability to describe challenges with complex noun phrases containing gerunds*

A *Group work*

- Explain the task. Ask Ss to read the goals and qualities. Elicit or explain any new vocabulary.
- Ask two Ss to model the conversation.
- Give Ss time to think of ideas.
- Ss work in small groups and decide on two qualities for each goal.

B *Group work*

- Explain the task. Ask two Ss to model the conversation. Point out that B keeps the conversation going by making a comment and then asking a question.
- Ss work in the same groups or different ones. Ss take turns making statements and asking follow-up questions.
- Go around the class and note use of gerunds, both correct and incorrect.
- Write your notes on the board. Elicit whether the gerunds are used correctly or not. If not, ask the class to correct them.

4 **ROLE PLAY**

Learning Objective: *assess one's ability to talk about one's own accomplishments and goals using the present perfect and future perfect*

- Explain the task.
- Divide the class into pairs, and assign A/B roles. Student As are going to be interviewed. Student Bs are the interviewers.
- Give Ss time to plan what they are going to say. Student As think of their accomplishments and goals. Student Bs read the interview questions and write two more.

- Ss role-play in pairs.
- Ss change roles and repeat the role play.
- **Option:** Ask Ss to write an article about the interview for an imaginary newspaper. The paragraphs can be posted around the room or turned in for you to check.

WHAT'S NEXT?

Learning Objective: *become more involved in one's learning*

- Focus Ss' attention on the Self-assessment again. Ask: "How well can you do these things now?"

- Ask Ss to underline one thing they need to review. Ask: "What did you underline? How can you review it?"
- If needed, plan additional activities or reviews based on Ss' answers.

3 DISCUSSION *What does it take?*

A GROUP WORK What qualities are good or bad if you want to accomplish these goals? Talk with the group and decide on two qualities for each.

Goals	Qualities		
hike across your country	adaptable	dependent	self-sufficient
conduct an orchestra	compassionate	insensitive	timid
make a low-budget movie	courageous	resourceful	unimaginative
become a salsa instructor	cynical	rigid	upbeat

A: To hike across your country, you need to be courageous.
B: Yeah, and you can't be dependent on anyone.

B GROUP WORK What do you think would be the most challenging things about achieving the goals in part A? How would you overcome the challenges?

A: I think the most challenging thing about hiking across your country would be feeling lonely all the time.
B: I agree. So how would you cope with loneliness?

4 ROLE PLAY *Interview*

Student A: Student B is going to interview you for the school website. Think about your accomplishments and goals. Then answer the questions.

Student B: Imagine you are interviewing Student A for the school website. Add two questions to the notebook. Then start the interview.

Change roles and try the role play again.

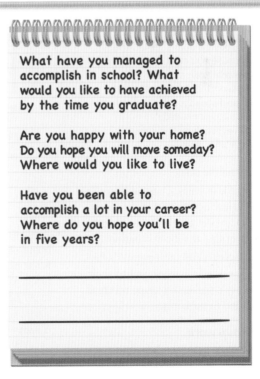

What have you managed to accomplish in school? What would you like to have achieved by the time you graduate?

Are you happy with your home? Do you hope you will move someday? Where would you like to live?

Have you been able to accomplish a lot in your career? Where do you hope you'll be in five years?

_____

_____

WHAT'S NEXT?

Look at your Self-assessment again. Do you need to review anything?

Interchange activities

Learning Objective: speak more fluently about personality in discussion

A Pair work

- Ask: "Have you ever taken a personality quiz in a newspaper or magazine?" If so, ask Ss to describe the quiz (e.g., *where they took it, what it was about, whether it seemed accurate*).
- Give Ss time to read the quiz individually. Tell Ss to circle unfamiliar words.
- Elicit or explain any new vocabulary.

Vocabulary

put off: wait until later to do something

facing: doing something even though it is difficult

avoid: stay away from something

give up: stop doing something because you can't do it

superachiever: a person who always likes to be best or first

cool and steady: calm and not nervous or excited

carefree: not worried about anything

- Explain the task.
- Ss work in pairs. They take turns interviewing each other. Encourage Ss to answer quickly, choosing the answer that fits most situations.
- Then Ss add up their partner's "a," "b," and "c" answers. Ss find their partner's personality type and read it aloud to him or her.

B Group work

- Each pair joins another pair to compare scores. Ss also suggest four characteristics for each of the three personality types in part A.

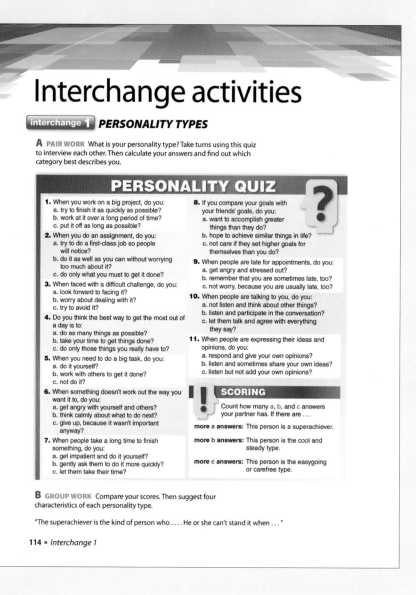

- Write the example phrases on the board. Ask Ss to complete them. Elicit phrases for the other two types. Write them on the board (e.g., *The cool and steady person is someone who . . . . The person who is easygoing doesn't mind it when . . . .*). Remind Ss to use the language from the Grammar Focus boxes on pages 3 and 6.
- Groups discuss their scores and whether they feel the test was accurate.

- Bring the class back together, and help Ss summarize the scores. Ask how many people had more than 6 "a" answers? more than 7? more than 8? Then ask about "b" and "c" answers.

A PAIR WORK Imagine you and your partner are professional party planners and have been hired to organize an important dinner party. Read about each person on the guest list.

 Joanie Van Buren is 42, single, and the host of the party. Wealthy and sociable, she is an art museum volunteer. She has never been married and is rarely seen without her beloved dog.

 John Pradesh is 28, single, and a computer software company owner. He was recently voted "Most Promising Entrepreneur" by *Tech* magazine. He puts his career ahead of dating and marriage.

 Madge Mathers is 45, married, and a gossip columnist. She's nosy, talkative, and likes to dominate the conversation. She has a good sense of humor and is Joanie's oldest friend.

 Buck Eubanks is 54, a widower, and an oil tycoon. This millionaire is bossy and straightforward. His companies have been accused of destroying land to make money.

 Emma Smart is 30, single, and a nuclear physicist. She's currently working on top-secret military projects. She's shy, introverted, and recently broke up with her boyfriend of four years.

 Pierre is 25, single, and Joanie's favorite chef. He's friendly and ambitious, but can be very moody. He's coming to the party to get celebrities and powerful business executives to invest in his new restaurant.

 Sebastiana Di Matteo is 23, single, and a world-famous movie star. She's secretly engaged to her costar in her new movie, and is often followed by photographers.

Ralph Larson is 32, married, and a "green" politician. He's egotistical, outspoken, and tends to start arguments. He's running for public office on an environmental platform.

B PAIR WORK Discuss the possible seating arrangements for the party. Then complete this seating plan.

A: Let's seat Buck next to Pierre. Pierre is interested in finding investors for his new restaurant.
B: It might be better to put Buck next to Joanie. He's a widower and she's single, so . . .

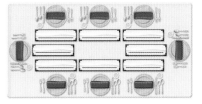

Interchange 2 ▪ 115

---

widower: a man whose wife has died
tycoon: a very powerful, rich business owner
straightforward: direct
ambitious: having a strong desire for success
moody: often unfriendly because of feeling angry or unhappy
green: working to conserve resources or do things in an environmentally-friendly way
outspoken: always saying what one thinks
platform: a politician's set of beliefs

B *Pair work*

- Ask two Ss to model the conversation.
- Explain the task. Ss will complete a seating plan. They should seat guests next to people they will want to talk to and will not argue with.
- Ss work with the same partner from part A. Tell Ss to make brief notes about their decisions.
- Each pair joins another pair to compare seating plans, or call on a few pairs to present their plans to the class. Ss should give reasons for their choices.
- *Option*: Ss form new pairs, and work out seating plans for groups of students in the class or for a group of popular celebrities. Ss share their plans with another pair.

---

interchange 2

Learning Objective: *speak more fluently about personalities in discussion*

A *Pair work*

- Explain the task. Elicit or explain that professional party planners plan and organize important social events. Ss read about the guests. In part B, Ss will decide where these people should sit at the dinner party.
- Ss can read individually, or pairs can take turns reading paragraphs aloud. Encourage Ss to work together to figure out new vocabulary. If they can't figure out a word, they can check with you, another pair, or a dictionary.

- Elicit or explain any new vocabulary.

Vocabulary

host: the person who is having a party
beloved: loved very much
gossip columnist: someone who writes an article regularly for newspapers or magazines, giving information about famous people's private lives
nosy: always trying to find out private things about other people
dominate: control
oldest: for the longest time
introverted: quiet and shy
entrepreneur: business owner

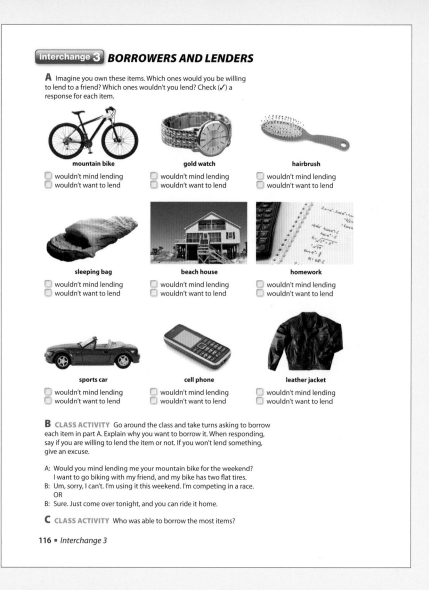

A Imagine you own these items. Which ones would you be willing to lend to a friend? Which ones wouldn't you lend? Check (✓) a response for each item.

mountain bike
☐ wouldn't mind lending
☐ wouldn't want to lend

gold watch
☐ wouldn't mind lending
☐ wouldn't want to lend

hairbrush
☐ wouldn't mind lending
☐ wouldn't want to lend

sleeping bag
☐ wouldn't mind lending
☐ wouldn't want to lend

beach house
☐ wouldn't mind lending
☐ wouldn't want to lend

homework
☐ wouldn't mind lending
☐ wouldn't want to lend

sports car
☐ wouldn't mind lending
☐ wouldn't want to lend

cell phone
☐ wouldn't mind lending
☐ wouldn't want to lend

leather jacket
☐ wouldn't mind lending
☐ wouldn't want to lend

B CLASS ACTIVITY Go around the class and take turns asking to borrow each item in part A. Explain why you want to borrow it. When responding, say if you are willing to lend the item or not. If you won't lend something, give an excuse.

A: Would you mind lending me your mountain bike for the weekend? I want to go biking with my friend, and my bike has two flat tires.
B: Um, sorry, I can't. I'm using it this weekend. I'm competing in a race.
OR
B: Sure. Just come over tonight, and you can ride it home.

C CLASS ACTIVITY Who was able to borrow the most items?

116 ▪ Interchange 3

---

interchange 3

Learning Objective: *speak more fluently about borrowing and lending*

- Note: The exercise title comes from the proverb "Neither a borower nor a lender be," which means that both borrowing and lending can cause trouble between friends.

A

- Books closed. As a warm-up and review, go around the classroom asking different Ss if you can borrow certain items (e.g., *a pen, watch, comb, dictionary, moped*):

T: Can I borrow your watch for a minute?

S1: Well, OK, but please be careful with it.

T: I will. Thanks. And, uh, Joe, don't you come to school on a moped?

S2: Yes, I do.

T: Would you mind lending it to me for about half an hour? I need to take a book back to the library.

S2: Gee, I'm sorry, but . . .

- Books open. Explain the task. Make sure Ss understand that *be willing* means "would agree to do something."

- Discuss the pictures. Ask different Ss to read the names of the items. Point out the same two choices under each one.

- Give Ss time to decide whether they would be willing to lend each item. Remind Ss to check one of the two boxes. Tell Ss to make sure they have at least three items checked they would rather not lend.

B *Class activity*

- Ask two Ss to model the conversation. Elicit additional responses to the request about borrowing the mountain bike. Write them on the board.

- Ss go around the class and take turns asking to borrow the items in part A.

- Set a time limit of ten minutes. Tell Ss to make requests of as many classmates as possible. Remind Ss to give the reason they need to borrow each item. Also remind Ss to give an excuse for not lending something.

- Tell Ss to check off each item that someone agrees to lend them.

- Go around and note problems Ss are having. When time is up, go over the most common problems with the class.

C *Class activity*

- Find out who was able to borrow every item or the most items on the list.

- ***Option:*** If time allows, ask Ss to give quick summaries of who was willing to lend them each item and why they needed to borrow it.

interchange 4 · A DOUBLE ENDING

A Read the beginning and the two possible endings of this story.

Beginning

Ken Passell grew up in a small, working-class family in Detroit, Michigan. His father was an auto mechanic and

his mother worked in a factory. When Ken was a child, he was very good with his hands.

Ending 1

The wedding was the biggest in the history of Los Angeles. After the ceremony, Ken and Cindy left on their private yacht for a honeymoon cruise to Baja, Mexico. When they return, they will live in their twenty-room mansion in Beverly Hills.

Ending 2

Ken and his wife, Cindy, were arrested in London last week. Police found more than $250,000 in cash in their suitcase. The couple insists they are innocent. "I don't know how the money got in our luggage," Ken told the police.

B PAIR WORK Choose one of the endings. What do you think happened during the middle part of the story? Discuss and take notes.

C GROUP WORK Tell your story to another pair. Answer any follow-up questions they have.

Interchange 4 ▪ 117

---

interchange 4

Learning Objective: *develop discussion and storytelling skills*

A

- Explain the task.
- Ss read individually. Remind Ss that there is no middle to the story yet.
- Elicit or explain any new vocabulary.

Vocabulary

working-class: the social class that includes people who don't have much money and do physical work

factory: a building where people use machines to produce products

good with his hands: skilled at making or doing things by hand

yacht: an expensive pleasure boat

cruise: a vacation on a boat

mansion: a large, expensive home

B *Pair work*

- Explain the task. Ss choose one ending and make up the missing middle part of the story. With the whole class, brainstorm what they might include (e.g., Cindy's background, their high school and college years, how they met, what jobs they had).
- Ss work in pairs. They discuss and take notes on their ideas. Go around the class and give help as needed.
- ***Option:*** Ss can write the middle of the story in paragraph form.
- Pairs practice telling their stories.

C *Group work*

- Each pair joins another pair. They take turns telling their stories. Ask pairs to ask follow-up questions and make comments. If time allows, form new groups at least once.
- Elicit from the class at least two stories with Ending 1 and two stories with Ending 2.

Interchange activities ▪ **T-117**

interchange 5

Learning Objective: *speak more fluently about customs*

A

- Focus Ss' attention on the pictures. Ask: "What do you think is happening in each picture? Do you have similar customs in your country?"
- Model the task by reading the first two or three statements. Ss check those statements that apply to their own culture. Elicit that *socializing* means "spending time with people."
- Ss work individually. Remind Ss to mark any words they are unable to guess from context. They can consult their dictionary after they finish. Go around the class and give help as needed.
- Elicit or explain any new vocabulary.

Vocabulary

housewarming gift: a small gift, often food or something for the home, that people give to a new neighbor

dropping by: visiting someone without calling first

split the cost: share the bill

bargain: ask a store owner to lower the price of something

reception: the party after the wedding ceremony

B *Pair work*

- Ss compare their answers with a partner. They discuss how many answers are the same and how many are different.
- **Option:** If your background is different from your Ss', go through the chart and explain which statements are true in your own culture.

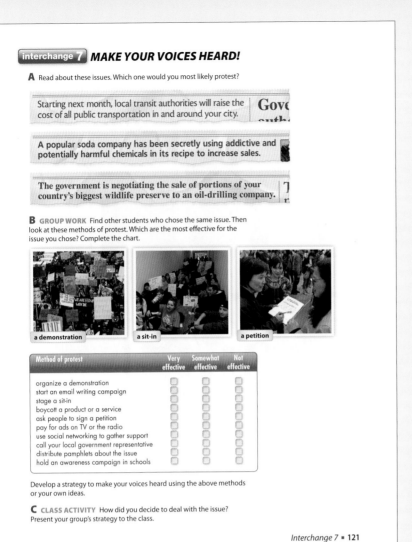

interchange 7 *MAKE YOUR VOICES HEARD!*

A Read about these issues. Which one would you most likely protest?

> Starting next month, local transit authorities will raise the cost of all public transportation in and around your city.

> A popular soda company has been secretly using addictive and potentially harmful chemicals in its recipe to increase sales.

> The government is negotiating the sale of portions of your country's biggest wildlife preserve to an oil-drilling company.

B GROUP WORK Find other students who chose the same issue. Then look at these methods of protest. Which are the most effective for the issue you chose? Complete the chart.

a demonstration · a sit-in · a petition

Method of protest	Very effective	Somewhat effective	Not effective
organize a demonstration	☐	☐	☐
start an email writing campaign	☐	☐	☐
stage a sit-in	☐	☐	☐
boycott a product or a service	☐	☐	☐
ask people to sign a petition	☐	☐	☐
pay for ads on TV or the radio	☐	☐	☐
use social networking to gather support	☐	☐	☐
call your local government representative	☐	☐	☐
distribute pamphlets about the issue	☐	☐	☐
hold an awareness campaign in schools	☐	☐	☐

Develop a strategy to make your voices heard using the above methods or your own ideas.

C CLASS ACTIVITY How did you decide to deal with the issue? Present your group's strategy to the class.

Interchange 7 ▪ 121

---

interchange 7

Learning Objective: *speak more fluently about social, public, and environmental problems*

A

▪ Explain the task. Give Ss time to read the issues.

▪ Elicit or explain any new vocabulary.

Vocabulary

local transit authorities: people and/or organizations in charge of a city's public transportation

addictive: causing an unhealthy dependence on something

potentially harmful chemicals: chemicals that might do damage

negotiate: try to make or change an agreement by discussion

portion: part of something

wildlife preserve: an area where wild animals and plants are protected

▪ Ask Ss to check the issue that would upset them the most.

▪ Books closed. Ask the class to brainstorm methods of protest. You may need to give them one or two examples (use ones from the book) to get them started. Write Ss' ideas on the board.

B *Group work*

▪ Books open. Ask Ss to go around the class to find other Ss who chose the same issue. Limit group size to five Ss.

▪ Read the methods of protest in the chart. Note which are the same as the ones the class came up with. Answer any vocabulary questions.

▪ Groups complete the chart. Encourage Ss to discuss their ideas before checking (✓) any boxes. Explain that it is OK for Ss in the same group to check different columns.

▪ Ask the groups to plan a strategy for their protest. Tell the groups to choose one S as a secretary to write down the group's ideas.

C *Class activity*

▪ Group secretaries take turns sharing their group's solutions for each problem. Let other Ss ask questions.

▪ *Option:* Take a quick class poll (through a show of hands) to find out which solution is the best for each problem.

interchange 6A *FIXER-UPPER*

Student A

A Look at this apartment. What's wrong with it? First, make a list of as many problems as you can find in each room.

B PAIR WORK Compare your lists. What are the similarities and differences in the problems between your picture here and your partner's picture? Ask questions to find the differences.

A: What's wrong in the living room?
B: Well, in my picture, the sofa has a hole in it. And the carpet . . .
A: Oh, really? In my picture, the sofa has a hole in it, but the carpet . . . , and the wallpaper . . .

Interchange 6A ▪ 119

---

interchange 6A/B

Learning Objective: *speak more fluently about problems in the home*

A

- Books closed. Read the subtitle, "Fixer-upper." Ask Ss to guess what it means. (It describes a place for sale at a lower price because it needs a lot of repairs.) *Fix up* means "to improve or restore to good condition."
- Divide the class into pairs, and assign A/B roles. Tell Student As to look at Interchange 6A, and Student Bs to look at Interchange 6B.

- Give Ss a few minutes to look at their picture. Tell Ss not to look at their partner's picture.

> **TIP** In information gaps, have partners sit across from each other so they can't see their partner's page. Alternatively, have them sit back-to-back.

- Explain the task. Say that the instructions and conversations in Interchange 6A and 6B are the same; only the pictures have slight variations.
- Model the task. Write these examples on the board:

What's wrong in the living room?
The sofa is torn. OR
The sofa has a tear in it. OR
There's a hole in the sofa. OR
The sofa has a hole in it. OR
The sofa needs to be repaired. OR
The sofa needs repairing.

- Then Ss work individually. Set a time limit of about five minutes to list all the problems they see. Ss may use their dictionaries if necessary.
- Go around the class and give help as needed.

interchange 6B *FIXER-UPPER*

Student B

A Look at this apartment. What's wrong with it? First, make
a list of as many problems as you can find in each room.

B **PAIR WORK** Compare your lists. What are the similarities and
differences in the problems between your picture here and your
partner's picture? Ask questions to find the differences.

A: What's wrong in the living room?
B: Well, in my picture, the sofa has a hole in it. And the carpet . . .
A: Oh, really? In my picture, the sofa has a hole in it, but the carpet . . . ,
and the wallpaper . . .

120 ▪ *Interchange 6B*

B *Pair work*

▪ Explain the task. Ask two Ss to
read the conversation. Ss find
similarities and differences between
the two pictures.

▪ Ss work in pairs. Set a time limit of
ten minutes. Tell Ss to make notes
on their lists about which problems
are the same (S) and which are
different (D).

TIP To check answers at the end of an
information gap activity, it's helpful
to ask Ss to exchange answers, rather
than going over the answers as a
class.

Possible Answers

Two problems are the same (S), and
nine are different (D):
What's wrong in the living room?
Pictures A & B: The sofa is torn./The
sofa has a tear in it./There's a hole
in the sofa./The sofa needs to be
repaired./The sofa needs repairing.
(S)
Picture A: The wallpaper is peeling./
The wallpaper needs to be
replaced./The wallpaper needs
replacing. (D)
Picture B: The carpet is stained./There
are stains on the carpet. (D)
What's wrong in the kitchen?
Picture A: The refrigerator door
is falling off./The refrigerator
door needs to be repaired./The
refrigerator door needs repairing.
(D)
Picture A: The stove needs to
be repaired./The stove needs
repairing./The stove doesn't work.
(D)
Picture B: The sink/faucet is leaking./
The sink has a leak./The sink needs
to be fixed./The sink needs fixing.
(D)
What's wrong in the bedroom?
Pictures A & B: The walls need to be
painted./The walls need painting.
(S)
Picture A: The curtains are torn. (D)
Picture B: There's a crack in the
window./The window is cracked/
broken. (D)
What's wrong in the bathroom?
Picture A: A pipe is leaking./A pipe
has a leak./A pipe needs to be
fixed./A pipe needs fixing. (D)
Picture B: The toilet needs to be
fixed./The toilet needs fixing. (D)

A Complete this chart with information about yourself. Add one idea of your own.

two foreign languages I'd like to speak
two musical instruments I'd like to play
two dances I'd like to learn
two types of cuisine I'd like to learn how to cook
two evening courses I'd like to take
two sports I'd like to play
two skills that I'd like to improve
two

B CLASS ACTIVITY Ask three classmates to help you choose between the things you wrote down in part A. Write their recommendations in the chart.

Names:			
foreign language			
musical instrument			
dance			
cuisine			
evening course			
sport			
skill			

A: I don't know if I'd rather learn Portuguese or Turkish. What do you think?
B: Hmm. If I were you, I'd learn Portuguese.
A: Why Portuguese and not Turkish?
B: Well, you already know Spanish, so Portuguese might be easier to learn.

C GROUP WORK What are your final choices? Who gave the best advice? Why?

---

interchange 8

Learning Objective: *speak more fluently about learning new things*

A

- Explain the task. Ask Ss to read the items in the chart. Focus Ss' attention on the picture. Ask: "What does this person want to learn?" (Answers: play the electric guitar and drums, speak Portuguese and Turkish, cook Chinese food and Spanish food, play badminton and soccer)

- To help Ss get started, model like this:

  T: "Two foreign languages I'd like to learn." Let's see . . . I've always wanted to learn how to speak Japanese, and I'd also like to study French again. So I'll write down those two foreign languages here in my chart. And how about you, Cecilia?

  S: Well, someday I'd really like to learn Russian and . . .

- Ss complete the chart individually. Tell Ss to use dictionaries to check spelling and pronunciation of new words they want to use.

- Go around the class and give help as needed.

B *Class activity*

- Explain the task. Ss ask three classmates for help choosing between things in part A. Ss write classmates' preferences and reasons in the chart. Ask two Ss to model the conversation.

- Write these additional questions on the board:

  Would you rather . . . ?

  Would you prefer to . . . ?

- Ss go around the class interviewing one another. Remind Ss to include

the interviewees' names in the chart. Set a time limit of about ten minutes.

- Go around the class and give help as needed. Make sure Ss are completing their chart.

C *Group work*

- Give Ss some time to read over their chart and decide who gave the best advice.

- Ask Ss to tell the class about the best advice they received. In a large class, Ss can do this activity in groups.

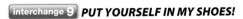

interchange 9 *PUT YOURSELF IN MY SHOES!*

A PAIR WORK Read these comments made by parents. Why do you think they feel this way? Think of two arguments to support each point of view.

> Our daughter wants to get her ears pierced. We think she should wait until she's 16.

> Our son wants to get his computer upgraded, but it's not necessary. We just bought it last year!

> If our daughter insists on having her nails done, she has to pay for it herself.

> Our son wants to buy a motorcycle. He has the money, but we feel he should save it for college.

> Our daughter wants to go to a rock concert with her friends. Absolutely not!

> Our son wants to have his hair cut at an expensive salon. What's wrong with a regular barber?

> Regardless of the color, we refuse to let our kids get their hair dyed.

A: Why do you think they won't let their daughter get her ears pierced?
B: They probably think she's too young.
A: They may also feel that she . . .

B PAIR WORK Now put yourselves in the children's shoes. One of you is the daughter and the other is the son. Discuss the parents' decisions, and think of two arguments against their point of view.

A: Why do you think mom and dad won't let me get my ears pierced?
B: They probably think you're too young.
A: That's crazy! My friend got her ears pierced when she was 10. It's not a big deal.

C CLASS ACTIVITY Take a vote. Do you agree with the parents or the children? Why?

Interchange 9 ▪ **123**

---

interchange 9

Learning Objective: *speak more fluently about having things done and giving reasons*

A *Pair work*

- Explain the task. Ss will think of reasons to support the parents' views.
- Give the class some time to read the parents' comments.
- Elicit or explain any new vocabulary.

Vocabulary

get her ears pierced: have holes made in her ears for earrings
get his computer upgraded: get new, up-to-date software for his computer
have her nails done: get her fingernails painted at a salon
barber: a person who cuts men's hair and boys' hair
get their hair dyed: have their hair colored

- Model the conversation with a S. Complete the conversation with an idea of your own. Then elicit other ideas from the class.

- Ss work in pairs. Remind Ss to think of two arguments to support each point of view. Ss can take notes of their arguments.
- Each pair joins another pair to compare arguments.
- *Option:* Ask Ss to share their arguments with the whole class or write them on the board.

B *Pair work*

- Elicit or explain that *put yourself in the children's shoes* means "imagine you are the children." Ss think of the children's arguments. Elicit some examples from the first situation.
- Ss work with the same partner from part A. Ss can take notes of their arguments.
- Each pair joins another pair to compare arguments.
- *Option:* Ask Ss to share their arguments with the whole class or write them on the board.
- *Option:* Ss suggest additional parent-child conflicts for the class to discuss and vote on.

C *Class activity*

- For each issue, have a class vote on whether Ss agree with the parents or the children. Tally the results on the board for each issue.
- Ask Ss to share their reasons with the class.

interchange 10A HISTORY BUFF

Student A

A PAIR WORK Ask your partner these questions. Put a check (✓) if your partner gives the correct answer. (The correct answers are in **bold**.)

2000 Sydney Olympics

3D movie from the 1950s

Cleopatra

Test Your Knowledge

1. Was Julius Caesar emperor of Athens, **Rome**, or Constantinople?

2. What did Thomas Edison invent in 1879? Was it the television, the telephone, or the **lightbulb**?

3. In which year did Mexico gain its independence? Was it in 1721, **1821**, or 1921?

4. Where were the 2000 Olympics held? Were they in Athens, **Sydney**, or Beijing?

5. When did World War I take place? Was it from 1898 to 1903, from 1911 to 1915, or **from 1914 to 1918**?

6. What sculptor made the famous statue of David? Was it Leonardo da Vinci, Auguste Bartholdi, or **Michelangelo**?

7. Who was the first human in space? Was it **Yuri Gagarin**, Neil Armstrong, or John Glenn?

8. When were the first audio CDs put on the market? Was it in 1973, **1983**, or 1993?

9. In what decade did 3-D movies first gain wide popularity? Was it the **1950s**, 1960s, or 1970s?

10. Was Cleopatra the queen of **Egypt**, Rome, or Greece?

B PAIR WORK Answer the questions your partner asks you. Then compare quizzes. Who has the most correct answers?

C CLASS ACTIVITY Think of three more questions of your own. Can the rest of the class answer them?

124 ▪ Interchange 10A

---

interchange 10A/B

Learning Objective: *speak more fluently about world events*

A Pair work

- Find out if any Ss know what *history buff* means. (Answer: A history buff is someone who is interested in and knows a lot about history.)
- Explain the task.
- Divide the class into pairs, and assign A/B roles. Ask the Student As to look at Interchange 10A and the Student Bs to look at Interchange 10B. Tell Ss not to look at their partner's page.
- Tell Ss to read their ten quiz questions. Ask Ss to mark any words they don't understand or know how to pronounce. Point out that the quiz answers are in boldface.
- Now gather all the Student As and quietly explain any words they ask about. Ss may also use their dictionary.
- Elicit or explain any new vocabulary.

Vocabulary

Student A's quiz (Interchange 10A)
emperor: the ruler of an empire, which is a group of countries controlled by one ruler or government
gain: get, win, or achieve something important
sculptor: an artist who makes pieces with marble, clay, wood, metal, etc.
put on the market: made available for someone to buy

- Model rising and falling intonation patterns in these questions of choice. If needed, ask the Student As to repeat quietly in unison. Remind Ss not to give away the correct answer by reading it differently from the other choices.

- Now work with the Student Bs in the same way.
- Elicit or explain any new vocabulary.

Vocabulary

Student B's quiz (Interchange 10B)
penicillin: a medicine used to kill bacteria
magnetic compass: an instrument used for finding direction as it always shows magnetic north
theory of relativity: the relationship between time, space, and movement, which changes with increased speed

- Set a time limit of about five minutes. Ask the Student As to start. Tell Ss to read each question on their quiz to their partner. Remind Ss to write a check (✓) when their partner gives the correct answer.

Student B

A PAIR WORK Answer the questions your partner asks you.

B PAIR WORK Ask your partner these questions. Put a check (✓) if your partner gives the correct answer. (The correct answers are in **bold**.) Then compare quizzes. Who has the most correct answers?

The Wright Brothers

Mary Shelley's *Frankenstein*

Hong Kong, 1997

Test Your Knowledge

☐ **1.** When did the Wright brothers make their first airplane flight? Was it in 1893, **1903**, or 1923?

☐ **2.** What was the former name of New York City? Was it New England, New London, or **New Amsterdam**?

☐ **3.** When did Walt Disney make his first cartoon movie? Was it in 1920, **1938**, or 1947?

☐ **4.** In which century did the composer Mozart live? Was it the seventeenth, **eighteenth**, or nineteenth century?

☐ **5.** Who was the novel *Frankenstein* written by? Was it Jane Austen, John Keats, or **Mary Shelley**?

☐ **6.** Who discovered penicillin? Was it **Alexander Fleming**, Marie Curie, or Albert Einstein?

☐ **7.** When was the first Volkswagen "Beetle" car built? Was it during the 1920s, the **1930s**, or the 1940s?

☐ **8.** Who used the first magnetic compass? Was it the Portuguese, **the Chinese**, or the Dutch?

☐ **9.** When did the British return Hong Kong to China? Was it in 1995, 1996, or **1997**?

☐ **10.** Was the theory of relativity created by **Albert Einstein**, Charles Darwin, or Isaac Newton?

C CLASS ACTIVITY Think of three more questions of your own. Can the rest of the class answer them?

B *Pair work*

- Now tell the Student Bs to ask their quiz questions. Again, set a time limit of about five minutes.
- When time is up, tell pairs to total their quiz scores to find out who had more correct answers.
- Designate these winners as the class "history buffs."
- Remind Ss to tell their partners the correct answers to items they missed.

C *Class activity*

- Explain the task. Ss write three more questions of choice like those in the quiz.
- Ss work individually or in pairs to write the questions.
- Ss take turns standing up and asking their questions. Tell Ss to call on others who have raised their hands to answer them.

interchange 11 **WHEN I WAS YOUNGER, . . .**

A **PAIR WORK** Play the board game. Follow these instructions.

1. Use small pieces of paper with your initials on them as markers.
2. Take turns by tossing a coin:

Heads Move two spaces.　　**Tails** Move one space.

3. When you land on a space, tell your partner what is true. Then say how things would have been different. For example:

"When I was younger, I didn't pay attention in class. If I had paid attention in class, I would have gotten better grades."
OR
"When I was younger, I paid attention in class. If I hadn't paid attention in class, I wouldn't have won a scholarship."

B **CLASS ACTIVITY** Who was sensible when they were younger? Who was rebellious? Tell the class.

Interchange 11 ▪ 125

---

interchange 11

Learning Objective: *speak more fluently about things you wish you could change*

A *Pair work*

▪ Explain the task. Read the example sentences as a model. Then show Ss how to toss a coin and advance on the game board.

▪ Ss play the board game in pairs.

▪ Go around the class and give help as needed.

B *Class activity*

▪ Read the questions. Elicit or explain the meaning of *sensible* (showing good judgment, making good choices) and *rebellious* (refusing to follow rules).

▪ Give Ss time to plan what they will say.

▪ Ask different Ss if they were sensible or rebellious when they were younger. Encourage Ss to give examples to explain why, and

encourage other Ss to ask follow-up questions.

▪ ***Option:*** Ss write a paragraph about things people have done that they wish they could change. Ss hand it in to you to check, or ask Ss to share their paragraphs in pairs or small groups.

interchange 12 *CATCHY SLOGANS*

A PAIR WORK Read these popular slogans for products.
Match the slogans with the product types.

1. It's the real thing.	a. an amusement park
2. The happiest place on earth	b. a soft drink
3. Good to the last drop	c. coffee
4. All the news that's fit to print	d. a daily newspaper
5. Just do it!	e. potato chips
6. Bet you can't eat just one.	f. sports clothing

7. You're in good hands.	g. fast food
8. Reach out and touch someone.	h. automobiles
9. Alarmed? You should be.	i. security systems
10. M'm! M'm! Good!	j. insurance
11. Built for the road ahead	k. soup
12. Have it your way.	l. telephone service

B PAIR WORK Join another pair and compare your answers.
Then check your answers at the bottom of the page.

C GROUP WORK Think of a product. Then create your
own slogan for it and add a logo. Consider a design
and colors that are suitable for the product.

A: Any idea for a product?
B: What about a pizza delivery service?
C: That's good. Let's try to think of some catchy slogans.
D: How about "Delicious and dependable"? Or maybe . . .

D CLASS ACTIVITY Present your slogans to the class.
Who has the catchiest one?

Answers: 1.b; 2.a; 3.c; 4.d; 5.f; 6.e; 7.j; 8.l; 9.i; 10.k; 11.h; 12.g

Interchange 12 ▪ 127

---

interchange 12

Learning Objective: *speak more fluently about using slogans to advertise products*

- Note: Bring some magazine ads to class, or ask Ss to bring some.

A *Pair work*

- Focus Ss' attention on the subtitle. Elicit or explain that *catchy* means "pleasant and easy to remember" (e.g., *a catchy song*).
- Explain the task. Ss try to identify what product each slogan is advertising.
- Ask Ss to read the slogans. Point out that these slogans are real. All have been used to advertise well-known companies or products.

- Ss work in pairs to match the slogans to the products. Set a time limit of about seven minutes. Go around the class and give help as needed.

B *Pair work*

- Ss join another pair and compare their answers. Then they check their answers at the bottom of the page.

C *Group work*

- Explain the task. Elicit or explain that a logo is a picture, design, or symbol that represents a business or helps to advertise a product. Point out the logos in the four pictures.
- Have four Ss read the example conversation.

- Tell Ss they can imagine the slogan, logo, and any other design elements as part of a print ad, an online ad, or some other type of ad.
- **Option:** To further prepare Ss for the task, show examples of advertisements with slogans and logos. Have Ss discuss what they like and dislike about them, including the design and colors. Or have Ss find their own examples outside of class and bring them in for discussion.
- Ss work in groups to think of a product, slogan, and logo. One S records the group's ideas.
- Go around the room and offer help as needed.

D *Class activity*

- Groups present their ideas to the class. Give Ss time to practice their presentations. Encourage Ss to draw a mock-up or draft of the advertisement.
- Each S presents a different aspect of their advertising campaign (the slogan, the logo, and the design and color of the ad). Encourage Ss to ask for more information.
- **Option:** The class votes on the business that is (1) most interesting and (2) most likely to succeed.

Interchange activities ▪ **T-127**

A PAIR WORK Look at these pictures. What do you think might have happened in each situation? Talk about possibilities for each picture.

A: Maybe the woman thought of something funny that had happened earlier.
B: Or, she might not have understood . . .

useful expressions

Maybe he/she was . . . when . . .
Or perhaps he/she was . . .
He/She may have . . . when . . .
He/She might have . . .

B GROUP WORK Agree on one interpretation of each situation and share it with the class. Be ready to answer any questions.

128 ▪ Interchange 13

---

interchange 13

Learning Objective: *speak more fluently about what might have happened*

A Pair work

▪ Explain the task. Focus Ss' attention on the pictures. Ask two Ss to model the conversation.

▪ Write questions on the board to help guide Ss:

<u>Describe the situation or event</u>.

What's the situation in the first picture?

What are the people doing? Why are they doing it?

<u>Guess what happened</u>.

What do you think happened? Why did it happen?

▪ Read the useful expressions.

▪ Ss work in pairs. Ss take turns talking about what might have happened.

▪ ***Option:*** After pairs discuss the pictures, they choose one of the pictures and write a paragraph about what might have happened.

▪ Set a time limit of about ten minutes. Go around the class and give help as needed.

▪ ***Option:*** If pairs have trouble coming up with vocabulary, brainstorm with the whole class on each picture. Write Ss' suggestions on the board.

▪ ***Option:*** Ss can do part A for homework. In the next class, pairs

compare their interpretations and stories. Then they choose the four most interesting ones for part B.

B Group work

▪ Explain the task.

▪ Each pair joins another pair. Ss take turns telling their stories for each picture.

▪ Groups choose their favorite story about each situation. Groups practice telling their stories.

▪ Groups then take turns sharing their best stories around the class.

▪ ***Option:*** Take a quick class poll to find out which group's story was the best or most creative for each picture.

T-128 ▪ *Interchange activities*

---

interchange 14 *WHO MAKES IT HAPPEN?*

A GROUP WORK Here are some additional jobs in the movie industry.
What do you think each person does?

art director   costume designer   makeup artist   sound-effects technician
cinematographer   lighting technician   set designer   special-effects designer

A: What does an art director do?
B: I know. An art director manages the people who build the sets.

B GROUP WORK Imagine you are going to make a movie. What kind of
movie will it be? Decide what job each person in your group will do.

A: You should be the art director because you're a good leader.
B: Actually, I'd prefer to be the producer.
C: I think I'd like to be one of the actors.

C CLASS ACTIVITY Tell the class what kind of movie you are going to make.
Explain how each person will contribute to the making of the film.

a cinematographer

a makeup artist

a lighting technician

a sound-effects technician

Interchange 14 ▪ 129

---

interchange 14

Learning Objective: *speak more
fluently about the movie industry*

A Group work

- Explain the task.
- Give Ss time to read the list of
  occupations and think about what
  those people do. Ask two Ss to
  model the conversation.
- Ss work in small groups. Tell Ss
  to use a dictionary only as a last
  resort. Go around the class and give
  help as needed.

Possible Answers

art director: person who is in charge
of the overall visual appearance of
the movie

special-effects designer: person
who creates costumes, props, or
scenarios for special characters or
situations

cinematographer: person who
shoots the scenes

lighting technician: person who
arranges the lights according to
the needs of a scene

costume designer: person who
creates clothing for actors to wear

set designer: person who creates
and designs the surroundings
where scenes are shot

sound-effects technician: person
who creates special sounds and
noises

makeup artist: person who applies
makeup according to a character's
needs in a scene

B Group work

- Explain the task. Ask two Ss to
  model the conversation. Then
  brainstorm with the class additional
  jobs in the movie industry
  (screenwriter, actor, etc.)
- Ss work in the same groups as in
  Exercise A or in new groups. One
  S in each group takes notes on the
  movie idea. Another S takes notes
  on jobs.
- Set a time limit of about seven
  minutes. Go around the class
  and listen in. Note any problems,
  especially with relative clauses.
- When time is up, write some of the
  problems on the board. Elicit Ss'
  help in correcting them.

C Class activity

- Explain the task. Give groups time
  to plan what to say.
- Ask the groups to present their
  ideas to the class. Ask Ss to share
  the speaking.
- **Option:** Each group writes up its
  movie plans to hand in to you.

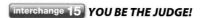
interchange 15 YOU BE THE JUDGE!

A PAIR WORK What punishment (if any) is appropriate for each possible offense? Complete the chart.

Offense	Punishment
1. failing to clean up after a dog	
2. crossing the street in dangerous places	
3. leaving trash on public streets	
4. using a cell phone while driving	
5. buying pirated DVDs and video games	
6. driving without a seat belt	
7. riding a motorcycle without a helmet	
8. painting graffiti on public property	
9. stealing from your company	
10. shoplifting	
11. hacking into a government computer	
12.	
(your own idea)	

A: What do you think should be done about people who don't clean up after their dogs?
B: They should be required to pay a fine.
A: I don't agree. I think . . .

possible punishments

receive a warning
spend some time in jail
pay a fine
lose a driver's license
get suspended
do community service

B GROUP WORK Join another pair of students. Then compare and discuss your lists. Do you agree or disagree? Try to convince each other that you are right!

130 ▪ Interchange 15

---

interchange 15

Learning Objective: *speak more fluently about offenses and punishments*

A Pair work

- Explain the task. Ask Ss to read the offenses and possible punishments. Ask two Ss to model the conversation.
- Elicit or explain any new vocabulary.

Vocabulary

pirated: illegally copied and distributed
shoplifting: stealing things from a store
hacking into: illegally gaining access to a computer system
fine: money paid as punishment for breaking a rule or law
get suspended: be forced to stay away from a job or school for a period of time
community service: unpaid work that benefits the city or town you live in

- ***Option:*** Ask Ss to identify as many offenses as they can in the picture.
- Ss work in pairs to discuss ideas and complete the chart. Tell Ss they can write more than one punishment if they wish.

B Group work

- Explain the task. With the class, brainstorm phrases to agree, disagree, and convince others.
- Each pair joins another pair. Remind Ss to use a variety of expressions. Go around the class and give help as needed.
- ***Option:*** Ask groups to come to an agreement on one punishment for each offense. Then ask groups to share a few punishments they agreed on. Ask Ss to explain their choices. This can be done as a written assignment and turned in.

A Complete this survey with your viewpoints on communities, charities, and volunteering.

WHAT DO YOU THINK?

1 Do you help out in your community?
- ☐ Yes, I do regularly.
- ☐ Yes, I do from time to time.
- ☐ No, I don't right now.
- ☐ other: _____
_____

2 Would you consider working in a developing country?
- ☐ Yes. It would be an interesting experience.
- ☐ Maybe when I'm older.
- ☐ No. That's definitely not for me.
- ☐ other: _____

3 What's the best way to raise money for charities?
- ☐ through donations
- ☐ through taxes
- ☐ through special fund-raising activities
- ☐ other: _____

4 Who do you think has the greatest responsibility to support charities?
- ☐ the government
- ☐ all citizens
- ☐ the wealthy
- ☐ other: _____

5 What's the best way to improve a community?
- ☐ through education
- ☐ by creating more jobs
- ☐ by protecting the environment
- ☐ other: _____

6 Which of these things are you most concerned about?
- ☐ the environment
- ☐ crime and safety
- ☐ unemployment
- ☐ other: _____

7 Which of these activities would you prefer doing?
- ☐ helping the elderly
- ☐ helping the poor
- ☐ helping the sick
- ☐ other: _____

8 What advice would you give someone who wanted to work for a charitable organization?
- ☐ Go for it! It can be very rewarding.
- ☐ Be selective about who you decide to work for.
- ☐ Don't do it. It's a waste of time.
- ☐ other: _____

B PAIR WORK Compare your responses. Do you and your partner have similar viewpoints?

C CLASS ACTIVITY Take a class poll. Which choice was the most popular for each question? Talk about any "other" responses people added.

Interchange 16 ▪ **131**

---

interchange 16

Learning Objective: *speak more fluently about volunteering*

A
- Explain the task. Read the subtitle. Elicit or explain that "Viewpoints" means the same as opinions. Ask Ss to read the survey questions.
- Elicit or explain any new vocabulary.

Vocabulary

raise money: collect money so it can be used to help people

charities: official organizations that give money, food or help to people who need it

donations: money given to help a person or an organization

fund-raising: collecting money for a special purpose

the elderly: old people

Go for it!: said to encourage someone to do or try something

selective: careful about what you choose to do or give

a waste of time: using time on something that isn't worth it

- Tell Ss to check (✓) one of the four choices. If they choose "other," they should write their answer on the line.

- Ss complete the survey individually. Go around the class and give help as needed.

B *Pair work*
- Explain the task. Ask two Ss to model the task:

  S1: Well, for number 1, I checked *No, I don't right now* because I'm a student and I don't have much money. But when I get a job, I'd like to . . .

  S2: I checked *Yes, I do regularly*. I volunteer at a local school as a tutor every Friday.

- Ss work in pairs. Set a time limit of ten minutes. Then ask which pairs had the most responses in common.

C *Class activity*
- Conduct a class poll. Ask Ss to read each question and the four choices while you count how many Ss (through a show of hands) checked each one. Ask Ss who checked *other* to explain their responses.

Grammar plus

Unit 1

1 Relative pronouns (page 3)

> ▶ A relative pronoun – *who* or *that* – is necessary when the pronoun is the subject of the clause: I'd love to meet someone **who/that** is considerate. (NOT: I'd love to meet ~~someone is considerate.~~)
> ▶ When the pronoun is the object of the clause, *who* and *that* can be left out: I'd like a roommate **who/that** I have a lot in common with. OR I'd like a roommate I have a lot in common with.

Complete the conversation with *who* or *that*. Put an **X** when a relative pronoun isn't necessary.

A: Ana, have you met Clint – the guy ....**X**........ Laurie is going to marry?

B: Oh, Clint and I have been friends for years. In fact, I'm the one .... introduced Laurie and Clint.

A: Do you think they're right for each other?

B: Definitely. They're two people .... have a lot in common – but not *too* much.

A: What does that mean?

B: Well, you don't want a partner .... doesn't have his or her own interests. Couples .... do everything together usually don't last very long.

A: I guess you're right, but the opposite isn't good, either. My last girlfriend was someone .... I had nothing in common with. She wasn't the kind of girl .... I could talk to easily.

B: Well, you can talk to *me* easily. . . .

2 *It* clauses + adverbial clauses with *when* (page 6)

> ▶ In sentences with an *it* clause + an adverbial clause with *when*, the word *it* refers to and means the same as the adverbial clause with *when*. The *it* in these sentences is necessary and cannot be left out: I hate **it when** people talk on a cell phone in an elevator. (NOT: I ~~hate when~~ people . . .) **It** bothers me **when** people talk on a cell phone in an elevator. (NOT: ~~Bothers~~ me when people . . .)

Rewrite the sentences using the words in parentheses.

1. I can't stand it when people call me before 8:00 A.M. (it really bothers me)
   It really bothers me when people call me before 8:00 a.m.

2. It upsets me when I don't have enough time to study for an exam. (I hate it)

3. I don't mind it when friends talk to me about their problems. (it doesn't bother me)

4. I don't like it when I forget a co-worker's name. (it embarrasses me)

5. It makes me happy when my friends send me emails. (I love it)

6. I hate it when I have to wait for someone. (it upsets me)

Unit 2

1 Gerund phrases (page 9)

> ▶ A gerund phrase as a subject takes a singular verb: Taking care of children **is** a rewarding job. (NOT: Taking care of children ~~are~~ a rewarding job.)
> ▶ There are some common verb + preposition expressions (for example, *dream about, feel like, talk about, think about*) and adjective + preposition phrases (for example, *good/bad at, excited by/about, interested in, tired of, used to*) that are followed by a gerund: I'**m thinking about looking for** a new job. I'm **tired of working** long hours.

Complete the sentences with the correct gerund forms of the verbs in the box.

✓ become	have	make	stand	travel
change	learn	solve	take	work

1. My brother's very interested in ..*becoming*.. a flight attendant. He dreams about .... to new places.
2. I'm excited about .... a Japanese class next semester. I enjoy .... languages.
3. You wouldn't like .... in a restaurant. You'd get tired of .... on your feet throughout the long shifts!
4. Our teacher is very good at .... problems. Maybe she should think about .... careers to become a guidance counselor.
5. .... a living as a photographer could be challenging. .... an impressive portfolio is really important to attract new clients and employers.

2 Comparisons (page 11)

> ▶ When making general comparisons with count nouns, use *a/an* + singular noun or no article + plural noun: **A pilot** earns more than **a flight attendant**. **Pilots** earn more than **flight attendants**. (NOT: ~~The~~ pilots earn more than ~~the~~ flight attendants.)

Make comparisons with the information below. Add articles and other words necessary.

1. architect / more education / hairstylist
   An architect needs more education than a hairstylist.
2. college professor / earn more / elementary school teacher
   ....
3. nurses / worse hours / psychiatrists
   ....
4. working as a police officer / as dangerous / being a firefighter
   ....
5. taxi driver / not as well paid / electrician
   ....
6. being a tour guide / less interesting / being an actor
   ....

Unit 3

1 Requests with modals, *if* clauses, and gerunds (page 17)

▶ Use the simple past form – not the gerund or simple present form – after *if* with *Would you mind . . . ?* and *Would it be all right . . . ?*: **Would you mind if I used** your car? **Would it be all right if I used** your car? (NOT: Would you mind if I ~~using~~ your car? OR Would it be all right if I ~~use~~ your car?)

Read the situations. Then complete the requests.

1. You want to borrow a friend's underwater camera for a diving trip.
   A: I was wondering <u>if I could borrow your underwater camera.</u>
   B: Sure. That's fine. Just please be careful with it.
2. You want to use your roommate's computer.
   A: Is it OK _____
   B: You can use it, but please save my work first.
3. Your neighbor has a car. You need a ride to class.
   A: Would you mind _____
   B: I'd be glad to. What time should I pick you up?
4. You want your brother to help you move on Saturday.
   A: Can you _____
   B: I'm sorry. I'm busy all weekend.
5. You would like a second piece of your aunt's cherry pie.
   A: Would it be all right _____
   B: Yes, of course! Just pass me your plate.
6. You want to borrow your cousin's red sweater.
   A: Could you _____
   B: Sorry. I don't like it when other people wear my clothes.

2 Indirect requests (page 20)

▶ In indirect requests with negative infinitives, *not* comes before – not between – the infinitive: Could you tell Allie **not to be** late? (NOT: Could you tell Allie ~~to not be~~ late?)

Complete the indirect requests. Ask someone to deliver the messages to Susie.

1. Are you busy this weekend? → Could <u>you ask Susie if she's busy this weekend?</u>
2. Do you want to hang out with me? → Can _____
3. Email me. → Can _____
4. Do you know my address? → Can _____
5. Don't forget to write. → Could _____
6. What are you doing Saturday? → Can _____
7. Do you have plans on Sunday? → Could _____

Unit 4

1 Past continuous vs. simple past (page 23)

> ▶ Verbs for non-actions or states are rarely used in the past continuous: I **wanted** to stop, but I couldn't. (NOT: I ~~was wanting~~ to stop . . .)

Circle the best forms to complete the conversations.

1. A: How **did you break** / **were you breaking** your arm?
   B: It's a crazy story! Ramon and I **rode** / **were riding** our bikes in the park when a cat **ran** / **was running** out in front of me. I **went** / **was going** pretty fast, so when I **tried** / **was trying** to stop, I **went** / **was going** off the road and **fell** / **was falling**.
   A: That's terrible! **Did you go** / **Were you going** to the hospital after it **happened** / **was happening**?
   B: Yes. Luckily, we **weren't** / **weren't being** too far from City Hospital, so we **went** / **were going** there.

2. A: You'll never guess what **happened** / **was happening** to me this morning!
   B: What?
   A: Well, I **brushed** / **was brushing** my teeth when suddenly the water **went** / **was going** off. I **had** / **was having** toothpaste all over my mouth, and I couldn't wash it out.
   B: So what **did you do** / **were you doing**?
   A: Fortunately, I **had** / **was having** a big bottle of water in the refrigerator, so I **used** / **was using** that water to rinse my mouth.

2 Past perfect (page 25)

> ▶ Use the past perfect to show that one past action happened before another past action: I **wasn't able to** pay for lunch because I **had left** my wallet at work.
>
> PAST _____X_____X_____ NOW
>   had left   wasn't able
>   my wallet   to pay

Combine the two ideas into one with a past event and a past perfect event. Use *when* or *because*.

1. The museum closed. A thief stole a famous painting earlier.
   The museum closed because a thief had stolen a famous painting earlier.

2. We finished cleaning the house. Then our guests arrived.
   ....

3. Someone robbed my house yesterday. I left the window open.
   ....

4. There was no food in the house. We forgot to stop at the supermarket.
   ....

5. I called her three times. She finally answered.
   ....

6. I knew about the problem. Your brother told me about it.
   ....

Unit 5

1 Noun phrases containing relative clauses (page 31)

▶ The relative pronoun *who* or *that* can be left out in noun phrases as subjects and as objects. These four sentences have exactly the same meaning: One thing I'd be nervous about is getting lost. One thing that I'd be nervous about is getting lost. Getting lost is one thing I'd be nervous about. Getting lost is one thing that I'd be nervous about.

Answer the questions using the words in parentheses. Write each sentence two ways. Leave out the relative pronouns.

If you went to live in a foreign country, . . .

1. Who would you miss a lot? (person: my best friend)
   a. *One person I'd miss a lot is my best friend.*
   b. *My best friend is one person I'd miss a lot.*
2. What would you be very interested in? (things: the food and the music)
   a. ....
   b. ....
3. What would you be worried about? (something: not understanding the customs)
   a. ....
   b. ....
4. Who would you stay in touch with? (people: my brother and sister)
   a. ....
   b. ....
5. What would you feel insecure about? (thing: speaking a new language)
   a. ....
   b. ....

2 Expectations (page 33)

▶ Use the base form of a verb – not the gerund – after these expressions for expectations: *be the custom to, be supposed to, be expected to, be acceptable to*: It's the custom to **arrive** a little late. (NOT: It's the custom to ~~arriving~~ a little late.)

Complete the sentences with the clauses in the box.

> it's not acceptable to show up without calling first
> it's the custom for them to sit across from each other
> you're expected to reply within a few days
> you're supposed to bring a gift.
> ✓ you're supposed to shake his or her hand

1. When you meet someone for the first time, *you're supposed to shake his or her hand.*
2. When a friend sends you an email, ...
3. If you want to visit someone, ...
4. If you invite a married couple to dinner, ...
5. When you go to a birthday party, ...

Unit 6

1 Describing problems 1 (page 37)

▶ The simple past and the past participle of regular verbs are the same: I **chipped** the vase. The vase is **chipped**. BUT Many irregular verbs have different simple past and past participle forms: I **tore** my jacket. My jacket is **torn**.

Complete the conversations with the correct words from the box.

are stained	has a dent	✓ have a tear	is broken	is scratched
has a chip	has a stain	is a hole	is leaking	some damage

1. A: Oh, no! These jeans ....*have a tear*.... in them.
   B: And they .... , too.
2. A: This table has .... on top.
   B: I know. The wood .... because my son drags his toy cars on it.
3. A: Why are you drinking out of that glass? It .... in it.
   B: Oh, I didn't see it. That's why it ....
4. A: Someone hit my car today. Look! The door .... in it.
   B: I see that. Your back light .... , too.
5. A: I bought this blouse yesterday, but I have to take it back. There .... in it.
   B: It's really cute, but that's not the only problem. It .... on it, too.

2 Describing problems 2 (page 39)

▶ Use the past participle – not the present participle or gerund – with passive forms: The oven needs to be **fixed**. (NOT: The oven needs to be ~~fixing~~.)

A Complete the conversation with the verbs in parentheses. Use *need* + passive infinitive in A's lines and *need* + gerund in B's lines.

A: Look at this place! A lot of work ....*needs to be done*.... (do) before we move in.
B: You're not kidding. Let's make a list. First, the walls ....*need painting*.... (paint).
A: Right. And the windows .... (wash). Add the rug to your list: It really .... (clean). Do you think it .... (dry-clean)?
B: No, I think we can do it ourselves. It .... (shampoo). We can rent a machine for that.
A: And what about the ceiling fan? I think it .... (replace). Fans aren't too expensive.
B: OK. I've added it to the list. And what should we do with all this old furniture?
A: It .... (throw out)! I think the landlord should take care of | that, though.

B Complete the blog with the correct form of *keep* and the verb in parentheses.

I ....*keep having*.... (have) technical problems. My computer .... (crash), and my printer .... (jam). I have to .... (put) a new battery into my mouse because it .... (die). The letters on my keyboard .... (stick), too. I .... (think) things will get better, but they just .... (get) worse. Time for some new electronics!

Unit 7

1 Passive with prepositions (page 45)

▶ The prepositions *by, as a result of, because of, through,* and *due to* have similar meanings. They are used in sentences that describe cause and effect; they introduce the cause.

Match phrases from each column to make sentences. (More than one answer may be possible.)

Subject	Effect	Cause
1. The environment	is being contaminated due to	improper disposal of medical waste.
2. Our soil	is being harmed by	deforestation to make paper products.
3. Infectious diseases	are being endangered due to	hybrid cars.
4. Many different species	has been affected because of	the use of pesticides on fruits and vegetables.
5. Our air quality	has been reduced as a result of	the destruction of their habitats.
6. Smog pollution	have been spread through	climate changes like global warming.

2 Infinitive clauses and phrases (page 47)

▶ The form of *be* that follows the first infinitive must agree with the subject: The best way to reduce pollution **is** to improve public transportation. BUT The best ways to reduce homelessness **are** to build more public housing and provide free health care.

A Match the phrases.

1. What are the best ways to make ....e....
2. And the best way to do that is ....
3. The best ways to reduce ....
4. One way to improve ....
5. Another way to make ....

a. people happier is to make the air healthier.
b. to create a larger police force.
c. people's quality of life is to help them feel safe.
d. air pollution are to ban cars and control industry.
e. this city a better place to live?

B Complete the conversation with the sentences above.

A: What are the best ways to make this city a better place to live?
B: Well, ...
A: That's right. ....
B: I agree. ....
A: Yes. Good air quality is key. ....
B: Maybe it's time to share our ideas with the mayor. Hand me my laptop.

Unit 8

1 *Would rather* and *would prefer* (page 51)

▶ In negative statements with *would rather* and *would prefer*, the word *not* comes after the verbs: I'**d rather not**/I'**d prefer not** to take any courses this semester. (NOT: I ~~wouldn't rather~~/I ~~wouldn't prefer~~ to . . .)

Write questions and responses using the words in parentheses.

1. A: *Would you prefer to take classes during the day or at night?*
      (prefer / take classes / during the day / at night)
   B: ....
      (rather / take classes / at night)

2. A: ....
      (rather / study / business / education)
   B: ....
      (prefer / major in / education)

3. A: ....
      (prefer / sign up for / a biology course / an engineering course)
   B: ....
      (rather / not / take / either)

4. A: ....
      (rather / take / computer science / history)
   B: ....
      (prefer / not / take / a class this semester)

2 *By* + gerund to describe how to do things (page 53)

▶ In negative sentences that express comparison with *by* + gerund and *but*, *not* comes before *by*: A good way to improve your accent is **not by watching** TV **but by talking** to native speakers. In negative sentences with *by* that give advice without a comparison, *not* comes after *by*: A good way to improve your accent is **by not imitating** non-native speakers.

Combine the two ideas into one sentence using *by* + gerund.

1. There is a good way to learn idioms. Learners can watch American movies.
   A good way to learn idioms is by watching American movies.

2. You can build your vocabulary. Write down new words and expressions.
   ....

3. Students can improve their listening skills. They can listen to English-language radio.
   ....

4. Hardworking students improve their grammar. They don't repeat common mistakes.
   ....

5. You can become fluent. Don't translate everything. Try to think in English.
   ....

6. You can become a good conversationalist. Don't just talk with others. Talk to yourself when you're alone, too.
   ....

Unit 9

1 Get or have something done (page 59)

▶ Sentences with *get/have* + object + past participle are passive. BUT Don't use any form of *be* before the past participle: Where can I **have** my watch **fixed**? (NOT: Where can I have my watch be fixed?)

Rewrite the statements as questions with *Where can I get/have . . . ?* Then complete B's answers with the information in parentheses.

1. I want to have someone shorten this skirt.
   A: Where can I have this skirt shortened?
   B: You can have it shortened at Cathy's Cleaners. .... (at Cathy's Cleaners)
2. I need to get someone to repair my computer.
   A: ....
   B: .... (at Hackers Inc.)
3. I need to have someone prepare my taxes.
   A: ....
   B: .... (by my accountant)
4. I'd like to get someone to cut my hair.
   A: ....
   B: .... (at Beauty Barn)
5. I need to have someone paint my apartment.
   A: ....
   B: .... (by Peter the Painter)

2 Making suggestions (page 61)

▶ Use the base form of a verb – without *to* – after *Maybe you could . . .* and *Why don't you . . . ?*: Maybe you could **join** a book club. (NOT: Maybe you could to join a book club.) Why don't you **join** a book club? (NOT: Why don't you to join a book club?)

Complete the conversations with the correct form of the verbs in parentheses.

A: I'm having trouble meeting people here in the city. Any ideas?
B: I know it's hard. Why don't you ......join...... (join) a gym? That's usually a good place to meet people. Or maybe you could .... (take) a class at the community college.
A: What about .... (check out) the personal ads? Do you think that's a good way to meet people?
B: I wouldn't recommend doing that. People never tell the truth in those ads. But it might be a good idea .... (find) a sports team. Have you thought about .... (play) a team sport – maybe baseball or volleyball?
A: I'm not very good at most sports, but I used to play tennis.
B: There you go! One option is .... (look up) tennis clubs in the city and see which clubs have teams people can join.
A: Now, that's a great idea. And I could always use the exercise!

Unit 10

1 Referring to time in the past (page 65)

> ▶ Use *since* with a particular time: The UN has been in existence **since** 1945. Use *for* with a duration of time: The UN has been in existence **for** about the last 70 years.
> ▶ Use *in* and *during* with a specific period of time: Rock 'n' roll became popular **in/during** the 1950s.
> ▶ Use *from* and *to* to describe when something began and ended: World War II lasted **from** 1939 **to** 1945.

Complete the conversation with the words in the box. (Use some of the words more than once.)

ago	during	for	from	in	since	to

A: Hey, Dad. Did you use to listen to the Beatles?

B: Of course. In fact, I just listened to one of their records a few days
.......*ago*....... . Do you realize that the Beatles' music has influenced
other musicians .... over 50 years? They were the greatest!

A: Well, I just found some interesting information about them. I'll read it
to you: "The Beatles were a well-known British band .... the
1960s. They performed together .... ten years – ....
1960 .... 1970. .... 2003, the Beatles released another
album, even though one of the original members had been dead
.... 1980 and another had died .... 2001. The album
had been recorded .... 1969 and was in the studio safe
.... 34 years before it was released."

B: That *is* interesting. It's pretty amazing that people have listened
to the Beatles .... both the twentieth and the twenty-first
centuries, isn't it?

2 Predicting the future with *will* (page 67)

> ▶ In sentences referring to time, the preposition *by* means "not later than." Don't confuse *by* with *within*, which means "some time during." Use *by* with points in time; use *within* with periods of time: **By** 2050, we will have eliminated starvation around the world. (NOT: ~~Within~~ 2050, . . .) **Within** the next five years, people will have invented mobile phone applications for nearly everything! (NOT: ~~By~~ the next five years, . . .)

Circle the correct verb forms to complete the conversation.

A: What do you think you **will do** / (**will be doing**) five years from now?

B: I'm not sure. Maybe I **will get** / **will have gotten** married by then.
How about you?

A: I **will be finishing** / **will have finished** medical school, so I
will be doing / **will have done** my internship five years from now.

B: So you **won't be living** / **won't have lived** around here in five years,
I guess. Where do you think you **will live** / **will have lived**?

A: Wherever I get my internship.

Unit 11

1 Time clauses (page 73)

> ▶ Use the past perfect in the main clause with *until* and *by the time*. This shows that one of the past events happened before the other: Until I got my driver's license, I **had** always **taken** public transportation. By the time I got my driver's license, all of my friends **had** already **gotten** theirs.

Circle the correct time expression to complete each sentence.

1. **After /** (**Until**) I traveled overseas, I hadn't known much about different cultures.
2. **After / Before** I got a full-time job, I had to live on a very limited budget.
3. **By the time / Once** I finished high school, I had already taken three college courses.
4. **As soon as / Before** I left for college, my mother turned my room into her office.
5. **Once / Until** I left home, I realized how much my family meant to me.
6. **By the time / The moment** you have a child, you feel totally responsible for him or her.

2 Expressing regret and describing hypothetical situations (page 75)

> ▶ Conditional sentences describing hypothetical situations often refer to both the present and the past:
> If I'**d finished** college, I'**d have** a better job now.
>   past   present
> (NOT: If I'd finished college, I'd ~~have had~~ a better job now.)

A Write sentences with *should (not) have* to express regret about each person's situation.

1. Sarah was very argumentative with her teacher, so she had to stay after school.
   Sarah shouldn't have been argumentative with her teacher.
2. Ivan didn't save up for a car, so he still has to take public transportation.
   ....
3. Jon was very inactive when he was in college, so he gained a lot of weight.
   ....
4. Lisa didn't stay in touch with her high school classmates, so now she has very few friends.
   ....
5. Tony didn't study Spanish in school, so he's not bilingual now.
   ....

B Rewrite your sentences in Exercise A, changing them to hypothetical situations.

1. *If Sarah hadn't been argumentative with her teacher, she wouldn't have had to stay after school.*
2. ....
   ....
3. ....
   ....
4. ....
   ....
5. ....
   ....

Unit 12

1 Describing purpose (page 79)

▶ Don't use *for* immediately before an infinitive: **To have** a successful business, you need a lot of luck. (NOT: ~~For~~ to have a successful business, you need a lot of luck.)

A Complete the sentences with *in order to* or *in order for*.

1. ......In order for...... a supermarket to succeed, it has to be clean and well organized.
2. .... stay popular, a website needs to be accurate and visually attractive.
3. .... run a profitable furniture store, it's important to advertise on TV.
4. .... a restaurant to stay in business, it needs to have "regulars" – customers that come often.
5. .... establish a successful nail salon, it has to have a convenient location.
6. .... an online business to survive, it's a good idea to have excellent pictures of the merchandise it's selling.

B Rewrite the sentences in Exercise A without *In order*.

1. .....For a supermarket to succeed, it has to be clean and well organized.....................
2. ....
3. ....
4. ....
5. ....
6. ....

2 Giving reasons (page 81)

▶ *Because* and *since* have the same meaning, and they can begin or end a sentence: **Because/Since** the food is always fantastic, Giorgio's is my favorite restaurant. = Giorgio's is my favorite restaurant **because/since** the food is always fantastic.
▶ Don't confuse *because* and *because of*. *Because* introduces an adverb clause and is followed by a subject and verb, while *because of* is a preposition and is followed by a noun object: **Because** Giorgio's is so popular, we should get there early. Giorgio's is popular **because of** its food and service.

Circle the correct words to complete the conversation.

A: I had to go downtown today **because / because of / due to** I needed to mail a package at the post office. **Due to / For / Since** I was only a few blocks from Main Street, I went over to Martin's. Did you know that Martin's has gone out of business? I'm so upset!

B: That's too bad, but I'm not surprised. A lot of family-owned shops are closing **because / because of / since** the construction of shopping malls.

A: Yeah, and don't forget about all the megastores that are popping up everywhere. **Because / For / The reason why** people prefer to shop there is to save money. Everyone loves a megastore **because / due to / since** the low prices and the huge selection.

B: Not me! I loved Martin's **for / since / the reason that** their beautiful clothes and friendly salespeople. When you were there, you almost felt like family. You'll never get that at a megastore!

Unit 13

1 Past modals for degrees of certainty (page 87)

▶ Use the past modal *could have* to express possibility. BUT Use *couldn't have* when you are almost 100% sure something is impossible: I suppose he **could have gotten** stuck in traffic, but he **couldn't have forgotten** his own birthday party.

Complete the conversations with past modals *must (not) have, could (not) have,* or *may/might (not) have*. Use the degrees of certainty and the verbs in parentheses. (More than one answer may be possible.)

1. A: Yoko still hasn't called me back.
   B: She ....*might not have gotten*.... your message. (it's possible – not get)
2. A: What's wrong with Steven?
   B: Oh, you .... the news. His dog ran away. (it's almost certain – not hear)
3. A: I went to see the Larsens today, but they didn't answer the door.
   B: Was their car there? If so, they .... in the backyard. (it's possible – be)
4. A: Fabio said he was going to the party last night, but I didn't see him.
   B: Neither did I. He .... there then. (it's not possible – not be)
5. A: I can't find my glasses, but I know I had them at work today.
   B: You .... them at the office. (it's possible – leave)
6. A: Marc's new car looks really expensive.
   B: Yes, it does. It .... a fortune! (it's almost certain – cost)

2 Past modals for judgments and suggestions (page 89)

▶ In advice with *would have*, the speaker means, "If I were you, ..."

Read each situation and choose the corresponding judgment or suggestion for an alternative past action.

Situation
1. Sue forgot her boyfriend's birthday. ...*b*...
2. Tim got a speeding ticket. ....
3. Ruth still hasn't paid me back. ....
4. Bill lied to us. ....
5. I spent an hour making Joe dinner, and he didn't even thank me. ....
6. Carol came over for dinner empty-handed. ....

Judgment/Suggestion
a. I wouldn't have lent her money.
b. She should have put it on her calendar.
c. He should have told the truth.
d. He shouldn't have gone over the limit.
e. She should have brought something.
f. I wouldn't have cooked for him.

Unit 14

1 The passive to describe process (page 93)

> ▶ The modals *have to* and *need to* must agree with the subject; other modals, like *may be*, have only one form: Each scene **has to/needs to** be filmed from several different angles.

Put the words in the correct order to make sentences.

1. overnight / business / A / started / small / isn't / .
   A small business isn't started overnight.
2. to / plan / business / a / written / First, / be / has / .
   ....
3. research / Next, / done / be / market / should / .
   ....
4. needs / competition / to / the / Then / identified / be / .
   ....
5. online / ads / posted / be / Classified / may / .
   ....
6. work / are / employees / be / hired / can / started / the / so / Finally, / .
   ....

2 Defining and non-defining relative clauses (page 96)

> ▶ Use either *who* or *that* in defining relative clauses about people: A set designer is an artist **who/that** makes important contributions to a theater production. BUT Use only *who* in non-defining relative clauses about people: A set designer, **who** makes important contributions to a theater production, has to be very creative. (NOT: A set designer, ~~that~~ makes . . .)
> ▶ Use commas before and after a non-defining clause: A gossip columnist**,** who gets to go to fabulous parties**,** writes about celebrities and scandals.

Combine these sentences with *who* or *that*. Add a comma wherever one is necessary.

1. A prop designer makes sure everything on a movie set looks realistic.
   He or she is good with details.
   A prop designer, who is good with details, makes sure everything on a movie set
   looks realistic.
2. A screenwriter is a talented person. He or she develops a story idea into a
   movie script.
   A screenwriter is a talented person that develops a story idea into a movie script.
3. A script doctor is a writer. He or she is used when a screenplay needs
   more work.
   ....
4. Casting directors choose an actor for each part in a movie. They have
   usually been in the movie business for a long time.
   ....
   ....
5. High-budget movies always use big stars. The stars are known around
   the world.
   ....
6. Movie directors are greatly respected. They "make or break" a film.
   ....

Unit 15

1 Giving recommendations and opinions (page 101)

> ▶ *Ought to* has the same meaning as *should*, but it's more formal: Traffic signs **ought to** be obeyed. = Traffic signs **should** be obeyed.

A student committee is discussing rules for their school. Complete speaker B's sentences with appropriate passive modals. (More than one answer is possible.)

1. A: Students must be required to clean off the cafeteria tables after lunch.
   B: I disagree. Students ....*shouldn't be required*.... to do that. That's what the cafeteria workers are paid to do.
2. A: Teachers shouldn't be allowed to park in the student parking lot.
   B: Why not? Teachers .... to park wherever a space is available. After all, they're here for us.
3. A: A rule has to be made to ban the use of cell phones in school.
   B: I don't think a rule .... Students may need their phones for emergency purposes.
4. A: Students mustn't be permitted to use calculators during math exams.
   B: Sometimes we .... to use them, especially when we're being tested on more complicated concepts than simple arithmetic.
5. A: Something has got to be done to control the noise in the hallways.
   B: Students .... to talk to each other between classes, though. They aren't disturbing anyone when classes aren't in session.
6. A: Teachers must be required to remind students about important exams.
   B: That's unnecessary. On the contrary, students .... to follow the syllabus and check important dates on the course websites.

2 Tag questions for opinions (page 103)

> ▶ Tag questions added to statements in the simple present and simple past use the corresponding auxiliary verb in the tag: You **agree** with me, **don't** you? You **don't agree** with me, **do** you? You **paid** the rent, **didn't** you? You **didn't pay** the electric bill, **did** you?

Check (✓) the sentences if the tag questions are correct. If they're incorrect, write the correct tag questions.

1. Food is getting more and more expensive, ~~is it~~? ....*isn't it*........
2. Supermarkets should try to keep their prices down, shouldn't they? ....✓........
3. People don't buy as many fresh fruits and vegetables as they used to, do we? ....
4. We have to buy healthy food for our children, don't we? ....
5. Many children go to school hungry, won't they? ....
6. Some people can't afford to eat meat every day, don't they? ....
7. We can easily live without eating meat every day, can we? ....
8. A lot of people are having a hard time making ends meet these days, haven't they? ....

Unit 16

1 Complex noun phrases containing gerunds (page 107)

> ▶ Complex noun phrases usually contain gerunds. Often they are also followed by gerunds: One of the most challenging things about **being** a teacher is **not becoming** impatient with difficult students.
>
> ▶ Different prepositions follow different nouns. Use *about* with *thing(s)*: What's the best thing **about** working from home? BUT Use *of* after *challenge(s), reward(s)* and *aspect(s)*: What's one of the rewards **of** being a social worker? One of the best aspects **of** being a social worker is helping people. NOTE: Use *of* or *about* with *part(s)*: What's the best part **about** being a mom? The best part **of** it is being a witness to your children's lives.

Read each situation. Use the words in parentheses to write a sentence with a noun phrase containing a gerund.

1. I work in an office. (one challenge = getting along with co-workers)
   One of the challenges of working in an office is getting along with your co-workers.

2. I have a job abroad. (most difficult thing = dealing with homesickness)
   ....

3. I work in a nursing home. (best aspect = helping people feel more positive about life)
   ....

4. I work in a rural clinic. (most frustrating part = not having enough supplies)
   ....

5. I'm a child-care worker. (one reward = making the children feel safe)
   ....

2 Accomplishments and goals (page 109)

> ▶ When talking about past accomplishments and including a specific time, use the simple past – not the present perfect: I **was** able to complete my degree last year. (NOT: I've been able to complete my degree last year.)

A Complete the sentences about Ana's accomplishments. Use the verbs in parentheses. (More than one answer is possible.)

In the last five years, Ana . . .
1. *managed to finish* .... (finish) college.
2. .... (pay) all her college loans.
3. .... (start) her own company.
4. .... (move) to the city.
5. .... (make) some new friends.

B Complete the sentences about Ana's goals. Use the verbs in parentheses. (More than one answer is possible.)

Five years from now, Ana . . .
1. *would like to have expanded* ...... (expand) her business.
2. .... (meet) the man of her dreams.
3. .... (travel) to South America and Asia.
4. .... (get) married.
5. .... (buy) a house.

Unit 1 Language summary

Vocabulary

Nouns
acceptance
accomplishment
affection
(positive) attitude
capabilities
companionship
compassion
compliments
cyberfriend
phenomenon
respect
responsibility
roommate
sense of humor
trust
understanding
wedding

Pronouns
anyone
herself
himself
others
someone
something

Adjectives
Personalities
carefree
considerate
direct
easygoing
egotistical
encouraging
friendly
inflexible
modest
neat
(un)pleasant
(un)predictable
(un)reliable
sensitive
serious
sociable
steady
stingy
stubborn
supportive
temperamental
Other
close (friend)
drastic
ideal
nasty
(un)wanted

Verbs
Modals
can
could
should
will
would
Other
accomplish
achieve
bother
brag
can't stand
dump
eliminate
find
get (along/angry/annoyed/rid of)
go out (with)
have (a sense of humor/in common/fun [with])
make (friends)
put (someone on hold)
remove
treat (someone to dinner)

Adverb
endlessly

Preposition
during (a movie)

Expressions

Expressing likes and dislikes
What kind of . . . do you like?
  I like people who/that . . .
  I'd prefer someone who/that . . .
I like/love (it when) . . .
I'd really like to . . .
I don't mind it when . . .
It makes me happy when . . .

Asking for more information
What else?
Complaining
I can't stand it when . . .
It annoys/bothers/upsets
  me when . . .
I hate it when . . .

Making an offer
Let me . . .
*Expressing agreement and
  disagreement*
For me, . . .
I think . . .
I agree.
I'm not sure I agree.
I feel the same way.

    Interchange Teacher's Edition 3 © Cambridge University Press 2013 Photocopiable

Unit 2 Language summary

Vocabulary

Nouns

Jobs/Occupations/Careers
accountant
air traffic controller
bank teller
(high school) coach
(gossip) columnist
comedian
(guidance) counselor
(clothing) designer
(TV) director
doctor
(truck) driver
(simulation) engineer
entrepreneur
(organic food) farmer
firefighter
flight attendant
headhunter
(diagnostic) imaging
intern
landscaper
(social media) manager
pharmacist
(nuclear) physicist
pilot
police officer
politician
(TV) reporter
(green) researcher
supervisor
(health informatics) technician
telesales
veterinarian
(social) worker
zookeeper

Other
(dis)advantage
brand
fields (of research)
landscaping
(job) lead
pesticides
representation
salary
(flight) simulator
tan
volunteer work

Adjectives
ambitious
beloved
bossy
environmentally friendly
harmful
in demand
introverted
moody
nosy
outspoken
rewarding
satisfying
social
straightforward
suited to
sustainable
talkative
virtual
wealthy

Verbs
diagnose
dominate
earn
relocate
seem
sound
train
treat (a patient)

Adverbs
overseas
probably

Conjunctions
as
but

Expressions

Giving an opinion
In my opinion, . . .
Interpreting information
It sounds like . . .
Expressing personal preferences
I'd be interested in . . .
I'd get tired of . . .
I'm very excited by . . .
I'd enjoy . . .
I think I'd be good at . . .
I wouldn't be very good at . . .

Disagreeing
I'm not so sure.
That's not true.
I disagree!
Beginning a series
First of all, . . .
Adding information
In addition, . . .
For example, . . .
Furthermore, . . .
However, . . .
On the other hand, . . .
In conclusion, . . .

Expressing surprise
Really?
Expressing enthusiasm
Guess what . . . .
That's great!

Unit 3 Language summary

Vocabulary

Nouns

apology
favor
miscommunication
mountain bike
sleeping bag
vending machine

Adjectives

broke
complicated
free (= not busy)
ready

Verbs

accept (an apology/an invitation/
   a request)
act (out)
decline (a request)

do (a favor)
find (out)
finish
give (a gift)
give up
have (a party)
help (out)
ignore
look at
make (a phone call/a request/noise)
move (away)
nod
offer (an apology)
owe (an apology)
receive (a compliment/a gift/an
   invitation/a phone call)
rephrase

return (a favor/a phone call/
   a compliment)
shake
take back
take care (of)
turn down (an invitation)

Adverbs

before
completely
eagerly
recently

Expressions

Talking on the telephone
Hi, ... This is . . .
   Oh, hi, ... What's up?
**Making, accepting, and declining
   requests**
Can I . . . ?/Could you. . . , please?
   Yes./Sorry, but . . .
Is it OK if I . . . ?
   Of course.
Would it be all right/OK if I . . . ?
   Fine. No problem.
Do you mind if I . . . ?/Would you mind
   if I . . . ?
   No, I don't mind.
I was wondering if I could . . .
   Sure, that's fine.

Thanking someone
Thanks a million./Thanks. I really
   appreciate it.
   Sure.
Making indirect requests
Could you tell . . . (that) . . . ?
Please tell . . . (that) . . .
Would you ask . . . if/whether/
   to . . . ?
Can you tell . . . (not) to . . . ?
Can/Could you ask . . . if/
   whether . . . ?
Please ask . . . if/whether . . .
Can/Could you ask . . . what/
   when . . . ?

Apologizing
I'm sorry.
I'm really sorry.
Sorry.

Unit 4 Language summary

Vocabulary

Nouns

Events
coincidence
dilemma
disaster
emergency
lucky break
misfortune
mystery
triumph

Other
achievement
ambulance
blog(ger)
broadcaster
camcorder
carjacker
coast
destruction
diver
(revolving) door
driver
e-commerce
elevator
(good) fortune
freeway
gold
honeymoon
journalist
(driver's) license
locker

mailbox
mansion
pain
police
(hair care) product
(coral) reef
robbery
shipwreck
software
species
stuff
(hair)stylist
suffering
surprise
thief
videophone
yacht

Adjectives
connected
entire
interactive
puzzling
quick
strange
sudden
unexplained

Verbs

Modal
be (un)able to

Other
arrest
break into
come back
e-publish
get (caught/stuck)
insist
interrupt
involve
kick
(un)lock
move on
perform
propose
reach
rob
run out (of)
score
supersede
trip
vanish

Adverbs
accidentally
fortunately

Preposition
off

Conjunction
even though

Expressions

Reacting to a story
What happened?
Oh, no!
That's terrible!

Exclaiming
What a (pain/. . .)!

Unit 5 Language summary

Vocabulary

Nouns
behavior
(religious) belief(s)
challenge
climate
cooking
culture
custom
shock
housewarming
host
language
mosque
pamphlet
(wedding) reception
temple
tip

Adjectives
Feelings
anxious
(un)comfortable
confident
curious
embarrassed
enthusiastic
fascinated
homesick
insecure
nervous
uncertain
worried
Other
unique

Verbs
avoid
behave
blow (your nose)
communicate
drop by
eat out
end up
feel
get used to
get sick
have (a baby)

keep (in mind)
plan
shout (out)
split (= divide evenly)
take (photographs)

Adverbs
afterward
along
appropriately
especially
(the) most
whenever

Prepositions
by (bus/train)
for (a while/example)
in (public)

Expressions

Expressing emotions
One thing/Something (that) I'd be
    (anxious/excited/ . . .) about is . . .
Asking for permission
Is it all right to . . . ?

Describing expectations
You're supposed to . . .
You aren't supposed to . . .
You're expected to . . .
It's the custom to . . .
It's not acceptable to . . .

Expressing an opinion/a feeling
Oh, how (nice/awful/ . . .)!

Interchange Teacher's Edition 3 © Cambridge University Press 2013 Photocopiable

Unit 6 Language summary

Vocabulary

Nouns

Electronics
battery
computer (screen)
DVD player
(ceiling) fan
joystick
oven
printer
refrigerator
remote/temperature control
telephone
TV (screen)
washing machine

Other
asset
bit
complaint
crack
damage
denim
discount
dry cleaner
evidence
lamp shade
leaf (leaves)
lens(es)
(jacket) lining
mosaic
mug
pair (of)
pitcher

receipt
refund
roof
scratch
shirt
signal
skin
stain
stool
store credit
straw
tablecloth
tabletop
tear
temperature
vase
wastebasket
wireless service
wrapper

Pronoun
everything

Adjectives

Past participles
chipped
cracked
damaged
dented
made
scratched
stained
torn
worn

Other
dirty
solar-powered
throwaway
undercooked

Verbs
adjust
break (down)
charge
crash
deliver
die
endanger
flicker
have (an eye for)
jam
leak
purchase
repair
replace
reuse
shrink
skip
work (= function)

Adverbs
by hand
even
right away/now
throughout

Expressions

Offering help
Can I help you?
What can I do for you?

Describing problems
What's wrong with it?
  It's torn/stained/damaged/
  scratched/cracked/chipped/worn.
What exactly is the problem?
  It has a tear/a hole/a stain/
  some damage.
  There are a few scratches.
  There's a crack.
  It's leaking./It has a leak.

Adding information
In fact, . . .

Unit 7 Language summary

Vocabulary

Nouns

World problems
acid rain
cancer
drug trafficking
e-waste
extinction
famine
global warming
government corruption
(the) homeless
inflation
overcrowding
overbuilding
overpopulation
political unrest
pollution
poverty
unemployment

The Earth
air
bacteria
birds
coral reef
ecosystem
fish
lake
land
marine life
ocean
oil
plant
rain forest
river
soil
wildlife

Other
chemicals
cyanide
demonstration
dependence
destruction
executive
explosives
factory
farm(land)
fumes
growth
health
industry
landfill
law
livestock
management
overuse
petition
(training) programs
publicity
recycling
reduction
run (a story)
sanctuary
shelter
sit-in
source
(TV) station
suburbs
supply
(heavy) traffic

Adjectives
alarming
free
illegal
innovative

major
underground
unemployed
urban
vocational
wasteful

Verbs
boycott
conserve
contaminate
create
deplete
develop
displace
dispose (of)
educate
erode
harm
ignore
improve
pollute
pump
reduce
threaten
voice (= share/talk about)

Adverbs
inevitably
moreover
outside

Prepositions
against (the law)
as a result of
because of
due to
on (the street)

Expressions

Describing problems
The . . . are being . . . by . . .
(The) . . . is being . . . because of/
   due to . . .
The . . . have been . . . through . . .
(The) . . . has been . . . as a
   result of . . .

Offering solutions
One thing to change things is to . . .
Another way to stop them is to . . .
The best way to help is to . . .

Talking about what will happen
What if . . . ?
   Well, then . . .

Identifying something
What's the name of . . . ?
   It's called . . .

Unit 8 Language summary

Vocabulary

Nouns
College majors
biology
business
communications
computer science
education
engineering
English
geography
history
journalism
nursing
psychology
social sciences

Language learning
accent
grammar
idiom
learner's dictionary
pronunciation
translation
(private) tutor
vocabulary

Personal qualities
artistic appreciation
communication skills
competitiveness
concern for others
cooperation
courtesy
creativity
perseverance
self-confidence
tolerance

Other
application (of skills)
ballroom dancing
commerce
computation
cuisine
curriculum
finance
formula
foundation
fundamentals
marketing
martial art
new media
presentation
principle

Adjectives
interpersonal
intrapersonal
kinesthetic
native
practical
private
right (= correct)
theoretical
useful

Verbs
acquire
analyze
attend
encounter
grasp
join
learn (about)
sign up (for)
take (a class/a course [on/in])
volunteer

Adverb
correctly

Expressions

Asking about preferences
Would you rather . . . or . . . ?
  I'd rather (not) . . .
Would you prefer to . . . or . . . ?
  (I think) I'd prefer . . . to . . .
  I'd prefer (to) . . .
Let's . . .
  I'd rather not./I'd prefer not to.

Asking for personal information
How's (your French class/ . . .)
  going?
  Not bad.

Talking about learning methods
You could . . . by . . .
  That's a good idea.
I . . . by . . .
  Maybe I should try that!
A good way to . . . is by . . .

Admitting something
To tell you the truth, . . .

Unit 9 Language summary

Vocabulary

Nouns

Services

beauty services
computer services
(house) cleaning
dry cleaning
financial services
language tutoring
laundry
moving services
music lessons
online-dating service
pet-sitting
(home) repairs

Other

bias
consultant
fingernail
photo

prejudice
priorities
reunion
shyness
vending machine

Adjectives

critical (thinking)
fake
fatty
overweight
sufficient
various

Verbs

Phrasal

break up with
come up with
cut down on
get along with

look forward to
keep up with
put up with
take care of

Other

crack (your knuckles)
examine
guarantee
integrate
overcome
quit
react
upgrade

Adverbs

absolutely
objectively
professionally
subjectively

Expressions

Talking about things you need to have done

Where I can have/get . . . ?
   You can have/get . . .

Asking for and giving advice

What can I do?
   What about . . . ?
   Have you thought about . . . ?
   Why don't you . . . ?
   Maybe you could . . .
   One option is (to) . . .
   It might be a good idea to . . .

Replying to advice

I don't think that's a very good idea.
Actually, I've tried that.

Expressing frustration

This is so depressing!

Interchange Teacher's Edition 3 © Cambridge University Press 2013 Photocopiable

Unit 10 Language summary

Vocabulary

Nouns
Historic events
achievement
assassination
discovery
election
epidemic
invention
natural disaster
terrorism/terrorist act
Other
baldness
billion
century
compass
connectivity
contributor
craze
debate
disco

existence
fad
feather
fusion
horn
human
ice cap
impact
microchip
penicillin
sculptor
sensation
spacecraft
summit
thought
vaccine
voice command

Pronouns
everyone
everywhere

Adjectives
coastal
polar

Verbs
age
downgrade
hijack
prevent
release
set up
translate

Adverb
so far

Prepositions
for (44 years)
in (existence/1989)
within (20 years)

Expressions

Talking about historical events
When did . . . begin?
  During/In the (1940s/ . . .).
  About . . . years ago.
How long was the . . . ?
  From . . . to . . . ./For . . . years.
How long has the . . . been in
  existence?
  Since . . ./For about the
  last . . . years.
  For over . . . years.

Saying you do something well
I'm good at . . .
Offering to solve a problem
Let me give it a try.
Making a prediction
I bet . . .

Unit 11 Language summary

Vocabulary

Nouns
attendee
bank account
bouquet
bungee jumpers
ceremony
cradle
evil
girlhood
ground
high school
importance
manhood
(safety) net
paycheck
pharaoh
promotion
relationship
rite of passage
sense
Sweet 15/16
turning point
vine
womanhood

Pronouns
myself
themselves

Adjectives
Behavior and personality
ambitious
argumentative
carefree
conscientious
(im)mature
naive
pragmatic
rebellious
(ir)responsible
selfish
sensible
sophisticated
spectacular
Other
ancient
broke
ready
wooden

Verbs
appreciate
ensure
demonstrate
distribute
find out
hurl
look back
prove
retire
rock
save (money)
scatter
symbolize

Adverbs
gently
not . . . anymore
plenty

Expressions

Describing yourself in the past
By the time I was 15, . . .
The moment I got my first
  paycheck, . . .
Before I had my first job, . . .
Once you get a credit card, . . .
After I finished college, . . .
As soon as I left home, . . .
Until I graduated, . . .

Describing regrets about the past
I should have . . ./I shouldn't
  have . . .
*Describing hypothetical
  situations*
If I had . . . , I would have . . .
If I had . . . , I wouldn't be . . .
Asking for clarification
What do you mean?

Interchange Teacher's Edition 3 © Cambridge University Press 2013 Photocopiable

Unit 12 Language summary

Vocabulary

Nouns

Businesses
athletic center
(clothing) boutique
coffee bar
concert hall
dance club
health club
megastore
supermarket

Other
acoustics
advertising
ancestors
coincidence
packaging
reason
slogan
trainer
wait

Adjectives

Qualities for success
affordable
charming
clever
convenient
countless
dependable
effective
entertaining
fashionable
industrious
informative
knowledgeable
muscular
persuasive
slender
tough
well written

Other
alarmed
brand new

catchy
crowded
diverse
dumb
funny (= strange)
packed
profitable
shocking
trendy

Verbs
attract
be seen
operate
overlook
plead
succeed
turn out

Adverbs
literally
worldwide

Expressions

*Describing the purpose of
    something*
In order to . . . , you need to . . .
(In order) for a/an . . . to . . . , it
    has to . . .
To . . . , it's a good idea to . . .

Giving reasons
I like . . . because . . .
It's so popular because of the . . .
The reason people . . . is to . . .
Due to . . .

Hypothesizing
I think another reason why . . .
    is . . .
It could be . . .

Accepting an invitation
I thought you'd never ask!

Unit 13 Language summary

Vocabulary

Nouns

Reactions
assumption
criticism
demand
excuse
prediction
suggestion
suspicion
warning

Other
(recycling) bin
explanation
graveyard
helmet
locksmith
mining town
mood
radioactivity/radioactive ore
pet peeve
tombstone
voice mail

Pronoun
one

Adjectives
complicated
eerie
inconsiderate
guilty
messy
prosperous
rotting

Verbs
accuse
burst (out laughing)
check (e-mail/one's messages)
chew
dent
fire
impress

interrupt
miss out (on)
slip (one's mind)
turn up
vanish
yawn

Adverbs
all the time
constantly
ethereally
slowly

Conjunction
however

Expressions

Expressing curiosity
I wonder what happened.
Offering to do something
Why don't I . . . ?

Saying you can't be exact
. . . or something.
Expressing approval of someone's action
. . . did the right thing.

Interchange Teacher's Edition 3 © Cambridge University Press 2013 Photocopiable

Unit 14 Language summary

Vocabulary

Nouns

Movies
actor
angle
costume
detail
director
editor
film
location
outline
review
scene
screen
screenplay
script
set
shot
special effects
studio
(movie) theater

Media professions
cinematographer
computer programmer
(art/casting/editorial) director
dialect coach
(photo) editor
film composer
location scout
makeup artist
movie extra
movie producer
network installer

newscaster
(costume/page/prop/set/software/
    special-effects) designer
screenwriter
sitcom writer
script doctor
stagehand
stunt person
talk show host
(lighting/sound-effects) technician

Other
computer graphics
(rock) concert
fashion show
industry
spooky
stage
(TV) sitcom
    (= situational comedy)
thousands (of)
villain

Adjectives

advanced
beloved
computer-animated
defenseless
deserted
elaborate
final
flashy
melodramatic
three-dimensional (3-D)

Verbs

complete
depend
divide
expand
gross (= earn)
pack into
pick
prepare
rehearse
run (= last)
shoot (a [movie] scene)
stand in (for)
stick out
twirl
write out

Adverbs

separately
soon after

Prepositions

in (order/sequence)
on (stage)

Expressions

**Explaining or identifying
    someone**
. . . is the person who/that . . .
Asking for an explanation
Why is that?

Saying you haven't decided yet
It depends.
Talking about an opportunity
I get to . . .

Unit 15 Language summary

Vocabulary

Nouns

Social issues
bullying
child care
company outsourcing
graffiti
homelessness
health care
noise pollution
stray animals
street crime

Other
big deal
break (from work)
car alarm
footpaths

handgun
horn
(health) insurance
offense
royalties
(sales) tax
source
telemarketing

Adjectives
clear-cut
high-rise
inadequate
periodic
pirated
severe
significant

Verbs
deserve
flush
go off
hack
honk
impose
make ends meet
pass
permit
pretend
resign
shoplift

Adverb
in protest

Expressions

Making a recommendation
People ought to/should be
    required to . . .
People shouldn't be allowed to . . .
Something has (got) to be
    done to . . .
A rule has to be made to . . .
Laws must be passed to . . .
People mustn't be permitted to . . .

**Acknowledging an opinion and
    offering a different one**
That sounds interesting, but
    I think . . .
That's not a bad idea. On the other
    hand, I feel that . . .
You may have a point. However,
    I think . . .

Asking for and giving reasons
Why?/Why not?
    Well, I don't think . . .
    Well, for one thing, . . .
    I'll tell you another thing that . . .
Talking about the past
. . . used to . . . when I . . .

Interchange Teacher's Edition 3 © Cambridge University Press 2013 Photocopiable

Unit 16 Language summary

Vocabulary

Nouns

aspect
circumnavigation
claim
donation
(the) elderly
emergency room
energy
fund-raising
grade
nonprofit organization
nursing home
orphanage
playfulness
senior citizen
waste of time
weakness

Adjectives

adaptable
challenging
compassionate
courageous
cynical
dependent
developing (country)
frustrating
gifted
(un)imaginative
(visually) impaired
insensitive
life-or-death
nautical
nonstop
polyglot
resourceful
rigid

selective
self-sufficient
timid
underprivileged
upbeat
youthful

Verbs

deal with
determine
empower
manage (to)
sail

Adverb

ahead

Prepositions

on (a regular basis)
on (one's own)

Expressions

Describing challenges, frustrations, and rewards

The most challenging/frustrating/
rewarding thing about . . . is . . .

Describing past accomplishments

I've managed to . . .
I managed to . . .
I've been able to . . .
I was able to . . .

Talking about future accomplishments

What do you hope you'll have achieved?
I hope I'll have . . .
I'd like to have . . .

Expressing birthday wishes

Happy birthday.

Appendix

Irregular verbs

Present	Past	Past Participle	Present	Past	Past Participle
(be) am/is, are	was, were	been	leave	left	left
become	became	become	lend	lent	lent
begin	began	begun	let	let	let
bite	bit	bitten	light	lit	lit
blow	blew	blown	lose	lost	lost
break	broke	broken	make	made	made
bring	brought	brought	meet	met	met
build	built	built	pay	paid	paid
burn	burned	burned	put	put	put
buy	bought	bought	quit	quit	quit
catch	caught	caught	read	read	read
choose	chose	chosen	run	ran	run
come	came	come	say	said	said
cost	cost	cost	see	saw	seen
cut	cut	cut	sell	sold	sold
do	did	done	send	sent	sent
dream	dreamed/dreamt	dreamed/dreamt	shine	shined/shone	shined/shone
drink	drank	drunk	shoot	shot	shot
drive	drove	driven	show	showed	shown
eat	ate	eaten	sink	sank	sunk
fall	fell	fallen	sit	sat	sat
feel	felt	felt	speak	spoke	spoken
fight	fought	fought	spend	spent	spent
find	found	found	stand	stood	stood
fly	flew	flown	steal	stole	stolen
forget	forgot	forgotten	stick	stuck	stuck
forgive	forgave	forgiven	sweep	swept	swept
get	got	gotten	swim	swam	swum
give	gave	given	take	took	taken
go	went	gone	teach	taught	taught
grow	grew	grown	tear	tore	torn
have	had	had	tell	told	told
hear	heard	heard	think	thought	thought
hold	held	held	throw	threw	thrown
hurt	hurt	hurt	upset	upset	upset
keep	kept	kept	wake	woke	woken
know	knew	known	wear	wore	worn
lay	laid	laid	write	wrote	written

Interchange Teacher's Edition 3 © Cambridge University Press 2013 Photocopiable

Audio scripts

1 *That's what friends are for!*

2 CONVERSATION (p. 2)

B Listen to Chris and Kim discuss Bob after they met for coffee. How did Kim like him?

CHRIS: So, what's the verdict? What did you think of Bob?

KIM: Well, I was worried at first – especially when I saw that he rode a huge motorcycle. I thought he might be one of those guys who is into heavy metal music and stuff like that. You know what I mean?

CHRIS: But he's just a regular kind of guy, right?

KIM: Yeah, we got along really well!

CHRIS: I knew you'd like him.

KIM: Yeah, I do. And he's really funny. He had me laughing so hard at the coffee shop, remember? I think the people sitting next to us thought we were crazy.

CHRIS: So are you two going to get together again?

KIM: Definitely. In fact, we're going to the wedding together!

CHRIS: That's great!

5 LISTENING (p. 4)

A Listen to conversations that describe three people. Are the descriptions positive (P) or negative (N)? Check the box.

1. Andrea

MAN: So, have you seen Andrea lately?

WOMAN: Yeah, I see her once in a while.

MAN: How's she doing? I've been meaning to call her.

WOMAN: Well, to be honest, she's kind of been getting on my nerves lately.

MAN: What do you mean?

WOMAN: She's changed a lot since we've started college. She talks about herself all the time, and she always manages to mention how good she is at everything she does.

MAN: Really? That would be annoying.

WOMAN: It is. You know, she asked me to be roommates with her next semester but I don't think I want to live with her. She used to be really generous but now she's just the opposite. And it's not just with money, but her time as well.

MAN: Well, college can be stressful. You two are good friends. Maybe you need to talk more.

2. James

WOMAN: Are you going to James's party on Saturday?

MAN: Of course. James always gives the best parties! And there are always lots of interesting new people to meet.

WOMAN: It's true. I don't know where he manages to find them all.

MAN: Well, you know what he's like. He makes friends very easily. He really likes talking to people – and he loves inviting people over.

WOMAN: Uh-huh. He invited me for dinner last Saturday. What a feast!

MAN: Yeah. He's a great cook, too.

WOMAN: After dinner, I offered to help clean up, and he told me not to worry about it. He said he'd take care of it later. He was, like, "It's nothing . . . no big deal."

MAN: Yep, that sounds like James.

3. Mr. Johnson

WOMAN 1: Have you met the new apartment manager?

WOMAN 2: Mr. Johnson? Yeah, I met him last week. He's . . . a little strange.

WOMAN 1: Yeah, he is. I'm not sure I like him. He's hard to predict. Sometimes he's pretty cheerful and talkative, and the next day he doesn't even say hello. I think he must have personal problems or something.

WOMAN 2: I think you're right. And have you noticed that half the time when he says he's going to do something, he never actually does it? He told me three times he'd come to fix the light in my kitchen, and he still hasn't done it.

B Listen again. Write two adjectives that describe each person in the chart.

2 *Career moves*

7 CONVERSATION (p. 11)

B Listen to the rest of the conversation. What is Tracy going to do at the amusement park?

MARK: So what will you be doing at the amusement park, exactly?

TRACY: Actually, I'll have two jobs. First, I'll be working at a place called Children's World. They have all kinds of interesting games and educational activities for young kids. I have to go to a training program for three days before I start.

MARK: Three days? Wow, the equipment must be pretty high-tech!

TRACY: Oh, it is – a lot of computers and interesting devices. It's just the kind of stuff that kids love.

MARK: Well, it sounds like the perfect job for you. I know how much you love kids. So what's your other job?

TRACY: Well, I'll also be one of the people who walks around the park greeting people.

MARK: Do you mean you'll have to dress up in a costume?

TRACY: Yes, as a cartoon character! I know, I know. It sounds silly. And it's certainly not as rewarding as working in Children's World, but it's part of the job.

10 LISTENING (p. 12)

A Listen to three people talk about their summer jobs. Number the pictures from 1 to 3.

1.

WOMAN: So where are you working this summer, Carlos?

CARLOS: Oh, I'm working as a tutor in a learning center for kids.

WOMAN: Interesting. What kinds of things do the kids do there?

CARLOS: Well, they work on subjects they need help in, uh, mainly math and English.

WOMAN: Is your job hard?

CARLOS: No, not at all. The kids work on computers most of the time. We have to help them get started and be there when they run into problems.

WOMAN: Do you enjoy it?

CARLOS: Oh, yes. Working with kids is so much more fun than working with adults. And I get to choose my own hours. As long as I work eight hours a day, I can come in at any time from 8 A.M. to 9 P.M.

WOMAN: Lucky you!

2.

WOMAN: Paul, did you find a summer job yet?

PAUL: Yeah, I'm working in a restaurant.

WOMAN: Oh, how's it going?

PAUL: Oh, the money's not bad.

WOMAN: What are you doing? Are you waiting tables?

PAUL: I wish! No, I'm working in the kitchen. I cut up stuff for the chef – vegetables and meat and things. I also wash the dishes.

WOMAN: Oh, yuck.

PAUL: Yeah. It's pretty hard work. I didn't realize how hot it is in a restaurant kitchen until I took this job.

WOMAN: So why don't you quit?

PAUL: I'd love to, but I need the money.

3.

MAN: So what kind of job did you find for the summer?

WOMAN: I'm working for a marketing company. I'm doing telephone marketing.

MAN: Oh, so you're one of those people who drives me crazy by calling me up and trying to persuade me to buy something that I have absolutely no need for.

WOMAN: Exactly.

MAN: Do you like it?

WOMAN: Believe it or not, I do. It's mostly a bunch of students working there, and we have a lot of fun when we're not making calls. It's really easy, too, since we just have to read from a script.

MAN: Are you doing this full time?

WOMAN: Yeah, but I work from two in the afternoon until eleven at night, so I get to sleep as late as I want to in the morning.

B Listen again. Do they like their jobs? Why or why not?

Units 1–2 Progress check

▶ LISTENING (p. 14)

A Listen to Ann and John discuss these topics. Complete the chart.

1. Taxi drivers

MAN: It really upsets me when taxi drivers drive so fast. I'm always terrified of having an accident.

WOMAN: That doesn't really bother me. I like to get where I'm going quickly. But I can't stand it when they have their radios turned up all the way. You can't even hear yourself think!

2. People with dogs

WOMAN: I hate it when people take their dogs to a park and let them make messes all over the place. It's so irresponsible.

MAN: You know what bothers me? I hate it when they go out and leave their dogs at home, barking all day.

3. TV commercials

MAN: I can't stand it when they turn up the volume on TV commercials. They're so loud. Why do they do that?

WOMAN: Yeah, that is annoying. But it bothers me more when they interrupt a ball game at the most exciting moment to show some stupid commercial.

4. Store clerks

WOMAN: It really upsets me when store clerks are rude. Sometimes, if they think that you aren't going to buy anything, they aren't helpful and won't answer your questions.

MAN: Yeah. But on the other hand, I can't stand it when store clerks give you the hard sell and try to get you to buy something you don't really want.

3 Could you do me a favor?

▶ CONVERSATION (p. 16)

B Listen to two more calls Jana makes. What else does she want to borrow? Do her friends agree?

1.

CARRIE: [*phone rings*] Hello?

JANA: Hi, Carrie. This is Jana.

CARRIE: Oh, hi, Jana.

JANA: I was wondering if you could do me a favor.

CARRIE: That depends.

JANA: Well, I have to go to a concert this weekend. Would it be OK if I borrowed that shirt of yours that I like so much?

CARRIE: That silver one? Oh, sure.

JANA: Thanks a lot. I'll come by and pick it up tonight.

CARRIE: That's fine.

2.

ANDY: [*phone rings*] Andy Parker.

JANA: Hi, Andy. It's Jana.

ANDY: Oh, hello. How are you?

JANA: Pretty good, thanks. Listen, the reason I'm calling is I have a really big favor to ask you.

ANDY: Yes?

JANA: Remember I told you about that friend of mine who's doing a show this weekend?

ANDY: Yeah, I remember. And?

JANA: Well, the concert's this Saturday afternoon, and it's out of town – about an hour's drive from here – and I was wondering if I could borrow your car for the afternoon to get there.

ANDY: Gee, Jana, I'd really love to help you out, but I'm going to need my car all weekend. I've got a friend coming in from out of town, and I promised to show her around.

JANA: Oh, OK. I understand. Anyway, how are things? I haven't seen you for ages.

ANDY: Oh, you know, work, work, work!

▶ LISTENING (p. 18)

A Listen to three telephone conversations. Write down what each caller requests. Does the other person agree to the request? Check Yes or No.

1. Tina

ROBERT: [phone rings] Hello?

TINA: Hi, Robert. This is Tina.

ROBERT: Hi, Tina. What's up?

TINA: Well, actually, would you mind lending me your camera for a few days? I want to take some photos of my new apartment to send to my folks.

ROBERT: No problem. You can borrow it.

TINA: Oh, thanks a million.

2. Kyle

MAGGIE: [phone rings] Hello?

KYLE: Hi, Maggie. This is Kyle.

MAGGIE: Oh, hi. How are things with you?

KYLE: Pretty good. Listen, I was wondering if I could borrow your bread maker.

MAGGIE: My bread maker? Don't tell me *you* are going to bake!

KYLE: I know. I'm planning to cook dinner for my girlfriend this weekend and I want to bake bread. And I want it to be perfect. I remember you baked some amazing bread with that thing. So what do you say? Can I borrow it? I'll be careful.

MAGGIE: Well, I have bad news. It's broken. I've been meaning to get it fixed, but I haven't gotten around to it yet.

KYLE: Oh, too bad.

MAGGIE: But you know, you can always just bake bread on your own.

KYLE: Hmm, I don't know. Maybe I'll just go to a bakery.

3. Phil

LI-LING: [phone rings] Hello?

PAUL: Hi, Li-ling. It's Phil.

LI-LING: Hi Phil, what's up?

PAUL: Not much, but I was wondering if I could ask you for a favor.

LI-LING: Hmm . . . maybe. Try me!

PAUL: Well, I have to go out of town for a few days next week.

LI-LING: Uh-huh.

PAUL: Could I leave Polly with you while I'm gone?

LI-LING: Polly? Who's Polly?

PAUL: You know – Polly, my bird.

LI-LING: Oh, yeah. I forgot. Your bird. I don't know, Phil. I really don't like birds very much. They're messy, and they make a lot of noise, and . . .

PAUL: No, not Polly. She's really a great bird. She's really clean and very quiet. She won't bother you – I promise.

LI-LING: Oh, all right. I'll do it.

PAUL: Thanks. I really appreciate it. I'll bring her over on Tuesday night.

LI-LING: OK. But you owe me one!

4 What a story!

5 LISTENING (p. 24)

A Listen to three news stories. Number the pictures from 1 to 3. There is one extra picture.

1.

MAN: A man was seriously injured on Sunday by a three-and-a-half-meter snake in a town in Thailand.

It seems that the man ran over to see the snake after friends told him that it was beside one of the town's main roads. The man put it around his neck, and while he and his friends were walking home, the snake squeezed more and more tightly. Luckily, the man got the snake off his neck in time.

2.

WOMAN: Two teenage girls who disappeared from a ship were found alive and well. The girls turned up on Friday, near a small town on the northeast coast of Australia. The girls said they were visiting a friend on the ship and fell asleep in their friend's cabin. When they woke up, the ship was heading for Singapore. So, they jumped off the ship, swam to shore, and had to walk for several days to get to the nearest town.

3.

MAN: Early Tuesday morning in California, two police officers were chasing a car thief when they suddenly lost control of their vehicle and drove into a river. Surprisingly, the thief went back to the scene of the accident and helped rescue the officers from the river. The local police department dropped all charges against the thief for saving the officers' lives.

B Listen again. Take notes on each story.

7 CONVERSATION (p. 25)

B Listen to the rest of the conversation. What did Kathy have stolen once? Where was she?

KATHY: I had something similar happen last year.

BRIAN: Really?

KATHY: Yeah. It was when I was in Belgium. I was on my way to the airport, so I was standing on the side of the road with my bags, trying to figure out the bus schedule. Anyway, this group of guys came by and asked if they could help me. They spoke very broken English, and I couldn't really understand what they were saying. Finally, they left, and when I looked down, I realized my purse had disappeared. It had my wallet in it with all my money and my credit card. Luckily, I had put my airline ticket and my passport in one of my carry-on bags.

BRIAN: How awful! So what did you do?

KATHY: I did just what I had seen people do on TV. I called the police and reported the theft. Then I called my credit card company. I was able to get some cash, and by the time I got home I had a new credit card waiting for me.

Units 3–4 Progress check

4 LISTENING (p. 29)

Listen to each situation. Number the events from 1 to 3.

1.

MAN 1: Even though she had hurt her ankle while she was running, she went to work anyway.

2.

WOMAN 1: John wrote to me last year, but I didn't get the letter. I'd moved away.

3.

WOMAN 2: I'd been very scared about the flight, so when the plane landed, I was relieved.

4.

MAN 2: When my cousin stopped by, I was watching a movie. We went out for coffee to catch up.

5 Crossing Cultures

7 CONVERSATION (p. 33)

B Listen to the rest of the conversation. If you are invited to someone's house in Germany, when are you expected to arrive? What can you bring as a gift?

KAREN: What are some of the customs in Germany?

MARTA: Well, when you're invited to someone's house, you can also take flowers. Not red roses, chrysanthemums, carnations, or lilies, but most others flowers are fine.

KAREN: When should you arrive? Should you arrive a little early?

MARTA: No, never. You're expected to arrive on time. Punctuality is very important in Germany. If you're going to be more than 15 minutes late, it's important to call the host. It's also the custom to write a short thank-you note the following day.

KAREN: I like that. I wish we did that here more often. To me, it shows good manners.

9 LISTENING (p. 34)

Listen to people describe customs they observed abroad. Complete the chart.

1. Alice

ALICE: One thing that I had to get used to when I was traveling in South Korea was the way people make noise when they drink soup. I think it's because they want to show that they're really enjoying their food so they make a slurping noise. It bothered me at first, but then I got used to it. I guess it's because my parents spent years when I was a kid telling me not to make noise while I was eating.

2. John

JOHN: When I lived in Spain, I was surprised at how late people eat in the evening. When you're invited to dinner, you're asked to come around nine o'clock and you usually don't start dinner until ten. And people stay really late – sometimes until two in the morning or even later. I found that difficult. How do you get up and go to work or school the next day after eating and talking until three in the morning?

3. Susan

SUSAN: I lived in Saudi Arabia for a while, and when I went out, I had to obey the local custom of putting something over my head and wearing clothing that covered my whole body. At first, I found it a real nuisance, but after a while, I got used to it and even started to like it. You feel really secure, and also you don't have to worry about what to wear all the time.

6 What's wrong with it?

4 LISTENING (p. 38)

A Listen to three customers return an item they purchased. What's the problem? Take notes. Then complete the chart.

1.

CLERK: Can I help you?

MAN: Yes, I bought this briefcase here last week, but there's something wrong with the lock. I can't get it to close properly.

CLERK: Let me see. Yes, I see what you mean. The lock seems to be jammed or something. No problem. I'll get you another one. Sorry about that.

2.

WOMAN: Excuse me.

CLERK: Yes?

WOMAN: I wonder if you could take a look at these shoes I bought here. They're pretty new, but they seem to be falling apart.

CLERK: Hmm. Let me see. Yes, this doesn't look right. The stitching is coming out. How long did you say you've had them?

WOMAN: Only about a month. Here's the receipt.

CLERK: Hmm . . . yes. Well, let me exchange these for you. I'm sorry for the inconvenience.

3.

MAN: Excuse me.

CLERK: Yes, how can I help you?

MAN: You see this shirt? I bought it here a few weeks ago, but the first time I washed it, the color changed: It went from bright red to light pink.

CLERK: How did you wash it?

MAN: Well, I just tossed it into the washing machine with my other clothes.

CLERK: What temperature did you use?

MAN: I usually wash my clothes in hot water, so I guess hot.

CLERK: Well, did you check the washing instructions?

MAN: Um . . . maybe not.

CLERK: Well, you see here on this label? It says, "Wash in cold water only."

MAN: Uh-huh.

CLERK: So I'm really sorry, but since you didn't follow the washing instructions, I can't really do anything for you.

6 CONVERSATION (p. 38)

B Listen to another tenant calling Ms. Lock. What's the tenant's problem?

MS. LOCK: [*phone rings*] Hello?

MRS. HARRIS: Hello. Is this the manager?

MS. LOCK: Yes, this is Ms. Lock.

MRS. HARRIS: This is Lula Harris in Apartment 216.

MS. LOCK: Yes. How can I help you, Mrs. Harris?

MRS. HARRIS: I'm having a problem with the electricity.

MS. LOCK: What sort of problem with the electricity?

MRS. HARRIS: Well, it keeps going off and coming back on again.

MS. LOCK: I see. Is it just the lights, or is it the appliances, too?

MRS. HARRIS: Let me check. . . . No, the refrigerator is OK, so it must be just the lights.

MS. LOCK: I guess the fuse box needs to be checked. I'll come up and take a look at it right away.

MRS. HARRIS: Thanks so much.

10 LISTENING (p. 40)

Listen to three people talk about their jobs. Complete the chart.

1. Joe

JOE: I work in the watch repair center at a large department store. I repair all kinds of watches, but nowadays, most of them are pretty easy to fix because they all run on batteries. The most common problem is they need a new battery. Since that only takes a minute or so to fix, I always have plenty of time to tell my watch jokes – like this one: What time is it when an elephant sits on your watch? Time to buy a new watch! And here's another one: What time is it when the big hand . . . ?

2. Louise

LOUISE: I repair luggage – mostly suitcases. I have a little shop at the airport. People spend a lot of money on luggage, and often all it takes is one flight for a suitcase to get damaged. The most typical problem, I guess, is the wheels. I fix the wheels on about 20 suitcases a week. It's not surprising, really, with the way those baggage handlers throw people's luggage around. You'd think they were playing ball, the way they toss the suitcases.

3. Sam

SAM: I repair household appliances. The most frequent calls I get are from people who are having trouble with the garbage-disposal system in their kitchen sink. Usually the thing gets jammed because people put too much food into it at one time, or something metal or plastic has fallen down into it. It's usually pretty easy to fix a garbage disposal, but every once in a while, you run into situations that aren't exactly typical. One time, a little girl put her doll down into the disposal – she thought the doll would enjoy the ride. She couldn't get it back out again, and she was afraid to tell her mother. So when the mother went to use the disposal, it made a horrible noise and then died – and so did the doll.

Units 5–6 Progress check

3 LISTENING (p. 43)

A Listen to three tenants complain to their building manager. Complete the chart.

1.

TENANT 1: Hello, Mr. Smith. I was wondering if you could change the lightbulb out front. It went out again.

MR. SMITH: I'll take care of it later. I'm really busy right now, and besides, it's still light outside.

TENANT 1: But it'll be dark when I get home tonight.

MR. SMITH: I'd love to help, but somebody borrowed my ladder.

TENANT 1: Well, you know, I have a chair! And if you give me a lightbulb, I wouldn't mind doing it myself, OK?

MR. SMITH: Oh! OK. Here. Take a lightbulb from one of my lamps. So you know it works.

TENANT 1: Thank you!

2.

TENANT 2: Uh, excuse me. Mr. Smith.

MR. SMITH: Yeah?

TENANT 2: Uh, I was wondering if you could do something about my next-door neighbor's dog? It's been barking and keeping me up all night.

MR. SMITH: Dogs bark. That's what they do.

TENANT 2: Yes, but they don't have to bark all night. This is three nights in a row.

MR. SMITH: Have you seen the size of that dog? You want me to go up there? That dog could hurt me!

TENANT 2: Well, I need my sleep!

MR. SMITH: Look, look. I tell you what. I'll call your neighbor on the phone and ask if he can keep his dog quiet.

TENANT 2: OK. Thank you!

3.

TENANT 3: Mr. Smith.

MR. SMITH: Mrs. Taylor.

TENANT 3: I have a problem.

MR. SMITH: What is it now?

TENANT 3: It's my kitchen window. It's jammed shut. I can't open it anymore.

MR. SMITH: Mrs. Taylor, I'm not sure how I can help you.

TENANT 3: Well, can you at least try to open it for me?

MR. SMITH: That's not really part of my job. Maybe you could try putting some vegetable oil on it.

TENANT 3: I don't think so. I'll call my cousin George to come over to take a look at it. He's a weight lifter.

7 The world we live in

5 LISTENING (p. 46)

A Listen to three people describe some serious environmental problems. Check the problem each person talks about.

1. Jenny

JENNY: Wait, don't throw that out!

MAN: Why not?

JENNY: Recycle it. I've been reading a lot about how much trash we produce and what happens to all of it – and it really has me worried.

MAN: Why?

JENNY: Well, it seems that the easiest way to dispose of trash is by burying it in landfills, land that could be used by farmers to grow food and other things. The problem is that in many countries the dumping areas have already been filled up, and it's hard to find places to start new ones. Of course, no one wants trash buried in their neighborhood, but it has to go somewhere!

MAN: So what's the solution?

JENNY: Well, there is no easy solution; however, many cities are trying to do more recycling so that they can reduce the amount of stuff that goes into the landfills.

2. Adam

WOMAN: I love my new phone, but I don't know what to do with my old one. It's so outdated. I know I shouldn't just throw it away.

ADAM: Well, you're right about that. Not disposing of electronic devices and other appliances properly is a huge problem these days, not just here but all over the world. Many people don't know what to do with their old phones, computers, video game systems, TV sets, refrigerators. . . . There are dangerous chemicals in these products and they have to be handled in the right way.

WOMAN: So what are we supposed to do?

ADAM: Well, e-waste is not going away. With all the new technology these days, there's more e-waste than ever before. The solution is just to dispose of it responsibly. The good news is that there are more and more e-waste processing centers where professionals take these products and separate them into their various parts. Many of the parts can be re-used of course.

3. Katy

KATY: You know, you always hear about air pollution, but not many people are aware of the problem of water pollution.

MAN: You mean in the oceans?

KATY: No. I mean polluted drinking water. It's a problem in almost every major city in the world. Almost all our rivers and lakes – where we get our drinking water from – are being polluted in some way by businesses, farms, homes, industries, and other sources. And even though the water most of us drink is treated, it's still not a hundred percent pure.

MAN: So what's the solution?

KATY: Well, it's a complicated problem to solve, but basically what's involved is treating all waste products more carefully so that dangerous chemicals and bacteria don't get into our water supply.

B Listen again. What can be done to solve each problem? Complete the chart.

7 CONVERSATION (p. 47)

C Listen to the rest of the conversation. What do Andy and Carla decide to do?

CARLA: Wait a minute. Before we do anything, shouldn't we make sure that we've got our facts straight?

ANDY: Absolutely. The best thing to do is to monitor the situation over the next several weeks to see what exactly is happening.

CARLA: How do we do that?

ANDY: Well, we can take pictures of the river and even take water samples to see how bad the situation is. We can get some friends to help.

CARLA: OK. And then maybe I should talk to my uncle about it.

ANDY: That would be fantastic.

8 Lifelong learning

5 LISTENING (p. 52)

A Listen to three people talk about the part-time courses they took recently. What course did each person take?

1. Linda

MAN: So, Linda, what have you been doing with yourself?

LINDA: Not much. Oh, wait! That's not true. I took this great dancing class last semester.

MAN: Oh, yeah? What kind of dancing?

LINDA: We learned African dance and samba.

MAN: Wait . . . why would you want to learn African dance and samba? It sounds exhausting. And it's not like you would dance that way in clubs!

LINDA: Oh, just for fun. You should try taking the class. You'll see that you learn more than just dancing. You also learn how to be more confident and how to interact better with other people.

MAN: Hmm. I think with all that dancing around I'd be too exhausted to interact with anyone.

2. Rich

WOMAN: So, how did you enjoy your cooking course?

RICH: It was great.

WOMAN: What kinds of things did you learn to cook?

RICH: Well, it was a course on vegetarian cooking.

WOMAN: I didn't know you were a vegetarian.

RICH: Oh, I'm not, but a lot of people are these days. So I thought it would be useful to know how to make some interesting dishes without meat for times when I invite friends over for dinner.

WOMAN: Hmm. Well, I guess that makes sense.

RICH: Oh, but we learned more than just cooking. They also taught us all kinds of useful things about, you know, the health value of different kinds of vegetables, and how to prepare them so that you don't remove all the vitamins they contain.

WOMAN: So . . . uh . . . when's dinner?

3. Gwen

GWEN: I just got my grade in the mail. I got an A!

MAN: Wow! That's terrific. Congratulations. What kind of course was it?

GWEN: It was an online course on how to open and run a small business.

MAN: An online course? How interesting! Did it help?

GWEN: Yes, absolutely. We learned a lot of general principles, and a lot about finance. Even if I don't open a business, I learned a lot about investing and managing money!

MAN: Great! Can you manage my money? My finances are a mess!

B Listen again. What additional information did each person learn?

8 CONVERSATION (p. 52)

B Listen to two other people explain how they learn new words in a foreign language. What techniques do they use?

1.

MAN: I keep a record of new words I come across. Then I make up study cards. I write the word on one side of the card and the meaning on the other side. Oh, and I always include at least one sentence with the word in it. Then I go through the cards whenever I have some spare time – like when I'm waiting for my laundry to dry, or on the bus – and study the words until I know them by heart. Every week or so, I organize the cards into categories: you know, I put all the words together that have to do with food . . . or work . . . or home . . . or school . . . whatever I can find that my new words have in common.

2.

WOMAN: I keep a vocabulary list on my computer. It's organized alphabetically. Whenever I hear or read a new word, I add it to the list. Then when I have time, I look it up in my dictionary. I also try to put down some key information about the word – you know, whether it's a noun or a verb, and some examples of how it's used. I go through the list and study the words as often as I can. I really believe that the only way to learn new words – even in your own language – is by memorizing them.

10 DISCUSSION (p. 53)

A Listen to Todd and Lucy describe how they developed two skills. How did they learn? Complete the chart.

1. learn to play a musical instrument

TODD: I play the guitar. I haven't played for very long, maybe about two years. The way I learned was by practicing by myself with a "how to" video my girlfriend bought for me. It takes a lot of patience to teach yourself how to do something, especially a musical instrument, but it works for me. I'm still learning, and I can practice as little or as much as I want, and I'm slowly getting better and better. There are even free video lessons online I check out sometimes.

LUCY: I could never teach myself a musical instrument. I need a teacher, and one who makes me practice. That's how I learned the piano. I started taking lessons when I was in middle school. I'd go to a neighbor's house after school twice a week and she'd teach me for an hour or so. She was a good teacher, strict, but she knew how to get me to play. I suppose it helps that I've always wanted to play the piano. I don't take lessons anymore, but I still practice at least once a week. You know that saying – if you don't use it, you lose it.

2. become a good conversationalist

TODD: I guess I learned how to communicate with people when I was a flight attendant. I worked as a flight attendant for five years. The most important thing you have to do in that job is to talk to passengers – especially during long flights. You learn to talk about all kinds of stuff, and you find out just how interesting some people's lives are. I think the key to being a good conversationalist is to be sincerely interested in other people and to try to get them to talk about themselves as much as possible.

LUCY: I had always been really shy. I was the sort of person who could go to a party and never talk to anybody. And when you don't talk to anybody, it's hard to make friends. Anyway, my sister suggested I take an acting class. She said it might help me become more outgoing. So I did it. I was really frightened in that first acting class. But you know, it really helped. The teacher was very kind and taught me that I could talk to anybody just by pretending I had confidence.

Units 7–8 Progress check
③ LISTENING (p. 57)

A Listen to people talk about recent events and activities in their lives. What events and activities are they talking about? What quality does each person's behavior demonstrate? Complete the chart.

1. Mark

MARK: I could just kick myself.

WOMAN: Come on, Mark, it could happen to anyone.

MARK: I lost the game for us. All I had to do was kick it past the goalie.

WOMAN: Yeah, but that goalie is tough to get by.

MARK: No way. I'm a much better player. And there was no one in the way. Everybody else was at the other end of the field.

WOMAN: Yeah, but we all miss one sometimes.

MARK: Yeah, and I won't let that happen again.

WOMAN: How are you going to do that?

MARK: By playing the game better.

2. Joan

JOAN: I did it! I did it!

MAN: Oh my gosh, Joan, what happened?

JOAN: I did it! I did it!

MAN: Joan! Calm down! What happened?

JOAN: I got into the company I auditioned for!

MAN: Really? That's fantastic! But I thought you auditioned and didn't make it.

JOAN: I did! I felt really bad about not making it for a while, but then I decided I couldn't be depressed forever, so I started dancing again on my own. I worked really hard. And by practicing every day, I got better and better. Then I saw in the newspaper that they were having auditions again. So I went in, I auditioned, and I got in!

MAN: That's great. Congratulations!

3. Kim

MAN: Kim, when did you start doing this?

KIM: Oh, a few months ago. I'd never picked up a brush before.

MAN: What made you start?

KIM: I'm not sure. I've always wanted to paint or draw, but my brother was the artistic one. I was on the basketball team. Last month, I decided I wanted to take a class at the community center. It was this or yoga. I decided on this. I feel like I've learned how to relax by painting.

MAN: You're not bad, you know.

KIM: Thanks.

MAN: Who is it?

KIM: It's you.

9 Improvements
⑩ LISTENING (p. 62)

A Listen to people give different suggestions for each problem. Put a line through the suggestion that was *not* given.

1. How to overcome shyness

MAN 1: Well, I think if you're really shy it might be a good idea to see a therapist or someone like that – you know, to get some professional help. You can't always change by yourself.

WOMAN: Or how about getting one of those self-help books from the library? I'm sure there are books around with lots of good suggestions that you can try.

MAN 2: I think the best thing is to join a club and do activities where you have to meet and talk to different people. Like if you join a theater group and work on putting on a play, you'll probably be able to overcome your shyness.

2. How to stop biting your fingernails

MAN 1: I think biting your fingernails is just a sign of anxiety, so the first thing to do is to find out what's making you nervous. Once you've identified that problem and then solved it, the nail biting will disappear.

WOMAN: My sister used to bite her nails all the time, so she started wearing bright red nail polish. She bought the really expensive kind, so she felt that she had made an investment in quitting her bad habit. I think the polish made her think about what she was doing, too. Anyway, after a few months, it worked, and she has really nice nails now. I guess if you're a guy, it's a little more difficult, though.

MAN 2: Maybe you could find something else to do when you're stressed out, like tapping your fingers or counting to 100. You have to try to transfer your habit into a different activity – one that doesn't cause such a problem.

3. How to organize your busy schedule

MAN 1: To organize a busy schedule, one thing you could do is make a list. I usually make a list of all the things I have to do. Then I prioritize them. Then I decide which days I'm going to get the things done based on which errands are the most important.

WOMAN: Maybe you could use electronic reminders. Put all the things you need to do into your calendar on your phone or your email. Then program it so you have reminders sent to you. For some things you might get a reminder 15 minutes before, but for other things it might be better to get a reminder a few hours or even days before. I use that to help me remember people's birthdays.

MAN 2: If your schedule is really busy, it might be a good idea to get help. There are plenty of professional consultants who organize people's lives. It's expensive, but if you're too busy, it's the only way to get everything done!

10 *The past and the future*
2 CONVERSATION (p. 64)

B Do you know the answers to the three questions in part A? Listen to the rest of the conversation. What are the correct answers?

STEVE: So what are the correct answers, then?

EMMA: Well, World War I began in 1914 and ended in 1918.

STEVE: Oh, that's right.

EMMA: And the United Nations was formally established in 1945, following the end of World War II.

STEVE: And the Beatles?

EMMA: Well, they started back in 1960, and they broke up in 1970. So they were together for 10 years, not 15.

STEVE: Did I say I was good at history? Uh, I meant geography.

11 LISTENING (p. 68)

A Listen to people discuss changes that will affect these topics of interest in the future. Write down two changes for each topic.

1. Work

WOMAN: Work? In the future? Well, I think unemployment will keep getting worse.

MAN: I agree. As companies get more efficient and more computerized, they're finding ways of using less staff.

WOMAN: So I guess people will find it hard to get a good job unless they have excellent qualifications.

MAN: Hmm, yeah. I think that's probably true. But I also think that because of computers, more and more people will be telecommuting instead of going into an office.

WOMAN: Wow, I'd really love that. Can you imagine – spending most of your workweek in the comfort of your own home?

MAN: Personally, I would get so much more done. And with email, instant messaging, and video conferencing, you can still keep in touch with everyone you need to.

WOMAN: Well, I'd certainly enjoy it, but I don't know if I'd get more done or not. I'm afraid I might just turn on the TV and zone out!

2. Transportation

WOMAN: As far as transportation is concerned, I think there will be huge changes in the way people use cars. They'll probably have made laws about what kind of car you can own and when you can use it.

MAN: And I bet it'll be impossible for people to use cars whenever they like. There'll just be too many of them on the roads.

WOMAN: Exactly. People will have to take other modes of transportation – especially trains.

MAN: Why do you say that?

WOMAN: Well, we won't be able to use cars, and airports take up too much space. With the supply of land for airports shrinking around the world, there will be fewer airports and fewer plane flights. That leaves trains.

MAN: Huh. So do you think there will be more efficient train systems between cities?

WOMAN: Sure. There may even be trains going under the oceans to connect the major continents.

MAN: Under the oceans? Get out of here! I get nervous enough flying on a plane.

3. Education

WOMAN: How do you think education will change in the future?

MAN: I think kids are going to have to stay in school until they're older – maybe until they're 20 or 21.

WOMAN: Why?

MAN: Well, one reason is that there won't be enough jobs for everyone, so it will be necessary to keep kids in school longer.

WOMAN: Hmm. I think they will have found a way for us to learn without teachers. There will be computer-learning programs that can teach you much more quickly than a teacher, and they'll also make learning much more fun.

MAN: Are you saying that our teachers weren't any fun?

WOMAN: Well . . . OK. Maybe some of them were fun.

4. Health

WOMAN: Every day you hear about some new medical breakthrough on the news.

MAN: Yeah. And who knows what will happen in the next 50 years.

WOMAN: I think in the next 50 years there will be new drugs that will help people lose weight permanently – without dieting!

MAN: And hopefully they will have found cures for many of the diseases that are around today, so people will live longer.

WOMAN: How much longer do you think?

MAN: I bet that within the next 50 years, most people will live to be over 100.

Units 9–10 Progress check
3 LISTENING (p. 71)

A Listen to people discuss the questions. Write the correct answers.

1.

MAN: What are you reading?

WOMAN: I'm reading an article about the Iditarod.

MAN: What's the Iditarod?

WOMAN: It's a sled-dog race in Alaska.

MAN: I didn't know you liked dog racing.

WOMAN: Well, not exactly, but it's interesting to read about, anyway.

MAN: Are you learning anything?

WOMAN: Well, they've been doing it since 1973. And the race covers 1,150 miles.

MAN: Wow! That's pretty far to go in all that snow and ice.

2.

WOMAN: How long did apartheid exist in South Africa?

MAN: Hmm. Let's see. I know apartheid ended in 1991, but I'm not sure when it began.

WOMAN: Well, I know it was after World War II.

MAN: Yes, yes. You're right. It wasn't long after the war ended. I think it was in 1948.

WOMAN: You're right. So apartheid existed from 1948 to 1991. Huh. Wow.

3.

GIRL: Dad! Can you help me?

MAN: What do you need?

GIRL: I'm writing this report for school. It's about the space program. I did my research at the library, but I forgot to look something up.

MAN: What do you need to know?

GIRL: When did a spacecraft first land on Mars?

MAN: Oh, I remember that. Mom was pregnant with you! It was in 1997.

GIRL: 1997! Thanks! I'm done!

4.

MAN: What's that?

WOMAN: It's a book about the Berlin Wall.

MAN: Oh, wow! Look at these pictures. They're amazing.

WOMAN: Yes. It's incredible to think about. The wall divided the city in half.

MAN: How long was it up?

WOMAN: For almost 30 years.

MAN: Wow!

5.

WOMAN: What are you doing?

MAN: I'm working on this crossword puzzle.

WOMAN: Oh, I love crossword puzzles! What clue are you working on?

MAN: Well, here. The clue is "began in 1896." It starts with an "O."

WOMAN: I know this one! It's the Olympics!

MAN: The Olympics have only been around since 1896?

WOMAN: Well, yes. The modern Olympics.

11 *Life's little lessons*

2 *CONVERSATION (p. 72)*

B Listen to the rest of the conversation. What was another turning point for Carol? For Alan?

CAROL: Another turning point for me was when I got my dog, Pepper. I know that sounds silly, but it was really important to me.

ALAN: Why was that so important?

CAROL: Well, I was about 18, my first semester at college. Having a dog of my own made me feel really responsible. He was always waiting for me when I came home from class.

ALAN: I never got to have a dog, but I remember when I got my first bicycle. That was a very important day for me.

For the first time, I could go out on my own and go as far as I wanted to. I took really good care of it. Of course, that only lasted a few months, and then I lost interest in it!

4 *LISTENING (p. 74)*

A Listen to three people describe important events in their lives. Complete the chart.

1. Sally

SALLY: One thing that was really a turning point for me was when I learned Spanish. I was always kind of scared of learning a foreign language, yet I was really envious of kids who could speak another language. But when I started learning Spanish, I found I was actually pretty good at it, and the moment I reached that breakthrough stage – you know, when you discover you can actually speak and communicate with people in the language – I felt really proud of myself. I realized that learning a foreign language wasn't an impossible thing after all. Now I can speak three: Spanish, Italian, and German. And I'm taking Korean this year.

2. Henry

HENRY: I'm a twin, and my twin brother and I have always been very close. We always did everything together, and we were never apart for any time at all – until we were 18. Then we went to different colleges in different towns, and that was the first time we had ever really had to cope on our own. I think it was good in a way, because we both became more confident and independent. Until then, I'd always had my brother to depend on whenever I ran into a problem. But once I went away to college, I realized I was actually capable of working things out on my own.

3. Debbie

DEBBIE: I guess I was always pretty shy in school, and I didn't share a lot of things with people – not even with my parents. Then one time it was Awards Day at school. I didn't think I was getting any prizes or anything, and neither did my parents. So we were all pretty surprised when the principal announced that I was the top student in my class. Afterward, I didn't think too much about it, but then people suddenly started treating me differently. You know, I think some of the kids in school started looking up to me, and I became a lot more outgoing after that.

B Listen again. What do these three people have in common?

11 *LISTENING (p. 76)*

A Listen to people describe their regrets. What does each person regret?

1. Alex

ALEX: I should never have stopped exercising. It's the dumbest thing I've ever done. I've been trying to lose weight for the last year and a half, and it's really difficult. I guess I was just like everyone else at my age. I thought I would be thin forever, and I ate junk food all the time. It was OK then because I was playing tennis, hockey, and soccer. Then after college I got busy and quit playing sports. But now I'm determined to join a gym because I know I can't get healthy by just dieting. Besides, I love potato chips!

2. Yi-yun

YI-YUN: If I'd had a choice, I would have learned to play the guitar when I was a kid. My parents made me study the piano, and I only studied classical music. I love the piano, but it's not very practical. I mean, you can't take a piano with you to a party. But I love it at a party when someone brings a guitar and they can play songs and everyone sings along. I wish I could do that.

3. Jacob

JACOB: I regret something I didn't do. I regret not going to Europe with my friends when I had the chance. It was the summer after we all graduated from college. I started to look for a job right away but my friends went backpacking in Europe for a few weeks. I should have gone because I didn't get a job right away anyway, and my friends had an unforgettable time together. I regret it because they all had this amazing experience without me, and looking back, I could have . . . and should have gone.

B Listen again. Why does he or she regret it?

12 *The right stuff*
9 LISTENING (p. 82)

A Listen to radio commercials for three different businesses. What are two special features of each place?

Maggie's

WOMAN 1: Oh, Denise, what a great suit! It looks just like the one I saw in the latest fashion magazine. Is . . . that . . . a . . . ?

WOMAN 2: Uh-huh.

WOMAN 1: Wow! But her clothes are so expensive. How can you afford designer clothes? And on our salary? Hey, did you get a raise?

WOMAN 2: No way! You know I'd tell you if I did.

WOMAN 1: Well, there's something you're not telling me.

WOMAN 2: OK, OK. Well, I found this really great store. They have all the latest fashions – not last year's stuff that's already out of style. And their prices are just unbelievable!

WOMAN 1: They must be. That's the second new outfit you've worn this week! Where is this place?

WOMAN 2: It's called Maggie's, and it's just around the corner. I'll take you there at lunchtime.

ANNOUNCER: Don't wait for your lunch hour – come to Maggie's now! We've got all the best designer fashions at the lowest prices. And we accept all major credit cards. Remember: If you don't see what you want in your closet, come check out ours!

Sports Pro

ANNOUNCER: Hey, people, what are you going to do this summer? A little fishing? Camping? Maybe finally learn how to play tennis instead of just watching it on TV? Yeah, I know how much you'd like to do these things . . . if only you had the right equipment . . . if only you knew what you were looking for when you walked into one of those big sporting goods stores. Well, here at Sports Pro, we want to help you, not confuse you. Our experienced salespeople are knowledgeable; they really know what they're talking about. So, feeling inspired? Good! Now, come on in – no excuses, because we're open every day. Sports Pro: We're here to help you have fun!

Mexi-Grill

ANNOUNCER: Excuse me. Was that your stomach I just heard growling? Hmm . . . feeling hungry, right? Only . . . you're not sure what you want? Well, close your eyes and picture this: A huge tortilla filled with sizzling pieces of chicken. Should you add fried onion and peppers? Or maybe crispy lettuce and tomato? Or guacamole and spicy salsa? Well, you know what! You can have any of these, because we'll add any combination of fillings you want. In a hurry? No problem. We have lots of people waiting to serve you. And check out our low prices. Mexi-Grill: You won't find a cheaper, tastier meal – anywhere!

B Listen again. Complete each slogan.

Units 11–12 Progress check
3 LISTENING (p. 85)

A Listen to a business consultant discuss the factors necessary for a restaurant to be successful. Check the ones she says are important.

WOMAN: Well, there are many factors that go into making a restaurant successful. I think one of the most important ones is to develop a concept for the restaurant – something that makes the restaurant different from its competitors, like a theme. It could be a hip-hop or jazz restaurant, or a Hollywood movie star café. Something that makes it unique. This is important, since the restaurant business is very competitive.

There's an old joke that asks, "What are the three most important factors needed for a successful business?" The answer? "Location, location, location." And it's true. It's important to do some research. Find out how many cars drive past the site every day, and also how many pedestrians walk by. Why? Because you want people to know about your restaurant. So it needs to be in a place that's visited by businesspeople, people who live in the area, as well as tourists.

Finally, promotion and advertising are absolutely necessary. Because your restaurant is new, you need to find a way to attract customers into the restaurant. They don't know about the restaurant. You have to find a way to tell them about it. For example, you might advertise through radio, or magazines, or online. Or maybe you mail out advertising to potential customers, offering them a coupon for a free drink or a meal, or something like that.

B Listen again. In your own words, write the reason why each factor is important.

13 *That's a possibility.*
2 CONVERSATION (p. 86)

B Listen to the rest of the conversation. What happened?

BILL: Oh, here comes Beth now.

BETH: Hey, guys. Sorry I'm late. I had an emergency.

JACKIE: Oh. Nothing serious I hope.

BETH: Well, kind of. It was Sally.

JACKIE: Sally, your dog? What happened?

BETH: Well, I was just about to leave when she started acting strange. Then she just passed out.

JACKIE: Oh, my gosh.

BETH: I panicked. I thought she had died at first. I had to rush her to the emergency clinic.

JACKIE: But is she OK? I hope she's all right.

BETH: Yeah, she's going to be fine. The vet said it was some kind of virus. So he gave her an injection, and I had to leave her with him. I'll go by later and pick her up. Oh, but guess what!

JACKIE: What?

BETH: She's going to have puppies!

BILL: Congratulations! You're going to be a grandmother!

JACKIE: Very funny, Bill!

BETH: Yeah, Bill. Very funny!

5 LISTENING (p. 87)

B Listen to the explanations for the two events in part A and take notes. What *did* happen? How similar were your explanations?

1.

MAN: I was on a cruise and saw something funny one morning. I was walking on the deck and I saw three people all bent over the railing. I thought maybe they were seasick or someone had an accident or something, so I went over to see if I could help. It turns out they were all bent over the railing because they were looking at some dolphins that were following the cruise ship. There were about eight of them and they followed us for a while. It was an amazing thing to see.

2.

WOMAN: I'm so embarrassed! I can't imagine what people must have thought when they saw me out in my front yard in my pajamas. See, I had opened my front door to get the morning newspaper. But the wind accidentally blew the door shut behind me, and the door locked. I couldn't get back in the house. I saw that my bedroom window upstairs was open so I went into the garage and got a ladder. I was able to climb up the ladder and into the window. I'm afraid some of my neighbors might have seen me. I'll have to explain to them what I was doing the next time I see them.

11 LISTENING (p. 90)

A Listen to descriptions of three situations. What would have been the best thing to do in each situation? Check the best suggestion.

1.

DENNIS: Oh, no! Arrgh!

WOMAN: Dennis accidentally locked his keys in his car when he went shopping. When he returned to his car, he couldn't get in. So he decided to try to force the door open. He damaged the door, and it cost him $200 to get it repaired.

2.

DIANA: Hello, police? This is an emergency!

MAN: Diana heard the sound of people fighting in the apartment next door. Then she heard a loud scream. She called the police, but when they arrived, it turned out the neighbors' kids were watching television and had the sound turned up very loud.

3.

SIMON: Hey, what's this? Wow! A gold ring!

WOMAN: Simon found a gold ring on a busy sidewalk. It looked like an expensive ring. He wanted to give it back

to the owner, but he thought the person who lost it might return to look for it. So he left the ring on the sidewalk.

14 *Behind the scenes*

2 CONVERSATION (p. 92)

B Listen to the rest of the conversation. What else makes working on movies difficult?

NINA: So you see, it's not really as glamorous a job as people think.

RYAN: I guess not.

NINA: For example, the hours are dreadful.

RYAN: So it's not exactly a nine-to-five job.

NINA: Not at all! Sometimes we shoot a scene right through the night. Or we may start work early in the morning. We have to get everything ready for a shoot – the lighting and everything – and that can take hours. So if we're going to start filming at eight in the morning, we usually have to be on the job by three or four A.M. to get ready.

RYAN: Three in the morning! That's unbelievable!

NINA: Oh, no, it's not! Believe me. It happens all the time.

4 LISTENING (p. 93)

A Listen to an interview with a TV producer. Write down three things a producer does.

RITA: Welcome to another edition of "Behind the Scenes," the show that profiles fascinating jobs and the people that do them. I'm Rita Roberts. Our guest today is Scott Jasper, a local TV producer. Hello, Scott. Welcome.

SCOTT: Hi. Thank you for inviting me, Rita.

RITA: Let me begin by saying that I asked a few people what they thought a producer does, and I was surprised at all the different responses I got.

SCOTT: Ahhh . . . yeah . . . you're so right! When I tell people I'm a producer, I often get a slightly confused reaction – sort of like, "Oh . . . really?"

RITA: Well, let's clear up the mystery.

SCOTT: I'd love to! First off, let me say that not every producer does exactly the same things. But I can say that they are all tired and stressed out, but probably love their job! For myself, I can tell you that my job allows me to be in charge of things and at the same time – work as part of a team. There's a lot of responsibility to this job, too. I have to see that everything is done correctly, on time, and within the budget.

RITA: Most people probably think of the producer as the "money person." Is there a creative side to the job, too?

SCOTT: Oh, absolutely. For example, I do research and think up ideas for shows with the writers. And then I work with the directors and the performers. You have to have a strong personality to be a producer – you have to be in charge of everyone, get them to do what you want – but you still have to be nice to them!

RITA: That can't be easy!

SCOTT: Oh, no, not at all. Also, you have to be able to make quick decisions . . . and if something you thought was great isn't working, you can't waste time. You have to let it go and start again. This isn't the job for someone who is indecisive or hates being under pressure! I love the excitement and the opportunity to work with very interesting people.

RITA: Well, this has been very informative, Scott, but I'm afraid we're out of time. Thank you so much for being our guest today.

SCOTT: Oh, it's been my pleasure!

RITA: Speaking for "Behind the Scenes," I'm Rita Roberts.

B Listen again. What are three personality traits a producer should have? Complete the chart.

Units 13–14 Progress check

1 LISTENING (p. 98)

A Listen to three conversations. Where do you think each conversation takes place? What do you think might have happened? Take notes.

1.

MAN 1: Well. I'll certainly never eat here again! And I'll tell all my friends not to come here either!

MAN 2: I do apologize. I . . . I'm afraid he's just started working here, but I don't think he's going to last long . . . not after this!

2.

MAN: Help! Help! Would someone call the manager? Can anyone hear me? Help!

WOMAN: Oh! Is someone in there?

MAN: Yes! I'm stuck between the second and third floors! Please help me get out!

WOMAN: Won't it open?

MAN: No! Get the manager, please!

WOMAN: OK! I'll get some help! Uh . . . don't go away!

3.

MAN: Oh, no! Not again! Listen to that funny noise. I thought you just had it checked.

WOMAN: Well, I did! The mechanic said everything was OK now.

MAN: Good grief! Well, let's stop and check the manual again. Maybe we can fix it ourselves.

WOMAN: Let's have a look under the hood and see what we can do.

15 There should be a law!

5 LISTENING (p. 102)

A Listen to people discuss problems. What solutions do they suggest? Take notes in the chart.

1. People talking loudly on cell phones in restaurants

PATRON: [*phone rings*] Hello? Yes. Oh, oh, hi…hi…! No, no….

WOMAN: Ugh. I hate it when people use cell phones in restaurants.

MAN: Me, too. It's so unnecessary. And so rude to everybody else!

WOMAN: I agree. I think people with cell phones should be asked to leave them at the door – you know, like coats and umbrellas. They can always check their voice mail later to see if there are any messages.

MAN: Exactly. That's a great idea.

2. Car alarms going off at night

MAN: I tell you another thing that drives me crazy – when people's car alarms go off in the middle of the night.

WOMAN: Yeah. Don't you hate it when an alarm wakes you from a deep sleep? It's such an awful sound – and it just goes on and on!

MAN: I think people who park regularly on the street ought to be required to let their neighbors know their license plate number and their telephone number. Then if their alarm goes off, someone can call them to come down and turn it off.

WOMAN: Good idea. At least that way they'd be sure to get woken up, too.

3. Telemarketing salespeople calling too often

WOMAN: And I really hate it when people call me at home and try to sell me stuff.

MAN: Me, too. I think the telephone companies should offer a service that automatically blocks telemarketing calls.

WOMAN: That's an interesting idea. That way, we might pay a little bit more, but we'd have peace.

MAN: Right!

8 CONVERSATION (p. 103)

B Listen to the rest of the conversation. What is Todd concerned about?

SARAH: Oh, listen to me. I'm always complaining, aren't I? Anyway, how are things with you?

TODD: Oh, not bad, but I'm still not sure what I'm going to do after I graduate.

SARAH: Yeah, it's hard to find a job these days, isn't it?

TODD: It's not that. I'm just not sure if going to law school was the right thing to do.

SARAH: What do you mean?

TODD: I only have a few more months before I graduate, and now I'm wondering why I did this. I don't want to be a lawyer. It all seems like a waste of time now.

SARAH: So what are you going to do?

TODD: Well, I'd like to move to Mexico and open a coffee shop, but I think my parents would flip.

11 LISTENING (p. 104)

A Listen to people give their opinions about current issues in the news. What issues are they talking about?

1.

MAN: I see some students are planning to hold a protest march downtown tomorrow.

WOMAN: Well, there's no law against protesting, is there?

MAN: No, no, of course not.

WOMAN: What are they protesting about?

MAN: I think they're trying to get the university to stop all research using animal subjects.

WOMAN: Oh, yeah. I definitely support them. I hate to think of monkeys and other animals being used for research. It's so cruel, and it's unnecessary as well. I don't see why animals should be killed just so some professor can publish a bunch of papers and get promoted.

MAN: Well, I don't think it's quite as simple as that. The fact is that a lot of advances in medical research on diseases like cancer and AIDS depend on animal research. You simply can't do that kind of research on humans, so they have to use animals. I'm afraid there's no other way.

2.

MAN: I saw a really interesting program on TV last night. It talked about the types of things that people have to be careful about when they download music and movies off the Internet.

WOMAN: What do you mean?

MAN: Well, they have to be careful not to download things that are protected by copyright.

WOMAN: How can that be avoided?

MAN: Well, some people download things illegally. They use file-sharing services so they don't pay anything for them. People should have to pay for their music and movies. Not doing so is unethical, and some people would say a form of stealing.

WOMAN: I don't understand. Let's say I downloaded a movie, and I paid for it. Don't I have the right to share this with other people? My friends, for example?

MAN: Not really. Some people think that sharing songs and movies is OK, but it's not. It's taking away money from the artists. These people have the right to make money off of their own work. You agree with that, don't you?

WOMAN: I don't know. I think the whole thing is ridiculous. Musicians and actors make tons of money as it is. I mean, who can afford to have a good music collection when you have to pay for every single song? And movies have gotten really expensive lately. When music and movies are more affordable, people will stop sharing them or downloading them illegally.

B Listen again. What opinions do you hear? Complete the chart.

16 *Challenges and accomplishments*

6 *LISTENING (p. 108)*

Listen to these people talk about their work. What is the biggest challenge of each person's job? What is the greatest reward? Complete the chart.

1. Psychologist

WOMAN: Maybe the biggest challenge for me is listening to people talk about their problems all day. At the end of the day, I'm usually pretty worn out. At times, it can be depressing as well. On the other hand, I do see patients making real progress. It's great to see people really turn their lives around and get on top of problems that they never thought they could deal with.

2. Camp counselor

MAN: As a camp counselor, it's difficult to find a way to get through to kids with problems and win their trust. Sometimes kids are very suspicious and find it hard to trust an adult – even a young adult. So getting them to open up is the hardest part. Once you've done that, they almost become different people. One of the things I find most rewarding is seeing kids develop confidence and a sense of self-worth. It's especially great to see that happen in a kid who started out the summer with low self-esteem.

3. Firefighter

MAN: It sounds pretty obvious, but in my job, the biggest challenge is going into a burning building that's full of smoke when you can barely see a few inches in front of you. It's really difficult – especially when you know there are people in there, and it's your job to get them out. Once

you do get someone out safely, then you feel really great, and you forget about how dangerous the work is.

11 *LISTENING (p. 110)*

A Listen to three young people discuss their plans for the future. What do they hope they'll have achieved by the time they are 30?

1. Rick

RICK: What do I hope I'll have achieved by the time I'm 30? Well, I hope I'll have opened my own restaurant by then. I've been working a 9-to-5 job the past two years, and I can't say it's really for me. I'd much rather work for myself and run my own place. So, I started taking cooking classes at night, and I'm getting pretty good at it!

2. Jasmine

JASMINE: I plan to be a doctor. I'm not in medical school now – I'm in pre-med, taking a lot of science classes. But I'm sure this is what I want to do with my life. By the time I'm 30, I hope I'll have finished medical school and will have started my career as a pediatrician – you know, a doctor who works with children. I've always loved working with kids.

3. Bianca

BIANCA: By the time I'm 30, I hope I'll have had a successful modeling career. I've already had some modeling experience, and after I graduate, I hope I can get a job with a big agency in New York or Los Angeles. I'm only 20 now, and I'd only like to model when I'm in my twenties. After that, I want to get married and start a family.

Units 15–16 Progress check

2 *LISTENING (p. 112)*

A Listen to people give opinions. Check the correct responses.

1.

WOMAN: It's difficult to find good housing around here, isn't it?

2.

MAN: They should do something about the graffiti in this city, shouldn't they?

3.

WOMAN: We have to pay way too much for child care these days, don't we?

4.

MAN: This city needs more youth centers, doesn't it?

5.

WOMAN: Company outsourcing isn't good for employment, is it?

6.

MAN: You can never find a parking space downtown, can you?

Workbook answer key

1 *That's what friends are for!*

Exercise 1

2. The Chans like meeting new people and having friends over for dinner. They're one of the most <u>sociable</u> couples I know.
3. You can't trust Jane. She always promises to do something, but then she never does it. She's pretty <u>unreliable</u>.
4. Alex wants to be an actor. It's hard to break into the business, but his family is very <u>supportive</u> of his dream.
5. I never know how to act around Tina! One minute she's in a good mood, and the next minute she's in a bad mood. She's *so* <u>temperamental</u>.

Exercise 2

A

(Note: Words in *italics* were given as examples.)

Opposites with in-

incompetent	inexperienced	informal
independent	inflexible	insensitive

Opposites with un-

unattractive	unpopular	unreliable
uncooperative	unreasonable	unsociable

B

Answers will vary.

Exercise 3

B: Hmm. So what kind of person are you looking for?

A: I want to travel with someone <u>who/that</u> is easygoing and independent.

B: Right. And you'd probably also like a person <u>who/that</u> is reliable.

A: Yeah, and I want someone ✗ I know well.

B: So why don't you ask me?

A: You? I know you *too* well!

B: Ha! Does that mean you think I'm someone <u>who/that</u> is high-strung, dependent, and unreliable?

A: No! I'm just kidding. You're definitely someone ✗ I could go on vacation with. So, . . . what are you doing in June?

Exercise 4

Answers will vary.

Exercise 5

A
The Snake and the Tiger
B
1. Sign: <u>The Dragon</u>
2. Sign: <u>The Boar</u>
3. Sign: <u>The Rooster</u>
4. Sign: <u>The Tiger</u>

Exercise 6

1. b   I like it when people are easygoing and friendly.
2. d   I don't mind it when people are a few minutes late for an appointment.
3. c   It upsets me when rich people are stingy.
4. a   It embarrasses me when someone criticizes me in front of other people.

Exercise 7

Answers will vary. Possible answers:
2. I love it when someone gives me a gift.
3. It bothers me when someone calls too early in the morning.
4. It makes me happy when I finish work for the day.
5. I can't stand it when I'm stuck in traffic.
6. It upsets me when I can't see at the movies.

Exercise 8

Answers will vary. Possible answers:
2. *It bothers me when* someone yells at me.
3. *I really don't mind it when* people eat at their desk.
4. *It upsets me when* people don't clean up after themselves.

Exercise 9

Answers will vary.

Exercise 10

1. I can tell Simon anything, and I know he won't tell anyone else. I can really <u>trust</u> him.
2. Brenda has a very high opinion of herself. I don't like people who are so <u>egotistical</u>.
3. It bothers me when people are too serious. I prefer people who are <u>easygoing</u> and have a good sense of humor.
4. I like it when someone expresses strong <u>opinions</u>. Hearing other people's views can really make you think.
5. Jackie is very rich, but she only spends her money on herself. She's very <u>stingy</u>.

2 Career moves

Exercise 1

A

2. green researcher <u>a</u>
3. guidance counselor <u>b</u>
4. organic food farmer <u>e</u>
5. social media manager <u>c</u>
6. zookeeper <u>d</u>

B

Answers will vary. Possible answers:

1. *An accountant is someone who* keeps records of income and expenses.
2. A fashion designer is someone who designs stylish clothing.
3. A flight attendant is someone who takes care of passengers in flight.

Exercise 2

A

Positive	Negative
challenging	*awful*
fantastic	boring
fascinating	dangerous
interesting	difficult
rewarding	frightening

B

Answers will vary.

Exercise 3

A

work for an airline – *travel to different countries*
with computers – learn new software programs
as a high school coach – teach discipline and fitness

be a university professor – do research
a writer – work independently

B

ANN: Hmm. I don't know if I'd like that because I'd have to write every day.

TOM: What do you want to do, then?

ANN: Well, I'm not sure, either! I'd love <u>working as a high school coach</u>. I'd really enjoy being with teenagers all day and <u>teaching discipline and fitness</u>. On the other hand, I'd be interested in <u>working for an airline</u>.

TOM: Really? What would you like about that?

ANN: Well, I'd love <u>traveling to different countries</u> all over the world.

TOM: Oh, I could never do that! I think it would be very tiring work.

C

Answers will vary. Possible answers:

A: So what kind of career would you like?

B: Well, I'm not exactly sure. <u>Working with computers could be interesting. You know, learning new software programs.</u>

A: That sounds interesting. But I wouldn't like it because <u>I'd get tired of staring at a computer screen.</u>

B: What do you want to do, then?

A: Well, I'd love <u>being a university professor.</u>

B: <u>Why is that?</u>

A: <u>I'd enjoy doing research.</u>

Exercise 4

A

1. self-employed builder
2. freelance artist
3. house painter
4. orchestra conductor
5. aerobics instructor
6. child-care worker

B

Answers will vary.

Exercise 5

2. A chef's <u>assistant</u> has <u>worse hours than</u> a waiter.
3. A dog <u>walker</u> is <u>better paid than</u> a student intern.
4. A house <u>painter</u> earns <u>more than</u> a camp counselor.
5. A park <u>ranger</u> is <u>not as well paid as</u> a landscaper.
6. Being a yoga <u>instructor</u> is <u>not as difficult as</u> being a professor.
7. Being an interior <u>decorator</u> is <u>more interesting than</u> being a sales assistant.
8. A guidance <u>counselor</u> has <u>more responsibility than</u> a gardener.

Exercise 6

1. Wai-man works <u>at</u> the best Chinese restaurant in Vancouver.
2. I think working <u>with</u> other people is more fun than working alone.
3. I would hate working <u>in</u> the media. It would be nerve-racking!
4. Working <u>as</u> a dance instructor sounds great.
5. Working <u>in</u> an office is less interesting than working <u>on</u> a cruise ship.

Exercise 7

Answers will vary. Possible answers:

2. A: *Working in a* travel agency has better benefits than working at a private summer school.
   B: *Yes, but working* as a tutor is more challenging than being a travel agent.
3. A: A tennis instructor doesn't make as much money as a tour guide.
   B: Yes, but a tour guide works longer hours than a tennis instructor.
4. A: A taxi driver has a shorter work week than an office assistant.
   B: Yes, but working as an office assistant is less boring than being a taxi driver.

Exercise 8

Answers will vary.

3 *Could you do me a favor?*

Exercise 1

A

2. *Would you mind* giving me a ride home?
3. *Is it OK if* I turn down the TV?
4. *Do you mind if* I use your cell phone?
5. *I was wondering if* I could borrow your car for the weekend.
6. *Could* you tell me how to get to the subway?

B

Answers will vary. Possible answers:
1. Can you pick up my mail?
2. I was wondering if you could take care of my cat.
3. Could you feed my fish?
4. Would you mind taking me to the airport?

Exercise 2

Answers will vary.

Exercise 3

Answers will vary. Possible answers:
2. A: Would you mind doing the dishes? I'm exhausted!
   B: Sorry, but I have to take out the trash.
3. A: Could you take care of these things? I have to leave early today.
   B: Sorry, but I have to leave early today, too.

Exercise 4

A

People make formal requests if the speaker thinks the listener will decline. People make less formal requests if the speaker thinks the listener will accept.

B

	Less formal	More formal	Type
1. Close the door.	✓		2
2. It's really cold in here.		✓	10
3. Could you possibly move your car?		✓	4
4. May I borrow your dictionary?		✓	5
5. I was wondering if you could help me with this assignment.		✓	7
6. I need some help moving to my new apartment.	✓		1
7. I'm sorry but I can't stand loud music.		✓	9
8. Do you have a camera?	✓		3

Exercise 5

A

Noun	Verb	Noun	Verb
apology	*apologize*	invitation	invite
compliment	compliment	permission	permit
explanation	explain	request	request

B

1. giving a compliment
2. accepting an apology
3. asking for a favor
4. declining a request
5. making a request

Exercise 6

1. My phone didn't work for a week. The phone company <u>offered</u> an apology and took $20 off my bill.
2. A friend of mine really loves to <u>receive</u> compliments, but he never gives anyone else one. I don't understand why he's like that.
3. Carol is always talking on the phone. She makes a lot of calls, but she rarely <u>returns</u> mine. Maybe she never listens to her voice mail!
4. I need to <u>ask for</u> a favor. Could you please give me a ride to school tomorrow? My bike has a flat tire!

Exercise 7

Answers will vary. Possible answers:
1. A: Is Rosa Sanchez there, please?
   B: No, she isn't. Would you like to leave a message?
   A: Yes, please. This is Anita Jensen calling from Toronto. Could you tell her *that my flight arrives at 7 p.m. on Tuesday?* Would <u>you ask her to meet me in the International Arrivals area</u>?
   B: OK, I'll give her the message.
2. A: Can I speak to Eric, please?
   B: I'm afraid he's not here. Do you want to leave a message?
   A: Yes, please. This is Kevin. Please <u>ask him if I can borrow his scanner. And if it's OK, could you ask him when I could pick it up</u>?
   B: Sure, I'll leave him the message.
3. A: Could I speak to Alex, please?
   B: I'm sorry, but he's not here right now.
   A: Oh, OK. This is Mr. Todd. I'd like to leave a message. Could <u>you tell him that the meeting is on Thursday at 10:30 a.m.? Could you tell him not to forget to bring his report</u>?
4. A: I'd like to speak to Jenny, please.
   B: She's not here right now. Can I take a message?
   A: Yeah. This is Philip Lim. Can <u>you ask Jenny if she's going to the conference tomorrow? And would you ask her what time it starts</u>?
   B: OK. I'll give Jenny your message.

Exercise 8

CHRIS: Sure. And I'll bring two extra speakers. We'll have amazing sound.
LEN: Thanks.
CHRIS: No problem. Now, what about food?
LEN: Well, I thought maybe a salad. Would you mind <u>bringing a big salad</u>, too?
CHRIS: Well, OK. And, how about drinks?
LEN: Well, could you <u>ask Jill to get some soda</u>? And please tell her <u>not to be late</u>. Last time we had a party, she didn't arrive till eleven o'clock, and everyone got really thirsty!
CHRIS: I remember.
LEN: One more thing – I was wondering if you could <u>buy dessert</u>.
CHRIS: Um, sure. All right. But, uh, would you mind if I <u>borrowed some money</u> to pay for it?

Exercise 9

2. Would you please ask Penny to stop by and talk to me?
3. I was wondering if I could borrow your guitar.
4. Could you ask Adam when he's coming over?
5. Would you mind lending me your hairbrush?

4 What a story!

Exercise 1

1. A 69-year-old grandmother in Paris _went_ to the bathroom – and <u>stayed</u> there for twenty days. What happened? As she was <u>locking</u> the door, the lock <u>broke</u>. She could not open the door. She <u>shouted</u> for help, but no one <u>heard</u> her because her bathroom had no windows. After nearly three weeks, the woman's neighbors <u>wondered</u> where she was. Firefighters broke into her apartment and <u>found</u> her in a "very weakened" state. While she was <u>waiting</u> to be rescued, she <u>drank</u> warm water.

2. A woman was <u>behaving</u> strangely when she <u>entered</u> Bangkok Airport. While she was <u>checking in</u> for an overseas flight, she <u>had</u> difficulty with a very large bag. The check-in clerk <u>became</u> suspicious and <u>decided</u> to X-ray the bag. The X-ray <u>showed</u> an image that looked like an animal. When airport staff <u>opened</u> the bag, they saw that a baby tiger was <u>sleeping</u> under lots of toy tigers. The tiger was taken to a rescue center for wildlife, and the woman was arrested.

Exercise 2

Sentences may vary. Possible sentences:

2. While/As I was using my computer, it suddenly stopped working. (_or_ I was using my computer when it suddenly stopped working.)
3. While/As we were playing tennis, my racquet broke. (_or_ We were playing tennis when my racquet broke.)
4. While/As I was taking a shower, the water got cold. (_or_ I was taking a shower when the water got cold.)
5. While/As I was cooking dinner, I burned my finger. (_or_ I was cooking dinner when I burned my finger.)

Exercise 3

1. A: Guess what happened to me last night! As I _was getting_ into bed, I <u>heard</u> a loud noise like a gunshot in the street. Then the phone <u>rang</u>.
   B: Who was it?
   A: It was Mariana. She always calls me late at night, but this time she had a reason. She <u>was driving</u> right past my apartment when she <u>got</u> a flat tire. It was very late, so while we <u>were changing</u> the tire, I <u>invited</u> her to spend the night.
2. A: I'm sorry I'm so late, Kathy. I was at the dentist.
   B: Don't tell me! While you <u>were sitting</u> in the waiting room, you <u>met</u> someone interesting. I know how you are, Tom!
   A: Well, you're wrong this time. The dentist <u>was cleaning</u> my teeth when she suddenly <u>got</u> called away for an emergency. So I just sat there waiting for two hours with my mouth hanging open!

Exercise 4

A

Text message saves 18 people

B

Answers will vary. Possible answers:

1. Eighteen people (twelve tourists from the U.K., Australia, and New Zealand, and six Indonesian crew members)
2. Because there were waves nearly five meters high, the engine broke down and there was power for only three lights on board. The boat had no marine radio.
3. Because she had a cell phone; it was the only chance they had to get help.

4. He called her and then called a branch of the British coast guard.
5. The high waves
6. Maybe the weather improved and the coast guard pulled the small boat with a rope.

Exercise 5

Answers will vary.

Exercise 6

Bob and I _had just gotten_ engaged, so we went to a jewelry store to buy a wedding ring. We <u>had just chosen</u> a ring when a masked man <u>came in</u>. After the robber <u>had taken</u> Bob's wallet, he <u>demanded</u> the ring. I <u>had just handed</u> it to him when the alarm <u>started</u> to go off, and the robber <u>ran off</u>. We were so relieved! But then the sales assistant <u>told</u> us we had to pay for the ring because I <u>had given</u> it to the robber. We <u>had just told</u> her that we wouldn't pay for it when the police <u>arrived</u> and <u>arrested</u> _us!_ What a terrible experience!

Exercise 7

A

1. What an emergency!
2. What a triumph!
3. What a dilemma!

B

Answers will vary. Possible answers:
remote: far away from populated areas
mainland: the main part of a country or continent, not including the islands belonging to or surrounding it
skip: miss; not to do
remarkably: incredibly, surprisingly
promotion: a better paid job, usually with more responsibility, in the same company
resign: leave a job

Exercise 8

1. After an art show _opened_ in New York, it was discovered that someone <u>had hung</u> a famous painting by Henri Matisse upside down.
2. In 2003, Italian workers <u>found</u> important archeological remains while they <u>were constructing</u> a new parking lot in Vatican City. There were mosaics dating from 54 to 68 CE.
3. Russia <u>had</u> a very hot summer in 2010. The country <u>had not experienced</u> such hot weather for at least 130 years.
4. In 2011, two divers <u>discovered</u> the remains of a 200-year-old shipwreck while they <u>were diving</u> off the coast of Rhode Island, in the eastern United States.

Exercise 9

Reporters' countries and arrival days

Sunday	Name:	Mr. Swire
	Country:	Singapore
	Name:	_____
	Country:	_____
Monday	Name:	Ms. Anderson
	Country:	the United States
	Name:	Mr. Marks
	Country:	Canada
Tuesday	Name:	Mr. Jackson
	Country:	Australia
	Name:	Ms. Benson
	Country:	Italy

5 Crossing cultures

Exercise 1

2. The first time I traveled abroad, I felt really <u>depressed</u>. I was alone, I didn't speak the language, and I didn't make any friends.
3. I just spent a year in France learning to speak French. It was a satisfying experience, and I was <u>fascinated</u> by the culture.
4. At first I really didn't like shopping in the open-air markets. I felt <u>uncomfortable</u> because so many people were trying to sell me something at the same time.
5. When I arrived in Lisbon, I was nervous because I couldn't speak any Portuguese. As I began to learn the language, though, I became more <u>confident</u> about living there.
6. Before I went to Alaska last winter, I was very <u>worried</u> about the cold. But it wasn't a problem because most buildings there are well heated.
7. When I was traveling in Southeast Asia, I couldn't believe how many different kinds of fruit there were. I was <u>curious</u> to try all of them, so I ate a lot of fruit!
8. It was our first trip to Latin America, so we were <u>uncertain</u> about what to expect. We loved it and hope to return again soon.

Exercise 2

Answers will vary. Some possible answers:
1. Public transportation is one thing I'd be uncertain about. I'd be uncomfortable with reading unfamiliar maps.
2. The architecture is something I'd be enthusiastic about. Looking at buildings is one of my favorite things to do in a new city.
3. The climate is something I'd be uncomfortable with. I hate being cold!
4. The food is something I'd be curious about. I love tasting new things.
5. The language is one thing I'd be nervous about. I'd worry that people wouldn't understand me.
6. The money is something I'd be comfortable with. I'm very good with numbers.
7. The music is one thing I'd be curious about. I always love to hear new groups!
8. Meeting people my age is something I'd be uncertain about. I'm pretty shy.

Exercise 3

A
Answers will vary.
B
You can find articles like this one on websites and in magazines.
Anyone may want to read it but the most likely readers would be people who are thinking of working, studying, or traveling abroad.
C
1. culture: customs that are particular to a specific country or group of people
2. culture shock: discomfort caused by experiencing a culture different from one's own
3. appreciate: to recognize and value
4. stereotypes: generalizations about a group of people

D
Answers will vary.

Exercise 4

Answers will vary.

Exercise 5

A
2. Denmark and Spain
3. Egypt and New Zealand
4. France and the United States
B
Answers will vary. Possible answers:
1. *In Spain, you're expected to* arrive late for most appointments.
2. *In France*, you're not expected to leave tips in restaurants.
3. *In Egypt*, you're supposed to allow your hosts to treat you to meals in restaurants.
4. In Japan, it's not the custom to kiss people on the cheek.
5. In Indonesia, it's not acceptable to wear shorts in temples.

Exercise 6

Answers will vary.

Exercise 7

Answers will vary.

6 What's wrong with it?

Exercise 1

A

chipped	cracked	dented	leaking
glasses	chair	car	car
plate	glasses	bike	sink
	plate		

scratched	stained	torn
bike	blouse	blouse
car	carpet	carpet
chair	chair	tablecloth
glasses	tablecloth	

B

2. The blouse is torn. (*or* There's a tear in the blouse.)
3. The carpet is stained. (*or* There's a stain on the carpet.)
4. The bike is scratched and dented. (*or* There's a scratch/dent on the bike.)
5. The sink is leaking. (*or* The sink has a leak.)
6. The chair is cracked. (*or* There's a crack in the chair.)
7. The plate is chipped. (*or* There's a chip on the plate.)
8. The tablecloth is torn. (*or* There's a tear in the tablecloth.)
9. The glasses are cracked and scratched. (*or* There's a crack in/scratch on the glasses.)

Exercise 2

A

Answers will vary. Possible answer:
People who are thinking of buying similar products would probably read articles like these because they would want to avoid these kinds of problems.

B

	Problems	What Consumer magazine did	Paid back? Yes	No
Sharon's laptops	*fuzzy screen* scratched cover loose keys crashed	Wrote a letter explaining Sharon was losing work because of the computer problems	✓	
Chris's car	engine damaged locks broken insurance company wouldn't pay 40%	Asked the insurance company to prove the new engine would increase the car's value	✓	

Exercise 3

2. The screws on these glasses are too loose. They need <u>to be tightened (*or* tightening).</u>
3. The blades on these scissors are too dull. They need <u>to be sharpened (*or* sharpening).</u>
4. This faucet is too tight. It needs <u>to be loosened (*or* loosening).</u>
5. These pants are too long. They need <u>to be shortened (*or* shortening).</u>
6. This street is too narrow. It needs <u>to be widened (*or* widening).</u>

Exercise 4

TIM: Guess what? Someone broke into my car last night!

JAN: Oh, no. What did they take?

TIM: Nothing! But they did a lot of damage. The lock <u>*needs to be repaired*</u>. And the window <u>needs to be replaced (*or* needs replacing).</u>

JAN: It was probably some young kids having "fun."

TIM: Yeah, some fun. I think they had a party in my car! The seats <u>need to be cleaned (*or* need cleaning).</u>

JAN: How annoying. Does the car drive OK?

TIM: No, it feels strange. The gears <u>keep sticking</u>, so they <u>need fixing (*or* need to be fixed)</u>. And the brakes <u>need to be checked (*or* need checking)</u> right away.

JAN: Well, I guess you're lucky they didn't steal it!

TIM: Yeah, lucky me.

Exercise 5

Answers will vary.

Exercise 6

A

2. c
3. b
4. e
5. d
6. a

B

2. The DVD in the DVD player is stuck. The DVD needs to be removed.
3. The wire for the speakers is damaged. The wire needs to be repaired. (*or* The wire needs repairing.)
4. The screen on the TV is cracked. The screen needs to be replaced. (*or* The screen needs replacing.)
5. The metal door of the stove is scratched. The door needs to be repainted. (*or* The door needs repainting.)
6. The table legs are loose. The legs need to be tightened and glued. (*or* The legs need tightening and gluing.)

C

Answers will vary.

Exercise 7

7 The world we live in

Exercise 1

2. The taste of our drinking water has been ruined by chlorine and other additives.
3. New illnesses have been caused by certain agricultural pesticides.
4. Our crops are being destroyed because of traffic pollution.
5. Dangerous chemicals are being released by factories.
6. People's health has been damaged as a result of breathing smog every day.
7. More severe droughts have been created through a lack of rainfall.
8. Our forests and wildlife are being threatened by global warming.

Exercise 2

A

Verb	Noun	Verb	Noun
contaminate	contamination	educate	education
contribute	contribution	pollute	pollution
create	creation	populate	population
deplete	depletion	protect	protection
destroy	destruction	reduce	reduction

B
Answers will vary.

Exercise 3

2. One way to inform the public about factories that pollute the environment is through educational programs on TV.
3. In many countries of the world, threatened animal and plant species are being protected by strict laws.
4. Agricultural pesticides are damaging the soil in many countries.
5. Poverty is an enormous problem in many large cities where whole families can only afford to live in one room.

Exercise 4

A

Bills and coins are being replaced by plastic money: banks are issuing debit cards; stores and businesses are issuing charge cards. Cards that used to be made of paper are being replaced by plastic ones. An additional reason could be that customers choose to use them because they are convenient.

B

1. False: Most cards are made from polyvinyl chloride (PVC). Harmful chemicals, such as dioxin, are released into the atmosphere when PVC is produced.
2. False: Most plastic cards do not biodegrade.
3. True.
4. False: It's difficult to make wood both flexible and unbreakable; some people say it's dangerous to put metal objects into electronic equipment.
5. True.
6. False: Many people complain that it's wrong to turn a food crop, such as corn, into plastic.

Exercise 5

A

2. f   3. d   4. b   5. a   6. c

B

1. As a result of overfishing, we are losing more and more species as well as entire ecosystems.

2. In some major cities, the problem of overbuilding is a result of too many skyscrapers and too little land area inside the city limits.
3. There is an overuse of fossil fuels when we should be looking for other natural sources of energy like wind and solar power.
4. City officials are trying to stop development in areas with overburdened roads and schools.
5. The best way to prevent the overflowing of our landfills is to have better and more efficient recycling programs.
6. Another way to help reduce the overcrowding of our schools is to build more schools and hire more teachers.

Exercise 6

Answers will vary. Possible answers:

1. A: A big housing developer wants to build apartments in Forest Hill Park. I think that's terrible, but what can we do?
   B: _One thing to do is to complain to the Parks Department about it._
   A: That's a good idea.
   B: Another thing to do is to organize a public meeting to protest the threat to public property.
2. A: Personally, I'm worried about drug trafficking. It puts lots of children and young people at risk.
   B: One way to help is to educate young people about its dangers.
3. A: You know, there's a lot of corruption in our city government.
   B: The best way to fight corruption in our city government is to report it to the local newspaper.
   A: Yeah, the bad publicity might help to clean things up a bit.
4. A: There are so many unemployed people in this city. I just don't know what can be done about it.
   B: One thing to do is to create more government-funded jobs.
5. A: What worries me most is the number of homeless people on the streets.
   B: One way to help is to create more public housing projects.
   A: I agree.
   B: Another thing to do is to donate money to charities that provide shelters and food.

Exercise 7

Answers will vary. Possible answers:

2. These days, a lot of endangered animals are being killed by hunters and poachers. The best way to stop this practice is to have more police to arrest the poachers.
3. During the past few years, lots of trees have been destroyed by acid rain. One thing to do about it is to stop factories from polluting the air.
4. Underground water is being contaminated by agricultural pesticides. The best way to deal with the problem is to create safe agricultural pesticides.
5. Too many young people's lives are being ruined through the use of illegal drugs. The best way to fight drug traffickers is to enforce the laws against selling drugs.

Exercise 8

Answers will vary.

8 Lifelong learning

Exercise 1

1. I'm interested in human behavior, so I'm planning to take a class in <u>psychology</u>.
2. I want to take a course in <u>business</u>, such as commerce or accounting.
3. I'd prefer not to study <u>nursing</u> because I'm not very comfortable in hospitals.
4. I'd really like to work in Information Technology, so I'm thinking of taking courses in <u>computer science</u>.

Exercise 2

A

Answers will vary. Possible answers:
2. Would you rather study part time or full time?
3. Would you prefer to have a boring job that pays well or an exciting job that pays less?
4. Would you prefer taking a long vacation once a year or several short vacations each year?

B

Answers will vary.

Exercise 3

Answers will vary.

Exercise 4

Answers will vary. Possible answers:
1. *I'd rather stay home than go out because* I rarely get to spend time at home.
2. I'd prefer to have a bird because I'm not home enough to have a cat.
3. I'd rather live in the city than in the country because there is more to do in a city.
4. I'd rather invite them over for dinner than take them out to a restaurant. I love to cook, but don't get to do it that often.
5. I'd prefer to download a movie and watch it at home than see a new movie at the theater because movie ticket prices have gotten so expensive lately.

Exercise 5

A

Answers will vary.

B

1. There are between 1.5 and 1.9 million homeschoolers in the United States today.
2. Some parents prefer to teach their children at home because they do not believe that schools teach the correct religious values. Others believe they can provide a better education for their children by teaching them at home.
3. The Gutersons start with their children's interests and questions.
4. Critics say that homeschoolers can become social outsiders who are uncomfortable mixing with other people in adult life. Another criticism is that many parents are not well qualified to teach.

C

Answers will vary.

D

Answers will vary.

Exercise 6

Answers will vary. Possible answers:
2. A good way to keep in touch with old friends is <u>by using social networks.</u>
3. You can make new friends <u>by going out more often.</u>
4. The best way to save money is <u>by not eating out.</u>
5. You could stay in shape <u>by exercising regularly.</u>
6. I stay healthy <u>by eating good food.</u>
7. One way to learn self-confidence is <u>by studying dance.</u>

Exercise 7

1. Miriam shows her <u>concern for others</u> by volunteering to help people with cancer.
2. My parents' love of art, poetry, and music taught me <u>artistic appreciation</u> from a very young age.
3. I learned <u>courtesy</u> from my parents. They taught me the importance of being polite to both family and friends.
4. Barbara always gets upset with people who disagree with her. I wish she would show more <u>tolerance</u>.
5. I recently joined a choir, and I love it. But you need a lot of <u>perseverance</u>, because you have to practice the same piece of music for weeks before you're ready to perform it!

Exercise 8

A

1. John is very good at most school subjects, but he has no interest in being "the best." Instead, he likes to work with others in a group to complete a job together. The world would be a better place if everyone showed as much <u>cooperation</u> as John.
2. Felix finds school very hard, but no one tries harder than he does. He always spends the whole weekend in the library trying to keep up with his studies. He shows great <u>perseverance</u>.
3. Caitlin always wants to do better than everyone else. In school, she always tries to get the best grades. Her favorite sport is badminton because she's the best player in the school. No one needs to teach Caitlin <u>competitiveness</u>.
4. Andrea has more <u>creativity</u> than any of her classmates. She writes fascinating stories that show she has a wonderful imagination. She's also very artistic and does very interesting paintings.

B

Answers will vary.

Exercise 9

Answers will vary.

9 Improvements

Exercise 1

2. house painting
3. dry cleaning
4. pet sitting
5. language tutoring
6. home repairs

Exercise 2

A

2. do/cut my hair
3. do/cut my nails
4. fix my computer
5. print my photos
6. remove a stain
7. shorten my pants

B

Answers will vary. Possible answers:

2. A: Where can I get/have my hair cut?
   B: You can get/have it cut at Mike's Salon.
3. A: Where can I get/have my nails done?
   B: You can get/have them done at Nail Hut.
4. A: Where can I get/have my computer fixed?
   B: You can get/have it fixed at Techies.
5. A: Where can I get/have my photos printed?
   B: You can get/have them printed at Photo Plus.
6. A: Where can I get/have a stain removed?
   B: You can get/have it removed at Harry's Dry Cleaning.
7. A: Where can I get/have my pants shortened?
   B: You can get/have them shortened at Lily's Clothing Alterations.

Exercise 3

2. You can have/get your shoes repaired at Kwik Fix.
3. You can have/get your clothes dry-cleaned at Dream Clean.
4. You can have/get your carpets cleaned at Carpet World.
5. You can have/get your nails done at Nail File.
6. You can have/get your car washed at Jimmy's.
7. You can have/get your washing machine serviced at Hal's Repairs.
8. You can have/get your eyes examined at Eye to Eye.

Exercise 4

A

Answers will vary.

B

1. True
2. False: All the energy is burned off through the roof of a round building. That is bad for business.
3. False: Feng shui has become popular in many western countries only in recent years.
4. False: The principles of good feng shui were not respected when the building was designed.
5. True

Exercise 5

Answers will vary. Possible answers:

2. Maybe you could <u>see a doctor. Or why don't you get a more comfortable chair?</u>
3. Why don't you try <u>gardening? Another thing you could do is go walking every day.</u>
4. It might be a good idea <u>to slow down. Have you thought about staying home with friends?</u>
5. What about <u>staying in your house? Have you thought about refusing to open the door?</u>

Exercise 6

1. I don't know how my grandmother <u>keeps up with</u> all the new technology. She's better at understanding new gadgets than I am!
2. My cousin didn't know what to do for her mother's 60th birthday, but she finally <u>came up with</u> the idea of a surprise picnic with the whole family.
3. Judy has done it again! She only met Sam two months ago, and already she has <u>broken up with</u> him. Why doesn't she try to work out any problems?
4. After Pat saw her doctor, she decided to <u>cut down on</u> eating fast food. She wants to lose some weight and start exercising again in order to keep fit.
5. We're really lucky in my family because we all <u>get along with</u> each other very well.
6. I've done pretty badly in my classes this semester, so I'm not really <u>looking forward to</u> receiving my grades.
7. I can't <u>put up with</u> that loud music anymore! I can't stand hip-hop, and I'm going to tell my neighbor right now.
8. I've been getting sick a lot lately, and I often feel tired. I really need to start <u>taking care of</u> my health.

10 *The past and the future*

Exercise 1

2. discovery
3. terrorist act
4. achievement
5. assassination
6. natural disaster

Exercise 2

2. The cell phone was invented about 40 years <u>ago</u>.
3. Brasília has been the capital city of Brazil <u>since</u> 1960.
4. The first laptop was produced <u>in</u> 1981.
5. Mexico has been independent <u>for</u> more than 200 years.
6. World War II lasted <u>from</u> 1939 <u>to</u> 1945.
7. Vietnam was separated into two parts <u>for</u> about 20 years.
8. East and West Germany have been united <u>since</u> 1990.

Exercise 3

A

Noun	Verb
achievement	*achieve*
assassination	assassinate
demonstration	demonstrate
discovery	discover
discrimination	discriminate
election	elect

Noun	Verb
existence	exist
exploration	explore
explosion	explode
invention	invent
transformation	transform
vaccination	vaccinate

B

2. In World War I, many soldiers were <u>vaccinated</u> against typhoid, a deadly bacterial disease.
3. Aung San, the man who led Myanmar to independence, was <u>assassinated</u> in 1947. No one is certain who killed him.
4. The European Union has <u>existed</u> since 1957. There are now 27 member states.
5. Until the 1960s, there were many laws that <u>discriminated</u> against African Americans in certain regions of the United States.
6. In 1885, Louis Pasteur <u>discovered</u> a cure for rabies when he treated a young boy who was bitten by a dog.
7. In recent years, teams of experts in countries such as Cambodia and Angola have been safely <u>exploding</u> land mines in order to rid those countries of these dangerous weapons.
8. One of the few parts of the world that has not been <u>explored</u> much is Antarctica. The extreme climate makes it dangerous to travel far from research centers.

Exercise 4

A

Vaccinations are injections intended to prevent diseases such as smallpox.

B

2. End of the 18th century	Smallpox was responsible for the deaths of about one in ten people around the world.
3. 1796	Jenner vaccinated a boy with cowpox and smallpox. The boy did not get smallpox.
4. 1800	The Royal Vaccine Institution was founded in Berlin, Germany.
5. 1801	Napoleon opened a vaccination program in Paris.
6. 1967	WHO started an ambitious vaccination program.
7. 1977	The last case of smallpox was recorded.
8. Future challenge	Discover new vaccines for other diseases

Exercise 5

A

2. many people <u>will be wearing</u> temperature-controlled body suits.
3. most people <u>will be driving</u> cars that run on fuel from garbage.
4. people <u>will be competing</u> in a new Olympic event – mind reading.
5. Answers will vary.
6. Answers will vary.

B

2. ties for men <u>will have gone</u> out of fashion.
3. scientists <u>will have discovered</u> a cheap way of getting drinking water from seawater.
4. medical researchers <u>will have found</u> a cure for cancer.
5. Answers will vary.
6. Answers will vary.

Exercise 6

Answers will vary.

Exercise 7

Answers will vary.

Exercise 8

Answers will vary.

11 Life's little lessons

Exercise 1

Answers will vary.

Exercise 2

2. I just spent a horrible evening with Kendra. She questioned and criticized everything I said. I wish she weren't so <u>argumentative</u>.
3. My sister is very <u>naive</u>. She trusts everyone and thinks everyone is good.
4. Once I turned 16, I became less <u>rebellious</u>, and my parents started to let me do what I wanted.
5. Paul is really <u>ambitious</u>. He wants to own his own business by the time he's 25.
6. I wish I could be like Celia. She's so <u>carefree</u> and never seems to worry about anything.

Exercise 3

Answers will vary.

Exercise 4

A

She learned not to sprint too early to the finishing line.

B

Answers will vary. Possible answers:
1. launched herself into: began her career in
2. record time: the fastest ever time
3. prestigious: well-known and respected
4. sprint: run faster for a short time
5. runners-up: participants who don't win a race but finish in second place (or do pretty well)
6. ecstatic: extremely happy

C

Answers will vary. Possible answers:
Her siblings are athletes; her father is a trainer; she seems to learn lessons from her mistakes; her coach says she trains hard and with determination.

Exercise 5

Answers will vary. Possible answers:
2. I shouldn't have been argumentative with my boss.
3. I shouldn't have changed jobs.
4. I should have waited and paid for the TV with cash.
5. I should have studied computer science in school.
6. I should have been more serious in school.
7. I shouldn't have given my homework to my friend.
8. I should have put the party in my calendar with a reminder.
9. I shouldn't have lent money to people I couldn't trust.
10. I should have complimented my friend on her hairstyle.

Exercise 6

A

2. If we'd made a reservation, we would have eaten already.
3. If I'd put on sunscreen, I wouldn't have gotten a sunburn.
4. If you'd let me drive, we would have arrived by now.
5. If I'd ignored your text in class, I wouldn't have gotten in trouble.

B

Answers will vary.

Exercise 7

ANDY: I've made such a mess of my life!

JOHN: What do you mean?

ANDY: If I *hadn't accepted* a job *as soon as* I graduated, I <u>could have traveled</u> around Europe all summer – just like you did. You were so carefree.

JOHN: You know, I shoul<u>dn't have gone</u> to Europe. I should <u>have taken</u> the great job I was offered. <u>After</u> I returned from Europe, it was too late.

ANDY: But my job is so depressing! <u>The moment</u> I started it, I hated it – on the very first day! That was five years ago, and nothing's changed. I should <u>have looked</u> for another job right away.

JOHN: Well, start looking now. I posted my résumé online last month and five companies contacted me right away. If I <u>hadn't posted</u> my résumé, no one <u>would have contacted</u> me. I accepted one of the job offers.

ANDY: Really? What's the job?

JOHN: It's working as a landscape gardener. <u>The moment</u> I saw it, I knew it was right for me.

ANDY: But for me right now, the problem is that I get a very good salary, and I just bought a house. If I <u>hadn't bought</u> the house, <u>I'd be able to</u> take a lower-paying job.

JOHN: Well, I guess you can't have everything. If I <u>had</u> a better salary, <u>I'd buy</u> a house, too.

12 The right stuff

Exercise 1

2. <u>In order for</u> a movie to be entertaining, it has to have good actors and an interesting story.
3. <u>In order to</u> succeed in business, you often have to work long hours.
4. <u>In order to</u> attract new members, a sports club needs to offer inexpensive memberships.
5. <u>In order to</u> speak a foreign language well, it's a good idea to use the language as often as possible.
6. <u>In order for</u> a clothing store to succeed, it has to be able to find the latest fashions.

Exercise 2

Answers will vary. Possible answers:

2. *For a clothes store to be profitable,* you have to hire talented salespeople.
3. In order to manage your own business, you need to work extremely long hours.
4. For an advertisement to be persuasive, it needs to be clever and entertaining.
5. In order to run a successful automobile company, you have to provide excellent customer service.
6. For a reality TV show to be successful, it needs to have drama and interesting characters.

Exercise 3

2. I learned a lot about how to run a successful bookstore from taking that class. I found it very <u>informative</u>.
3. Linda has so many interesting ideas, and she's always thinking of new projects. She's very <u>clever</u>.
4. Rosie is a salesperson, and she's good at her job. She's so <u>persuasive</u> that she sells three times as much as her co-workers.
5. Daniel is one of the top models in Milan. He goes to the gym every day so he looks really <u>muscular</u>.
6. For a restaurant to succeed, it has to <u>maintain</u> a high level of quality in both food and service.
7. If a department store improves its <u>decor</u> and looks really fashionable, it can attract a lot of new customers.

Exercise 4

Answers will vary.

Exercise 5

A

Answers will vary. Possible answers:

1. *I like this park because it's clean and there are a lot of trees. I don't like this park since* there is a lot of trash.
2. I like this outdoor café since it's in a sunny location. The reason I don't like this outdoor café is its noisy location right next to the street.
3. This gym is nice because of its size and its modern environment. I don't like this gym due to its small size and old equipment

B

Answers will vary.

Exercise 6

A

Muji's philosophy is to provide good quality but simple products at low prices and to avoid logos. They seek to maximize their use of suitable raw materials and to minimize waste and packaging.

B

Answers will vary. Possible answers:

1. competitors: companies or people who compete in the same market or business
2. basic principle: philosophy or way of working
3. raw materials: natural, unprocessed materials that can be used in manufacturing (e.g., cotton)
4. minimal packaging: the least possible amount of packaging or materials for wrapping products
5. product range: the number and variety of items available for sale
6. the bottom line: the essential, or most important, thing

Exercise 7

Answers will vary. Possible answers:

2. I don't like the second ad because it's not very interesting. *or*
   I like the second ad because you have to think about it. Another nice thing is that it makes the product look tasty.

Exercise 8

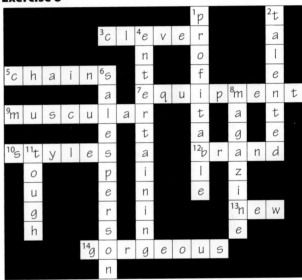

13 *That's a possibility*

Exercise 1

Answers will vary. Possible answers:
2. The storeowner may have left due to an emergency.
3. She might have gotten five of the same wedding present.
4. They could have forgotten the time.
5. He may have won something in a contest.
6. A cat must have eaten the chicken.

Exercise 2

Answers will vary.

Exercise 3

Answers will vary.

Exercise 4

A

Answers will vary. Possible answers:
The Missing Link
The Abominable Snowman
Half-man, Half-beast
The Yeti

B

1. It is about 2.5 meters tall, covered with hair except on the face, and walks upright on two feet.
2. He lives near the top of Mount Everest, in the Himalayas.
3. Another name for the Abominable Snowman is "Yeti."
4. In 1951, Shipton took photographs of enormous tracks in the snow.
5. Scientists say they need more and better evidence. The tracks Shipton saw could have been bear tracks.

Exercise 5

A

Answers will vary. Possible answers:
1. He should have walked to the nearest pay phone and called a tow truck.
2. She should have asked them to throw away their trash.
3. He could have asked them not to make any noise in the evenings.
4. She shouldn't have done anything. It was an accident.
5. She could have written him a nice email asking for the money.

B

Answers will vary.

Exercise 6

A

Noun	Verb	Noun	Verb
advice	*advise*	excuse	excuse
assumption	assume	prediction	predict
criticism	criticize	suggestion	suggest
demand	demand	warning	warn

B

2. Bart bought an expensive ring and gave it to Millie for her birthday. A year later, he asked her to marry him. When she said no, he made an outrageous demand. He said he wanted his ring back!
3. I shouldn't have warned my co-worker not to be late for work so often. It was really none of my business.

4. Last year, some economists said that food and gas prices wouldn't increase. Those predictions were wrong! Both food and gas are more expensive now.
5. Jill said she was late because she got caught in traffic. Hmm! I've heard that excuse before.
6. Philip shouldn't have assumed I would still be awake at midnight. I was asleep when he called.
7. My professor shouldn't have advised me to take a course in English literature. I have absolutely no interest in it.
8. Josh shouldn't have criticized me for wearing jeans and a T-shirt to a friend's party.

Exercise 7

Answers will vary. Possible answers:
2. A: Nina never responded to my invitation.
   B: She may not have received it. You should have called her.
3. A: Jeff hasn't answered his phone for a week.
   B: He might have gone on vacation. He should have told you, though – sometimes he's very inconsiderate.
4. A: I can never get in touch with Susan. She never returns phone calls or answers texts!
   B: Yeah, I have the same problem with her. Her voice mail might have run out of space. She should have gotten a new phone service by now.
5. A: Martin is strange. Sometimes he works really hard, but sometimes he seems pretty lazy. Last week, he hardly did any work.
   B: Well, you know, he might not have felt well. Still, he could have told you that he was sick.
6. A: I ordered a book online a month ago, but it still hasn't arrived.
   B: They may have had a problem with the warehouse, but they should have let you know.

14 *Behind the scenes*

Exercise 1

VERA: Putting on a fashion show must be really challenging!

ISAAC: Yeah, but it's also fun. All the clothes have to *be numbered* so that the models wear them in the right sequence. And they also have to be marked with the name of the right model.

VERA: What happens if something is worn by the wrong model?

ISAAC: Well, if it doesn't fit, it looks terrible! First impressions are very important. A lot of clothes are sold because they look good at the show.

VERA: Do you have to rehearse for a fashion show?

ISAAC: Of course! There's more involved than just models and clothes. Special lighting is used, and music is played during the show.

VERA: It sounds complicated.

ISAAC: Oh, it is. And at some fashion shows, a commentary may be given.

VERA: A commentary? What do you mean?

ISAAC: Well, someone talks about the clothes as they are shown on the runway by the models.

VERA: It sounds like timing is really important.

ISAAC: Exactly. Everything has to be timed perfectly! Otherwise, the show may be ruined.

Exercise 2

1. Often, special music has to be composed for a film.
2. A play may be rehearsed for several weeks before it is shown to the public.
3. Designing costumes for actors to wear requires a lot of creativity.
4. Newspapers are distributed to stores after they are printed.
5. Sound effects are added after the film has been put together.

Exercise 3

1. Nowadays, all sorts of things *are produced* in factories, including lettuce! At one food factory, fresh green lettuce is grown without sunlight or soil. Here is how it is done.
2. Lettuce seedlings are placed at one end of a long production line. Conveyor belts are used to move the seedlings slowly along. The tiny plants are exposed to light from fluorescent lamps.
3. They have to be fed through the roots with plant food and water that is controlled by a computer.
4. Thirty days later, the plants are collected at the other end of the conveyor belts.
5. They may be delivered to the vegetable market the same day.

Exercise 4

A

1. a shadow puppet
2. a marionette
3. a hand puppet
4. a rod puppet

B

	Hand puppets	Rod puppets
Size	50 cm (20 inches)	1 meter (40 inches)
How they're constructed	large head that has a costume with arms attached	similar to hand puppet, but bigger
How they're moved	puppets worn like gloves, puppeteer operates puppets with his or her fingers	operates the puppet with rods
Position of puppeteer	stands below the stage	stands below the stage
Where they're commonly used	European countries, such as Italy, France, Britain	Japan, Italy, Eastern Europe

	Shadow puppets	Marionettes
Size	50 cm (20 inches)	varies
How they're constructed	similar to rod	constructed from several small parts
How they're moved	shadows on a screen	moved by strings
Position of puppeteer	controlled from below or beside the stage	controlled from above
Where they're commonly used	China, Java, Indonesia, Turkey, Greece	Myanmar

Exercise 5

1. A photo editor, who tells the photographers what news stories to cover, selects only the best photos.
2. A website designer is a skilled artist who/that creates computer files with text, sound, and graphics.
3. A network installer is a skilled person who/that responds to calls from people with computer problems.
4. Movie extras, who almost never have any lines, appear in the background scenes.
5. TV sitcoms include actors and actresses who/that are recognized by television viewers around the world.

Exercise 6

2. c		6. f	
3. a		7. d	
4. h		8. e	
5. b			

Exercise 7

Answers will vary.

Exercise 8

2. Next, new walls are built.
3. Then the walls are painted.
4. After that, new lighting is installed.
5. Then new furniture is delivered.
6. Finally, the restaurant is reopened.

15 *There should be a law!*

Exercise 1

Answers will vary. Possible answers:
2. Something ought to be done to stop people from eating on the subway.
3. A law should be passed to make people turn down their music at night.
4. Dogs shouldn't be allowed to run without leashes.

Exercise 2

Answers will vary. Possible answers:
2. A law must be passed to limit the number of cars.
3. People mustn't be allowed to park their bikes near subway entrances.
4. Something has to be/has got to be done to repair our sidewalks.

Exercise 3

Answers will vary.

Exercise 4

Answers will vary. Possible answers:
2. B: That's not a bad idea. On the other hand, I feel that freedom of speech is important.
3. B: You may have a point. However, I feel that the public transportation wouldn't be as well maintained.
4. B: Do you? I'm not sure it's possible to produce enough hybrid cars.
5. B: That's interesting, but I think it would take a long time to ban all of them.

Exercise 5

A

Answers will vary. Possible answers.
Revenge stories are about people who had something bad happen to them and then did something to make the person stop what they were doing. In the first story, the people did the same thing to the other person that the other person did to them – not paying. In the second story, the person stopped the situation by taking away the rabbits. In the third story, the person turned the dripping water from the air conditioner against his neighbor.

B

Problem	First attempt to solve it	Final solution
1. friend never paid her own way	offered to pay for her friend at first	Marcy pretended that she had forgotten her wallet in order to force friend to pay
2. neighbors kept rabbits in their yard and treated them badly	complained to the neighbors, but they wouldn't listen; complained to animal protection, but they did nothing	stole the rabbits and gave them to a local pet store
3. dripping air conditioner kept Chad awake	called a technician to repair it, but there was nothing wrong; asked neighbor to check air conditioner, but he said it wasn't his problem	flooded neighbor's apartment with water from the dripping air conditioner

C

Answers will vary.

Exercise 6

3. You can easily spend all your money on food and rent, <u>can't you</u>?
4. Some unemployed people don't really want to work, <u>do they</u>?
5. Health care is getting more and more expensive, <u>isn't it</u>?
6. There are a lot of homeless people downtown, <u>aren't there</u>?
7. Some schools have overcrowded classrooms, <u>don't they</u>?
8. Laws should be passed to reduce street crime, <u>shouldn't they</u>?

Exercise 7

A

Noun	Verb	Noun	Verb
advertisement	*advertise*	permission	<u>permit</u>
<u>bullying</u>	bully	<u>pollution</u>	pollute
<u>improvement</u>	improve	prohibition	<u>prohibit</u>
offense	<u>offend</u>	provision	<u>provide</u>
<u>outsourcing</u>	outsource	<u>requirement</u>	require

B

Answers will vary.

Exercise 8

Answers will vary.

Exercise 9

KATE: You know, I just moved into this apartment building, and I thought everything would be really great now.

TONY: What's the problem?

KATE: Well, yesterday, the manager gave me a copy of the house rules. I found out that I can't park my moped on the sidewalk in front of the building anymore.

TONY: But people shouldn't <u>be permitted</u> to park their bikes or mopeds there.

KATE: Why not? There isn't any other place to park, <u>is there</u>? I guess I'll have to park on the street now.

TONY: I'm sorry that parking somewhere else will be inconvenient, but don't you agree that people shouldn't <u>be allowed</u> to block the sidewalk or the entrance to the building?

KATE: Well, you may have a point, but parking spaces for all types of cycles need <u>to be provided</u> for renters here. All renters with a car have a parking space, <u>don't they</u>?

TONY: Well, yes, you're right. You should go to the next renter's meeting and discuss the issue with everyone else.

KATE: That's not a bad idea. My voice ought <u>to be heard</u> as much as anyone else's – I think I will!

16 Challenges and accomplishments

Exercise 1

Answers will vary. Possible answers:

2. The most challenging thing <u>about doing volunteer work is finding the time.</u>
3. One of the rewards <u>of being unemployed is having a lot of time for yourself.</u>
4. One of the most difficult things <u>about being a student is having to take final exams.</u>
5. The most interesting aspect <u>of being a parent is seeing your children develop into adults.</u>
6. One of the least interesting aspects <u>of acting in movies is waiting around a lot.</u>

Exercise 2

Answers will vary.

Exercise 3

Answers will vary.

Exercise 4

A

Médecins Sans Frontières won the Nobel Peace Prize in 1999 for providing emergency medical relief.

B

Suggested answers:

Challenges	*Rewards*
Organizing a team to open a hospital	Reduction of deaths and gratitude of the local people
Test personal and professional skills to the limit	Travel
Working in politically sensitive areas with limited resources	Making even a small or temporary difference to people

C

1. The aim of Médecins Sans Frontières is to provide emergency relief for people who have suffered badly in wars or natural disasters.
2. More than 60 countries receive foreign volunteers through MSF.
3. The average ratio of local staff members to foreign volunteers is seven to one.
4. Volunteers must be able to deal with stress and work independently as well as in a team.
5. MSF needs medical professionals as well as technical staff such as building engineers and food experts.

Exercise 5

1. It's not good to be <u>rigid</u> if you're an emergency-room nurse.
2. If teachers are going to be successful, they have to be <u>resourceful</u>.
3. You have to be <u>adaptable</u> if you work as a volunteer.
4. If you take a job far from your family and friends, you have to be <u>self-sufficient</u>.
5. One of the most important things about working with children is being positive and not <u>cynical</u>.
6. Being a role model for troubled youths requires someone who is strong and <u>compassionate</u>.

Exercise 6

2. By the time I'm 35, I'd like to have lived in a culture that's very different <u>from</u> my own.
3. For me, the most difficult aspect <u>of</u> working abroad is learning a foreign language.
4. Working <u>for</u> an organization like the Peace Corps is very rewarding.
5. I'd like to have gotten another degree <u>in</u> two years
6. I hope I'll have gotten married <u>by</u> the time I'm 30.

Exercise 7

A

Possible answers:

2. get a promotion
3. learn new skills
4. make a change
5. meet someone special
6. pay off debts

B

Answers will vary.

Exercise 8

Answers will vary.

Credits

Illustrations

Jessica Abel: 119, 120; **Andrezzinho:** 87, 94; **Mark Collins:** v;
Carlos Diaz: 24 (*top*); **Jada Fitch:** 5 (*bottom*), 25, 64 (*bottom*), 109, 122;
Tim Foley: 76; **Travis Foster:** 14, 18, 95 (*right*), 105 (*center*), 117;
Chuck Gonzales: 2 (*bottom*), 6, 33, 52, 72 (*bottom*), 103, 128;
Jim Haynes: 11, 61; **Dan Hubig:** 125; **Trevor Keen:** 5 (*top*), 75, 83, 102;
KJA-artists: 29, 68, 88 (*bottom*); **Shelton Leong:** 47; **Scott MacNeill:** T23,
T60; **Karen Minot:** 2 (*top*), 16 (*top*), 36 (*bottom*), 49, 63, 72 (*top*), 86 (*top*),
95 (*left*), 105, 117 (*background*); **Jeff Moores:** 59

Rob Schuster: 8 (*top*), 23, 24 (*bottom*), 32, 56, 58 (*bottom*), 78 (*bottom*),
92, 100, 113, 115 (*bottom*),121, 131; **Daniel Vasconcellos:** 28, 36 (*top*),
43, 44 (*bottom*), 67, 91 (*top right*), 96, 99, 101; **Brad Walker:** 16 (*bottom*);
Sam Whitehead: 10, 20, 21 (*center*), 38, 39, 86 (*bottom*), 115 (*top*);
Jeff Wong: 30; **James Yamasaki:** 19, 79, 88 (*top*), 112, 123, 130;
Rose Zgodzinski: 7, 13, 22 (*top*), 27, 40, 44 (*top*), 55, 62, 64 (*top*),
66, 77, 97, 100, 111, 124, 126; **Carol Zuber-Mallison:** 21 (*top*), 22 (*bottom*),
34, 35, 41, 50 (*top*), 57, 58 (*top*), 69, 78 (*top*), 91, 106 (*top*), 114, 118

Photos

4 (*middle right*) © Ariel Skelley/Photographer's Choice/Getty Images;
(*bottom right*) © Smart Creatives/Flame/Corbis;
8 © Douglas Graham/Roll Call Photos/Newscom
9 (*right, top to bottom*) © OtnaYdur/Shutterstock; © Morgan Lane
Photography/Shutterstock; © Ablestock.com/Getty Images/Thinkstock;
© Slaven/Shutterstock
12 (*middle, left to right*) ©Tetra Images/Alamy; © Bob Daemmrich/Alamy;
© fStop/SuperStock
13 (*left, top to bottom*) © Exactostock/SuperStock; © iStockphoto/
Thinkstock; © Exactostock/SuperStock; © Rui Vale de Sousa/Shutterstock;
© Andres Rodriguez/Alamy; © Perfect Pictures/FogStock/Alamy
15 (*bottom right*) © ester22/Alamy; © Hill Street Studios/Blend Images
17 © Andy Ryan/The Image Bank/Getty Images
19 © sozaijiten/Datacraft/Getty Images
22 ©Tim Laman/National Geographic Stock
23 © Ocean Image Photography/Shutterstock
26 © Tanya Constantine/Blend Images/Getty Images
27 © Michael Caulfield/WireImage/Getty Images
30 © Travelscape Images/Alamy
31 © Ian Cumming/Axiom Photographic Agency/Getty Images
32 © Meeyoung Son/Alamy
34 (*middle left*) © Dana White/PhotoEdit; (*bottom left*) © Bill Bachman/
Alamy
35 © Hemis.fr/SuperStock
37 (*bottom, left to right*) © Craig Dingle/iStockphoto; © Jeffrey Hamilton/
Stockbyte/Thinkstock; © Michael Wells/Getty Images; © Epoxydude/
Getty Images
40 © ewg3D/iStockphoto
41 (*bottom, left to right*) © Don Farrall/Photodisc/Getty Images;
© Andy Crawford/Dorling Kindersley/Getty Images; (*lamp*) © Courtesy
of Khader Humied/Metaform Studio; (*coffee table*) © Courtesy of
Joel Hester/The Weld House; © Suzanne Long/Alamy
42 © arabianEye/Getty Images
43 © Hemera/Thinkstock
44 © inga spence/Alamy
45 (*middle, clockwise*) © Lincoln Rogers/Shutterstock; © luoman/
iStockphoto; © Tim Roberts Photography/Shutterstock; © UNEP/Still
Pictures/The Image Works; © Mark Leach/Alamy; © Barnaby Chambers/
Shutterstock
46 © Phil Crean A/Alamy
48 (*top, left to right*) © Bob Daemmrich/The Image Works;
© altrendo images/Getty Images; © JK Enright/Alamy; (*middle right*)
© Joel Stettenheim/Corbis
49 © Travel Pix/Alamy
50 © Jack Sullivan/Alamy
51 (*middle right*) © Science Photo Library/Alamy; (*bottom right*)
© Diego Cervo/Shutterstock
53 © Bailey-Cooper Photography 4/Alamy
54 (*top right*) © Bob Ebbesen/Alamy; (*bottom right*) © Hans Martens/
iStockphoto
55 © Blue Jean Images/Alamy
57 © Image Source/Corbis
60 © Eddie Linssen/Alamy
62 (*middle, left to right*) © Juanmonino/iStockphoto; © Paul Ridsdale/
Alamy; © Chris Rout/Alamy
63 © Tetra Images/Getty Images
64 (*top, left to right*) © Teenage doll/Alamy; © Selyutina Olga/
Shutterstock; © Hemera/Thinkstock; © Stan Honda/AFP/Getty Images/
Newscom; © Hachette Book Group. Used by permission. All rights
reserved. © Reisig and Taylor/ABC/Getty Images
65 (*top right*) © Handout/MCT/Newscom; (*middle right*) © De Agostini/
SuperStock

66 © Chung Sung-Jun/Getty Images
69 © David Livingston/Getty Images
70 © Image Source/Corbis
71 (*top right*) © Al Grillo/ZUMA Press/Corbis; (*bottom right*)
© Maisant Ludovic/Hemis/Alamy
73 © Ariwasabi/Shutterstock
74 © Gene Chutka/iStockphoto
77 (*top, left to right*) © El Sebou' - Egyptian Birth Ritual (1986) by
Fadwa El Guindi. Image courtesy of Documentary Educational Resources;
© Jeremy Woodhouse/Blend Images/Alamy; © James Strachan/
Robert Harding Picture Library Ltd/Alamy
80 (*top right*) © rudy k/Alamy; (*bottom right*) © Ethan Miller/Getty Images
81 © Ethan Miller/Getty Images
84 © Image Source/SuperStock
85 © Max Montecinos/LatinContent/Getty Images
86 © Elena Elisseeva/Shutterstock
89 © iStockphoto/Thinkstock
92 © Macpherson/Prahl/Splash News/Newscom
93 (*middle right*) © Corbis Bridge/Alamy; (*bottom right*) © Bill Aron/
PhotoEdit
94 © Myrleen Ferguson Cate/PhotoEdit
97 © DreamPictures/Taxi/Getty Images
99 (*top left*) © David Young-Wolff/PhotoEdit; (*top right*) © iStockphoto/
Thinkstock
100 (*top left*) © Joao Virissimo/Shutterstock; (*top right*) © Gillian Price/
Alamy
102 © Greg Balfour Evans/Alamy
104 © B.O'Kane/Alamy
106 (*top, left to right*) © Getty Images/Photos.com/Thinkstock;
© Daniel Jones/Alamy; © Design Pics/Newscom
108 (*bottom right*) © Mike Greenlar/Syracuse Newspapers/The Image
Works
109 © Payless Images, Inc./Alamy
110 (*top, left to right*) © Rui Vale de Sousa/Shutterstock; © leolintang/
Shutterstock; © Carl Stewart/Alamy
111 (*top right*) © Courtesy of Ali Pirhani (*middle left*) © AP Photo/
Rob Griffith; (*middle right*) © Gallo Images/Getty Images
113 © Maridav/iStockphoto
116 (*top, left to right*) © Kayros Studio Be Happy/Shutterstock; © Karkas/
Shutterstock; © Jovan Svorcan/Shutterstock; (*middle, left to right*)
© Klaus Mellenthin/Westend61/Alloy/Corbis; © Stacie Stauff Smith
Photography/Shutterstock; © iStockphoto/Thinkstock; (*bottom, left to
right*) © Zedcor Wholly/PhotoObjects.net/Thinkstock; © Ragnarock/
Shutterstock; © Alaettin Yildirim/Shutterstock
118 (*top, left to right*) © Webphotographer/iStockphoto;
© Stuart O'Sullivan/Fancy/Corbis; © BananaStock/Thinkstock
121 (*middle, left to right*) © AP Photo/Joshua Trujillo; © David Bacon/
Alamy; © Directphoto.org/Alamy
124 (*top, left to right*) © Hauke Dressler/LOOK Die Bildagentur der
Fotografen GmbH/Alamy; © J. R. Eyerman//Time Life Pictures/Getty
Images; © ewg3D/iStockphoto
126 (*top, left to right*) © Library of Congress; © Heritage Images/Corbis;
©AP Photo/Pool
125 © Jeffrey Kuan/iStockphoto
127 (*bottom, clockwise*) © Don Nichols/iStockphoto; © Martin Thomas
Photography/Alamy; © Evox Productions/Drive Images/Alamy;
© Daniel Bendjy/iStockphoto
129 (*middle, left to right*) © Exactostock/SuperStock; © Hans Gutknecht/
ZUMA Press/Newscom; (*bottom, left to right*) © Jeff Greenberg/Alamy;
© Michael Newman/PhotoEdit